EXPERT

Intensive training. Intensive practice. Be an Expert.

Contents

Contents

IELTS Overview

Listening (30 Minutes + 10 minutes transfer time)

Discourse Types	Question Types	Skills
Section 1: a conversation between two people in an everyday context **Section 2:** a monologue in an everyday context **Section 3:** a conversation between up to four people in an educational setting **Section 4:** a monologue on an academic subject	40 questions, including: • Multiple choice • Short-answer questions • Notes/Table/Form/Flow chart completion • Diagram labelling • Matching • Classification • Sentence completion • Flow chart summary • Plan/Map/Diagram labelling	• Listening for gist • Listening for main ideas • Listening for specific information • Understanding opinions

Academic Reading (60 minutes)

Text Types	Question Types	Skills
General interest texts taken from journals, newspapers, textbooks and magazines. These non-specialist texts are graded in difficulty and are representative of reading requirements for undergraduate and postgraduate students. Total of 2,000–2,750 words	40 questions, including: • Multiple choice • Short-answer questions • Notes/Table/Form/Flow chart completion • Diagram labelling • Matching • Classification • Sentence completion • Flow chart completion • Matching paragraph headings • Matching lists/phrases • *True/False/Not given*	• Reading for gist • Skimming • Reading for main ideas • Reading for detail • Understanding logical argument • Recognising opinions, attitudes and purpose
General Training Reading (60 minutes) Texts and extracts taken from books, magazines, newspapers, notices, advertisements, company handbooks and guidelines that you would encounter on a daily basis.		

Academic Writing (60 minutes)

Task 1: a minimum of 150 words. A summarising description of a graphic or pictorial input. **Task 2:** a minimum of 250 words. An extended piece of discursive writing.	**Task 1:** Describe, summarise or explain information from a graph, table or chart. **Task 2:** Respond to a point of view, argument or problem. Formal register required.	• Using the appropriate writing conventions and register • Describing processes • Describing data • Expressing a point of view • Comparing and contrasting • Analysing problems and solutions
General Training Writing (60 minutes)		
Task 1: a minimum of 150 words. Writing a letter or email. **Task 2:** a minimum of 250 words. An extended piece of discursive writing.	**Task 1:** Write a letter or email to someone explaining a situation or requesting information. **Task 2:** Write an essay in response to a point of view, argument or problem. Can be personal in style.	

Speaking (11–14 Minutes)

Format	Nature of Interaction	Skills
Part 1: Introduction and interview (4–5 minutes) **Part 2:** Individual long turn (3–4 minutes) **Part 3:** Exploring a topic/discussion (4–5 minutes)	**Part 1:** Speaking on familiar topics like home, family, work, studies, interests, etc. **Part 2:** You will be given a card which asks you to talk about a topic. You have one minute to prepare before you speak for two minutes You will then be asked one or two questions on the same topic. **Part 3:** You will be asked more questions about the topic in Part 2 so you can discuss more abstract ideas.	• Giving personal information • Talking about everyday habits and issues • Expressing opinions • Organising ideas • Understanding the rules of conversation

Total test time: 2 hours and 45 minutes (+ 10 minutes transfer time for Listening)

Lifelong learning

1a Training
- **Reading:** Predict language; Scan for information (Note and table completion)
- **Vocabulary:** The language of learning; Collocations; Dictionary skills
- **Speaking:** Use a range of tenses; Use a range of vocabulary; Word stress (Part 1)
- **Listening:** Recognise paraphrasing (Section 2: Multiple choice; Select from a list)
- **Language development:** Synonyms; Prefixes; Word formation; Paraphrase sentences
- **Writing:** Structure your answer; Summarise features (Task 1)

1b Testing
- **Listening:** Section 2: Multiple choice; Select from a list
- **Language development and vocabulary:** Tense review; Describe trends
- **Speaking:** Part 1: Talk about studying
- **Reading:** Table completion; Note completion
- **Writing:** Task 1: Describe a line graph

Lead-in

1   Discuss the questions.
   1   How would you define intelligence?
   2   What different kinds of intelligence are shown in the photos? How do the people around you show different kinds of intelligence?
   3   Do you think intelligence can be measured? How?
   4   What different kinds of intelligence can people have? How do the people around you show different kinds of intelligence?
   5   In what areas (academic, social, practical, etc.) do you think you are most and least intelligent?

Reading (Note and table completion)

Before you read

1 Read the title and introduction to the article. Then follow the steps below.

  1 Predict what the passage will say and make notes.
  2 Read the passage quickly. Were your predictions mentioned?

Predict language; Scan for information

2a Look at question 1 in the test task below. Read around the gap and answer these questions.

  1 What class of word are you looking for? (verb, noun, adjective, adverb?)
  2 What will the meaning be of the missing word? What word would collocate with *highest*?

b Scan the passage to find the part which will give you the answer. Do not read every word.

  1 Use the title and the highlighted key words to find the correct place in the passage.
  2 Look for a word in the passage that will fit grammatically and has the correct meaning.

Test practice

3 Read the strategies and complete the test task.

➤ **TEST STRATEGIES** page 170

Questions 1–4

Complete the notes below.

*Choose **NO MORE THAN TWO WORDS** from the passage for each answer.*

Using your time effectively

- keep times of highest 1 _____ for most important work
- do not send an email that requires a non-urgent 2 _____ until main work done
- a drop in 3 _____ affects mental power – avoid early/post-lunch hours
- 4 _____ is a good way of 'switching off'

Questions 5–9

Complete the table below.

*Choose **NO MORE THAN TWO WORDS AND/OR A NUMBER** from the passage for each answer.*

Brain boosting

	ADVICE	BENEFITS
Exercise	• 5 _____ not necessary • run up steps or on spot	• reduces 6 _____ ; improves mood
Food	• have breakfast rich in 7 _____ ; • stop eating when 8 _____ full	• makes you calmer and more alert • you achieve more when a bit hungry
Study/ Work area	• remove unnecessary mess from your workspace	• prevents attention wandering; allows more freedom of 9 _____

Task analysis

4a Discuss these questions about the test strategies. Give reasons for your answers.

  1 How helpful was it to predict the kind of word(s) you were looking for before reading the passage?
  2 Which strategies helped you to scan the passage quickly rather than read every word?
  3 How did you identify the word(s) you needed to write? Did you get distracted by any other words you thought were possible?

b In which ways could you improve your performance in these tasks next time?

Discussion

5 Discuss these questions in groups.

  1 How effectively do you study? Give examples of the ways in which you could improve.
  2 At what time of day do you study best/worst? Give reasons.
  3 To what extent do you agree with the writer's comments on food, exercise and workspace? Why?
  4 What do you do when you take breaks? In what way does this help you?

Using neuroscience to manage your time

In the face of pressure, our instinct is to study or work as much as we can for as long as we can. So why do we still feel as if we have not accomplished enough at the end of the day?

Neuroscientist and professor at the Manhattan NeuroLeadership Institute, Josh Davis, suggests that, rather than focusing on what is urgent, people should decide what matters most and pinpoint the best time to do it. "It's really about being highly effective as far as it's reasonable for a human being," Davis says. He believes that, rather than making a to-do list and working through each item, people should decide on the main aim for the day and work out when they are most likely to achieve peak productivity. Then this time can be devoted to the task with the highest priority, such as writing an essay or revising.

It is obviously impossible to work intensively all the time, so simple tasks not requiring much attention – emails or paperwork – can be done in any 'downtime'. However, there are times when the extent to which small tasks can tax our brains is underestimated. Sending an email, for example, may appear simple on the surface but can involve a decision which, although trivial, can cause mental exhaustion. In this case, it is better to reorder the day and deal with less pressing concerns only after the work target has been achieved.

The time of day when people are most alert varies from person to person but as a general rule the first two hours after waking up are not conducive to serious study. Research measuring attention, verbal reasoning and reaction times has also shown that when our body temperature falls below 37 degrees C, the brain is not at its full potential so the worst time to do anything involving thinking is between midnight and 6am. This is almost as bad as the afternoon slump between 2pm and 4pm, which is more to do with feeling cold than a heavy lunch.

Rather than being afraid of getting distracted, just be careful how you do it. "These days, when people decide to take a break, they tend to go on social media", says Davis, "and then they spend too much time there." Instead, they should go back to day-dreaming, where it is possible to stop thinking about work without really focusing on anything else. This allows for creative thinking and the integration between different parts of the brain, which cannot occur when the mind is required to focus on something specific.

Neuroscience has revealed much about the mind-body connection and how exercise can be used as a tool. "It's a different way of seeing exercise," says Davis. "Usually we think about how in the long term it will make us healthy

and look better but this is focused on the short term." A short session – 20 minutes or so – of moderate exercise will be sufficient. It does not need to be a lengthy gym visit; just running up and down stairs or jogging on the spot can be an effective method of lessening tension and boosting positive emotions.

Food that keeps blood-sugar levels stable will also help people to work most effectively, says Davis. If people snack during the day, they should choose foods that contain fats such as nuts and cheese rather than carbohydrates, to avoid blood-sugar spikes. Starting the day with high-protein food such as eggs and toast will have a high impact on the neurotransmitters in the brain. The amino acid tyrosine, which is found in proteins, will stimulate the transmitters responsible for alertness and the calming protein tryptophan will relax the brain. On meal breaks, people should eat only to 80 percent capacity; people's best work will be done when they are slightly hungry but not starving. Keep hydrated and improve your mood by sipping water. Just remember not to overdo caffeine; it may improve your alertness but also minimizes concentration.

Ensure you have a well-lit study space and that your desk space is clear; clutter is a distraction and not a good one, as it reminds you of uncompleted work. A clear desk also gives you room for increased movement, whether sitting with your arms behind your head or your feet up. You could alternate between standing and sitting.

Finally, try to get eight hours sleep a night. While we sleep, our brains process and retain information, consolidating facts and reinforcing how to perform tasks. It also rejuvenates us both physically and mentally.

Vocabulary

The language of learning

1a Are the words below nouns, verbs or both?

acquire	capacity	focus	method	process
reaction	research	retain		

b Match the words above with the definitions. There are definitions for the words that are both nouns and verbs.

1 to remember information
2 a response to something
3 the thing that people pay attention to
4 to gain knowledge or a skill
5 someone's ability to do something
6 the activity of finding out information about something
7 to give special attention to one thing
8 a series of actions that are done in order to achieve a result
9 a planned way of doing something
10 to take in and think about information
11 to study something in detail, especially to discover new facts or test new ideas

c Choose the correct option in *italics* to complete the sentences.

1 It is impossible to *acquire / retain* everything you hear in a lecture, but taking notes can help.
2 Some students prefer to use visuals as a *capacity / method* for learning.
3 If you want to *focus / acquire* effectively, you should remove all distractions.
4 Controversial ideas can cause people to have widely differing *reactions / processes*.
5 Some areas of the mind are unexplained and will need further *research / methods*.

Collocations

2 Complete the text with the verbs below to make verb + noun collocations. There is one verb you do not need to use.

achieve	conducting	demonstrate	focused
process	study		

Child prodigies are young people who 1 _____ intelligence at a very early age. Such children probably do not have secret study methods in order to 2 _____ intellectual skill, rather they probably have an innate ability to 3 _____ information. Kim Ung-yong, considered by many to be the smartest man alive today, could read in four languages by the age of four. So, he then 4 _____ his attention on mathematics. He gained his PhD in physics by the age of 15, and during this time also started 5 _____ research at NASA.

3a Read the text and underline the verb + adverb, adjective + noun collocations.

The growing popularity of apps

People love to learn using their smartphones and this can often be achieved by using the many apps on the market. These apps provide a wide range of learning tools which cater for all interests and age groups. Apple was the first company to release apps for download. It started with just 500 but within three months this rose rapidly to 3,000 apps. In contrast, when Google began launching apps there was a slower increase in downloads. It began with a few and this gradually increased over the next few years. Now, there are thousands of apps on both operating systems. In the last few years, the number of apps has fluctuated slightly for Google, between 500,000 and 600,000, and there has been a steady increase to a million for Apple. Free apps tend to be downloaded the most, whereas the demand for ones which are paid for has fallen sharply in comparison.

It is likely that apps will remain a popular way for people to learn and Google and Apple will probably remain the market leaders. However, newer platforms may threaten the market in years to come.

b Put the verbs you underlined in Exercise 2b into the correct categories.

1 go up   2 go down   3 move up and down

Dictionary skills

4a Look at the dictionary entry below. What does the dictionary entry tell you about the word?

knowledge (n) /ˈnɒlɪdʒ/: the information, skills, and understanding that you have gained through learning or experience
collocations: (verbs) to acquire, retain, gain knowledge (adjectives) background, first-hand, in-depth, specialist knowledge
similar words: understanding, information
opposite words: ignorance
example: *My university degree gave me an in-depth knowledge of statistics.*

b Work in pairs and discuss the questions.

1 Do you record the same information as above when learning a new word? Why/Why not?
2 What do you think it is important to record? Why?
3 How can recording synonyms and collocations help you in IELTS?

c In pairs, choose a word from Exercise 1a and write down how you could record information about this word. Use a dictionary to help you.

Speaking (Part 1)

Lead-in

1 Discuss the following questions.

1 What did you want to do when you were growing up? Do you still feel the same? Are you doing something completely different now?

2 How have your goals and dreams changed throughout your life?

3 How do you plan to achieve these goals? Can education help you get there? How?

Use a range of tenses

2a 🔊 1.1 Listen to a candidate talking about what she wanted to do when she was younger. Did she achieve it?

b Listen again and complete the sentences with the correct verbs.

1 I always _____ to be a writer when I was younger.

2 I _____ by people like J.K. Rowling.

3 I was really dedicated and _____ short stories in my spare time.

4 I remember once I _____ a story to a publisher, and got a letter from them but it was a rejection.

5 I _____ about giving up, but then I decided to learn more about writing.

6 I _____ to go to university and study literature.

c Match the sentences (1–6) in Exercise 2b with the explanations (A–F).

A a past action that happened over a period of time

B a past completed action

C a habit or repeated action in the past

D a past action that happened before another past action

E an unfinished or recent action in the past

F a past action/event/emotion that happened to the speaker

d Tell your partner what you wanted to be when you were younger and why. Remember to use a range of tenses.

Use a range of vocabulary

3a Think of alternatives for the words in bold.

1 When I was younger I was a really **good** piano player.

2 I once cheated on a test and I felt really **bad** about it.

3 Once I started the course I realised that it was more **difficult** than I expected.

4 Joaquin is a really **good** student; He always does what the teacher tells him to do.

5 When I was younger I had really **big** plans for my future.

6 The punishments at my old school were really **bad**.

b Replace the words in bold in Exercise 3a with the words below. There are two extra words you do not need.

ambitious   beneficial   demanding   guilty   hopeless
obedient   severe   talented

c Match the adjectives from the audio (1–5) with their meanings (A–E).

1 eager   3 dedicated   5 uncertain
2 inspired   4 disheartened

A to be disappointed to the point where you want to stop doing something

B to be hard-working at something because you believe it is important

C to be provided with an idea (often by somebody or something)

D to be very excited about doing something

E to not be sure about something

d Work in pairs. Discuss when you last felt the emotions in Exercise 3c.

Pronunciation – Word stress

4a 🔊 1.2 Listen to different pronunciations of the word *beneficial*. Which one has the stress in the correct place?

b Mark the stress on the words.

hopeless   guilty   ambitious   talented
severe   demanding   obedient   eager
inspired   dedicated   disheartened

c 🔊 1.3 Listen and check your answers.

Test practice

➤ TEST STRATEGIES page 174

➤ EXPERT SPEAKING page 184

5 Read the questions and write some vocabulary to help you answer them. Work in pairs and discuss your answers to the questions. Record your answers if possible.

Reasons for learning

1 Why is learning English important to you?

2 What do you want to study at university? Why are you interested in it?

3 What inspires you to work towards these goals?

4 What difficulties have you experienced working towards your educational goals?

Task analysis

6 Think about your and your partner's answers and answer the questions.

1 Did you use a variety of tenses?

2 What interesting vocabulary did you use?

Listening (Section 2)

Before you listen

1a Look at the pictures of libraries. How do they compare to libraries you have visited? Where might you find each type of library shown? What could be the advantages and disadvantages of each one?

b What kinds of activities do people usually do in a library? Make a list.

c Compare your list with another student.

Recognise paraphrasing

2 🔊 1.4 Listen to a talk about a library and answer the questions.

1 Is the talk for new students or second-year students?
2 Do any of the points in the talk match your ideas in Exercise 1b?

3a Read the question and underline what you are listening for.

> 1 What was added to the library during the holidays?

b Read the options. Write some alternative ways of saying options A–C.

> A relaxation areas   C new IT equipment
> B study spaces

c Read the excerpt from the audio script. What is the answer to Exercise 3a?

> During the summer, some changes have been made to make the library even better for you all. We've always had some of the best IT services around, and now you'll find these on the 2nd instead of the 3rd floor. We've also added a more informal area in front of the study spaces on the ground floor. Here you'll be able to chat with your friends, have a coffee and take a break from your hard work.

d Look again at the audio script in Exercise 3c and answer the questions.

1 Did the audio script use any of the same words as the answer options (A, B, C)?
2 Were any of the options (A, B, C) expressed differently in the audio script?
3 What can this tell us about answering these types of questions?

4a Read the question below. What other ways can you say the underlined part? Which word(s) cannot be changed?

> Choose **TWO** services the students <u>need their library card for</u>.

b Read the options for the question. Think of some synonyms for them.

> A borrow books   D access the journal
> B use private study areas   archives
> C print an essay   E pay fines

c Listen to the library talk again and answer the question in Exercise 4a.

Task analysis

5 Look at audio script 1.4 on page 201 and discuss the questions.

1 Where can you find the answers to Exercise 4a?
2 How many answers were expressed with synonyms? Did you get these correct?
3 Did you choose any wrong options? Can you identify in the audio script why you thought it was correct and why it is wrong?

Discussion

6 How useful do you think libraries are these days? Do you think people generally prefer looking information up in books or online? Why? In what ways might the internet become a threat to libraries?

Language development

Synonyms

> EXPERT GRAMMAR page 176

1a Match 1–4 with their synonyms A–D.

1	order	A	up-to-date
2	explain	B	talk someone through something
3	recent	C	get something in
4	refill	D	top something up

b Complete the sentences in two ways: with both the words 1–4 and the synonyms A–D in Exercise 1a. Make any necessary changes.

1 If you cannot see the book on the shelves, we would be happy to _____ the book for you.
2 The magazines on this rack are the most _____ ones we have; they are all from last week.
3 When the photocopier runs out of paper, you can _____ it with this paper here.
4 There are a lot of facilities here so if you need more information, I will _____ further.

Prefixes

2a Complete the sentences with the correct prefixes below.

en   in   inter   mis   re   un

1 If we don't have what you want, we're happy to get it in for you from another library, as we have an _____-library loan policy.
2 But, you'll be _____able to use the automatic machines; you'll need to come to the desk.
3 If you have _____sufficient money on your card, you can top this up at the reception desk.
4 You can _____arrange any appointment or room booking up to 24 hours in advance.
5 This may seem severe, however it _____sures that the services and facilities aren't _____used.

b Match the sentences in Exercise 2a with the sentences with a similar meaning A–E.

A As long as you give a day's notice, you can change any of your reservations.
B Make sure you return to the reception desk as you don't have access to the electronic system.
C Although it may appear strict, it's to make sure people use the library properly.
D We have a system of sharing books between libraries so if the book isn't here, we can order it for you.
E The reception desk is the place to refill your card when you run out of credit.

c Which words helped you to match the similar sentences in Exercises 2a and 2b?

d How were the words with prefixes paraphrased in Exercise 2b?

Word formation

3a Read the text and decide which word form (noun, verb, adjective, adverb) should go in each space.

Internet v libraries

There is no denying that the internet has an astounding amount of information, but it **1** _____ is not the case that everything can be accessed **2** _____ online. All the books in the world still have not been **3** _____ , despite efforts by companies such as Google. There are many reasons for this, and one such reason is copyright; it is **4** _____ to fully reproduce many books online. Academically, libraries are **5** _____ too as they are a way to view scholarly material for free. Research articles and journals can be **6** _____ online with a subscription, yet go to any library and you can access these without charge. Also, you can usually guarantee that a library only stocks quality books and articles, whereas the quality of **7** _____ on the web can **8** _____ enormously.

b Complete the text with the correct form of the words below.

accessible   digital   easy   informative   legal
simple   valuable   various

Paraphrase sentences

4a Complete the sentences below using a different form of the word in bold. Write no more than three words.

1 There is no one best way to revise for an exam.
possible
It is _____ define a single best study method.
2 Getting to know yourself and how you study best is essential to your success.
valuable
If you know your study habits, it _____ your success.
3 Working at a steady pace, rather than cramming, is one key to success.
steady
You should _____ instead of cramming in order to be successful.
4 Rather than just reading your notes, you are more likely to remember information if you can connect it together logically.
likely
The _____ remembering information will increase if you connect information together, instead of just rereading notes.
5 Sleep is an essential part of studying effectively as it keeps your brain alert during the day.
concentrate
In order to study effectively, keep your _____ ensuring you get enough sleep.

b Do you agree with the advice given in Exercise 4a? Why/Why not?

Writing (Task 1)

Structure your answer

> EXPERT WRITING page 191

1a Look at the graph and answer the questions.
1 What do the blue, green and orange lines represent?
2 What is the date range shown on the graph?
3 Which group starts with the highest percentage?
4 Which group starts with the lowest percentage?
5 Which group remains the steadiest?
6 Are the groups more similar or different when comparing 2010 to 1950?

Percentage of women in employment from 1950–2010 by level of education

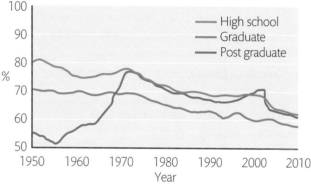

b Match the sections (1–4) with the structures (A–D) below.
1 In 1950 a high proportion of high school-educated women worked in comparison to women with a post-graduate qualification. Just over 80 percent of high school women were employed compared to around 55 percent of post-graduates. However, in the 1970s the percentage of women working in these two groups converged, at approximately 75 percent.
2 Overall, the graph shows that the level of education attained had a greater impact on women's employment in the past than more recently.
3 This graph shows the changes in employment of women with different levels of education from 1950 to 2010. The levels of education are separated into three categories: high school, graduate and post-graduate, and the data showing how many of each group were in employment is given in percentages.
4 During the given period, the percentage of women in employment from all three groups somewhat converged and then declined uniformly over the latter half of the period.

A Introductory sentences (what the graph shows, how it is measured).
B Description of the overall trends.
C Explanation of most important feature (with data).
D Overview (summarising the overall message of the graph).

Summarise features

2a Look at the graph below. Which of the sentences 1–3 gives the overview?
1 Women do not go to school for as many years as men.
2 The average time spent in education generally increased.
3 Korea is overtaking New Zealand in years spent in education.

b Which of the following sentences is a trend and which is a detail?
1 The number of years in education for Korean men and women increased.
2 In the 1950s Korean men and women spent around three to five years in education. However, in 2010 both groups spent around 11 to 12 years in education.

Average number of years of education, by country

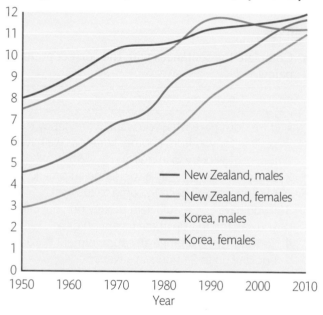

c Discuss what other trends you could write about in the graph above.

Test practice

3a Look at the graph in Exercise 2a and make a plan for your writing. Follow the structure A–D in Exercise 1b.

> TEST STRATEGIES page 173

b Compare your plan with a partner. Are the trends and overview accurate? Does your structure match the one in Exercise 1b? Why/Why not?

Listening (Section 2)

£2.99 Great for stargazers. You point your device at the sky and this educational app tells you what you are looking at. It labels the constellations, stars and satellites.

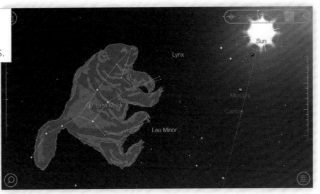

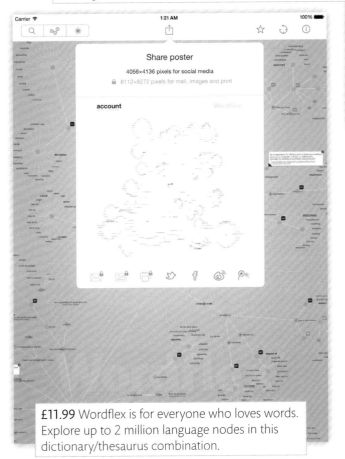

£11.99 Wordflex is for everyone who loves words. Explore up to 2 million language nodes in this dictionary/thesaurus combination.

Before you listen

1 Read the descriptions of the apps. Which ones would you like to use? Why? How might these apps help people learn? Do you think people should pay for good learning apps? Why/Why not?

Predict alternative language

2a Think of some alternative language for the question and options.

> What is the speaker's job?
> A An educational consultant
> B A teacher
> C A technology expert

b Compare your alternative language with a partner.

c 🔊 1.5 Listen and answer the question.

d Read audio script 1.5 on page 201 and find the section with the answer. How is the language in the question and options different?

Test practice

> **TEST STRATEGIES** pages 168 and 169

3 🔊 1.6 Complete the test task. Try to think of some alternative language for the questions and options.

Questions 1 and 2
*Choose the correct letter, **A**, **B** or **C**.*

1 The speaker thinks that free apps are
   A worse than paid apps.
   B full of advertising.
   C badly designed.
2 What does the speaker think of *Mathword*?
   A It is too expensive.
   B It is good for children.
   C It is easy to use.

Questions 3 and 4
*Choose **TWO** letters, **A–E**.*
*Which **TWO** subject areas does the speaker think are underrepresented?*

   A Foreign languages
   B Maths
   C Art and design
   D Music
   E Literature

Task analysis

4 Read audio script 1.6 on page 201. With a partner, discuss what language helped you choose your answers. How did you eliminate the distractors?

Discussion

5 Do you think technology benefits education? Why/Why not? In what ways can it be positive and negative?

Language development and vocabulary

Tense review

> **EXPERT GRAMMAR** page 176

1a Match the forms below with the underlined parts of the sentences.

past perfect   past simple   future with *will*
present perfect   present continuous   present simple
future with *going to*

1 I've had some excellent test results so far this academic year.
2 Next year I'll start learning the guitar.
3 My best friend Jun and I are students on the same university course.
4 I'm learning Spanish so I can live and work there.
5 I started playing tennis two months ago.
6 As soon as I started watching the film, I realised I'd seen it before.
7 Later this week I'm going to meet my friends for dinner.

b Complete the sentences with the correct form of the verbs in brackets.

1 Last week I _____ (complete) the application forms to the three universities I'm interested in.
2 My sister started an online English course last month and her vocabulary _____ (increase) every day.
3 When I saw my teacher smiling I knew I _____ (achieve) a high mark for my essay.
4 Since my friends and I started a band, I _____ (become) much less nervous about performing in public.
5 Next year, my tutor _____ (introduce) a new programming module into our course.
6 After speaking to my parents about the benefits, I now know that I _____ (go) abroad to study.

c Choose the correct option in *italics* to complete the text.

Hello everyone and welcome to our presentation. Today we **1** *'re going to show / show* you our app, which is a phrasebook app. We **2** *'ve outlined / 'll outline* the reasons why we chose it, and then give you a demonstration. So, firstly, we **3** *want / wanted* to make an app that could help us travel around. As students we often travel, so it'd be really useful. We **4** *'d thought / 're thinking* that there weren't many apps on the market for this, but we were surprised to find out that quite a few existed. We **5** *'ve tried / 'd tried* to make ours different though so we designed it like a cartoon. Students **6** *'re loving / love* gaming and cartoons so we thought this would appeal to them.

Describe trends

2a Write the words below in the correct place in the table.

climb   decline   decrease   drop   grow   lessen
plummet   reduce   remain stable   soar

Go up	Go down	No movement

b Read the sentences about the graph and underline the errors. Correct the errors.

Peak study times of UK secondary school students in a day

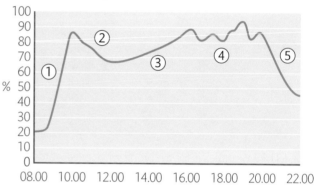

1 Firstly, the line remains stable then it falls sharply.
2 Next the line increases gradually.
3 Then the line rises sharply.
4 After this, the line plummets.
5 Finally, there is a slight drop.

c Look at the graph again. Write sentences to describe each stage of the graph. Discuss your ideas with a partner.

Speaking (Part 1)

Vocabulary development

1a Look at the picture above. What decision do you think the woman has to make? What would you do in this situation? Why?

b Complete the collocations (1–8) with the verbs below.

deal	draw up	change	come	consider	reach
resolve	take				

1 _____ a list
2 _____ the alternatives
3 _____ to a conclusion
4 _____ action
5 _____ your mind
6 _____ an issue
7 _____ with a problem
8 _____ a decision

c What big decisions have you had to make in your life? Choose ONE and describe the decision-making process to your partner. Use the vocabulary in Exercise 1b.

Focus on lexical resource

2a Turn to page 183 and look at the descriptors for lexical resource for bands 6, 7 and 8. With a partner, discuss the difference between the bands.

b 🔊 1.7 Work in pairs. Listen to the candidate. What are her strengths according to the criteria? How could she improve her responses?

Test practice

> TEST STRATEGIES page 174

3 Ask and answer the questions, taking turns to be the examiner and candidate. Record your answers if possible.

1 What was your favourite subject at school?
2 Why did you like it?
3 What did you enjoy about going to school?
4 What other activities did you take part in at school?
5 What do you want to study in the future?
6 Why did you decide to take the IELTS test?

Assess and improve

4a How did you perform in the interview? Complete the checklist.

1 I used a variety of tenses and vocabulary.
2 I avoided too much repetition in my answers.
3 I spoke fluently and with clear pronunciation.

b Discuss your answers in Exercise 4a with a partner. If applicable, listen to your recordings in Exercise 3. What advice would you give your partner to help him/her improve?

Reading (Table completion; Note completion)

Before you read

1a How much do you know about the brain? Decide whether these statements are true or false.

1 Hippocrates was the first person to discover how the brain works.
2 People used to believe the mind could be found in the heart.
3 Each brain comprises thousands of neurons.
4 The brain weighs an average of three pounds.

b Scan the first paragraph of the passage to find the answers to the questions.

Test practice

2a Read the strategies and complete the test tasks.

➤ **TEST STRATEGIES** page 170

Questions 1–5

Complete the table below.

*Choose **NO MORE THAN TWO WORDS AND/OR A NUMBER** from the passage for each answer.*

The structure of a neuron

PART	DESCRIPTION	FUNCTION
Cell body	• contains a nucleus	• origin of molecules • short electrical signals, known as 1 _____, pass through here
Dendrites	• projections similar in appearance to 2 _____	• gather incoming information from other cells
3 _____	• size varies • covered in 4 _____	• depends on distance needed to travel • helps increase range and speed of signals (up to potential of 5 _____ per second)

➤ **HELP**

1 Find another name for these electrically charged signals.
2 What is a verb meaning *similar in appearance to*?
3 Be careful: How many are there?

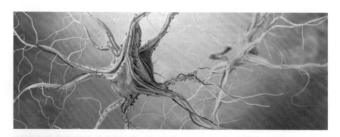

neuron: a type of cell that makes up the nervous system and sends messages to other parts of the body or the brain

Questions 6–9

Complete the notes below.

*Choose **NO MORE THAN TWO WORDS** from the passage for each answer.*

Synaptic transmission

• neurotransmitters – electrical signals change into 6 _____
• synapse – a 7 _____ keeping neurons apart
• neurotransmitters – connect to 8 _____ in new cells
• neurotransmitter 9 _____ can cause diseases

➤ **HELP**

6 Look for a paraphrase of *change*.
7 What is a verb meaning *keep apart*? How is a synapse described?
8 Think of a paraphrase for *connect*.

b Discuss your answers in pairs.

Task analysis

3 Work in pairs and discuss the questions.

1 What strategies did you use to quickly locate the information that you needed to find?
2 Is it better to use your own words rather than copy word(s) from the passage?
3 Why is it important to read the instructions carefully?
4 Why should you always read carefully around the gaps in the task?

Discussion

4 Discuss the questions.

1 Do you think male and female brains are different from each other? In what ways? What about teenage and adult brains?
2 Give a few examples of activities which can help to keep the brain functioning well.
3 Which of these functions of the brain do you think is most important at different ages: memory, cognitive ability (e.g. solving problems), motor skills (e.g. tying shoelaces), emotional intelligence (e.g. empathy)?

The learning brain

For centuries, scientists and philosophers have been fascinated by the brain, until recently viewed as nearly incomprehensible. Two thousand five hundred years ago Hippocrates argued that the brain rather than the heart, which is what his contemporaries believed, is the seat of thought, sensation, emotion and cognition. In the 17th and 18th centuries, anatomists began depicting the structure of the brain with increasing accuracy but it was not until the 19th century that it was confirmed that nerves and muscles generate electrical impulses. All of this paved the way for the modern era of neuroscience, beginning with the work of Spanish anatomist Ramon y Cajal at the dawn of the 20th century: he suggested that our abilities depend on the way neurons are connected, not to any special features of the cells themselves. And in recent years, due to the accelerating pace of research in neurological and behavioural science along with the development of new research techniques, scientists have begun to understand much more about the 100 billion neurons which, along with trillions of neural connections, construct the most intricate organ of the human body, weighing three pounds and using a fifth of a person's blood supply.

Reading, learning, pattern recognition and so much more, all begin with the main type of brain cell and fundamental building block of the brain – the neuron. All sensations, movements, thoughts, memories and emotions are the result of very rapid messages that one of these nerve cells sends to another. Neurons themselves consist of three parts: each one has an input area (the dendrites), an output area (the axon) and a cell body with a nucleus, where most of the molecules that the neuron needs in order to survive are manufactured. Each neuron extends into networks of many thousands of dendrites, thin short fibres resembling the branches of a tree, which receive incoming electrical signals from a neighbouring cell and pass them into the cell body. Once a signal arrives at the cell body, it may be suppressed or amplified by other signals: eventually, as a result of all the incoming signals converging, a new one is triggered.

The processed information then travels down the neuron's long nerve fibre, known as the axon, until it gets to another neuron, a muscle cell or cells in some other organ. Each neuron generally has only one axon but it may split and branch into as many as 10,000 knob-like endings that disperse signals across many cells. The axon may be very short, extending only to adjacent cells in the brain, or much longer, carrying electrical signals for up to a metre down to the spinal cord to move the arms, legs and feet. An insulating sheath formed of cells wraps around the axon: this includes a fatty molecule called myelin, which helps the signals travel faster and farther. The information is transmitted by brief impulses carrying only 0.1 volts and lasting just a few thousandths of a second but with the capacity – in just one second – to travel as far as 120 metres.

Arriving at the end of the axon, the electrical signals stop when they reach a synapse, the narrow gap which separates a neuron or cell from the next one. Then follows the process of synaptic transmission, in which the signal pauses to convert itself into chemical energy before crossing the synapse and reaching the next neuron. These neurotransmitters – as they are known – then attach themselves to receptors on the neighbouring cell, which may also change the properties of the receiving cell. If the receiving cell is also a neuron, the neurotransmitter then travels the length of the new cell until it reaches the synapse of another receptor cell and repeats the process. The electrical signals and sprays of neurotransmitter that send the messages somehow build into the complex mental feats that can perform functions such as understanding language, remembering experiences from the past, and comprehending the outside world. Disorders relating to neurotransmitters have been linked to depression, Parkinson's disease, Alzheimer's and a host of other conditions.

Both the brain and body need regular exercise if neurons are to remain sharp: to spur on the brain to make new neuronal connections and protect the ones it has, people should try activities such as learning a new language, solving mental puzzles and games, eating a healthy diet and getting regular physical exercise.

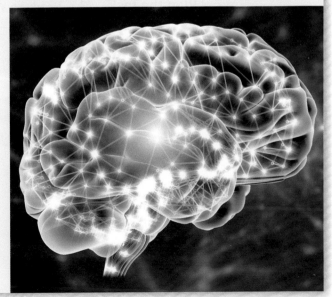

Writing (Task 1)

Lead-in

1 Discuss the following quotation. What do you think it means? To what extent do you agree or disagree with it?

'The true purpose of education is to make minds, not careers.'
William Deresiewicz

Understand the task

➤ EXPERT WRITING page 191

2a The line graph below has no title or key, but the trends can still be identified. Look at the graph and answer the questions.

1 What is unusual about the y-axis?
2 What do you notice about the time period?
3 Can you group any of the lines together? How and why?
4 Which line has increased more than the others?
5 Which line fluctuates the most?

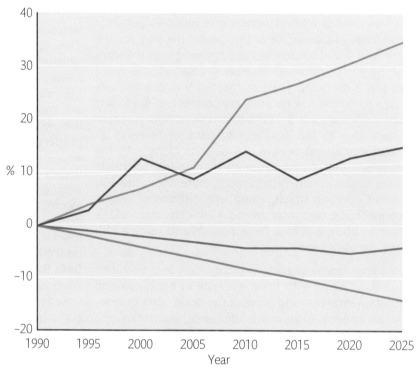

b Discuss your answers to Exercise 2a. How do the answers to the questions help you plan and write your report?

Plan the task

3 Read the Writing band descriptors for task achievement on page 190 and complete the sentences.

1 An overview is expected at band _____ and above.
2 The overall trend must be shown at band _____ and above.
3 You are expected to select the important features in the information at band _____ and above.

4 Look at the graph on page 21 and discuss the questions in pairs.

1 What is the topic of the graph?
2 How is the information in the graph categorised?
3 What key features can you pick out?
4 What is the overall trend?

The graph shows the actual and predicted percentage change in employment in the UK, by education level.

Summarise the information by selecting and reporting the main features, and make comparisons where relevant.

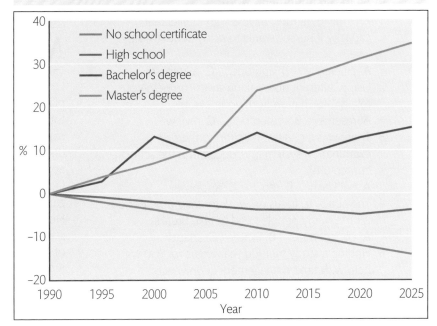

Language and content

5a Look at the graph above. What tenses could you use to write your answer? Why?

b Look at the graph again. What part is in the future? Is it definite or is it speculative?

c Which of these sentences could be used to express a future prediction in writing Task 1?

1 The number of people attending universities will probably double.
2 The number of people attending universities must double.
3 The number of people attending universities is likely to double.
4 The number of people attending universities is going to double.
5 The number of people attending universities would double.
6 The number of people attending universities is predicted to double.

d Look at the graph and talk about the predictions it makes.

Write your description

6a Plan your answer for the task in Exercise 4. Think about the following:

- Writing your introductory sentences
- Identifying trends
- Identifying key features
- Ordering information logically
- Choosing details as support
- Concluding with an overview sentence

b Write your answer to the task Exercise 4. Write at least 150 words.

Assess and improve

7a Work in pairs. Check your partner's description and answer the questions.

1 Does it have an introductory sentence? Is it accurate?
2 Are key features identified? Do you think they are the appropriate key features?
3 Is there any important information missing?
4 Does it conclude with an overview?

b Work with your partner to improve both of your answers.

Review

1a Choose the word with the closest meaning (A, B or C) to the underlined word.

1 An individual must have a high intellectual <u>capacity</u> if he/she wants to study at doctorate level.
A efficiency B aptitude C readiness
2 Using different note-taking styles can help you <u>retain</u> information from your lectures.
A reserve B remember C review
3 There was a positive <u>reaction</u> to the new examination system introduced into the school curriculum.
A backlash B reply C response
4 The ability to <u>focus</u> on work for long time periods is rare. Many people need to take breaks.
A concentrate B fixate C adapt
5 Finding a study <u>method</u> that works for you will help with time management at university.
A design B custom C system

b Match the verbs below with the correct parts of the graph (A–D). Some parts match more than one verb.

decline   drop   grow   plummet   remain stable
soar

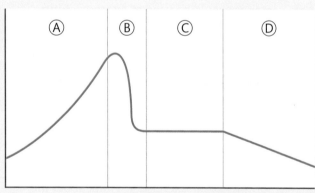

c Write sentences to describe the graph below.

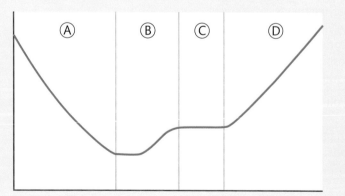

2a Complete the text with the correct form of the words below.

limit   view   assess   improve   inform   ease
vary

Methods of learning

Learning creative skills such as drawing, carpentry or playing an instrument is very different from learning topics or subjects based on acquiring 1 _____ . It can be argued that this type of learning involves distinct areas of our brain and also a 2 _____ of approaches to retaining information. When studying facts and figures the brain doesn't have an 3 _____ capacity for storing and therefore learning data. However, when people start to learn more creative skills, there are many opportunities for 4 _____ . One of these is based on practice. Through a process of 5 _____ and then doing these actions again we can become better at creative skills. One reason is due to the fact that we receive immediate feedback. We can compare two drawings and 6 _____ notice if one is better than the other. Then we are able to 7 _____ our competence and focus on particular aspects of what we are learning in order to plan how to carry on with our learning. This feedback loop ensures we continue to improve these creative skills.

b Complete the sentences with the correct form of the verbs in brackets.

1 Since this academic year started, the students' grades _____ (rise) steadily.
2 The number of students taking online higher education courses _____ (plummet) after the initial excitement had worn off.
3 In the future, the use of technology in all types of learning _____ (soar) beyond what we can now imagine.
4 The need for IT and science knowledge for the future workforce _____ (grow) considerably this century.
5 The popularity of media degrees _____ (decline) because there are now many unemployed media graduates.
6 The government has said that it _____ (reduce) funding for sport in primary and secondary education over the coming years.
7 At the end of the 20th century the importance of studying languages in the UK _____ (decrease).
8 The government has announced that they _____ (increase) tuition fees for the next academic year.

2 A world of change

2a Training
- **Reading:** Topic sentences and supporting details (*True/False/Not given*; Short-answer questions)
- **Vocabulary:** Academic verbs; Written and spoken vocabulary; Process verbs
- **Speaking:** Develop topic-specific vocabulary; Make notes and plan your answer (Part 2)
- **Listening:** Understand different ways location is expressed (Section 1: Label a map)
- **Language development:** Present simple, past simple and present perfect passives; Other passive forms
- **Writing:** Write introductions and processes; Use the active and passive (Task 1: Describe a process)

2b Testing
- **Listening:** Section 1: Form completion; Label a map
- **Language development and vocabulary:** Relative clauses; Sequencing with prepositions and adverbs
- **Speaking:** Part 2: Describe a place you visited
- **Reading:** *True/False/Not given*; Short-answer questions
- **Writing:** Task 1: Describe a process

Lead-in

1 Look at the photos and discuss the questions.

1 Would you agree that living standards are improving all around the world? Why/Why not?

2 Explain what 'development' means to you.

3 Are the following examples of personal or social development?
- studying at university
- improving healthcare
- reducing carbon emissions
- improving communication skills

4 How are personal and social development different?

5 Which do you think is more important – personal or social development? Why?

Reading (*True/False/Not given*; Short-answer questions)

Before you read

1   Discuss the questions in groups.

    1   Which of these developments have had the most impact on people's lives in your country?
      • industry   • agriculture   • technology   • science

    2   In what ways have these changes generally been positive/negative for a) your country b) the world?

Topic sentences and supporting details

2   Look at the highlighted topic sentence in the first paragraph of the article.

    1   Predict which of these details the rest of the paragraph will give about the Agricultural Revolution.
      •   when it took place
      •   where it began
      •   how people lived before that time

    2   Skim the paragraph quickly and tick which of these supporting details are mentioned.

3a   Highlight the topic sentences in the rest of the passage. Predict what the supporting details will be.

  b   Skim quickly and check.

Test practice

4   Read the strategies and complete the test task.

> **TEST STRATEGIES** pages 170 and 171

Questions 1–5

Do the following statements agree with the information given in the reading passage? Write

TRUE   *if the statement agrees with the information*

FALSE   *if the statement contradicts the information*

NOT GIVEN   *if there is no information on this*

    1   Studies prove that the Agricultural Revolution was prompted by a rise in the birth rate at the time.

    2   The Agricultural Revolution enabled people to eat more than the daily minimum requirement.

    3   An increase in illness amongst the population at that time is likely to have been caused by factors connected to the Agricultural Revolution.

    4   Not until modern times have people in Greece and Turkey reached the same average height as their hunter-gatherer ancestors.

    5   The superior strength of hunter-gatherers' bones is explained by the fact that they did a greater amount of work than agriculturalists.

Questions 6–10

Answer the questions below.

*Choose **NO MORE THAN TWO WORDS AND/OR A NUMBER** from the passage for each answer.*

    6   To what extent did people's teeth worsen as a result of an agricultural diet?

    7   What chemical element was lacking in the diet of agriculturalists?

    8   What physical evidence is there that catching illnesses from others at that time was common?

    9   What was greatly reduced as a result of diet and illness in post-agricultural times?

   10   What kind of food did the early farmers have problems processing?

Task analysis

5a   How useful were the test strategies? Decide which of these statements you agree/disagree with.

    1   Identifying topic sentences helped me to skim each paragraph quickly.

    2   Reading the passage quickly before doing the task meant that I could scan the passage more quickly to find the information I needed.

    3   It is hard to decide what the key words are in the statements/questions.

    4   Looking for paraphrases of the key words helped me to scan the passage rather than read every word.

  b   Compare and discuss which strategies you used and which were successful/unsuccessful.

Discussion

6   Work in pairs and discuss the questions.

    1   Which important social changes have you witnessed in your lifetime?

    2   Why might some groups of people (e.g. the young, the old) welcome or fear change? What kind of changes might they welcome and which might they fear, and why?

A better life?

For over two million years, humans foraged for wild plants and hunted wild animals: since no food was grown and little stored, these hunter-gatherers had to endure a daily struggle if they were to avoid starvation. Then 'progress' came, in the form of the Agricultural Revolution.

At the end of the Ice Age, 10,000-12,000 years ago, the Agricultural Revolution took place, something which was to transform people's lives forever. Whether this was a consequence or the cause of the dramatic population growth which we know occurred around this time is still unclear. What is beyond doubt, however, is that during this period, evidence of the domestication of select plants and animals began to emerge in the archaeological record. This happened more or less simultaneously in a number of regions throughout the world, the practice spreading until by the first century AD the vast majority of the global population were agriculturalists.

Perhaps the most significant consequence of this change was the ability to produce a surplus of food beyond the immediate needs of daily subsistence. The care and controlled breeding of selected species led to genetic changes that allowed greater production and increased the geographical ranges across which the domesticated species could be grown, thus greatly expanding the potential food resources available to humans.

These developments produced a revolution in human lives. Most notably, small communities that had previously been forced to make seasonal moves across the landscape to follow the shifting availability of naturally occurring resources could now settle in one place for long periods and expand in size. The negative aspect to this was that because agriculture encouraged people to settle together in crowded societies, it accelerated the spread of parasites and infectious diseases, whereas when populations were scattered in small bands that continually moved camp, epidemics could not take hold.

The health of agriculturalists of this time can in part be assessed by the newly emerging techniques of paleopathology, which study the remains of ancient peoples. One example of this work concerns historical changes in size: skeletons from Greece and Turkey show that around 10,000 years ago male hunter-gatherers were 5'9" tall, while women were 5'5". Following the adoption of agriculture, this dropped and by 3000 BC had reached an average height of only 5'3" tall for men and 5' for women before very slowly beginning to rise again.

Studies also show that hunter-gatherers living about 7,000 years ago had bone density proportionally similar to that seen in modern primates. By contrast, agriculturalists living 6,000 years later had significantly lighter and weaker bones. However, these findings do not imply that the latter worked fewer hours: data suggests that the differences can principally be attributed to changes in the pattern of physical activity, from being highly mobile foragers to relatively sedentary agriculturalists.

Another example of paleopathology at work is the study of Native American skeletons from burial mounds in the Illinois and Ohio River valley, when they assessed health changes that occurred when a hunter-gatherer culture changed to intensive maize farming around AD 1150. Studies by George Armelagos and his colleagues then at the University of Massachusetts show these early farmers paid a price for their new-found livelihood.

When compared with their hunter-gatherer ancestors, the farmers were found to have significant health deficiencies which indicated malnutrition. For example, a bone condition called porotic hyperostosis increased by four times indicating iron-deficiency anaemia, bone lesions were three times more evident which points to an increase in infectious diseases and a rise in degenerative spinal conditions was the result of the gruelling physical work. One expert observed that life expectancy dropped by about seven years from the pre-agricultural average of twenty-six years to just nineteen years in post-agricultural society indicating the negative impact of nutritional deficiencies and infectious disease on the population.

The evidence suggests that while hunter-gatherers enjoyed a varied diet including wild plants and protein, early farmers obtained most of their food from a limited amount of starchy crops such as wheat, gaining cheap calories at the cost of poor nutrition. Using new food sources such as dairy products proved difficult as humans had not adapted to digest it. In addition, dependence on a restricted number of crops meant the risk of starvation were one crop to fail.

The lasting impact of the Agricultural Revolution was to enable Homo sapiens to succeed as a species in direct proportion to the increase in the amount of food they produced. However, the short-term effect was that small groups of relatively healthy people disappeared, to be replaced by large villages of people suffering from disease and malnourishment.

Vocabulary

Academic verbs

1a Match the verbs with their meanings (1–6).

disappear   emerge   enable   progress   settle   transform

1 to improve or develop things so that they are at a more advanced stage
2 to make it possible for someone to do something or for something to happen
3 to go and live somewhere, usually permanently
4 to completely change the appearance, form or character of something or someone, especially in a way that improves it
5 to begin to be known or noticed
6 to stop existing or reduce rapidly

b Complete the text with the correct form of the verbs from Exercise 1a.

An alternative world?

One little-known revolution **1** _____ the future of the USA: the Haitian Revolution. In 1791, the black slaves on the island of Haiti rebelled against their French colonisers who had **2** _____ on the island as part of Napoléon Bonaparte's empire, which was growing rapidly. His ultimate plan was to conquer the United States as a French colony. This would **3** _____ France to have more power across the world. However, when he sent his army to stop this uprising, there was an outbreak of disease which killed many of his men. With his finances **4** _____ due to the expense of waging war on this island, he had to shift his attention from the United States. This has had far-reaching effects; perhaps French would have even **5** _____ as the prominent language.

Written and spoken vocabulary

2a Look at the sentences. Which is spoken and which is written? Why?

1 To better manage modern life, many people have to expand their skill sets.
2 It's important to build up a lot of different skills so you can deal with life these days.

b Adapt the questions into spoken English. Replace the verbs in bold with the correct form of a verb phrase below. There is one extra verb phrase you do not need to use.

die out   get on   make it possible for   put down roots   spring up

1 Are there any traditions in your country that you think are **disappearing**? Can you give any examples?
2 What changes have **enabled** people to have an easier life?
3 Why do people **settle** in new countries?
4 What changes in society have **suddenly emerged** in your country in the last 20 years?

c Work in pairs and discuss the questions in Exercise 2b.

Process verbs

3a Choose the correct option in *italics* to complete the text.

Humans: friend or foe?

A lot has changed in the world over the last 2000 years. Developments such as the **1** *construction / construct* of buildings, towns and cities, the ability to **2** *hot / heat* and **3** *cool / cold* the environments we live in, the ability to **4** *connect / connection* to people all around the world at the click of a button, have made our lives more comfortable and infinitely more enjoyable.

However, human **5** *adds / additions* to the planet have not always been positive. Although we have seen civilisations **6** *develop / development*, we have also seen the **7** *destruction / destroy* of some natural habitats and animal life due to human intervention.

b Complete the table.

Noun	Verb	Adjective
1 _____	2 _____	hot/heated
3 _____	cool	4 _____
5 _____	construct	6 _____
connection	7 _____	8 _____
9 _____	develop	10 _____
11 _____	add	12 _____
13 _____	14 _____	destroyed/destructible
15 _____	rise	16 _____
rotation/rotator	17 _____	18 _____
19 _____	transfer	20 _____
21 _____	extract	22 _____

Speaking (Part 2)

Lead-in

1 Look at the photo. Do you like this style of architecture? How would you describe these buildings? Are they similar to the buildings in your neighbourhood?

Develop topic-specific vocabulary

2a Read the test task. How many of the points on the card must you talk about?

Describe an old building that you particularly like. You should say:

    what the building looks like

    where the building is located

    what the building is used for

and why you like it.

b 🔊 2.1 Listen to two students' answers. Which student answers the question more fully? Which student uses more topic-specific vocabulary?

c Listen again to the second student, and look at audio script 2.1 on page 202. Write the words or phrases he uses to express the following things.

Time	Materials	Change	Place	Style
	stone		near my house,	carvings,

d Can you think of any other expressions you can add to the table in Exercise 2c?

Make notes and plan your answer

3a Read the test task and the notes below. How has the student organised his/her notes?

Describe a town or city that you would like to go to. You should say:

    where it is

    what you know about it

    what you would like to do there

and why you would like to go there.

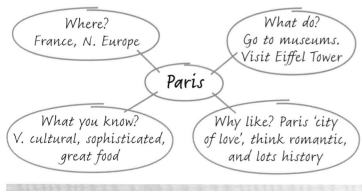

b Read the test task. Write notes on what you can say.

Describe a place that makes you feel happy. You should say:

    where it is

    what it is like

    when you first went there

and why it makes you happy.

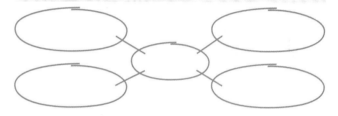

Test practice

➤ **TEST STRATEGIES** page 174

➤ **EXPERT SPEAKING** page 185

4a Look at the test task in Exercise 2a. You have 1 minute to prepare your topic and make notes.

Remember the following advice:
- Organise your notes into a logical system.
- Use your notes to make sure you answer all parts of the question.
- Think of some topic-specific vocabulary.

b Work in pairs and take turns to give your description. Speak for 2 minutes and record your answers if possible.

Assess and improve

5a Give feedback on your partner's performance in the exam task.

1 Did he/she make good notes to help answer the test task?

2 Did he/she answer all parts of the test task?

3 Did he/she use specific vocabulary for the topic?

b How could you improve?
- make clearer notes?
- make longer notes?
- organise your notes better?
- answer all parts of the test task?
- learn more topic-specific vocabulary?

Listening (Section 1)

Before you listen

1 Look at the photo and discuss the questions in groups.

1 Would you like to try this activity? Why/Why not?
2 What similar activities have you done?
3 Why do you think people choose to do this activity?

Understand different ways location is expressed

2 Look at the map. What places are shown on the map? With a partner, use the words below to talk about the locations.

along   across   adjacent to   at the end   beside
by   in the middle of   opposite   past   to the left of
on the edge of

A: The tables are to the left of the bridge.

3 🔊 2.2 Listen to two people describing their walks. Where do they go? Write the names of places they walk to.

Robert	Filipo
1 forest	1 campsite
2 _____	2 _____
3 _____	3 _____
4 _____	4 _____
5 _____	5 _____
6 _____	6 _____
7 _____	
8 _____	

4 Choose the correct option in *italics* to complete the text. Use the map in Exercise 2 to help you.

So, you want to go to the cabin, do you? It's quite far from the lake here. Cross **1** *over / around* the field with the cows in it. You'll see a bridge **2** *opposite / adjacent* you. Go **3** *past / along* the picnic area and **4** *through / over* the bridge. The cabin is to your right. It's **5** *on the edge / just north* of the forest.

5 Match the phrases 1–6 with their meanings A–F.

1 back on yourself   A straight in front
2 not too far   B keep going along
3 directly ahead   C quite near
4 a bit further on   D halfway down
5 don't go all the way   E back the way you came
6 follow it around   F just beyond

Test practice

> **TEST STRATEGIES** page 169

6a Look at the map. Describe the locations (A–E).

b 🔊 2.3 Listen and complete the test task.

Questions 1–4
*Label the map below. Write the correct letter, **A–E**, next to questions 1–4.*

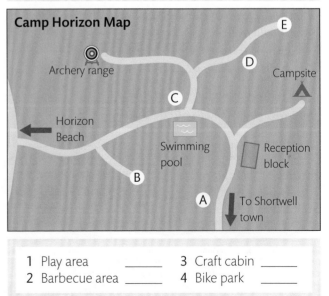

Camp Horizon Map

Archery range
E
D
Campsite
C
Horizon Beach
Swimming pool
Reception block
B
A
To Shortwell town

1 Play area   _____   3 Craft cabin   _____
2 Barbecue area   _____   4 Bike park   _____

Language development

Present simple, past simple and present perfect passives

> EXPERT GRAMMAR page 176

1a Read the resort description and underline the passive forms.

> Loxley Pines is a woodland resort for all the family. It is located on the shores of Creel Bay against the stunning backdrop of the mountains. Loxley Pines was built in 1971 with the aim of providing luxury accommodation for the adventurous. All our ten lodges are furnished beautifully and are equipped with wireless internet. All the lodges have been updated recently to include jacuzzi hot tubs and cinema-style TV screens. In addition, a barbecue area has been added so that our guests can enjoy eating in the great outdoors.

b Write an example of the following passive forms from Exercise 1a.
  1 Present simple passive
  2 Past simple passive
  3 Present perfect passive

c Rewrite these active sentences in the passive.
  1 People chose Hawaii as the most desirable holiday destination in 2013.
  2 Tourism has damaged the local wildlife in the nature reserve.
  3 People consider Thai beaches to be the best in the world.
  4 Walt Disney created the famous theme park Disneyland.
  5 Over 17,000 islands form Indonesia.
  6 The UAE has developed an indoor ski resort in the desert.

Other passive forms

2a Match the passive forms below with the sentences (1–5).

past perfect passive	present continuous passive
future simple passive	past continuous passive
modal passive	

  1 This wasteland area will be transformed into a new park for the community.
  2 The number of visitors to the attraction can be tracked by the new computer system.
  3 New ideas for regenerating the town were being considered, but no conclusion was reached.
  4 A considerable sum is being invested in upgrading transport facilities in the city.
  5 Although the hotel had been renovated five years ago, it recently closed due to lack of business.

b Choose the correct option in *italics* to complete the text.

> Until cameras became more widespread, photos **1** *are being taken / had been taken* mostly by explorers rather than tourists. The way we take photos now is almost unrecognisable from how it **2** *was done / has been done* when cameras **3** *were being invented / were invented* in the early 1800s. The very first photographs took a long time to develop, but nowadays, thousands of photos **4** *are taken / will be taken* by tourists all over the world. This can be seen by the huge number of photos which **5** *were uploaded / are being uploaded* daily.

c Complete the rest of the article with the correct passive form. The verb and form are given in brackets.

> Nowadays photos **1** _____ (modal/take) with not just cameras, but mobile phones and tablets too. There is no need to get any film developed as photos **2** _____ now _____ (present simple/ store) digitally. In the past, photos **3** _____ (past simple/keep) in albums, but now photos **4** _____ (present continuous/share) so quickly and easily online that there is an issue of privacy and ownership. When posting a photo, people have no idea where or to whom it **5** _____ (future simple/distribute). A recent estimate has suggested that over 250 billion photos **6** _____ (present perfect/upload) onto social media sites. Many of these are likely to be snaps shared in the blink of an eye.

3 Talk to your partner about these topics. Try to use the passive form where appropriate.
  1 A festival or celebration.
  2 The place where you now live.

Writing (Task 1)

Lead-in

1   What do you think is the greatest invention in your lifetime? Why?

Write introductions and processes

➤ **EXPERT WRITING** page 192

2a Look at the following process. With a partner, describe what is happening. Where does the process start? What is the final stage?

How wind turbines produce electricity

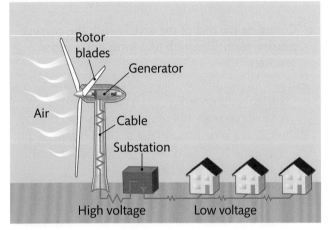

b   Put the words below in the order of the process shown in the diagram.

air   cable   generator   houses   rotor blades
substation

c   Number the sentences in the correct order to describe the process in Exercise 2a.

A   The electricity passes through a cable in the wind turbine.
B   The rotor blades are turned when air blows through them.
C   The voltage of the electricity is changed in the substation.
D   Electricity is produced by the generator.
E   The generator is turned by the rotor blades.
F   The low-voltage electricity is supplied to the houses.

d   Which introduction best describes the process in Exercise 2a?

1   The diagram shows how electricity is produced by wind turbines. There are several stages in the process which explain how the turbine generates electricity and how it is transmitted to houses.
2   This diagram demonstrates how wind turbines are constructed. It shows the parts of the wind turbine and the function of each part.
3   The process diagram explains the main use of wind turbines. This main use is to supply many houses with as much electricity as they require.

Use the active and passive

3a Which sentence is active and which is passive?

1   Electricity is produced by the generator.
2   The electricity passes through a cable in the wind turbine.

b   Look at the following sentences which describe the diagram in Exercise 2a. Change the passive forms to active and the active forms to passive.

1   The diagram shows how the wind turbine generates electricity.
2   The rotor blades are turned by the movement of the air.
3   The substation transforms the electricity from high voltage to low voltage.
4   The electricity is transmitted to houses along underground cables.

c   Work in pairs. Think of a process that you are familiar with and describe it using the active and/or passive.

Test practice

➤ **TEST STRATEGIES** page 173

4a Look at the process diagram below. Think of an introduction and the stages of the process. Make a plan of what to include.

The process of producing edible oils and fats, and margarine

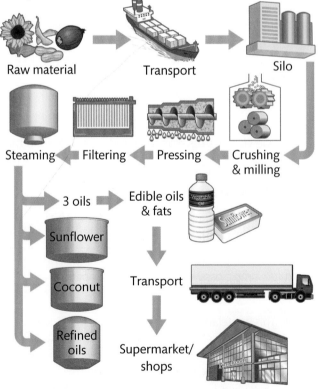

b   Read the strategies and write your answer. Remember to:

1   describe the overall process in the introduction.
2   stage your answer logically.
3   use the passive when appropriate.

Listening (Section 1)

Before you listen

1   Which of these ways of protecting endangered species do you think are more effective and why?

1   Creating national parks
2   Breeding programmes
3   Reducing human contact
4   Controlling invasive species

Accurate answers

2a   Read the audio script. What is Polly going to do?

Polly:	Hello, I'd like to book a flight, please.
Travel agent:	Certainly, do you have an account with us already?
Polly:	I do. My name's Polly Smith.
Travel agent:	OK. Let me look you up on the system … 14 Kingsland Terrace, Queensland?
Polly:	No, that's my old address. I now live at 243 Atlantic Avenue. It's still in Belletown, Queensland, 4399.
Travel agent:	Is your phone number still the same?
Polly:	Yes, it is. It's 61 565 9457.
Travel agent:	OK, thanks. And where do you want to travel to?
Polly:	I'd like to go to Borneo on Friday on the early flight if possible. I'm doing a conservation trip there.
Travel agent:	Yes, we've got availability on the 7.20 flight. Is that OK for you?
Polly:	Yes, that's fine.
Travel agent:	Great. That's flight number QA 785. The flight gives you 20 kilos. Do you need any more than this?
Polly:	No, that'll be fine.

b   Find and correct the errors in the answers. What kind of errors are they?

Questions 1–3
Complete the form below.
Write **NO MORE THAN TWO WORDS AND/OR A NUMBER** for each answer.

Name:	Polly Smith
Address:	243 1 *243 Atlantic Avenue*, Belletown, Queensland, 4399 Australia
Telephone number:	+61 565 9457
Travelling to:	2 *Borno*
Flight number:	QA 785
Baggage allowance:	3 *200 kilos*

Test practice

> TEST STRATEGIES page 169

3   🔊 2.4   Complete the test task.

Questions 1–5
Complete the form below.
Write **NO MORE THAN TWO WORDS AND/OR A NUMBER** for each answer.

Turtle Bay Safari Camp
Customer registration form

Customer name:	Cindy 1 _____
Telephone number:	09669 343123
Nationality:	2 _____
Length of stay:	One week
Accommodation type:	3 _____ cabin
Credit card number:	4 _____
Expiry date:	10/20
Additional comments:	5 _____

Questions 6–10
Label the map below.
Write the correct letter, **A–G**, next to questions 6–10.

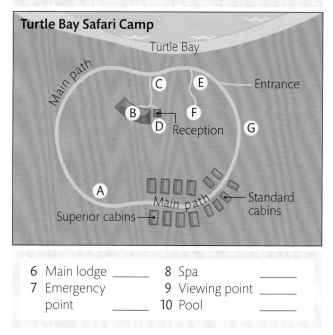

6	Main lodge _____	8	Spa _____
7	Emergency point _____	9	Viewing point _____
		10	Pool _____

Task analysis

4   Did you get any of the questions incorrect? Read audio script 2.4 on page 202 and locate your mistakes. How can you avoid making these mistakes in future?

Discussion

5   Do you think conservation efforts are making a positive change? Why/Why not?

Language development and vocabulary

Relative clauses

> EXPERT GRAMMAR page 177

1a Match the sentences 1 and 2 with the correct meanings A and B.

1 The islands which were likely to be flooded were evacuated.
2 The islands, which were likely to be flooded, were evacuated.

A All the islands were evacuated because they were likely to flood.
B Some of the islands were evacuated because they were likely to flood.

b Read sentences A and B and answer questions 1–4.

A The islands which were likely to be flooded were evacuated.
B The buildings, which were likely to be flooded, were evacuated.

1 In which sentence is 'which were likely to be flooded' essential information?
2 In which sentence is it extra information?
3 What are the differences in punctuation between the sentences?
4 In which sentence could you replace 'which' with 'that'?

2 Add more information to the student's description of their favourite place using relative clauses.

I think my favourite place must be the Musée d'Orsay. I went there once on a school trip. We went to all the well-known sightseeing places in Paris but I'll never forget the experience of going to the Musée D'Orsay. It was the first time and I was so excited. My art teacher had told me what to expect, but it was better than I'd expected. I saw loads of paintings. Almost every room has at least one inspiring painting in it. I think my favourites were the Van Gogh paintings. Especially *The Starry Night*. The colours in the painting are amazing! I think that I sat looking at that painting for about 30 minutes trying to imagine what it must have been like to be Van Gogh. I think Van Gogh was always poor when he was alive. Now I think that most people would consider him to be the most famous painter ever. The building is quite old and large. Although I thought it would feel old fashioned inside, it gives an impression of being really light and airy. It also has a huge clock in it. It reminded me of the clock in *Back to the Future*. I'm not sure why I liked it. I think it just made me feel happy being in there surrounded by so much beautiful artwork. I really hope that I can visit the Musée D'Orsay again someday.

3 Read the news report below and add punctuation to the relative clauses where necessary.

Disappearing islands

Residents of the Marshall Islands may be the first people to fall victim to climate change. The islands which are in the Pacific Ocean are likely to be underwater at some point in the near future. John Farrow who is a Marshall Island resident claimed that although there is pressure for other countries to reduce climate change, there is very little motivation when climate change has little effect on their daily lives. For Mr Farrow this is an issue which must be addressed by all nations that are still contributing to increasing global emissions. Only when the effects of sea level rises like this can be seen, may change actually occur.

Sequencing with prepositions and adverbs

4a Choose the correct option in *italics* to complete the sentences.

1 *While / During* the 20th Century, there have been many changes to women's rights.
2 People's lives became a lot easier *when / while* the computer was invented.
3 Television has developed so much that now we can watch events throughout the world *as / during* they happen.
4 *After / Before* commercial air travel became popular, people were able to travel more easily to new, far-flung destinations.
5 Many great authors thought of the idea for their novels *while / as* walking in the park.

b Complete the structures with the words in Exercise 4a.

1 _____	+ clause
2 _____	+ noun
3 _____ , _____	+ -ing, clause or noun
4 _____ , _____	+ -ing, clause

5 Work in pairs and discuss the questions. Use structures from Exercise 4b.

1 Have your opinions on society changed as you have become older?
2 Has your country changed much during the last 10 years?
3 How were social roles different when your parents were young?
4 How did people entertain themselves before the invention of the TV or internet?

Speaking (Part 2)

Catskill Mountains

Great Barrier Reef

Vocabulary development

1 How would you describe the places in the photos? Which of these do you think most deserves to be saved? Why?

2a Choose the correct option in *italics* to complete the text.

> Waikiki beach in Hawaii is one of the most 1 *devastating / stunning* places on earth. Its 2 *magnificent / contemporary* beaches attract visitors from all over the world. The Pacific island beaches feel so 3 *remote / obscure* that you can expect complete tranquillity, but just a few kilometres away is the 4 *fussy / bustling* town with its many restaurants and nightlife. It seems like the perfect place, 5 *unspoilt / distinguished* by the perils of modern tourism. However, this 6 *unique / privileged* environment is now being threatened by the construction of new homes and sea wall protection. Make sure you visit it while you still can!

b Choose ONE of the following and describe the place to your partner for 2 minutes. Use vocabulary from Exercise 2a and use relative clauses to provide extra details.

1 A place you find very tranquil.
2 The most remote place you've ever been to.
3 The most stunning view you have ever seen.

Focus on fluency and coherence

3a Turn to page 183 and read the fluency and coherence descriptors for the band score you want to achieve. Work in pairs and discuss what you need to do to achieve this score.

b 🔊 2.5 Listen to a student talking about the following test task. What are the student's strengths for fluency and coherence? Why?

> *Describe an important place in your country. You should say:*
> *what it is*
> *where it is*
> *why it is important*
> *and explain how you feel about this place.*

Test practice

> **TEST STRATEGIES** page 174

4 Work in pairs and take turns to complete the test task below. Speak for 2 minutes and time each other. Record your answers if possible.

> *Describe a beautiful place you visited when you were younger. You should say:*
> *where it is*
> *when you visited it*
> *what you did there*
> *and explain why you thought it was beautiful.*

Assess and improve

5a Assess your performance for fluency and coherence using the descriptors on page 183. How well did you and your partner do?

b What advice could you give in the following areas to help your partner improve?

1 The length of time he/she speaks for, overall
2 The development of his/her points by adding extra details
3 The logical ordering of the points he/she talks about
4 Correcting himself/herself if he/she makes mistakes

Reading (*True/False/Not given*; Short-answer questions)

A tiger

B bee

C bush baby

Before you read

1 Look at the photos and answer the questions.

    1 What might these creatures have in common?

    2 Which living creatures in your country do people most value and worry about losing? Why?

    3 What are the most common insects in your country?

    4 What purpose do insects serve?

Test practice

2 Read the strategies and complete the test tasks.

> **TEST STRATEGIES** pages 170 and 171

Questions 1–5

Do the following statements agree with the information in the reading passage? Write

TRUE   *if the statement agrees with the information*

FALSE   *if the statement contradicts the information*

NOT GIVEN *if there is no information on this*

    1 The majority of insects come from of a group of limited species.

    2 Every type of insect will feed off whatever is available, alive or dead.

    3 There is a significant variation in the life expectancy of different insects.

    4 The number of insects is falling despite the effort of humans.

    5 People become interested in conservation when they see the animals on television.

> **HELP**

1 How many insects are there altogether? What is the biggest proportion made up of?

2 Look carefully at these words in the passage: *almost, one sort or another, variously.*

4 Look carefully at both parts of the question.

Questions 6–9

Answer the questions below.

Choose NO MORE THAN THREE WORDS *from the passage for each answer.*

    6 With which animal are insects contrasted, in terms of their significance to mankind?

    7 By moving dead organic material around the ground, what are anthropods providing for the soil?

    8 What important aspect of a field do predator insects help to preserve?

    9 What are two examples of insects that keep the population of other insects in check?

> **HELP**

8 Find the part of the passage which gives names of anthropods typically found in the soil.

Task analysis

3 Work in pairs and discuss the questions.

    1 Did you highlight the key words in the questions/statements first? How did this help you to locate the information in the passage?

    2 Did identifying the topic sentences first help you to read the passage more quickly? How?

    3 In questions 6–9 did you
      • keep to the stated number of words?
      • copy down the word(s) with the correct spelling?
      • change the word(s) in any way?

Discussion

4 Discuss these questions, giving reasons.

    1 Do you agree with the writer that 'the extinction of the giant panda would be a terrible loss?' Why/Why not?

    2 Why do you think so many people are concerned about animals becoming extinct? Do you think it matters?

    3 Why do you think few people care about insects?

The Insect Empire

The insects were the last of the major anthropod* groups to arrive, about 400 million years ago, but they have become the masters of terrestrial life.

Today, of the roughly 1.5 million known species of plant and animal on Earth, 1.2 million are anthropods, of whom about one million are insects, and, of these, about 800,000 are beetles, flies, moths or wasps. And were you to go into any tropical forest with a butterfly net, you would almost certainly catch a handful of species that are new to science. For all of the last 500 million years almost every habitat on Earth has been dominated by insects, swarming in extraordinary diversity in the lakes, rivers, forests, grasslands and deserts, from the seashore to the top of the highest mountains.

Insects fill almost every conceivable ecological niche: they can be predators, parasites, herbivores or detrivores*. There is almost nothing of organic origin, alive or dead, that is not avidly consumed by insects of one sort or another, variously specializing in eating such things as blood, wood, seeds, the tongues of frogs, bacteria, leaves, spiders, fungi and, of course, other insects. They vary in size from Bornean stick insects, which can grow to over thirty centimetres, to speck-like parasitoid wasps that weigh in at just twenty-five millionths of a gram.

Some, such as ants and termites, live in vast social colonies, with workers specializing as soldiers, gardeners or nurse-maids, while others, such as the death-watch beetle, may spend ten years alone and in darkness, slowly munching through the timber of a dead tree. Nymphs of the periodic cicada in North America spend seventeen years living underground, sucking on tree roots, before all emerging together to mate and die, while a fruit fly dashes through its entire life cycle in a fortnight.

Just as their life cycles are infinitely diverse, so their mating habitats are extraordinarily varied and often bizarre. While butterfly males use their beautiful wings to attract a mate, male scorpion flies offer piles of dried saliva as an enticement to females. Crickets, cicadas and grasshoppers sing to impress, while other insects such as moths release pheromones that drift for kilometres on the wind.

In terms of numbers of individuals, insects rule supreme. In fact, at any one point in time there are currently thought to be very roughly ten million trillion individual insects alive on Earth. Whatever way you look at it we are seriously outnumbered. Some pest insects, such as house flies, are perhaps more common than ever because of the food we unwittingly supply for them. But most insects are declining, and many thousands of species have already become extinct.

In the minds of many, conservation is all about giant pandas, tigers, rhinos and blue whales: large charismatic, furry or feathery creatures, often living on the other side of the world, glimpsed only in television documentaries. What few people appreciate is that the vast majority of life on earth, in terms of both number of species and numbers of individuals, is comprised of insects and other anthropods, and that many of them are just as important, fascinating and worthy of our interest and of conservation as the larger creatures. Indeed, while the extinction of the giant panda would be a terrible loss, it would not have any major consequences. In contrast, the little creatures that inhabit the world around us are absolutely vital to human survival, yet we generally pay them little attention unless they annoy us.

The various flowers in the meadow need bees, hoverflies, butterflies and beetles to pollinate them, and many of those very same insects pollinate the peaches, apples and tomatoes in our gardens. Wild flowers and vegetables also need a healthy soil in which to grow, and so depend upon the worms and millipedes that live in it to break down dead plant and animal parts and return it to the earth in the form of nutrients to improve and aerate the soil. Without predators such as ladybirds and wasps, herbivorous insects would be uncontrollable, eradicating their host plants and therefore destroying the ecological balance of the meadow. Without grasshoppers, flies, crickets and moths, the birds and bats would have no food. Ugly or beautiful, it is the little creatures that make the world go round. We should celebrate and appreciate them in all their wonderful diversity.

*anthropods is a group which comprises crustaceans (e.g. woodlice), arachnids (e.g. spiders) and insects
*detrivores are insects which consume dead organic matter

Writing (Task 1)

Lead-in

1 What do you think is happening in the photo? What is the person doing? Why do you think he's doing it? Would you do this?

Understand the task

> EXPERT WRITING page 192

2 Look at the diagram of the formation of a supervolcano and answer the questions.

1 What is the process shown in the diagram?
2 Where does the process start and finish?
3 What information should you include in the introductory sentence(s) about the process?
4 How many stages are there in the process?
5 What is the order of these stages?

The diagram below shows the formation of a supervolcano and the stages involved.

Summarise the information by selecting and reporting the main features, and make comparisons where relevant.

Write at least 150 words.

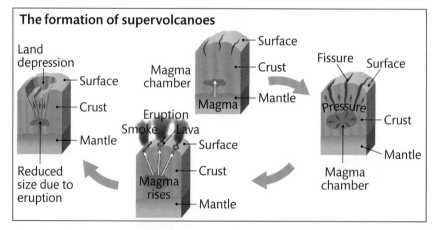

The formation of supervolcanoes

Plan the task

3a Read the coherence and cohesion descriptors on page 190. With a partner, discuss the differences between bands 6 and 7.

b Read the sentences below and tick those which are true about your own writing.

1 I organise my ideas/points logically.
2 I organise my ideas/points step-by-step and ensure I write about how these are connected.
3 I organise my ideas/points in a logical step-by-step way, referring back and forwards to show how they develop the overall idea/point.
4 I make an effort to move from one point to another using cohesive devices (*before*, *when*, etc.)
5 I know a few cohesive devices that I can use well.
6 I know a lot of cohesive devices and some I can use well.
7 I know a lot of cohesive devices and I can use them well.

4 Complete the text with the phrases below to make it more cohesive.

As they begin to melt   as well as   that have jet engines
When these particles stick

Danger in the skies

Volcanoes do not just affect those on land, they can also cause problems for those in the air. Volcanic ash can be particularly dangerous for airplanes **1** _____ . The ash particles from the eruption can be melted by the high temperatures of the jet. **2** _____ , they stick to the blades of the turbine, **3** _____ other parts of the plane. **4** _____ , they can change the shapes of parts, and block the engines.

Language and content

5a Look at the verbs below. What nouns do you think they go with in the diagram in Exercise 2? Discuss your answers with a partner.

break   cause   collapse   drop   expand   fall   fill   flow   force
push   reduce   rise   separate   tear

b Choose the correct option in *italics* to complete the sentences, according to the diagram in Exercise 2a.

1 The chamber is *filled / collapsed* with magma.
2 The magma *rises / breaks* to the surface.
3 The eruption is *pushed / caused* by pressure.
4 The fissures *reduce / separate*.
5 The surface is *torn / expanded*.

c Can you think of any other verbs you could use with this diagram?

Write your summary

6a Write your plan and check it. Have you included the following?

• An introductory sentence or sentences about the process
• A step-by-step description
• Passive and active tenses
• Verbs to accurately represent the picture
• Use of relative clauses to add information
• Sequential linking

b Write a description of the diagram in Exercise 2. Write at least 150 words.

Assess and improve

7a Work in pairs and review your answers, thinking about the criteria for Coherence and Cohesion. Answer the questions.

1 Is there an introductory sentence or sentences about the diagram?
2 Are all the stages included and in a logical order?
3 In your opinion, are all the sentences in the right order?
4 Have you grouped your ideas into clear paragraphs?
5 Are sequential linkers used well?
6 Are there enough words (150 or more)?

b Check your work using the checklist in Exercise 7a and the descriptors on page 190. Make a note of any key points you need to remember for this task.

Review

1a Complete the sentences with the correct word or phrase (A, B or C).

1 Due to climate change, it is likely that some species of animal will _____ over the next century.
   A transform   B die out   C emerge
2 The museum was greatly improved by the _____ of a new, larger gallery.
   A addition   B connection   C transference
3 I moved around a lot during my childhood, so it was nice when my family decided to come back to London and _____ .
   A spring up
   B make it possible
   C put down roots
4 The station is _____ here. It should only take you about ten minutes to walk there.
   A not too far from
   B directly ahead of
   C halfway down
5 At the end of a long winter, animals such as bears _____ from hibernation.
   A emerge   B transform   C progress

b Choose the correct option in *italics* to complete the text.

My favourite trip

One of the greatest places I've ever visited is the Masai Mara in Kenya. When I went there last year I stayed in a beautiful camp which had been renovated in traditional style. All the buildings were wooden **1** *constructions / constructed*. It was an amazing trip because it was so varied. **2** *During / While* my stay I was able to meet and spend time with some Masai people as well as seeing the animals on safari.

The Masai people **3** *settled / transformed* there in the 17th and 18th centuries. They are nomadic people, who farm the land and keep animals. They feel especially **4** *added / connected* to cattle, which are a central part of their lifestyle. I spent two weeks living this nomadic lifestyle. At first I found it unusual, but then I got used to their simple way of life. Spending time with the Masai **5** *enabled / progressed* me to rethink some aspects of my stressful lifestyle.

2a Complete the sentences with the correct passive form of the verbs in brackets.

1 Crops such as rice and wheat _____ (grow) all around the world for thousands of years.
2 Modern life, with all the machines and gadgets that we love, _____ (start) by the industrial revolution.
3 Nowadays great progress _____ (make) in finding treatments and cures for a variety of diseases.
4 Some people believe we _____ (develop) self-driving cars by the end of this decade.
5 Before the invention of the internet, ideas _____ (spread) by word of mouth.
6 The holiday resort _____ (construct) before the airport was built so very few tourists went there at first.
7 The building _____ (repair) when the builders found the old paintings in the cellar.
8 There is a new viewing platform on the hill and from here the animals in the park _____ (observe) more easily.

b Complete the text about the mission to Mars using the words below. There are more words than you need.

that   while   which   during   when   who   before
whose

A trip to Mars

Mars One is an organisation **1** _____ is based in the Netherlands. Its aim is to take the first humans to Mars and establish a permanent colony there by 2027. The project is being managed by a Dutch entrepreneur, **2** _____ announced the project to the world in 2012. The crew will be made up of people with a broad variety of skills including scientific knowledge, IT expertise and communication skills. In 2013, **3** _____ the initial application period closed, over 2,500 people had applied to be an astronaut on the programme. The applicants have to complete a series of rigorous tests **4** _____ being accepted onto the project. The applicants **5** _____ are chosen for the mission will then spend seven years training.

3 The feel-good factor

3a Training

- **Reading**: Identify the main idea (Matching headings; Multiple choice: select two answers)
- **Vocabulary**: Problems and solutions; Academic collocations; Idiomatic phrases for problems and solutions
- **Speaking**: Topic-specific vocabulary; Develop your answers (Part 3)
- **Listening**: Identify specific information required (Section 4: Sentence completion; Short-answer questions)
- **Language development**: Real and unreal conditionals review; Other ways to express conditionality
- **Writing**: Write about problems and solutions; Develop a paragraph (Task 2: Problem and solution essay)

3b Testing

- **Listening**: Section 4: Sentence completion; Short-answer questions
- **Language development and vocabulary**: Modal forms; Degrees of certainty; Adverbs of attitude
- **Speaking**: Part 3: Discussing health
- **Reading**: Matching headings; Multiple choice: select two answers
- **Writing**: Task 2: Problem and solution essay

Today's teenagers

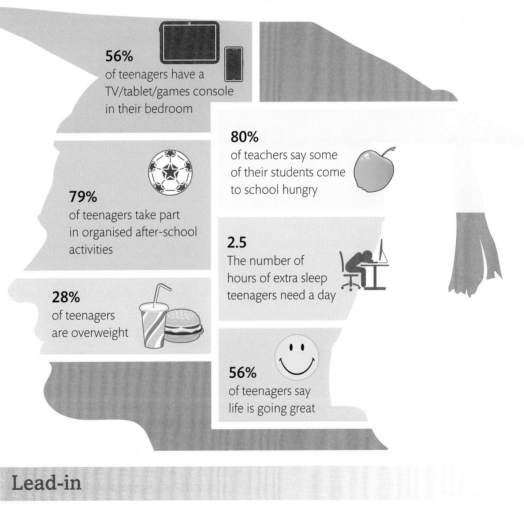

56% of teenagers have a TV/tablet/games console in their bedroom

79% of teenagers take part in organised after-school activities

28% of teenagers are overweight

80% of teachers say some of their students come to school hungry

2.5 The number of hours of extra sleep teenagers need a day

56% of teenagers say life is going great

Lead-in

1 Look at the infographic about school students in the USA. Discuss the questions.

  1 Which statistics would you say represent positive situations and which represent negative situations?

  2 Which factors might relate to psychological aspects and which to physical aspects?

  3 How do you think these factors might affect studying? Why?

  4 How do you think these statistics might compare to students in your country?

Reading (Matching headings; Multiple choice: select two answers)

Before you read

1   Work in pairs and discuss the questions.

   1   In what ways, if any, do you think people's lives are more stressful now than they were in the past?

   2   In what ways can stress affect people's lives?

Identify the main idea

2a Answer the questions.

   1   Read the title and subtitle of the passage. What do you think the article will be about?

   2   Skim paragraph A and underline the topic sentence. How is the rest of the paragraph structured?

   3   Choose the best summary (A, B or C) for the paragraph.

     A   The importance of nature throughout history

     B   The impact of change on people's lifestyles

     C   A comparison of town and country life

  b   Look at the list of headings in the test task below and choose the one which best matches the summary you chose in Exercise 2a.

Test practice

3   Read the strategies and complete the test task.

> TEST STRATEGIES pages 171 and 172

Questions 1–4

The reading passage has four paragraphs, **A–D**.

Choose the correct heading for each paragraph from the list below.

Write the correct number, **i–vii**.

List of Headings

i   Approaches to increasing young people's level of fitness

ii   Projects which form a connection with the natural world

iii   The high price being paid for progress in modern times

iv   The effect of too much pressure on people's well-being

v   Evidence for the value of strengthening links with nature

vi   Exploiting a country's natural resources to its advantage

vii   Positive outcomes of woodland therapy on global health and fitness

1 Paragraph **A**   3 Paragraph **C**

2 Paragraph **B**   4 Paragraph **D**

Questions 5–6

Choose **TWO** letters, **A–E**.

The list below contains some possible statements about health and environment.

Which **TWO** of these statements are made by the writer of the passage?

A   Individuals are programmed to want to live and work with other people.

B   Scientists believe that city living will always have a negative influence on our physical well-being.

C   Research in the USA has prompted town planners to surround new buildings with green spaces.

D   Studies confirm that prisoners are healthier if they are permitted to go outdoors.

E   It is not yet common practice for a doctor to recommend outdoor activities to their patients.

Task analysis

4a Which of these strategies refer to a) matching headings b) multiple choice: selecting two answers c) both?

   1   I summarised the paragraphs in my own words first.

   2   I highlighted key words in the task to help me find the correct place in the passage.

   3   I focused on the main idea in each paragraph.

   4   I scanned the passage to find where the information was located.

  b   Which strategies did you use? Which did you find useful?

Discussion

5   Work in groups and discuss the questions. Give reasons for your answers.

   1   In what ways can being in the countryside help people to feel better? Which outdoor activities would you recommend?

   2   What are the advantages and disadvantages of living in the city and the countryside?

   3   What aspects of modern life can cause stress? What strategies are useful for managing it?

Prescribing nature

Exciting new research shows how we can fight disease and improve mental health.

A Humans are hard-wired to be hunter-gatherers, an instinct so deep-rooted that we still feel a strong bond with nature; hunter-gatherers would also have had a clear purpose in life, and been responsible for set tasks upon which the community, who would have supported them, relied. In contrast, an inevitable consequence of the advances in industrialization and technology is a more sedentary and isolated life, where the average person spends more time on their computer or in their vehicle than they do in the outdoors, leading many people – including the unemployed, stay-at-home mothers or the elderly – to feel increasingly lonely, undervalued and stressed. In addition, the number of people on Earth living in urban settings is expected to rise to about 70 percent in the next three decades, bringing with it yet more artificial noise, air pollution and traffic. All of these factors will undoubtedly be a threat to both physical and psychological well-being and although the human body will eventually adapt to its changed circumstances, many people would agree with Paracelsus, the 16th-century German-Swiss physician, who wrote, "The art of healing comes from nature, not from the physician," a claim based less on science than on intuition but which has nevertheless been a pervasive sentiment throughout the ages.

B Health professionals have long expressed concern about the potential effects of chronic stress, which can lead to diabetes, obesity, depression, dementia and heart disease in two distinct ways. First, under stress we change our behaviour: we start to crave sugar and fat, we are too tired to exercise and we may indulge in bad habits such as smoking or alcohol. The second way in which we are affected is more direct. The hormone cortisol is released: this causes toxic fat to be laid down in our stomachs, which in turn may result in a malfunction of the bacterium present in our cells, known as mitochondria. This means we become more prone to disease and start to age more quickly.

C In recent years, as a result of the sharp rise in widespread health issues such as depression, obesity and nearsightedness, scientists have begun to investigate more closely the effects of nature on our physical and psychological state. Developments in neuroscience and psychology have meant that what once appeared solely intuitive can now be quantified; several research studies confirm that being surrounded by trees and flowers positively impacts on people's well-being. A team of Dutch researchers also found a lower incidence of 15 diseases, including stress and depression, in those who lived near a green space, and in a series of landmark studies in Chicago, it was found that residents living in large tower blocks surrounded by gardens were more likely to know and support their neighbours and experience less crime than those who overlooked concrete. In addition, being able to look out onto trees rather than concrete is believed to lead to increased concentration from office workers, a faster recovery for hospital patients, who also required less pain relief, a lower incidence of illness amongst inmates in prison cells and less bullying in playgrounds.

D Studies such as these make it clear that one of our main priorities in the modern world should be to make exposure to the outdoors an essential feature of healthcare, education, planning and community development. Inspiring initiatives are already underway, including tree planting, schemes which encourage people to walk or cycle and inventive ways to get children more involved in outdoor pursuits. A less widespread, but more innovative, approach empowers doctors to 'prescribe nature' to those requiring medical treatment, in the hope that this will help stem an increase in the prevalence of stress, chronic diseases and mental health issues; several pioneering schemes encourage patients and their families to visit nearby parks, providing them with transportation and programmes to follow, such as outdoor conservation work or 'health walks'. In Finland, a country which has high rates of depression, nature experiences have become part of government health policy, with people being recommended to spend five hours a month engaged in walking, mindfulness and reflection. We may never know the precise relationship between nature and health and perhaps it is irrelevant but we do know how nature makes us feel and the challenge is now to incorporate this into every aspect of our daily lives.

Vocabulary

Problems and solutions

1 Match the words below with the underlined words with a similar meaning in 1–6.

danger method outcome priority problem test

1 Knee injuries can be a frequent <u>result</u> of too much running.
2 One serious <u>issue</u> in society is how to take care of the growing number of elderly people.
3 Setting realistic weight-loss goals is a good <u>approach</u> for anyone wanting to diet.
4 Making sure children exercise regularly should be a <u>key concern</u> for parents.
5 Getting young people to eat vegetables can be a real <u>challenge</u>.
6 Pollution can be a <u>threat</u> to the health of people with allergies.

2 Choose the correct option in *italics* to complete the text.

Yoga – the perfect way to destress at work

Research shows that stress dominates the modern workplace and reduces productivity. The **1** *consequence / issue* of this stress is that employees who are overtired are less able to concentrate. As a result, some companies have started to introduce free lunchtime yoga classes. Doctors claim that reducing stress should be a **2** *priority / problem* for employers and they support the introduction of yoga as a **3** *method / concern* of relaxation. The **4** *approach / factor* which yoga takes is to increase our ability to remain calm by using physical exercises and teaching us how to control our breathing. The **5** *challenge / aspect* is to encourage people to take up yoga in the middle of the working day. However, studies show that the **6** *outcome / threat* of breaking up the day with yoga is almost always beneficial to employees.

Academic collocations

3a Complete the sentences with the correct verbs below to make collocations.

face find make pose tackle

1 It is the government's responsibility to _____ a **solution** to the obesity crisis.
2 It can be good to _____ a new **challenge** in order to learn new skills.
3 Society must find new ways to _____ **issues** relating to mental health.
4 Schools should _____ exercising every day a **priority** for children.
5 Eating a diet that contains a lot of sugar can _____ a **threat** to our health.

b Work in pairs and answer the questions.

1 What would you say are the biggest threats to people's health in developing nations?
2 How does the situation in developing nations compare to developed nations?
3 Which aspects of healthcare should be a priority in society? Why?
4 What are the main challenges in our everyday lives?

Idiomatic phrases for problems and solutions

4a Match the idioms (1–7) with the correct meanings (A–G).

1 the crux of the matter
2 a quick fix
3 the tip of the iceberg
4 a thorny issue
5 a vicious cycle
6 a knock-on effect
7 the last resort

A an easy solution which is often temporary and does not address the problem fully
B an issue which is difficult to deal with or solve
C a repeating situation where one problem leads to another problem which makes the first problem worse
D the final action used when all other possibilities have failed
E the basic or central point of a problem
F a small part of a larger problem which is hidden
G the effect that an action has on other situations

b Complete the sentences with idioms from Exercise 4a.

1 Using alternative medicine to treat serious illnesses is _____ for many people because there is conflicting evidence for its success.
2 A lack of exercise can have _____ on other areas of our lives.
3 The consumption of fast food is just _____ . People also eat many other foods which are bad for their health.
4 Telling people how to improve their health can be _____ because nobody likes to be criticised.
5 Increasing the number of doctors employed is often seen as _____ to healthcare problems although this fails to tackle the underlying issues.

Speaking (Part 3)

Lead-in

1a Work in pairs and do the quiz.

Positivity Quiz

1 I enjoy dealing with problems. Yes/No
2 When I have a good idea, I'm not surprised. Yes/No
3 After achieving a long-term goal, I congratulate myself. Yes/No
4 I don't complain much. Yes/No
5 Things don't worry me much. Yes/No

b What do you think 'half full' and 'half empty' in the photo means? Why do you think some people are more positive than others? Can people change how positive they are? How?

Topic-specific vocabulary

2a Complete the table with the correct word forms.

Noun	Adjective
1 _____	anxious
gratitude	2 _____
3 _____	inspiring
therapy	4 _____
5 _____	optimistic
6 _____	contented

b Read the examiner's question and think about how you could answer it. Choose some words below which are relevant to the question.

Examiner: What influences people's ability to think positively about life?

anxious attitude cheerful conceptualise contented gratitude inspiring optimistic outlook pessimistic prescribe self-awareness therapy treatment

c 🔊 3.1 Listen to a student answering the question. Tick the words she uses from Exercises 2a and 2b. Does she answer the question well?

d Complete the sentences with the correct form of the words from Exercises 2a and 2b.

1 Having a pet can be very _____ for elderly people who live alone.
2 Adults who have a positive _____ to life are more likely to have happier children.
3 Instead of aspiring to happiness, we should focus on achieving _____ .
4 Many doctors now _____ exercise to treat mental health conditions.
5 A lack of money and problems at work can cause _____ in lots of people.

e Work in pairs and discuss the following question using vocabulary from Exercises 2a and 2b.

Why are some people more positive than others?

Develop your answers

3a 🔊 3.2 Listen to two candidates. Who develops their answer more fully, Anya or Keigo?

b 🔊 3.3 Now listen to five students answer the question below. Match the students (1–5) with the way they develop their answers (A–E).

Examiner: What improves people's outlook on life?

1	Jing Lee	A	giving an example
2	Mario	B	making a comparison
3	Susanna	C	giving a reason
4	Heidi	D	giving alternatives
5	Mahmoud	E	explaining cause and effect

c Listen again. Write down examples of language for A–E in Exercise 3b.

4 Read the questions and make a brief note of your answer. Then write notes on how to develop your answer using the techniques in Exercise 3b.

1 Are people in your country generally optimistic or pessimistic?
2 Should we teach positive thinking in schools?

Test practice

▶ **TEST STRATEGIES** page 175

▶ **EXPERT SPEAKING** page 186

5a Read the questions and make notes on how you will develop your answers.

1 Do you think it's more difficult for adults to be positive than children?
2 Would you say that positivity is the key to happiness?
3 Do you believe that some cultures are more optimistic than others?

b Practise asking and answering the questions in pairs. Remember to develop your answers.

Listening (Section 4)

Before you listen

1 Look at the quotes about how people relax. What do you think they mean? Do you disagree with any of them? Which one do you think most accurately reflects your ideas?

> *'Tension is who you think you should be. Relaxation is who you are.'* Chinese proverb

> *'What you're supposed to do when you don't like a thing is change it. If you can't change it, change the way you think about it. Don't complain.'* Maya Angelou

> *'There is more to life than increasing its speed.'* Mahatma Gandhi

> *'He is richest who is content with the least, for content is the wealth of nature.'* Socrates

Identify specific information required

2a Read the questions. What do you think the main subject of the lecture will be?

Questions 1–2

Complete the sentences below.

Write **NO MORE THAN TWO WORDS AND/OR A NUMBER** *for each answer.*

1 There are <u>few</u> _____ on the <u>benefits</u> of meditation.
2 There is <u>some indication</u> that meditation <u>may be able to</u> <u>increase</u> our _____ .

Questions 3–4

Answer the questions below.

Write **NO MORE THAN THREE WORDS AND/OR A NUMBER** *for each answer.*

<u>In what ways</u> can meditation help us <u>physically</u>?
3 _____
4 _____

b Answer the following questions about the questions in Exercise 2a.

1 What kind of word or words should go in each space? A noun, adjective or verb?
2 Can more than one word go in any spaces? How many?
3 Which answers require a singular or plural noun?
4 What spaces definitely require more than one word? How do you know?
5 Which questions are asking for examples?

c Match the phrases below with the underlined words/phrases in Exercise 2a. Can you think of any others?

> a few signs   advantages   boost   could possibly   enhance in a more physical sense   in some manners   might even not many   positive points   preliminary evidence

d 🔊 3.4 Listen and answer the questions in Exercise 2a. You do not need pronouns (e.g. *it*) for your answers to questions 3 and 4.

Test practice

➤ **TEST STRATEGIES** page 168

3 🔊 3.5 Read the questions and complete the rest of the test task. Use the ideas in Exercises 2a–2c to prepare before you listen.

Questions 5–6

Answer the questions below.

Write **NO MORE THAN THREE WORDS AND/OR A NUMBER** *for each answer.*

What are two indirect benefits of meditation?
5 _____
6 _____

Questions 7–9

Complete the sentences below.

Write **NO MORE THAN TWO WORDS AND/OR A NUMBER** *for each answer.*

7 A lot of research has been done in the area of meditation and _____ .
8 _____ of daily meditation can improve a person's mental well-being.
9 In most cases, meditation should not be a replacement for _____ .

Task analysis

4a Read audio script 3.5 on page 203 and underline the sections with the answers.

b Analyse your answers using the questions.

1 Did you choose the correct part of speech?
2 Did you write the correct number of words?
3 Did you write singular and plural words correctly?

Discussion

5 Have you ever tried meditating? Why/Why not? To what extent do you believe that doing things like meditating can make mental or physical changes within a person?

Language development

Real and unreal conditionals review

> EXPERT GRAMMAR page 177

1a Read the sentences and decide if the conditionals are describing real situations or unreal (imaginary) ones.

1 If children eat too much sugar, they usually put on weight, which can have serious consequences.
2 If the government really wanted to tackle the problem of obesity, they would raise the price of unhealthy food and drink.
3 Elderly people will notice an improvement in their overall fitness if they add just 15 minutes of walking into their daily routine.
4 If cooking skills were a compulsory school subject, the overall health of young people could be improved.
5 When a person takes up a new hobby, they often report having a more positive outlook on life.

b Choose a sentence from Exercise 1a to match the conditional forms below.

1 Zero conditional   3 Second conditional
2 First conditional

c Answer the questions about real and unreal conditionals.

1 Which two conditionals express real situations?
   A zero and second   B zero and first
   C first and second
2 Which conditional expresses an unreal or imaginary situation?
   A zero   B first   C second

2 Complete the text using the correct conditional form of the verbs in brackets.

The perils of fast food

Supersize Me is a film about the effects of eating fast food. The director wanted to see what **1** _____ (happen) if he **2** _____ (consumed) nothing but fast food for a month. Each day he consumed 5,000 calories through eating three fast food meals. When humans **3** _____ (put) that much energy into their bodies, they **4** _____ (not use) most of it in one day. This means there is leftover energy, which is converted into fat and stored in the body. If the body **5** _____ (not need) this energy because the following day it receives another 5,000 calories, this fat **6** _____ (remain) in the body's fat cells. If this habit **7** _____ (continue), it is likely that the person **8** _____ (put on) more and more weight. This is exactly what happened and the film director put on 11 kilos. He made the documentary because he wanted to show how quickly fast food can cause weight gain. Doctors have suggested that if a teenager **9** _____ (eat) a diet of over 2,500 calories, they **10** _____ (increase) their body weight to obese levels within a few years.

Other ways to express conditionality

3a Match the beginnings of the sentences (1–5) with the endings (A–E).

1 Lifting weights is a good way to build body strength
2 People who have stressful jobs should find time to relax every day
3 **Supposing** everyone grew and ate their own fruit and vegetables,
4 There is no need to take vitamin supplements
5 **Unless** people get more than seven hours' sleep,

A they would improve nutrition levels easily.
B **otherwise** their health might suffer.
C **provided that** it is done safely.
D their brain will not function well.
E **as long as** you are eating a balanced diet.

b Which of the sentences in Exercise 3a express real situations and which express unreal (imaginary) ones?

4 Complete the sentences with the correct words below.

otherwise   provided that   supposing   unless

1 It is important to make time to learn new skills _____ life becomes boring.
2 We can all improve our outlook on life _____ we practise positive thinking.
3 _____ people use sunscreen, there is a danger of developing skin conditions.
4 _____ the world focused on generosity more, might society be happier?

5 Rewrite the sentences using the words in brackets. You may need to change the grammatical form or the order of the clauses.

1 People might be more productive and less stressed if they worked fewer hours per week. (supposing)
2 If children do lots of exercise, it does not matter what they eat. (as long as)
3 Improved health will not happen if people do not change their attitudes. (unless)
4 If governments do not limit the growth of supermarkets, small food shops will not be able to survive. (otherwise)

Writing (Task 2)

Lead-in

1   Work in pairs and discuss the questions.
1   What activities do you do that make you happy?
2   Why might being part of a community make people feel happier? Why might it not?

Write about problems and solutions

➤ EXPERT WRITING page 193

2   Read the essay title. Which of the following structures (1–3) are suitable for a problem and solution essay?

Nowadays many elderly people live alone and this can cause a variety of problems for society.

What are some of these problems and what solutions can you suggest?

1
> Introduction
> Paragraph 1: Issue 1: Problems and solutions
> Paragraph 2: Issue 2: Problems and solutions
> Conclusion

2
> Introduction
> Paragraph 1: Suggested solutions
> Paragraph 2: Discussion of problems
> Conclusion

3
> Introduction
> Paragraph 1: Discussion of problems
> Paragraph 2: Suggested solutions
> Conclusion

3a   Read the paragraph and underline the problems and the suggested solutions.

[A]One of the problems for older people living alone is often the isolation it brings. [B]Firstly, for these people, living alone can affect their health because there is no one around on a daily basis to notice any signs of bad health. [C]In addition, if older people live alone, they may feel less positive about life and therefore they might be less active. [D]One way of dealing with this would be for family and neighbours to make an effort to have regular contact with elderly people living alone. [E]Also, the elderly can be encouraged to join social groups for people of their age group. [F]Even though they live alone, they should focus on interacting with others as much as possible.

b   Match the sentences (A–F) in Exercise 3a with their functions (1–6).
1   First suggested solution
2   Further explanation of a solution
3   Description of the problem in more detail
4   Topic sentence to introduce the problem
5   Second suggested solution
6   Second problem and its effect

c   Think of another issue for the essay task in Exercise 2. Write a paragraph using the structure in Exercise 3b.

Develop a paragraph

4a   Put the sentences in order to make the second paragraph of the essay in Exercise 3a.
A   In addition, governments could give food subsidies to older people who live alone to encourage them to improve their diets.
B   Secondly, there is the problem of nutrition for elderly people living alone.
C   To reduce this problem, old people who live alone should make an effort to cook for themselves more often.
D   These people often eat more convenience food such as ready meals because cooking for one person is not that easy.
E   This is because supermarkets usually sell food in large packages and these are more suited to families than individuals.
F   For example, if they were to make large quantities of a meal, the remainder could be frozen and eaten at a later date.

b   Which sentence introduces the solution and which sentence supports the solution?

c   Can you think of any more solutions for the essay task in Exercise 2? How could you support these solutions?

Write your essay

➤ TEST STRATEGIES page 173

5a   Read the essay title. Make a plan of your answer listing the main problems and solutions.

In some parts of the world, people have become more focused on themselves than their communities. What problems can this situation cause and how can they be solved?

b   Write some ideas to support your solutions.

c   Decide which structure you want to use from Exercise 2 and organise your ideas into paragraphs.

d   Read the strategies and write your essay. Remember to write at least 250 words.

Listening (Section 4)

Before you listen

1   Read the ways of treating illness below. Which do you think are more effective? What are the advantages and disadvantages of these treatments?

medicine   herbs   acupuncture   homeopathy   change in diet

Identify correct answers

2   Read the excerpt from an audio script and the student's answers to a question. What is wrong with the answers? Why has the student made this mistake?

... So, there are plenty of health benefits to eating more healthily, but there's a lot of advice at the moment in the media to cut out all things like sugar or carbohydrates entirely. Now, this might not be a great idea. If a person just cuts out everything, instead of cutting down, this can have other consequences. For example, people who remove all sugars in their diets often complain of tiredness, especially in the first few weeks. There is also a chance of insomnia. Cutting out dairy products such as milk and cheese can make people feel sick.

What are TWO of the negative side effects of cutting out sugar?

1   *tiredness*
2   *feeling sick*

Test practice

> **TEST STRATEGIES** page 168

3a Read the questions and decide:
    1   exactly what is required in the questions.
    2   what kinds of words might form the answers (nouns, verbs, etc.).
    3   the maximum number of words for each answer.

b   🔊 3.6 Listen and complete the test tasks.

Questions 1–5
Complete the sentences below.
Write **NO MORE THAN THREE WORDS AND/OR A NUMBER** *for each answer.*

1   The term 'traditional' in regard to medicine seems _____ .
2   Modern scientific medicine began around _____ ago.
3   Over _____ of the world still rely on alternative medicine.
4   There is a growing trend for more natural treatment in _____ .
5   Scientists in the Western world claim that alternative medicine is _____ .

Questions 6–10
Answer the questions below.
Write **NO MORE THAN THREE WORDS AND/OR A NUMBER** *for each answer.*

What **TWO** things has acupuncture been shown to assist?

6   _____
7   _____

Where were parts of trees used as remedies?

8   _____

What are **TWO** possible benefits of fish oils?

9   _____
10 _____

Task analysis

4a Read audio script 3.6 on page 204 and check your answers.

b   Think about your incorrect answers. Tick the reasons why your answers were incorrect.
    • Incorrect spelling
    • Too many words
    • Wrong detail written down (wrong answer)
    • No answer written down

Language development and vocabulary

Modal forms; Degrees of certainty

> EXPERT GRAMMAR page 177

1a Put the modals below in the correct place on the line to show the degree of certainty each one expresses.

could   may   might   must   should   will   would

Certain		Certain
0%		100%

b Match the modal verbs below with the meanings they express. Some words have more than one meaning.

| can   can't   don't have to   may   must   need to
ought to   shouldn't   will |
| --- |

1 obligation   3 possibility   5 prediction
2 advice   4 ability

2 Choose the correct option in *italics* to complete the text.

According to a recent study, having strong leg muscles **1** *may / must* contribute to a healthy brain. It is thought that exercise **2** *will / could* be connected to brain health, but until recently this has been difficult to validate. This is because healthy brains can be determined by genes and childhood environment. In order to undertake research on this topic, scientists **3** *must / may* use identical twins because they have the same genes, which would mean that any differences in results **4** *should / would* not be related to genetics. The recent experiment showed that among the sets of identical twins, those who had the most powerful leg muscles ten years ago performed as well on cognitive tests as they had done a decade before. However, the study did not focus on how muscle power is connected to brain power although the scientists **5** *will / should* do research into this in the future. The scientists concluded that people **6** *might / should* exercise more if they want to increase their brain health.

3 Complete the sentences with the correct modal form below. There is one extra modal form.

might   must   should   won't   would

1 Teachers often suggest to parents that they _____ take their children out into nature more as a fun way to learn about the world.
2 In order to lose weight, you _____ do more exercise and eat less calorific foods.
3 Why not try spending some time alone reading fiction? This _____ help with relaxation.
4 Although the government plans to improve the quality of school meals, sceptics believe this _____ have a large impact on childhood obesity.

Adverbs of attitude

4a Match the sentences (1–2) with the speaker's opinion (A–B).

1 Unfortunately, it is really difficult to find time to exercise when you work full time.
2 Naturally, it is really difficult to find time to exercise when you work full time.

A The speaker thinks that this situation is obvious.
B The speaker thinks this situation is regrettable or unlucky.

b Read the sentence and choose the correct meaning for the underlined word.

Apparently, walking for 30 minutes a day has more health benefits than running or going to the gym.
1 I think this statement is wrong.
2 I really believe that this statement is true.
3 I have heard this statement, but I'm not sure if it's true.
4 I hope this statement is true.

c Match each underlined word to how it is used to show perspective.

1 Unfortunately I couldn't come to work because I was too ill.
   A you think the situation is unlucky
   B you think something is not important
2 Having regular health checks is undoubtedly helpful in detecting signs of serious illness.
   A you think something is definitely true
   B you have a negative opinion of something
3 Evidently, working too many hours causes people to become stressed.
   A you know something is wrong
   B you can see that something is true
4 Naturally, people put on weight when they eat lots of junk food.
   A you believe something is very important
   B you think something is normal and not surprising
5 Drinking water is undeniably good for your health.
   A you think something cannot be rejected
   B you cannot understand why others think this way

d Give your opinions on the following topics using the adverbs from Exercise 4c.

1 The best way to be healthy is to be vegetarian.
2 Happiness cannot be achieved through material wealth.
3 Self-confidence comes through being successful.

Speaking (Part 3)

Vocabulary development

1 What social problem does this photo show? To what extent do you think it can cause health problems? What other social problems have negative effects on people's health?

2 Complete the paragraphs with the words below.

bought   controlled   cope   exist

Global Health – problems and solutions

There are many health issues which affect broader society. One of these is stress; today, people have to 1_____ with lots of pressure in life in terms of work and finance. Another problem is obesity. This is because unhealthy food can be 2 _____ relatively cheaply. However, this problem is perhaps specific to certain countries. In other countries, the problem is a lack of food. Hunger and poverty still 3 _____ in many places in the world. Also, there are still many parts of the world that suffer from diseases which are not adequately 4 _____ .

aid   contracting   education   reflection   sanitation   vaccinations

Although there are solutions to these problems, they are not easy to implement. 5 _____ can prevent people from 6 _____ diseases, but there also needs to be improvements to 7 _____ to help with other kinds of diseases which may be passed on by things like water supply rather than from person to person. 8 _____ programmes also help people in poverty, yet these need to be more sustainable, perhaps by supporting food production in certain countries. In other countries, obesity could be managed by 9 _____ ; teaching people from a young age what is in their food and how to make better food decisions. Lastly, stress could be dealt with by exercise and 10 _____ on what is important in life.

3 Work in pairs and discuss the question. What possible solutions can you suggest to combat poor nutrition, contagious diseases and sanitation?

Focus on lexical resource

4 Turn to page 183 and read the descriptors for lexical resource for the band score you want to achieve. How can you achieve this score? Discuss your strengths and weaknesses with a partner.

5 🔊 3.7 Listen to two candidates talking about health and answer the questions.

  1 Which candidate uses vocabulary well to answer the examiner's question?
  2 Write down some vocabulary/phrases that the candidate uses.
  3 How could the other candidate improve? Read audio script 3.7 on page 204 and make some suggestions.

Test practice

> TEST STRATEGIES page 175

6a Read the questions below and discuss what kind of answers could be given.

List 1
1 What do you think are the most important health issues in society?
2 How can these health issues be addressed?
3 Do richer countries have a responsibility to help poorer countries in terms of health? Why/Why not?
4 How do you think health issues have changed over time?

List 2
1 In terms of health, how can people help themselves more?
2 To what extent is it the government's responsibility to look after people's health?
3 Should doctors focus more on preventing diseases rather than curing them? Why/Why not?
4 In your opinion, which health issues are under-addressed? What can be done about this?

b Work in pairs. Take turns to be the examiner and candidate, and ask and answer the questions. Use one list per student.

Assess and improve

7 Think about your speaking in Exercise 6b. Complete the checklist below about your lexical range.
  • I managed to answer the questions at length.
  • I did not have difficulty thinking of words.
  • I used some idiomatic vocabulary.
  • I used collocations.
  • I did not repeat phrases a lot.

Reading (Matching headings; Multiple choice: select two answers)

This year's winter flu deadliest ever

Sleeping too much shortens your life

Fat-free diets make you GAIN weight

Before you read

1 Work in pairs and discuss the questions.

1 Does your country have guidelines about what food you should and should not eat? To what extent do you follow these guidelines, and why?

2 What other advice and support is available to help you look after your health? Think about regular medical checks, access to advice on improving your diet, availability of preventive medicine, exercise classes and sports clubs, etc.

Test practice

➤ **TEST STRATEGIES** pages 171 and 172

2 Complete the test task. Read the instructions, the title and subtitle before reading more closely.

Questions 1–5.

The Reading Passage has FIVE sections, **A–E**.

Choose the correct heading for each section from the list of headings below.

List of Headings

i The importance of maintaining a sensible balance

ii The case in favour of adopting natural remedies

iii The role played by the media in generating panic about our well-being

iv The importance of consumer questionnaires in better health provision

v The potential for reaching the wrong conclusions about daily habits

vi The advantages of incorporating physical activity into daily routines

vii Realistic goals based on individual circumstances

viii Inflexible health principles which can be deceptive

ix The influence of modern lifestyles on our health prospects

1 Paragraph A _____   4 Paragraph D _____
2 Paragraph B _____   5 Paragraph E _____
3 Paragraph C _____

➤ **HELP**

1 What is a *hypochondriac*, and what is encouraging people to become one?

2 Has it been proved that insufficient sleep is a problem?

Questions 6–7

*Choose **TWO** letters, **A–E**.*

*Which **TWO** of the following claims are made in the passage?*

A The media frequently misinterprets academic findings.

B Being severely overweight causes people to have disturbed nights.

C Highly stressed people accomplish more than others.

D Plant-based medicines have only a psychological effect.

E Young people often underestimate their physical health and strength.

➤ **HELP**

A What conclusions do the authors reach about newspaper claims?

B Does one condition necessarily lead to the other?

Task analysis

3 Work in pairs and compare your answers to the questions.

1 For questions 1–5, did you read the list of headings before reading the passage? If so, did this help you to identify the main topic of each paragraph?

2 For questions 6–7, how was the information in the passage ordered? Were there any parts of the passage which were not tested? Did you choose the correct number of statements?

Discussion

4 Discuss these questions. Try to use some of the modal forms, degrees of certainty and adverbs from Language development and vocabulary on page 48.

1 What advice would you give to someone who wanted to become healthier?

2 Do you think it is an individual's responsibility to look after their own health or should the government have a role in this? Give reasons to support your opinion.

A growing preoccupation

Eat your five-a-day, take exercise, avoid alcohol, sugar, stress. Worrying about our well-being is dominating our lives, and it's bad for us.

A Nearly every day brings with it a new health scare headline. Whether it is about the dangers of using mobile phones, sleeping too much or too little or the risks involved in consuming wheat, it seems that there is always a newspaper story to evoke feelings of fear and guilt and encourage the hypochondriac in many of us. In their guide to healthy living, *Live a Little! Breaking the Rules Won't Break Your Health* author and clinical professor of surgery at UCLA, Dr Susan M. Love and co-author Alice Domar, explore whether these warnings can be substantiated, concluding that all too often, headlines misread research findings and percentages of risk are incorrectly understood and reported. Despite the fact that many people are driven by fear to take every medical test and new pill available, the authors make the case that many of us are leading healthier lives than we realise.

B Surveys suggest that the majority of people are getting too little sleep at night, to the point at which their normal activities are disrupted. The experts, however, think such polls give the wrong impression. "It would seem from these polls that you need at least six hours' sleep, with seven being ideal," says Love. "If you examine the data, you'll notice that those who sleep for seven hours a night throughout their entire lives tend to live the longest. But if you have a lot less sleep for a couple of days, you can catch up. It's all about the overall pattern over your lifetime." And although research conducted by the University of Warwick Medical School did discover that sleep deprivation is associated with an almost two-fold risk of obesity for both children and adults, Domar believes that a lot of work still needs to be done in the field. "No direct causal relationship has been found just yet. Unhealthy people tend to sleep a lot but we don't know if it's the disease making them sleep or vice versa."

C It is well reported that stress triggers heart attacks. According to an ongoing study of 735 American middle-aged or elderly men who had good cardiovascular health, those who scored the highest on four different scales of tension were far more likely to suffer heart attacks in later life. Yet there is a negative aspect to a low heart rate too: while anxiety may make you improve a bad area of your life, ignoring things might cause the situation to deteriorate. Even so, there is no doubt that avoiding the upper end of the stress spectrum is a good idea. "Stress improves your performance to a point, above which the way you handle things rapidly declines," says Domar.

D When it comes to a healthy diet, the rules are widely known: keep your saturated fats low, avoid too much salt and sugar, include a little of everything. But be wary of following overly prescriptive rules as there is no benefit from agonising about whether you have the recommended five portions of fruit or vegetables a day. "The data really isn't there to support such stringency," says Love. Scientific consensus also asserts that most vitamin supplements have little or no effect on those who eat a healthy range of food, apart from vitamin D, which does help those living in sunshine-poor environments. "It mirrors the proven effects of herbal remedies, which are mostly disputed," says Domar. "Even the benefits of remedies such as echinacea, for which there exists evidence in its favour, are just as likely to be due to the placebo effect as anything else."

E It is generally recommended that adults should do 30 minutes of moderate exercise, five days a week. However, a recent survey in the UK suggests that 94% of men and 96% of women fail to achieve this. "Some people can be naturally fit and not need to exercise so much," says Love. "If you are a young mother with a toddler, you probably don't need to spend so much time at the gym. It can depend a lot on your age." "But exercise is still the single best thing you can do for your health," says Domar. "It's good to be on the go the whole time. People in their late teens and twenties tend to be fitter than they think they are. Essentially, what we're trying to do is to remove the guilt if you can't achieve the lofty target of 30 minutes a day, five days a week."

Writing (Task 2)

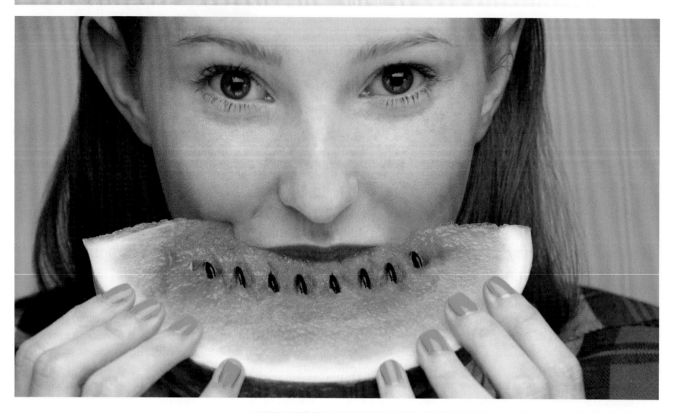

'The greatest medicine of all is teaching people not to need it.'

Lead-in

1 What do you think the statement above means? How can we teach people to avoid illness?

Understand the task

➤ EXPERT WRITING page 193

2a Read the essay question and look at the sample problem and solutions. Which solutions are appropriate for the essay?

Some people rely too much on doctors instead of taking care of their own health. They think all health problems can just be 'fixed' by visiting doctors.

What problems could this approach to healthcare cause and how might they be solved?

Problem	Solutions
Doctors may be overstretched and not be spending time with the patients who most need their help.	A People should be expected to pay to solve problems which they have created through their own lifestyle choices.
	B Greater healthcare provision is needed.
	C People need education to help them take responsibility for their own health.
	D If people visited their doctor more regularly, more health problems could be detected early and treated before they became serious.

b Note down another problem and possible solutions for the above task.

c Discuss your problem and solutions in groups. Are they key problems? Are the proposed solutions clear and relevant?

Plan the task

3a Look at the descriptors for grammatical range and accuracy on page 190. What's the difference between range and accuracy?

b Read the essay question in Exercise 2a again. Make a plan of your answer. What range of grammatical forms is suitable for this essay?

4 Read the paragraph and find six more mistakes.

One issue with people who ~~are believing~~ ^{believe} that doctors should be responsible for their health is that it creates a burden on the healthcare service this is because people go to the doctor more and more instead of think, how they can help themselves. This must possibly be solved by patients having to pay for treatment if they have contributed to the illness, such as smoker-related illnesses. Also, people could be given more education and advice on how they can make their lifestyles healthier by eat well and exercise. Governments could put money into encouraging people to do this more.

Language and content

5a Look at the extract below from Exercise 4. Decide which grammatical structure is being used in the phrase.

Also people *could be given* more education and advice ...
1 modal of deduction
2 modal passive
3 future modal

b Complete the rule below for forming the grammatical structure in Exercise 5a.

Modal verb + _____ + _____

c This kind of language is often used to write about solutions. Change the following sentences to reflect the structure above. The first one is done for you.
1 People must understand the benefits of eating well.
   The benefits of eating well must be understood.
2 Doctors cannot persuade people to try making lifestyle changes.
   People ...
3 People can find a lot of benefit in regular exercise and healthy eating.
   A lot of benefit ...
4 We should pay doctors more for the job that they do.
   Doctors ...
5 We could educate patients on healthy living.
   Patients ...

Write your problem and solution essay

6 Write your answer to the essay question in Exercise 2a. Write at least 250 words.

Assess and improve

7a Exchange your essay with a partner and review both essays using the following questions.
1 Does the essay present problems and solutions relevant to the title?
2 Are the problems explained?
3 Are the solutions clear?
4 Does the essay follow a clear structure?
5 Can you see any grammatical mistakes (e.g. tenses, articles, prepositions)?
6 Is the punctuation correct?
7 Can you see any spelling mistakes?

b Try to improve your answer. Focus on TWO areas you want to work on and use the list in Exercise 7a to help.

Review

1a Complete the sentences with one word. The first letter is given.

1 One m_____ of losing weight is to reduce carbohydrate intake.
2 Smoking is a real t_____ to good health.
3 The c_____ of poor sleep is a lack of concentration.
4 Exercising regularly can have positive o_____, both physically and mentally.
5 People who have a forward-looking a_____ to life are often happiest.
6 Investing money in medical technology should be a p_____ for the government.

b Complete the text with the words and phrases below.

challenges   evidently   pose   quick fix   tackle
the tip of the iceberg

Child food allergies are on the rise

One of the **1** _____ that the modern world faces is the rise in food allergies in children. In the UK alone, it has been estimated that approximately half of all children suffer from some type of food allergy. Some experts suggest that this number could be **2** _____ because not many parents have their children tested for allergies. Experts in child health suggest that the modern diet and lifestyle **3** _____ a threat to children's health and that we must work hard to find solutions that work. **4** _____ , there is no **5** _____ for this situation because people's lifestyles are different and a wide range of factors contribute to allergies. It is difficult to isolate which aspects are most problematic, which means that it is a challenge for doctors to **6** _____ the issue of food allergies in children. For example, a method that works for one child may not be suitable for another.

c Choose the correct attitude adverb in *italics* to complete the sentences.

1 *Unfortunately / Undoubtedly*, I wasn't able to attend the event because my friend was visiting me from overseas.
2 Climbing Mount Fuji was *evidently / undoubtedly* the most exciting experience of my life.
3 Children can become stressed when faced with competition at school. *Evidently / Unfortunately*, teachers should try to reduce this.
4 Making sure you get enough exercise is *unfortunately / undeniably* the best thing you can do to reduce stress levels.

2a Complete the sentences with the correct conditional form of the verbs in brackets.

1 If doctors _____ (visit) people at home, patients _____ (receive) better service.
2 Unless you _____ (stop) smoking, you _____ (have) serious health problems later in life.
3 I _____ (take up) horse riding if I _____ (have) enough money, but it's too expensive for me.
4 When I _____ (have) some free time at the weekends, I _____ (go walking) in the mountains.
5 If children _____ (learn) to cook, they are more likely _____ (grow up) to become healthier adults.
6 If I _____ (go) to the health food shop in my street, I _____ (buy) some nuts and dried fruit.
7 If people _____ (take) more care of their health, there _____ (not be) such pressure on healthcare services.
8 When I _____ (get) up early and go to the gym, it _____ (make) me feel good all day.

b Rewrite the sentences using modal passive forms.

1 The government should spend more money on medical research.
2 We could easily solve the problem of stress if we worked less.
3 People can take specific medicine to protect against allergies.
4 We might prevent the spread of flu by adopting more hygienic habits.
5 We could reduce the likelihood of obesity in adults by teaching children about the different types of foods and their nutritional value.
6 People can lift their mood if they take a short stroll in some green space such as a park.
7 The government should introduce a vaccination programme for children at primary school.
8 People becoming more self-sufficient might reduce the impact of the food industry on the environment.

c Choose the correct option in *italics* to complete the sentences.

1 I suggest that everyone *should / would* take a holiday once a year in order to destress from work.
2 Increasing the amount of protein and fibre in your diet *will / must* have beneficial effects.
3 Taking up a new hobby or sport *will / could* possibly help combat feelings of isolation.
4 Herbal medicine *may / must* be an alternative for people who don't like taking antibiotics.
5 In my opinion, schools *should / will* teach children how to cook so they understand more about nutrition.
6 In my opinion, everyone *will / should* take up yoga as a way to maintain good fitness levels.
7 Engaging in a new sport *may / must* help elderly people's brains remain healthy for longer.
8 In order to combat the spread of disease, hospitals *would / must* ensure that they are free of bacteria.

4 A consumer society

4a Training

- **Reading:** Identify functions (Matching information; Summary completion)
- **Vocabulary:** Academic verbs for thoughts and beliefs; Use an impersonal style in writing and speaking; Collocations for thoughts and beliefs
- **Speaking:** Develop topic-specific vocabulary; Expand your ideas using conjunctions and phrases (Part 3)
- **Listening:** Use questions to predict answers (Section 2: Note and table completion)
- **Language development:** Form clauses; Subordinate clauses; Express opinions with *that*
- **Writing:** Give your opinion; Develop your arguments (Task 2: Opinion essay)

4b Testing

- **Listening:** Section 2: Note and table completion
- **Language development and vocabulary:** Pronoun referencing; Signposting words
- **Speaking:** Part 3: Discussing consumerism
- **Reading:** Matching information; Summary completion
- **Writing:** Task 2: Opinion essay

I never buy lunch. I always take a packed lunch.	☐
I pay for lots of satellite TV channels but I don't want them all.	☐
I'm not a fan of brand names. I don't buy designer labels.	☐
I have a credit card and I don't always pay it off every month.	☐
I wait until there is a sale before I buy electronic goods.	☐
I get home late from work, so I usually have a take-away for dinner.	☐
I don't upgrade my mobile phone every year.	☐
If I see a jacket I like, I buy it before someone else does.	☐

Lead-in

1a Complete the quiz. How many blue boxes did you tick? How many green boxes did you tick?

b What do you think it means to be a 'responsible spender'? To what extent do people nowadays think about how much they spend and consume?

Reading (Matching information; Summary completion)

Before you read

1 Work in pairs and discuss the questions. Give reasons for your answers.

   1 What could be done to reduce waste in a) your country? b) the world?

   2 Who do you think should be responsible for helping to limit waste: the government, local councils, businesses, individuals? Why?

Identify functions

2 Read the title and skim the first and last paragraphs of the reading passage. What kind of passage is it? How do you know?

   1 descriptive   2 argumentative   3 factual

3a Match the underlined language (1–15) in the passage to the functions (A–E) below. The functions can be used more than once.

   A giving examples
   B comparing/contrasting
   C summarising
   D giving a reason/result
   E explaining/defining a word or phrase

  b Think of other ways to express the functions in Exercise 3a.

  c How does being aware of functional language help you to read efficiently for the information you need?

Test practice

4a Read the strategies and complete the test task.

➤ TEST STRATEGIES page 171

Question 1–5

The reading passage has FIVE paragraphs, A–E.

Which section contains the following information? Write the correct letter, A–E. You may use any letter more than once.

   1 A system in which resources would be exploited to their full potential through regeneration.

   2 A proposal to make manufacturers more accountable for the goods they produce.

   3 The cause of a wasteful approach to living.

   4 A realistic prediction for the future of our planet.

   5 The potential risks of a step-by-step approach towards economic change.

  b Work in pairs and discuss your answers.

Test practice

5a Read the summary below and decide whether it summarises the whole passage or just a part of it. If just a part, which part?

  b Read the strategies and complete the test task.

➤ TEST STRATEGIES page 170

Questions 6–9

Complete the summary below.

*Choose **NO MORE THAN TWO WORDS** from the passage for each answer.*

The consequences of progress

Many of the problems of our age can be blamed on the 6 _____ which took place over two centuries ago. People are soon expected to see a deterioration in their 7 _____ in addition to the current threat to the environment. Already, declining resources means that the world is having to limit its 8 _____ .
The 9 _____ is expected to expand two-fold worldwide by 2030, bringing with it a rise in spending power and an even greater use of resources.

  c Work in pairs and discuss your answers.

Task analysis

6 Work in pairs and discuss the questions.

   1 In the first task, did underlining the key words help you to identify the ideas in the paragraphs more quickly? Give examples.

   2 In the second task, did the title of the summary help you to find the part of the passage you needed? How successful were you in predicting the type of word you were looking for? Did you look for a grammatical fit as well as matching the meaning?

Discussion

7 Discuss these questions.

   1 How do you think people might be persuaded to change their mindsets and be convinced to be part of a 'sharing' system?

   2 What problems or drawbacks might occur with a 'sharing' economy and how might they be resolved?

Re-thinking an extravagant world

A These days many people around the world enjoy an unprecedented level of prosperity. **1** Yet this has come at a steep price: the creation of the so-called linear economy. **2** In other words, it is a "make, take and dispose" economy, in which we extract natural resources, exploit them and then dispose of them as soon as a more up-to-date alternative becomes available. At the moment, the world's growth model squanders the majority of the resources which we procure. Research in the US and Europe on consumption habits has shown the frequency in which scarcely used resources are found discarded in landfills. **3** In Germany, for instance, almost one third of household appliances disposed of in 2012 were still functioning, 89% of mobile devices in the US went straight to a landfill and in the UK, it is estimated that as many as 125 million phones languish in landfills, unused. Shamefully, cars in Europe remain parked 92% of the time; planned obsolescence is how we live.

B Mass and conspicuous consumption, the burning of fossil fuels, the creation of dense urban habitats and increased ownership of cars can largely be attributed to the Industrial Revolution of the 18th and early 19th centuries and has created huge environmental and social problems. **4** It not only endangers the natural world but will eventually have an adverse effect on our living standards; already, our economic productivity on a global level is being curbed by the rapid depletion of existing and readily accessible natural capital **5** such as clean sources of potable water and forests. In a recent study, it was found that perhaps 85% of Europe's soil has been degraded; mining for natural resources such as zinc has also become more expensive and the quality of the metal has diminished, **6** making it even more energy inefficient. At the same time, it is expected that the global middle class will double by 2030, **7** which means even higher consumption; given we consume more as we earn more. This path is simply not sustainable; **8** we cannot continue to grow as a species and live well without changing the way we operate.

C Many people are now considering how the global economy might function differently **9** in order that more value can be extracted from existing resources;

the thinkers behind these ideas have pioneered a new standard for how the world could be run: the "circular economy." The central aim of moving towards a circular economy is to improve resource productivity by keeping goods and resources in use for as long as possible, through recovery, reuse, repair, remanufacturing and recycling. **10** It is therefore not so much about "doing more with less" but rather doing more with what we already have by solving the problem of low resource utilisation: the goal would be to allow wealth to increase while using less oil, minerals and other spoils of the Earth.

D On a smaller scale, schemes are being conceived by many companies to use resources more efficiently. The so-called "sharing economy" represents a real move forward with enterprises such as car-sharing, (which may reduce the number of vehicles on the road, or at least limit their growth) and renting out spare rooms. This concept of leasing resources is not new but it is one of the business models which could help decrease the use of materials in the longer term. **11** If washing machines, for example, were rented, the makers of the products rather than consumers would be responsible for repair and replacement. **12** This would significantly decrease the use of materials and might, one assumes, also trigger a change in the design which would enhance the focus on longevity. It is true that consumers have well-established buying habits and that firms would encounter high costs when first establishing the new business models. **13** But the benefits could outweigh the immediate barriers, if people could be convinced to change their mindsets.

E However, solutions within a single industry or company are not going to be sufficient, because this practice of leasing effectively ignores the needs of the overall system. Moreover, if we resolve the problem in such a piecemeal way, we risk causing a "rebound effect." **14** That is, economic benefits gained in one area – such as driving less – being offset by all those savings being spent on another product or service. **15** For all these reasons we need the collaborative approach embodied in the circular economy so that we can maximise the benefits of these new technologies.

Vocabulary

Academic verbs for thoughts and beliefs

1a Match the verbs below with their meanings (1–8).

acknowledge   assume   conceive   consider
contradict   convince   define   speculate

1 To believe that something is true although you do not have definite proof.
2 To disagree with something, especially by saying that the opposite is true.
3 To describe something correctly and thoroughly.
4 To guess about the possible causes or effects of something.
5 To think about something carefully.
6 To admit or accept something is true or that a situation exists.
7 To make someone feel certain that something is true.
8 To imagine a particular situation.

b Complete the text with the correct form of the verbs in Exercise 1a.

Could you **1** _____ of a life without a mobile phone? Although it seems unlikely, there is a chance that mobile phone production could stop. This is due to the scarcity of the rare earth metals used to construct and power all smart phones. Rare earth metals are **2** _____ as 'lanthanides', which are 17 chemical elements in the periodic table. Most people **3** _____ that the resources needed to make smart phones will go on forever, however the evidence **4** _____ this. While companies try to **5** _____ us that everything is fine, scientists **6** _____ that this could change. Although rare earth metals are not that rare, they are difficult to extract so scientists predict that they could become too expensive to use in small gadgets in the future. This is a fact which companies and consumers have to **7** _____ as being a real problem. In the future we will probably need to **8** _____ alternatives to rare earth metals so our love of mobile phones can continue.

Use an impersonal style in writing and speaking

2a Read sentences 1 and 2. Which sentence uses an impersonal style and which uses a personal style?

1 It is thought that people buy many products that they do not use.
2 I think that people buy many products that they do not use.

b Read the example sentences and complete the grammatical rules with the correct words below.

adjective   adverb (x2)   noun   past participle
present simple verb

There is considerable evidence that fast fashion is contributing to rising consumption.
It is widely acknowledged that our generation is more wasteful than previous ones.
Some people strongly believe that governments need to make recycling compulsory.

1 *There is +* _____ *+* _____ *+ that + clause*
2 *It is +* _____ *+* _____ *+ that + clause*
3 *Some people +* _____ *+* _____ *+ that + clause*

3 Complete the sentences with the correct form of the words in brackets.

1 There is a _____ that the economy is more important than the environment. (widespread/believe)
2 There is an _____ that being eco-friendly is the best type of lifestyle. (underlie/assume)
3 Some experts have _____ that recycling isn't as effective as reducing waste. (formal/acknowledge)
4 There is a _____ that individuals cannot make a difference if they recycle. (common/misconceive)

4 Improve the sections of the text in *italics* using the structures in Exercise 2b and the prompts 1–3.

1 *Lots of people think* bottled water is the best kind of water to drink. Although 2 *definitely* bottled water is a necessity in some countries, in other places safe tap water is by far the best option. 3 *It is not true* that all kinds of tap water are of low quality; in some countries the tap water is safer than bottled water.

1 Many people/believe/general
2 It/true/undeniable
3 There/misconception/common

Collocations for thoughts and beliefs

5a Match 1–5 with A–E to form collocations.

1 to have   A something into consideration
2 to be   B oneself to something
3 to take   C a lot of faith in something
4 to pass   D judgement on something
5 to resign   E open to ideas

b Complete the sentences with the correct form of the collocations in Exercise 5a.

1 People often _____ large fashion companies that pay their workers low salaries.
2 It can be difficult to _____ the government's commitment to improving recycling facilities.
3 Students have to _____ not being able to afford luxury products during their studies.
4 So as to make society less focused on shopping, we have to _____ ideas about new ways of living.
5 When buying products, we should _____ the environmental cost of making them.

Speaking (Part 3)

'Infinite growth of material consumption in a finite world is an impossibility.' E. F. Schumacher

Lead-in

1 Read the quote above. What do you think it means? How far do you agree with this view?

Develop topic-specific vocabulary

2a Complete the definitions (1–6) with the words below.

landfill sites   ecological footprint   biodegradable
renewable resources   fast fashion   upgrades

1 _____ is the quick turnover of clothing styles.
2 _____ are areas where large amounts of rubbish are kept.
3 _____ describes substances which decompose over time.
4 _____ is the total impact that an individual or group has on the environment.
5 _____ are sources of fuel that do not run out.
6 _____ are newer or better versions of something.

b Think of some questions using the vocabulary in Exercise 2a. Discuss them with a partner.

Expand your ideas using conjunctions and phrases

3a Read the question and think of the answer you might give.

Do you think it is worth trying to recycle?

b Join together the words/phrases in columns B and C to complete one long answer to the question.

A	B	C
Absolutely. The people I know try to buy things which can be recycled ...	and	they know it'll be better for the environment.
	but	they try not to buy things which aren't biodegradable or recyclable.
	so	they aren't always easy to find.
	because	they buy things which are biodegradable.
	or	they don't generate lots of unnecessary waste.

Absolutely. The people I know try to buy things which can be recycled because they know it'll be better for the environment.

c Match the words below with the conjunctions in column B in Exercise 3b.

along with   alternatively   another thing   as well as
instead   in the end   on the grounds that
on the other hand   since

d Complete the sentences using the words and phrases in Exercise 3c.

1 I know recycling is something we should all be concerned with. _____ it can be so time-consuming and difficult to do.
2 Many people recycle by choice. In some areas the government enforces recycling _____ .
3 I imagine there are a lot of companies that don't bother to make their products biodegradable _____ it costs too much money.
4 There are many ways to be more environmentally aware. You can limit the amount of waste you throw away. _____ , you can buy fewer things in the first place.
5 One issue we need to think about is recycling and waste. _____ we should be concerned about is using up our limited fuel resources.

Test practice

➤ **TEST STRATEGIES** page 175

4a Read the questions below. Think of ways you can create a full answer by using conjunctions and phrases to add further ideas.

1 Do you think it is worth trying to recycle?
2 In what ways can people save/reuse resources?
3 Is it better to recycle or limit consumption?
4 Should recycling be voluntary or mandatory?

b Work in pairs and take turns to ask and answer the questions. Use the following:

• Subject-specific vocabulary
• Words and phrases to link and add further ideas and details
• Connected speech

Task analysis

5a Think about your and your partner's answers and respond to the statements.

1 I/My partner used some subject-specific vocabulary.
2 I/My partner gave a long answer for each question (more than 10 seconds).
3 I/My partner used some phrases and words to link ideas.
4 The phrases I/my partner used to link ideas were correct.
5 I/My partner used connected speech in the right places.

b Note down one area from the list in Exercise 5a that you need to improve.

Listening (Section 2)

Before you listen

1 What do you think 'upcycling' means? Look at the photo of an upcycled chair. What has happened? Why do you think people upcycle old objects? To what extent do you think this is a good idea? Why?

Use questions to predict answers

2a Read questions 1–4 in the test task opposite and answer the questions.

1 Do you need to follow the information downwards in columns or across in rows? How do you know?
2 What is the maximum number of words for the answers to questions 1–4?
3 Which questions do you think will require nouns as the answers?
4 Which questions might require verbs?
5 Which question(s) are about how often something happens?

b Is there anything else in the table that could help you when listening for the answers?

3a Read questions 5–7 in the test task opposite and predict the type of word you need to listen for.

b Answer the questions about questions 5–7 in the test task.

1 Can you change the words from what you hear in the recording?
2 Can you write three words to answer these questions? How do you know?

Test practice

> TEST STRATEGIES page 168

4 🔊 4.1 Complete the test tasks.

Questions 1–4
Complete the table below.
Write **NO MORE THAN THREE WORDS AND/OR A NUMBER** *for each answer.*

Upcycling workshops programme

Workshop topic	Date and frequency	Skills focus
How to reuse your furniture and make stylish pieces.	Mondays all day, weekly	• wood and metal care • 1 _____
Turning rubbish into useful things!	Twice monthly 2 _____ Tuesday 2.00p.m.– 6.00p.m.	• using craft tools • fixings – adhesive/ nails, etc.
Give your clothes a new life. (3 _____ required)	Tuesdays and Thursdays 8.00a.m.– 12.00p.m.	• advanced sewing stitches
Making gift boxes out of your old wood.	Fridays 8.00a.m.– 12.00p.m.	• 4 _____ • decoration ideas

Questions 5–7
Complete the notes below.
Write **NO MORE THAN TWO WORDS AND/OR A NUMBER** *for each answer.*

How to reuse your furniture and make stylish pieces
Workshop details:
5 _____ not necessary
Bring your own furniture so transport essential
Mention 6 _____ when applying
7 _____ essential for safety

Discussion

5 Discuss the questions. Why is it important to preserve the world's resources? In your view, do activities such as upcycling have a large impact on the future of the environment? Why/Why not?

Language development

Form clauses

> EXPERT GRAMMAR page 178

1a Read the text below and underline three incorrect sentences.

Cleaning up your home can actually save you money. If you have a lot of clutter, try to get rid of this. You can look around the house for items that you do not use and sell them off or give them away. One key way to reduce your spending and make money. This could also make your home a nicer place to be in. With the effect of being a more pleasant environment. This might also make your home a more enjoyable place to be in, which also saves you money. Because you will not go out as much.

b Match the mistakes you underlined with the reason for the mistake (A–F). There are more reasons than you need.

A No verb
B Wrong tense
C No subject
D Object needed
E A missing clause
F A missing conjunction

c Put the words and phrases in the correct order to make sentences. Add punctuation and capital letters where necessary.

1 use / unplug them / many electronic devices / a great deal of energy / so / when you can
2 these devices / when not in use / should unplug / you
3 you / it / hard / might seem / will save / money / but
4 they / the time / many people / this / because / neglect to do / simply do not have

Subordinate clauses

2 Which sentences (A or B) are NOT full sentences?

1 A There is no point in throwing away leftover food.
  B Although there is no point in throwing away leftover food.
2 A People buy too many things at the supermarket.
  B Whenever people buy too many things at the supermarket.
3 A If you have made too much dinner.
  B You have made too much dinner.
4 A Because food will keep a long time in the freezer.
  B Food will keep a long time in the freezer.

3 When a clause has a subordinating conjunction (e.g. *when, while, as, although*), the clause becomes subordinate and needs another clause to complete the sentence. Match the sentence beginnings (1–5) with the endings (A–E).

1 While many activities cost money,
2 Although going to the cinema or restaurant may be enjoyable,
3 Some people are good at managing money
4 People should do some kind of exercise every week
5 Unless people are sufficiently motivated,

A whether they want to or not.
B they will not be able to reduce their spending.
C exercise is free.
D while other people find controlling their finances more difficult.
E they can be quite expensive pastimes.

4 Punctuate the paragraphs below. The subordinating conjunctions are in bold.

life is not all about spending money thinking about saving money and resources can be really beneficial **if** you are careful with money and resources you may be able to afford some of the items you really want in the future you will be aiding the environment too **as** wasting resources is one of the largest environmental problems in the world

whenever you think about disposing of something consider whether you can do anything else with it think of activities you can do which do not involve resources **whereas** watching television for an hour uses power going for a walk does not consume any resources small steps like these can make a considerable difference.

5 Complete the sentences below. Work in pairs and discuss the reasons for your answers.

1 If I had enough money, …
2 While I don't always enjoy …
3 Although most people say …

Express opinions with *that*

6a Read the following sentence. What structure follows the word *that*?

There is widespread belief that reusing things saves money.
A a clause   B a noun phrase   C a verb

b Put the words and phrases in the correct order to express opinions using *that*.

1 by our / disagree / is being harmed / Many people / our planet / that / wastefulness.
2 double the amount / Experts speculate / of waste / that / we discard / we will soon
3 it might be easier / it will not help / the environment. / that / to just use resources freely, / We must take into consideration / whilst

Writing (Task 2)

Lead-in

1 Look at the cartoon. What is the joke?

Give your opinion

2 Read the essay task and number the paragraphs answering the question in the correct order.

Recycling is a waste of time. Individuals cannot do enough to make a significant contribution to the problem of rubbish.
To what extent do you agree?

A

Recycling is a straightforward way for people to contribute to conserving the Earth's resources. Recycling household waste does not require much effort from individuals since collection facilities are often provided by local governments. In addition, there are specialist recycling centres for larger objects such as domestic appliances. As a result, many people in lots of countries recycle as much as possible nowadays, therefore it should be acknowledged that individuals can make a difference.

B

In conclusion, it can be argued that recycling is effective. A large number of people in different countries now consider it to be a part of their everyday lives and make use of the recycling facilities provided for them. If this were further developed by local services and governments, the effects would be even greater.

C

Modern society produces a considerable quantity of waste which somehow needs to be disposed of. Although many people believe that recycling is a good idea, others claim that it is not effective. In my view, recycling is not a waste of time and should be encouraged. This essay will discuss why recycling is effective.

D

On the other hand, recycling cannot only be done by individuals. Some believe that until larger institutions start recycling their waste, whatever individuals do is merely a drop in the ocean. However, public opinion is shifting towards environmental awareness and every individual that recycles is now part of a larger movement. Further encouragement from governments and other institutions may ensure the effectiveness of individual contributions. For example, if local governments collected large items from people's houses, this would encourage further recycling.

Develop your arguments

3 Read the example essay in Exercise 2 and answer the questions.

1 Underline the writer's answer in the introduction paragraph.
2 What phrase introduces the writer's opinion in the introduction paragraph?
3 What is the main idea in the first content paragraph?
4 What kind of support (e.g. reason, example) does the writer use in the first content paragraph?
5 What is the main idea in the second content paragraph?
6 What kind of support does the writer use in the second content paragraph?
7 Does the conclusion agree with the answer in the introduction paragraph?

Write your opinion essay

> **EXPERT WRITING** page 194

4a Read the essay task below. Consider your opinion and plan your answer. Think about:
• how much you agree.
• what main reasons you have for this opinion.
• explanations and examples you can use to support your main reasons.
• how you can link your explanations and examples together.

Everyone should be encouraged to use fewer resources rather than recycle more.
To what extent do you agree with this statement?

b Now write your answer. Write at least 250 words.

c Work in pairs and answer the questions in Exercise 3 about your essays. How can you improve your answers?

Listening (Section 2)

Before you listen

1 Work in pairs and discuss the questions.

1 Is giving presents important in your culture? Why?
2 Are there any typical or traditional presents in your culture and when would you give them?
3 Are there any gifts which you should avoid giving in your culture? When/Why?

Identify links between ideas

2a Read the table. Discuss the order in which the information will be given.

Questions 1–3

Complete the table below.

Write **NO MORE THAN THREE WORDS AND/OR A NUMBER** for each answer.

Gift	Age range	Advantage	Disadvantage
Robot car	10+ (unsuitable for young children)	1 _____	High price
Talking doll	2 _____ years	Low price	Not lifelike, hair falls out, clothes 3 _____
Magic tricks game	12 and over, possibly more suited to teenagers	Easy to follow instructions	Batteries not supplied

b Match the words (1–4) with the functions (A–D).

1 firstly, then, lastly
2 however, but, on the other hand
3 which is, made for, aimed at
4 the good thing, a great bonus, fantastic for

A connecting the gift to the age range
B moving from one gift to the next
C introducing an advantage
D moving from an advantage to a disadvantage

c Read the note-completion questions in Exercise 3b. Why is it more difficult to predict the links between the ideas?

Test practice

➤ **TEST STRATEGIES** page 168

3a Work in pairs. Look at questions 1–10 below and discuss possible answers. What 'clues' are there in the questions?

b 🔊 4.2 Complete the test tasks.

Questions 1–4

Complete the table below.

Write **NO MORE THAN THREE WORDS AND/OR A NUMBER** for each answer.

Buying gifts for work colleagues

	Suggestion	Possible outcome
Cost	Make sure it is not too expensive	upsets 1 _____
	Spend a 2 _____ amount of money	Shows respect and thoughtfulness
Style	Buy something classic	Reduces risk of 3 _____
	Do not be overly 4 _____	Can be considered boring

Questions 5–10

Complete the notes below.

Write **NO MORE THAN ONE WORD** for each answer.

Gifts for stages of employment
Welcome – used to signify 5 _____ a new organisation
Anniversary markers – 6 _____ corresponds to the length of time working
Additional function – gives employees an 7 _____ to remain at the same company.
Leaving – co-workers 8 _____ to buy a gift for the leaver.
9 _____ – similar to leaving party
- Main difference – higher value of gift
- Importance indicated by 10 _____ from senior employee.

Task analysis

4 Work in pairs and discuss the question.

1 Which question type (table or note completion) were you able to answer more easily? Why?

Language development and vocabulary

Pronoun referencing

➤ **EXPERT GRAMMAR** page 178

1a Read the text. Match the underlined pronouns and phrases (1–10) with the nouns or phrases (A–J).

Most people will have heard of eBay, the buying and selling website. **1** <u>It</u> allows individuals and small companies to buy and sell products in a way which was not previously possible. eBay has been extremely successful and **2** <u>this</u> has encouraged people to set up similar websites. Some of them focus solely on one type of product whereas **3** <u>others</u> are more general. For example, Etsy predominantly focuses on handmade craft products, **4** <u>most of which</u> are made by artists, designers and jewellery makers. Because their skills are appreciated more by Etsy customers, **5** <u>they</u> are able to charge a fairer price for their time than they would on eBay, **6** <u>which</u> enables them to have a more viable business. There are also apps for individuals to buy and sell **7** <u>their</u> own possessions quickly and easily, such as Depop. **8** <u>This</u> lets you upload photos and share **9** <u>them</u> on social media. **10** <u>This</u> means that both buyers and sellers reach a wider audience.

A artists, designers and jewellery makers
B websites that allow you to buy products
C uploading photos and sharing them on social media
D being able to charge more money than on eBay
E eBay   H individuals
F the photos   I handmade craft products
G eBay's success J the app

b Answer the questions about pronouns.

1 Which pronouns can replace people's names?
2 What type of nouns can *these* and *those* replace?
3 Do *this* and *that* replace singular nouns, whole phrases/ideas or both?
4 What do relative pronouns (*which, who, where*) replace?

2 Complete the sentences with the pronouns below.

their   these   they   this   which

1 The internet is a selling tool _____ has given many people the opportunity to start small businesses.
2 Fashion companies regularly target teenage girls in advertising. _____ approach is considered unethical by many people.
3 People often overspend when it comes to buying presents for children. As a result, _____ often struggle to understand the value of possessions.
4 Around the world people have different attitudes towards spending money. _____ often stem from _____ culture and social values.

Signposting words

3a Write the signposting words below in the correct place in the table. Can you think of more examples of signposting words?

although   consequently   due to   despite   for instance   finally   furthermore   however   in addition   in conclusion   initially   in particular   nevertheless   on the contrary   therefore   whereas

To add more information	To show the order of things	To compare or contrast	To give examples	To show reasons and results

b Choose the correct option in *italics* to complete the text.

Foraged or field-to-table food is the latest trend in high-end restaurants around the world. Most of us believe that food in top restaurants is meticulously grown under special conditions. **1** *Whereas / On the contrary*, foraged food comes straight from fields in the countryside to restaurant kitchens. **2** *Although / Furthermore* some people predict it will be a short-lived fashion, others disagree **3** *for instance / due to* the philosophy behind the approach. The aim is to reduce the number of people who touch the food. **4** *In addition / Nevertheless*, it adds creativity and authenticity to the menu. **5** *Initially / Although*, it was popular in Denmark where Chef René Redzepi introduced the concept. **6** *Consequently / However*, it is now popular all over the world and people are willing to spend a fortune on this type of food. **7** *In conclusion / Furthermore*, chefs say that it changes how they cook, **8** *in particular / despite* how they prepare rare ingredients to enhance the natural flavours. This new style of sourcing food is all about focusing on high-quality, natural ingredients **9** *therefore / finally* it is easy for restaurants to charge extreme prices for their creations.

Speaking (Part 3)

Vocabulary development

1 Look at the photos. Can you name the items shown? How much do you think each item is worth?

2 Complete the text with the words below.

brand   gadgets   materialistic   possessions
status symbol   successful   value

Today, it can be argued that people do not understand the **1** _____ of money as much as they did in the past, spending so as to show off new things that are soon thrown away. The world is certainly becoming more **2** _____ as people see the latest **3** _____ and most famous **4** _____ names as a form of **5** _____ amongst their friends. However, we must remember that whilst these things may make you appear more **6** _____ , they do not necessarily bring you happiness. It is rare that joy is found in **7** _____ , for this feeling usually comes from within.

3 Work in pairs and discuss the questions.

1 What kinds of problems are associated with buying brand names? Why?
2 Do you think people are successful because of what they own? Why/Why not?
3 Would you say the world is becoming more materialistic? Why/Why not? Do you think this is true in only certain parts of the world? If so, which ones?
4 In what situations might materialism be beneficial? When could it be negative?

Focus on pronunciation

4a Turn to page 183 and read the level descriptors for pronunciation. Match the underlined words in (1–4) with the pronunciation features (A–D).

1 a new car   A Connected speech
2 I like brand labels.   B Weak forms
3 I'd love to be a millionaire.   C Sentence stress
4 important to   D Word stress

b 🔊 4.3 Listen and decide whether speaker 1 or speaker 2 is using correct features of pronunciation.

c 🔊 4.4 Listen to two candidates talking about shopping. Which of them (1 or 2) do you think is more likely to get a better band score? Why?

Test practice

> **TEST STRATEGIES** page 175

5a Read the questions below. Think about your answers and your pronunciation.

1 Are brands important? For what groups of people?
2 How are people influenced by advertising?
3 How much pressure is there on people to buy the latest gadgets these days?
4 Do you think the world is too materialistic these days? Why/Why not?

b Work in pairs and ask and answer the questions in Exercise 5a. Record your answers if possible.

Assess and improve

6a Work in pairs and discuss the questions.

1 Were there any words you could not understand?
2 Were there any sections that you did not understand?
3 Were the most important words stressed?
4 Was your partner's speech well connected?
5 Did he/she use strong and weak forms?

b Decide on TWO key features of pronunciation to try to improve.

Reading (Matching information; Summary completion)

Before you read

1 **Work in groups and discuss the questions.**

1 What are your three most precious possessions? Why do they mean so much to you?

2 What would you say makes one person more interested in money and possessions than another? How materialistic do you think you are compared to other people?

3 Do you prefer to spend money on possessions or on experiences such as holidays or tickets to events? Give reasons.

Test practice

2 **Read the strategies and complete the test task.**

➤ **TEST STRATEGIES** pages 170 and 171

Question 1-6

*The reading passage has **SIX** paragraphs, **A–F**.*

*Which section contains the following information? Write the correct letter, **A–F**. You may use any letter more than once.*

1 A comparison of what drives the desire for possessions across a range of communities.

2 Surprising research findings link personal well-being and the desire for possessions.

3 A reason why people might treasure something that cost very little.

4 An example of an inclination used to manipulate people into spending money.

5 The potential impact of depriving people of their possessions.

6 A warning of the possible consequences of 'retail therapy'.

➤ **HELP**

4 Who might use this technique?

5 In what situations might people have possessions taken away from them?

Questions 7–10
Complete the summary below.
*Choose **NO MORE THAN TWO WORDS** from the passage for each answer.*

How to spend money

People often find it difficult to stop buying things but they may be able to become happier with what they have bought. Clearly, people need money to live but having achieved a 7 _____ , more money will not mean it will get better. Psychologist Elizabeth Dunn recommends the more lasting benefits of spending money on 8 _____ and on doing something new rather than on buying things. Although our motive for buying something is often because we want 9 _____ in our lives, this idea will disappear as soon as we obtain the thing we wanted. Dunn's advice is to spend money on something which will improve the quality of the 10 _____ available to you.

➤ **HELP**

8 Will this noun be singular or plural/countable or uncountable? How do you know?

9 Find a word in this part of the passage which means *disappear*.

Task analysis

3 **Work in pairs and discuss the questions.**

1 Which of the strategies did you find helpful?

2 Which strategies would you like to try next time?

Discussion

4 **To what extent do you agree with the statements below? Give reasons and examples from your own experience.**

1 We expect new belongings not only to improve the quality of our lives, but also to enhance the way we are viewed by others.

2 Though we expect new belongings to bring change, this vague notion usually evaporates once we have acquired the new item.

3 Our belongings play an important role in bolstering our sense of identity.

4 Our materialistic desires are usually dictated not by what we need, but by what those around us possess.

MY PRECIOUS

Our belongings can have deep meaning, but do they make us happy, asks Michael Bond

A As we all know, our relationship with the items we own goes far beyond utility and aesthetics. As well as being useful, our possessions represent our extended selves. They are "repositories of ourselves", says Catherine Roster at the University of New Mexico in Albuquerque. "It might be a sweater, a lamp, an umbrella – an object doesn't have to have material value to have emotional value." Our ability to imbue things with rich meaning is a universal human trait that emerges early in life and develops as we age. The inclination to value material possessions beyond what others consider they are worth is known in psychology as the "endowment effect". It explains why we are more likely to buy a coat once we have tried it on as the mere act of imagining that something is ours in effect adds value to an object.

B Our ability to imagine the way new possessions will change our lives is what drives us to acquire them in the first place, states Marsha Richins at the University of Missouri in Columbia. Her research demonstrated that we have "transformation expectations" about new belongings: we expect them not only to improve the quality of our lives but also to enhance the way we are viewed by others. It is a tendency expertly exploited by advertisers, she claims.

C Our belongings also have an important role in bolstering our sense of identity, one made most apparent when we are forced to discard them. This can be difficult, even traumatic, since it is akin to relinquishing a part of ourselves. Institutions such as prisons and military camps strive for just this result by removing clothes and other personal effects from inmates and recruits and issuing them with standardised kit, which serves to diminish their individuality: they in effect become like clay, primed for reshaping.

D Our materialistic aspirations are usually dictated not by what we need, but by what those around us possess. Envy is a mover of markets. At a deep level it is all about equity and dignity, says Edward Fischer, an anthropologist at Vanderbilt University in Nashville, Tennessee. "Is it fair that I have less than others? And what does this mean to my sense of self-worth? This isn't just a feature of affluent societies," he adds. "It's also true among rural Maya farmers, Cairo's workers and various other groups of people around the world. The norms of those peer groups differ greatly but the influence of an individual's relative standing among them is equally important no matter where you are in the world."

E Our culture of hyper-consumerism can make it difficult to determine where normal behaviour ends and compulsion begins. Of course we are all materialistic to some extent and we do obtain a boost of happiness from a new possession. But it does not last and because it is so fleeting, there is a danger that many people immediately feel the need to make yet another purchase. Studies have clearly demonstrated that those who need material possessions to make themselves feel happier may in fact be struggling to find fulfilment in other key areas of their lives, such as relationships. But interestingly, the drive to attain greater material wealth may not itself be the cause of this discontentment: a study by Rik Pieters at Tilburg University in the Netherlands revealed that while loneliness tends to make people more materialistic, the inverse is not necessarily true.

F We may not be able to influence our drive for acquisition but we do have the power to alter the degree of happiness we derive from the purchases we make. It is widely understood that once you earn enough to maintain a comfortable lifestyle, additional money does not continue to improve your quality of life. But that could well be because people are spending it wrongly. Research by psychologist Elizabeth Dunn revealed that spending money on experiences and other people offers a more enduring boon than spending lavishly on other items. The price of the football boots that you purchase for your nephew, for example, matters far less than whether you accompany him to the park when he first wears them, she says. Though we expect new belongings to bring change, this vague notion usually evaporates once we have acquired that new item. So before making a purchase, Dunn suggests you pause to consider what you will be able to do differently once you have it and whether it will truly affect the way you spend your time – which in essence is your most precious commodity.

Writing (Task 2)

Lead-in

1 What brands do you tend to use or buy? Do you agree that branding encourages people to buy more than they need? Why/Why not?

Understand the task

> EXPERT WRITING page 194

2a Read the essay title and the opinions and ideas (1–7). Tick the opinions and ideas which are suitable for this essay.

Nowadays people value possessions more than other important aspects of life such as people and experiences.

To what extent do you agree or disagree?

1 People consume too much – this takes their attention away from other important aspects.
2 Consumerism is an important force which drives the world economy – without it our way of life would change.
3 Social media has brought people together – many communities are stronger nowadays.
4 Family and friends play a significant role in life – most people value spending time with them.
5 People should spend less money on possessions – buying cheaper products is much better.
6 It is important to value people in life – they support us through difficult times.
7 Some possessions are important and should be valued – gifts, house, necessary objects, etc.

b Work in pairs and discuss your answers with a partner. Explain why you think the ideas you chose are suitable for the essay.

3 Read the essay title below and complete the table with ideas and supporting arguments. One has been done for you.

Some people believe that consumerism is good for countries, whereas others argue that it has negative consequences.

Discuss both views and give your opinion.

Ideas	Supporting arguments
1 *Shopping generates business for companies and the development of new products.*	• *Brings wealth to businesses and therefore countries* • *Improves people's standard of living as new products can offer an easier life, e.g. microwave*
2	
3	
4	

Plan the task

4a Turn to page 190 and read the descriptors for coherence and cohesion. Work in pairs and discuss what the descriptors for each band mean.

b Which of the features of written language below contribute to text cohesion?

1 conjunctions (*and, so, but*)
2 paragraphing
3 the passive (*it was given*)
4 pronoun referencing (*it, these, they*)
5 signposting words (*however, firstly, although*)
6 articles (*a/an, the*)

c Discuss how well you use the cohesive features in Exercise 4b.

Language and content

5a Read sentences 1–3. Decide if they answer the essay question or describe the essay structure. Give reasons for your answer.

The rise of consumer culture in modern times has reduced the quality and craftsmanship of products compared to in the past. This has had many negative effects.
How far do you agree?

1 In my opinion the quality of products has reduced significantly in recent years.
2 This essay will explore two reasons for my view on consumer culture.
3 I will present two main arguments about the reduction of craftsmanship in this essay.

b Write another sentence to show your opinion and a sentence which describes the essay structure.

Write your opinion essay

6a Read the essay title and write some ideas and supporting points. Organise your ideas into paragraphs.

Young people spend too much money on expensive fashion brands and gadgets these days, many of which are not necessary.
To what extent do you agree?

b Write your answer to the question in Exercise 6a. Write at least 250 words.

Assess and improve

7a Work in pairs. Read and assess each other's essays using these questions.

1 Is the answer stated in the introduction?
2 Does each paragraph present an opinion?
3 Is there sufficient support for each opinion? What is the function of the support given (example, reason, result)?

b Give your partner some ideas on how he/she could improve his/her essay. Focus on the following areas:

• Answering the question in the introduction
• Explaining the essay content in the introduction
• Giving an opinion with support in the main body of the essay
• Restating the answer in the conclusion

c Rewrite your essay. Take into consideration the suggestions made by your partner.

Review

1a Choose the correct option in *italics* to complete the sentences.

1 Many people could not *conceive / speculate* of a life without the internet.
2 Evidence on the benefits of consumerism from academic sources *assumes / contradicts* many news reports.
3 It is easy to *pass / resign* judgement on the spending habits of others.
4 Although high street stores try to *speculate / acknowledge* on new fashions, they are notoriously difficult to predict.
5 Consumers tend to have a lot of *faith / judgement* in big-name brands, even though they may be more expensive and of comparable quality to other brands.
6 Success in fashion is the ability to constantly *define / convince* the consumer of the need to acquire more clothes.

b Match 1–5 with A–E.

1 A large proportion of rich people report being unhappy
2 Consumers demand new and exciting technology.
3 In many parts of the world owning a vehicle is becoming increasingly common
4 Consumerism can take many different forms,
5 Some sections of society see their possessions as temporary and disposable,

A Consequently, investment in this industry has grown considerably.
B for instance, demand for knowledge, services and goods.
C despite their accumulated wealth.
D whereas others buy goods that last even if they are more expensive.
E due to the expansion of the middle classes.

c Complete the sentences with the correct signposting words.

due to   despite   furthermore   in particular
for instance   consequently   initially   although

1 Internet shopping was _____ viewed as an unsafe shopping method, but nowadays payment security is much more secure.
2 Celebrities are often used to sell high-end fragrances. _____ , Beyonce has a range of perfumes which are globally successful.
3 _____ much of society becoming increasingly environmentally aware, fast fashion remains popular.
4 Many of the world's natural resources are being destroyed _____ increased manufacturing.

5 Consumerism is having a negative effect on many people. _____ , teenagers seem to be susceptible more than other generations.
6 Fashion today has a throwaway culture which is not financially beneficial for individuals. _____ , it is not beneficial for the environment.
7 Many parents give their children a lot of expensive gifts. _____ , they come to expect these things throughout their lives.
8 _____ people like having the latest versions of technology, this puts increasing demands on the world's natural resources.

2a Put the phrases in the correct order to make sentences. There may be more than one possible answer. Add any necessary punctuation.

1 it is cost effective / and replace goods frequently / many consumers believe that / to buy cheaply
2 is beneficial for consumers / has been negative / while the decreasing cost of fashion / the impact on factory workers' salaries
3 in this area / to keep up with the latest technology / because there are / so many rapid developments / it can seem difficult
4 the average household's consumption / this has not reduced / frequent complaints about rising prices / although there are
5 the better the quality / common belief / the more you pay / that / there is a
6 their electricity consumption / their house lights / people turned off / would be reduced / if
7 older people prefer / young people are interested in / whereas / things built to last / buying the latest products
8 demand it / ethically produced / unless / products / consumers / will not be

b Complete the text with the correct pronouns.

What are consumer rights?

Consumer rights are an important part of law, but 1 _____ vary from country to country. In the UK, for example, purchasers are protected. 2 _____ means that if 3 _____ buy a faulty product, 4 _____ are entitled to a refund. However, 5 _____ laws do not apply if the consumer simply changes 6 _____ mind about the product; there must be something wrong with 7 _____ .

5 Homes of the future

5a Training
- **Reading:** Recognise reference words (Matching features; Note completion)
- **Vocabulary:** The language of invention and innovation; Express quantity; Agreement and disagreement
- **Speaking:** Develop topic-specific vocabulary; Techniques for adding detail (Part 2)
- **Listening:** Listen for agreement and disagreement (Section 3: Matching)
- **Language development:** Reported speech patterns; Other reporting structures
- **Writing:** Interpret statistical data; Support trends with details (Task 1: Bar and pie charts)

5b Testing
- **Listening:** Section 3: Matching; Labelling a diagram
- **Language development and vocabulary:** Noun phrases 1; Reporting verbs
- **Speaking:** Part 2: Describe an experience
- **Reading:** Labelling a diagram; *True/False/Not given*
- **Writing:** Task 1: Describe a chart

Lead-in

1a Look at the photos. What aspects relating to the future do they predict? Which do you think are most likely to become reality? Why?

b Describe how you think the world will be in 50 years' time.

Reading (Matching features; Note completion)

Before you read

1   **Work in groups and discuss the questions.**

    1   Who does most of the housework in your house? Which chores do you dislike doing? Which chores would you like a robot to do? Why?

    2   In what ways are robots used in the modern world? What limitations do they have?

2   **Read the title and subtitle of the reading passage.**

    1   Predict what the reading passage will be about.

    2   Skim the passage to get an idea of its content and structure. Which of the scientists is working on a different kind of robot?

Recognise reference words

3   **When you are skimming and scanning, recognising words and phrases which refer back to *ones* mentioned earlier will help you to read more quickly and efficiently.**

    1   What does *ones* (in italics above) refer back to?

    2   Look at the words/phrases underlined in the passage (1–19). What do they refer back to?

    3   Look at paragraphs 4 and 5 and underline reference words or phrases.

Test practice

4   **Read the strategies and complete the test task.**

➤ **TEST STRATEGIES** pages 170 and 172

> **Questions 1–5**
>
> *Look at the following scientists and the list of statements below.*
>
> *Match each scientist (**A–D**) with the correct statement (**1–5**).*
>
> **List of scientists**
>
> A   Cynthia Breazeal   C   Colin Angle
> B   Jen McCabe   D   Jeremy Conrad
>
> 1   The next stage in robotic technology is for robots to become interactive companions.
> 2   A positive outcome for robots of the future would be expertise and reliability in specific tasks.
> 3   Robotic technology in the home is currently complicated to operate.
> 4   The fact that some current household products have a robotic action is not always apparent.
> 5   An approach which applies available technology to new products is beneficial.

> **Questions 6–9**
>
> *Complete the notes below.*
>
> *Choose **NO MORE THAN TWO WORDS** from the passage for each answer.*
>
> **The new wave of household technology**
>
> •   Nest thermostat – communicates with: 6 _____ at house and some 7 _____
> •   Echo – functions like a 8 _____ , i.e. obeys spoken instructions
> •   Roomba's 9 _____ facilitated by map-making ability

Task analysis

5   **Work in pairs and discuss the questions.**

    1   For the matching activity, which of the following strategies enabled you to do this quickly and accurately?

      A   Looking for paraphrases of the words and phrases in the statements. Give examples.

      B   Underlining the scientists' names in the passage.

      C   Reading the passage for gist first.

    2   For the note-completion activity, what do you need to check carefully

      A   before doing the task?

      B   after doing the task?

Discussion

6   **Discuss the questions, giving reasons.**

    1   What do you think of science-fiction films? Have you seen any which feature robots? If so, which ones?

    2   It is predicted that humanoid robots 'with a heart', which have already been introduced into some households in Japan, will soon become popular, in the same way as pets are in many places. How likely is it that they would become popular in your country?

    3   If humanoid robots were introduced into care homes for older people, what tasks might they be able to undertake? What might be the benefits and drawbacks of having such robots?

How robots are poised to take over our homes

A robot revolution has been predicted for years but are we really on the verge of a new era?

Robots are starting to change the way we live but not in the way that scientists predicted 50 or even 10 years ago. At a time when some technologists are worrying about the threat of killer robots being used on the battlefield, the coming wave of domestic robots are much more tame, or even mundane. Rather than having androids marching into our kitchens and living rooms, automation is stealthily entering our homes via appliances and security systems.

Defining what exactly a robot is, however, remains a controversial topic even among those who design and develop [1]them. "A huge variety of items in our homes or cars exhibit robotic behaviour – we just do not think of [2]them as [3]such because we have this vision of a humanoid robot," says Jen McCabe, director of electronics at manufacturer Flex's Innovation Unit which developed the self-learning thermostat control device, Nest. "The robotic movement of Nest is behind the thermostat. Just because [4]it is not visible does not make [5]it any less robotic."

The Nest thermostat, purchased by Google for $3bn last year, predicts when and how to set the temperature in the house, helping to save energy and ensure [6]it is comfortable for family members. It connects with [7]its home security cameras to determine when to switch [8]itself on and off. In addition to [9]this, there are certain makes of cars [10]which inform the heating system of [11]the driver's imminent arrival so that [12]it can increase the temperature. Other companies are pursuing [13]similar goals. Amazon's Echo, for instance, is an internet-connected music system [14]that responds to [15]the owner's voice. [16]In this way, the Echo can be used to turn on and off wifi-enabled light bulbs and electrical switches, not with mechanical arms but by putting [17]itself at the centre of a wireless network of connected devices. [18]This operates as a personal assistant would; playing whatever music is requested of [19]it, creating shopping lists and providing information about sports scores.

However, while the addition of wireless connectivity has brought a semblance of intelligence to our thermostats and light bulbs, using, installing and managing all these new devices remains a challenge. Even Colin Angle, the manager of the robotics company iRobot, says he struggles to corral the automatons in his home. He is frustrated with the expensive home automation system he has installed there; the heating cannot keep up with his oft-changing schedule and maintenance visits are required all too frequently. "There is an enormous amount of experimentation underway with wireless connectivity but it is largely unsuccessful."

In 2006, Bill Gates promised a future in which "robotic devices will become a nearly ubiquitous part of our day-to-day lives", thanks to advances in sensors, motors and processing power. Years later, Jeremy Conrad, an investor in early-stage hardware start-ups, observes that although automation and robotisation are major trends at present, it is not necessarily for the reasons that Gates predicted; the change is not in the core technology. Because sensors and other components are being widely used in smartphones and other mass-market devices, the costs are diminishing for other applications too. This means that a 'smart' device connected to an existing home wifi network is much more accessible and more competitively priced than a professional home automation system. He believes that the degree of success for the next generation of robots will depend on how specialized they are. "They must work every time and be absolutely dependable.

This was the approach adopted by iRobot when it released its first autonomous vacuum cleaner Roomba, thirteen years ago. Advances in computer vision and machine-learning technology now mean that the machines are capable of creating a digital map of our homes with assistance from low-cost cameras. As a result, their navigational skills will enable them to track where they have and have not yet cleaned."

However, for some in the robotics industry these kinds of ventures are not sufficiently ambitious. Cynthia Breazeal, a pioneer of social robotics at MIT's Media Lab, promises that her latest creation, Jibo, will not only be able to see, hear and speak but also relay messages between family members and make helpful suggestions and reminders. When released, it will have its own character that, she claims, will recognise users and understand speech. Such traits will differentiate it from smartphones because the secret is not powerful processors or better sensors but emotion, which, she maintains, should be the obvious subsequent development of this humanised engagement with technology.

Vocabulary

The language of invention and innovation

1a Complete the text with the words below.

accessible automation controversial experimentation
innovation intelligence

Self-driving cars

People used to think that self-driving cars were
a technical **1** _____ of the distant future but
thanks to the ambitious research and development
programmes of various tech giants such as
Google, they are likely to become a reality within
a few years. Currently there is a lot of **2** _____
taking place in order to ensure the cars will be
safe. There are several **3** _____ issues to be
discussed with this type of technology too. For
example, if the cars use artificial **4** _____ , does
this mean they are able to learn to make their
own decisions in order to avoid an accident? If an
accident were to occur, who would be responsible;
the owner or the manufacturer? Another question
centres on the cost of these cars and whether
they will be **5** _____ to everyone. Whatever the
answer, this type of technology is expected to
stay, and we are likely to see a large increase in
home **6** _____ such as smart heating systems and
fridges too.

b Match the definitions with the words in Exercise 1a.

1 (adj) causing a lot of disagreement because many
people have strong opinions about the subject
2 (n) a new idea, method or invention
3 (adj) easy to obtain or use
4 (n) the process of testing various ideas or methods
to determine how good or effective they are
5 (n) the ability to learn, understand and think about
topics and problems
6 (n) the use of computers and machines instead of
people to do a job

c Work in pairs and discuss the statements. Which
do you think are the most controversial? Why?

1 Increased automation in the home will make
people lazier.
2 Artificial intelligence will one day control the world.
3 Experimentation is the best way to learn.
4 Some innovations have had terrible
consequences.

Express quantity

2a Look at the table which shows the percentage of
gadget ownership for men and women. Complete
the sentences using the words below.

Percentage of gadget ownership among men and women		
	Men	Women
Smartphone	95%	87%
Home security system	4%	2%
Car satellite navigation system	78%	82%
Coffee machine	18%	25%
Digital camera	55%	35%

a third both few most the majority three quarters

1 _____ car satellite navigation systems and
smartphones are popular with men and women.
2 _____ men or women own a home security system.
3 _____ of men own a smartphone.
4 Approximately _____ of women own a digital
camera.
5 _____ of women do not own a coffee machine.
6 _____ men own a car satellite navigation system.

b Look at the list of futuristic technology. Ask
your classmates which they would like to see
invented. Write sentences about your class using
quantity words from Exercise 2a.

- Flying car
- Time travel machine
- Personal space rocket
- Weather controller

Agreement and disagreement

3a Write the words below in the correct place in the
table.

entirely firmly marginally partly slightly somewhat
thoroughly totally utterly wholeheartedly

Weak opinion	Strong opinion

b Look at the opinions below. Use the words
in Exercise 3a to say how much you agree or
disagree. Give reasons for your opinions.

1 I admit that smartphones are convenient but we
could use them a lot less.
2 I don't know what I'd do without my car satellite
navigation system. It's the most useful innovation
ever. I'd quite literally be lost without it!
3 In my opinion, technological advances have gone
too far and have become too expensive.
4 I think that inventions and gadgets are really just a
waste of money.

Speaking (Part 2)

Lead-in

1 Do you find objects like this are useful? Why/ Why not? What are the advantages and disadvantages of relying on a satnav (satellite navigation) device?

Develop topic-specific vocabulary

2a Complete the sentences with the words below.

labour-saving outdated revolutionary state-of-the-art
user-friendly versatile

1 The washing machine had a _____ impact on society. It totally changed the lives of many women, who as a direct result then had more time to go out to work.

2 Some devices are more _____ than others. My new phone, for example, is so much easier to use than the one I had before, which was awful.

3 People are always buying new gadgets these days. If you have had the same gadget for more than a couple of years, everyone considers it _____ .

4 My tablet is one of the most _____ pieces of equipment I possess. I can use it to call my family overseas, watch TV, surf the internet and do my homework.

5 Cooking used to be a lot of work in the past, but _____ devices like the microwave have transformed the amount of time people need to spend on preparing their meals.

6 Pablo has recently purchased a _____ watch. It works like a small tablet and is very fast.

b Work in pairs and discuss the questions.

1 Which gadget do you think is the most labour-saving? Why?

2 Which invention has revolutionised the world the most? Why?

3 What do you value most in a gadget; user-friendliness or versatility? Why?

4 What qualities does a state-of-the-art gadget possess for you?

5 Why do gadgets become outdated?

Techniques for adding detail

3a Read the following test task and response. Has the speaker answered all parts of the test task? Where?

Describe an electronic item which you think is essential in your home. You should say:

what it is

when you use it

what you use it for

and explain why it is so important.

The device that I think is essential for me is probably my computer, 1 *which is a new state-of-the-art gaming computer.* I use this pretty much every day and for quite a long time every day as well. You see I work from home and I do all my work on the computer. It's such an important tool for my work … perhaps the most important. 2 *For instance, I need it to send emails, have online meetings with clients and do research for my projects.* It basically makes my working life a lot easier. 3 *I don't just use it for work though;* I also stream the TV through the computer and I rarely leave the house to go shopping these days; I just buy everything online. It's so important to me because it really saves me time and makes my life so much more convenient. 4 *If I didn't have my computer at home, I don't know what I'd do. I'd feel a lot more isolated, and would be lost for entertainment.* My mum says I've become addicted to the internet and I can see her point, but if I'm addicted, then I think most of the world is too. 5 *Funnily enough, my mum's just got a computer herself. I've got to go and show her how to use it next week.*

b Match the underlined sections (1–5) with the techniques for adding detail (A–E).

A description   C aside   E contrast
B example   D conjecture

c In pairs, discuss how you could change the content in the underlined sections in Exercise 3a.

Test practice

> **TEST STRATEGIES** page 174

4a Look at the test task in Exercise 3a. You have exactly 1 minute to prepare your topic. Make notes on what you are going to talk about.

b Work in pairs and take turns to answer the test task in Exercise 3a. Speak for 2 minutes and record your answer if possible.

Task analysis

5 Did you both answer all parts of the test task? Were you both able to speak for 2 minutes? Was any extra information given? Could any extra information have been added? If so, where?

Listening (Section 3)

Picnic pants

LED slippers

Before you listen

1 Look at the inventions in the photos. Do you think any of these inventions have a practical use? How can they make our lives easier? Which one would you most like to possess and why?

Listen for agreement and disagreement

2 ◀) 5.1 You are going to listen to two students talk about inventions. Decide whether speaker 2 agrees or disagrees with speaker 1, then note down the reason given. The first one has been done for you.

Speaker 1 opinion	Speaker 2 opinion	Reason
1 Charlotte thinks the LED slippers will make life easier.	Scott *agrees / disagrees.*	
2 Scott thinks the picnic pants are completely useless.	Charlotte *agrees / disagrees.*	

Test practice

> TEST STRATEGIES page 169

3a You are going to listen to a student discussion about an innovation project. Look at the invention they are discussing. What do you think it is? What do you think is good/bad about it?

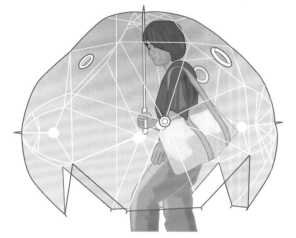

b Look at the test task below. Think of alternative ways to say the underlined expressions.

Questions 1–4
What do the students say about their innovation project? Match each student to their opinion.
*Write the correct letter, **A**, **B** or **C**.*

A Ben   B Debbie   C Phillip

1 <u>thought</u> their <u>initial idea was OK</u>.
2 thinks their design is <u>too complex</u>.
3 thinks they <u>don't need</u> to actually <u>make</u> their idea.
4 believes they'll <u>get a good mark</u>.

c ◀) 5.2 Complete the test task.

Task analysis

4 Read audio script 5.2 on page 206 and discuss the questions.
1 Where can you find the answers to Exercise 3c?
2 Which sections express similar ideas to the opinions in 3c?

Discussion

5 What is the strangest invention you have seen or heard about? Do you think all inventions help us in life? Why/Why not? If you could have anything invented for you to make your life easier, what would you choose and why?

Language development

Reported speech patterns

> EXPERT GRAMMAR page 178

1a Read the texts and underline the examples of reported speech.

> My lecturer told me that I'd get a better grade in my presentation on innovation in the workplace if I had more technology examples. I explained to her that I hadn't been able to find any good examples yet. She suggested that I looked in the *Journal of Technology and Industry*, which really helped me. I found this article about flexible computer screens. In it the author argued that one of the biggest benefits of this kind of technology was the possibility of saving office space.

> Yesterday, my friend mentioned that she'd found a great app to help manage reading. Apparently, the app information said that it was for people who come across interesting articles, but then forget about them! She said she thought it'd be useful for researching general information for our course and I promised that I'd look it up as soon as I got home.

b Answer the questions based on the examples you underlined in Exercise 1a.

1 What happens to tenses when they are transformed from direct to reported speech?
2 What happens to verbs like *will* and *can* when used in reported speech?
3 How do pronouns change?

2 Match the reporting verbs below with the speech patterns (1–3). Some verbs fit more than one pattern.

argue explain mention promise say suggest tell

1 Subject + reported verb + *that* + clause
2 Subject + reported verb + *to* + object + (*that*) + clause OR + infinitive verb
3 Subject + reported verb + object + (*that*) + clause OR + infinitive verb

3 Write sentences about what people have told you today. Use the verbs in Exercise 2 and follow the structures given.

4 Work in pairs and discuss the situations. Use reported speech in your answers.

1 Tell your partner a piece of good advice someone gave you.
2 Describe a time when you said something embarrassing.
3 Explain a time when you had to give someone some bad news.

Other reporting structures

5a Match the sentences (1–5) with the type of information they report (A–E).

1 She asked him to read the instructions on installing the new system.
2 The government instructed small businesses to change their working practices.
3 The lecturer asked the student if he wanted to discuss his research or his essay.
4 I asked her if she thought our lives would be easier in the future.
5 They asked me what I thought the next innovation in home music systems would be.

A Yes/No questions
B Requests
C Question word (*who, where, what*) questions
D Orders
E Either/Or questions

b Complete the sentences with the correct reported speech form.

1 The lecturer _____ people would live with robots in years to come and I said I thought we probably would.
2 The technology company _____ us _____ watch the demonstration before trying to use their new products. They made it clear it was not optional, as knowing how to work the products was essential and rather difficult at first.
3 Many people _____ we'll have self-cleaning homes but I think it'll probably not be for at least another 100 years.
4 I _____ my lecturer _____ explain more about genetic engineering as it was an extremely complex area of research.

Writing (Task 1)

Lead-in

1   How will technology change the homes of the future?

Interpret statistical data

> **EXPERT WRITING** page 195

2   Look at the pie chart and discuss the questions.
   1   How many paragraphs would you write if you were asked to describe the chart?
   2   How could you group the information?
   3   What order would you present the information in and why?

Energy use in Australian homes in 2008

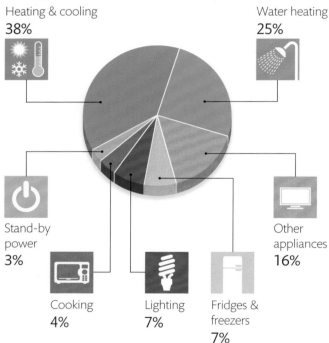

Heating & cooling
38%

Water heating
25%

Stand-by power
3%

Other appliances
16%

Cooking
4%

Lighting
7%

Fridges & freezers
7%

3a Look at the sentences giving specific details below. Which are correct and which are incorrect according to the data presented in the pie chart?
   1   <u>Exactly a quarter</u> of Australians spent their energy on water heating.
   2   <u>The smallest amount</u> of the total energy (3 percent) was used when appliances are put on standby.
   3   Over two-thirds <u>of all energy in Australian homes was used for heating and cooling</u>.
   4   More than <u>10 percent of home energy use was for lighting</u>.
   5   Other appliances accounted for <u>just over 25 percent</u> of total energy usage in the home.

   b   Correct the sentences above which you think are incorrect. Keep the underlined sections the same.

Support trends with details

Gadgets bought by men and women in the UK, 2013

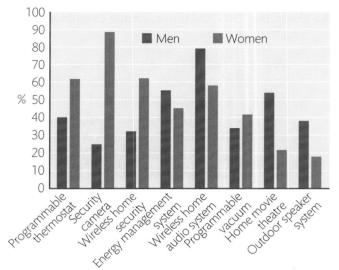

4   Look at the bar chart. Match the trends (1–3) with their supporting details (A–C).
   1   Women were more focused on safety gadgets for the home than men.
   2   Men tended to buy more entertainment-based gadgets for the home compared to women.
   3   Women spent more money on automated vacuums.

   A   Over forty percent of women purchased a vacuum system which is programmable.
   B   Almost 90 percent of women invested in security cameras, whereas only 25 percent of men bought these devices.
   C   For example, the chart shows that twice as many men as women purchased a home movie theatre.

Test practice

5   Choose one of the charts on this page and write a sample answer. Consider the following:
   •   How you can group the information
   •   What paragraphs you will use
   •   How you can describe the trends
   •   How you can outline the statistical details
   •   The accuracy of your sentences

Assess and improve

6   Work in pairs and compare your writing. Discuss the questions.
   1   Is there a clear structure?
   2   Are the paragraphs well organised?
   3   Are there both trends and details to support the trends?
   4   Are the details an accurate reflection of the data?
   5   Is the report over 150 words long?

Listening (Section 3)

Before you listen

1   Can you imagine space tourism becoming popular in future? Why/Why not? How might a hotel in space differ from those on Earth for holidaymakers?

Understand factual descriptions

2a   Look at the diagram of a space ship. Work in pairs and discuss what type of words could complete questions 1–4 below.

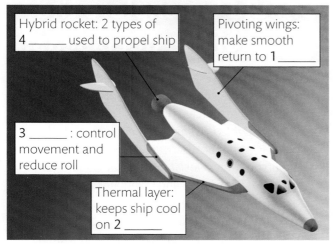

Hybrid rocket: 2 types of 4 _____ used to propel ship

Pivoting wings: make smooth return to 1 _____

3 _____ : control movement and reduce roll

Thermal layer: keeps ship cool on 2 _____

b   🔊 5.3 Listen and complete questions 1–4.

c   Read audio script 5.3 on page 206. How are the underlined phrases used to explain factual details about *Spaceship Two*?

Test practice

➤ **TEST STRATEGIES** page 169

3a   You will hear two students discussing their design project with a lecturer. Look at the questions and discuss what kind of information you will hear and possible answers.

b   🔊 5.4 Complete the test tasks.

Questions 1–5

What do the students say about their design project? Match each student to their opinion.

*Write the correct letter, **A**, **B**, **C** or **D**.*

   A Susie   **B** Brad   **C** Dr Kaye   **D** Dr Walters

1   believes the project may be too time-consuming.
2   disagrees that the project idea is too ambitious.
3   agrees with the presentation suggestion.
4   thinks the first draft of the plans are incorrect.
5   suggests a different approach to the next stage of the project.

Questions 6–10
Label the diagram below.
*Write **NO MORE THAN TWO WORDS** for each answer.*

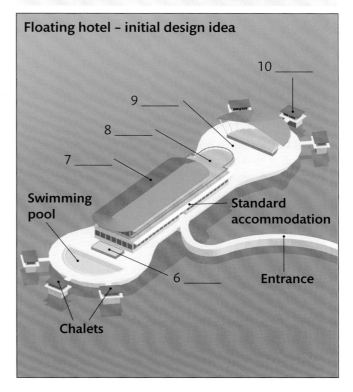

Floating hotel – initial design idea

10 _____
9 _____
8 _____
7 _____
Swimming pool
Standard accommodation
6 _____
Entrance
Chalets

Task analysis

4a   Read audio script 5.4 on page 206 and check your answers.

b   Analyse your answers by answering the following questions.

In the first set of questions:
1   How easy did you find it to identify the speakers? What helped you identify them?
2   Did you generally hear the phrases for agreement and disagreement? How many can you recall?
3   What paraphrases of the questions did you hear in the recording?

In the second set of questions:
4   Did you predict the correct type of word(s) for the spaces?
5   Were you able to follow the explanations of the different parts of the hotel?

Language development and vocabulary

Noun phrases 1

> **EXPERT GRAMMAR** page 179

1a Read the phrases (1–4) and match them with the noun phrase structures (A–D).

1 The television on the wall
2 Installation system
3 People who completed the survey
4 Luxury cars

A Noun + relative clause
B Adjective + noun
C Noun + noun
D Noun + prepositional phrase

b Quantities can also be used with noun phrases. Look at two example sentences and choose the correct option in *italics* to complete the rules (1–2).

A third of respondents said that they preferred using tablets to laptops.
The majority of countries which invest in space research have reported economic benefits.

1 When describing fractions, we use *a / the*.
2 With the words *majority* and *minority* we usually use *a / the*.

2 Put the words in the correct order to make noun phrases. Then match them to the sentence endings (A–D).

1 all / of / a / inventors / quarter
2 systems / new / alarm
3 design / futuristic
4 embrace / families / new / who / technology

A can already be seen in the minimalist look that some homes have.
B can monitor your home for movements.
C believe that the home will be unrecognisable in a hundred years' time.
D may benefit from a more convenient lifestyle.

3 Complete the second sentence so it has the same meaning as the first. Use a noun phrase.

1 Many older people do not like using new types of technology.
_____ is often resisted by many older people.
2 Most forms of technology makes our lives easier. These appliances soon become essential to us.
Technology _____ is often considered as essential within a few years.
3 Countless new inventions are created every year. Most of them do not make it to market though.
_____ do not proceed to market.

4 Complete the sentences using your own ideas.

1 The invention that I would like to see the most _____ .
2 One thing that scares me about the future _____ .
3 One place _____ is the moon.
4 Robots _____ would be an amazing invention.

Reporting verbs

5a Choose the correct option in *italics* to complete the text.

Should we explore the world of the deep seas?

Ocean exploration is a highly controversial issue. Critics **1** *illustrate / claim* that it is a complete waste of money and resources. However, some scientists have **2** *highlighted / denied* that exploration is the first step in scientific discovery and one which we must pursue. They **3** *insist / warn* that exploration expands our knowledge and stimulates ground-breaking discoveries. Recent deep sea expeditions have **4** *proved / suggested* beyond doubt that deep sea ecosystems can provide new innovations through the discovery of new substances which can be utilised for medicines and energy. However, scientists also **5** *claim / warn* that great care must be taken when reaching conclusions regarding ocean exploration, much more so than in other scientific research area, as around 95 percent of the underwater world is unchartered territory and completely unknown to mankind.

b Complete the sentences with the correct form of a suitable reporting verb from Exercise 5a.

1 Explorers have been _____ about the dangers of trying to reach the depths of the oceans.
2 Many companies who drill for oil in the seas _____ that their practices damage local environments.
3 Scientists have recently, through the use of time-lapse photography, _____ that the sea bed is in fact moving.
4 Recent finds during exploration of previously unexplored areas of deep sea strongly _____ that there are countless life forms we have yet to discover.
5 The newspapers _____ that a new species was recently identified on a recent expedition. However, scientists stated that it was simply an evolved species.

Speaking (Part 2)

Vocabulary development

1 Look at the two visions of the future. Which is utopian and which is dystopian? How likely do you think it is that either will become a reality? Why?

2a Complete the sentences with the adjectives below.

abundant arid dense overcrowded thriving
waterlogged

1 The Amazon has incredibly _____ forests, perhaps more so than anywhere else in the world, but they are in rapid decline due to deforestation.
2 Some people think that life on a space station would be uncomfortable because of limitations on the living space available, meaning that the ship would seem _____ with even a small number of people on board.
3 As a result of climate change, some regions of the world have become less habitable; in the hot seasons these places can be quite _____ , but in the rainy seasons entire areas can become _____ .
4 Recent research findings have revealed that coral reefs in the Pacific Ocean are _____ despite the water being incredibly acidic.
5 In order to succeed in colonising another planet, the human race would first need to discover one which has the _____ water supplies necessary to sustain human life.

b Work in pairs and use the words in Exercise 2a to describe places you know.

Focus on grammatical range and accuracy

3a Turn to page 183 and read the descriptors for grammatical range and accuracy. Answer the questions below.

1 At which band(s) do you need to speak without making many mistakes?
2 At which band should you begin producing more complex structures in speech?
3 At which band(s) should listeners be able to follow your speech easily?

b 🔊 5.5 Read the test task below. Listen and read the student's response in the audio script on page 206. How well do you think the student has answered the question? What do you think of her grammatical range and accuracy?

Describe a place where you would like to live in the future. You should say:

where it is

what you think it would be like

why you would like to live there

and explain what you have heard about it from other people.

c Find ONE example of each language feature below in the student's response.

Present perfect
Modal verb of deduction
Passive construction
Comparative
Second conditional
Modal verb for necessity
Future form
Imperative

Test practice

> TEST STRATEGIES page 174

4 Read the test task below and prepare. Work in pairs and take turns to speak for 2 minutes. Time each other and record your answers if possible.

Describe an experience that you would like to have in the future. You should say:

what it is

what you think it would be like

why you would like this experience

and say how likely you think it is to occur.

Assess and improve

5a Think about your partner's answers. Discuss the questions.

1 Did he/she speak for two minutes or more?
2 Did he/she answer all parts of the test task?
3 Could you understand all of his/her speech?
4 Did he/she use a wide range of grammatical structures? If so, which ones?
5 Did he/she make many errors with his/her grammar? What type of errors did you notice?

b What advice could you give your partner to improve? Use your answers in Exercise 5a to help you decide.

Reading (Labelling a diagram; *True/False/Not given*)

Before you read

1 Discuss the questions.

1 How likely is it that people will ever live under water? Why might they want to? Give reasons.
2 What might be the challenges of a) building homes underwater? b) living in an aquatic habitat?

Test practice

2a The first test task follows the same principles as note completion. Why is it important to

1 read the instructions carefully?
2 read the diagram heading?
3 skim the passage first?
4 look at the words around the gaps?

➤ **TEST STRATEGIES** page 170

b Complete the test task.

Questions 1–5
Label the diagram below.
Choose **NO MORE THAN TWO WORDS AND/OR A NUMBER** from the passage for each answer.

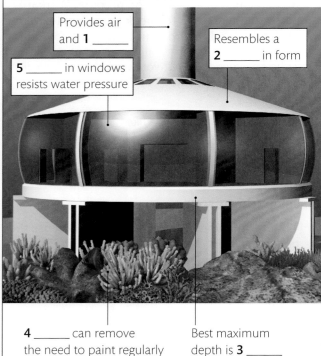

The structure of an H₂O Home

Provides air and **1** _____

Resembles a **2** _____ in form

5 _____ in windows resists water pressure

4 _____ can remove the need to paint regularly

Best maximum depth is **3** _____

➤ **HELP**

1 What else comes down the column?
2 Look for a word which describes a round flat shape.
4 What is the alternative to re-painting the structure if it needs to be protected from the surrounding salt water?

Questions 6–10
Do the following statements agree with the information in the reading passage? Write

TRUE *if the statement agrees with the information*

FALSE *if the statement contradicts the information*

NOT GIVEN *if there is no information on this*

6 Bruce Jones' house will be less dangerous to live in than previous undersea residences.
7 The H20me is less expensive to buy than any other undersea living quarters.
8 The underwater home is estimated to be habitable for up to 25 years.
9 There is still good visibility at a depth of 200 metres.
10 A lack of available resources will make entire underwater villages impossible.

➤ **HELP**

6 What makes this latest home more successful?
9 Is it an advantage or a disadvantage to live deeper in the sea?

Task analysis

3 In pairs, discuss the strategies which you used for both task types and ways in which you could improve next time.

Discussion

4 Discuss the questions.

1 How would you feel about the idea of living under the sea?
2 In what other kinds of places might people make their homes in the future?
3 Do you think there might be a move towards living in communities rather than in separate houses? What could be the benefits of this way of living?

How underwater living could soon be a reality

Fifty years after Jacques Cousteau's television programmes sparked our grandparents' imaginations, the idea, if not quite the practice, of underwater living is coming back into fashion with an ambitious and alluring vision for Katafinga Island in Fiji called the Poseidon Undersea Resort. The images circulating on the internet of luxurious rooms surrounded by shoals of exotic fish and colourful corals suggest that this is an established resort. However, this is not the case and the ongoing delays which have impeded the project attest to the specific issues encountered during the construction of an underwater environment.

The research and testing undertaken for the Poseidon resort have prompted L. Bruce Jones, the designer, to begin marketing an underwater house or the "H2Ome", which is billed on the company's website as "the most technologically advanced undersea residence ever designed." The plans show a disk-like structure, 20 metres in diameter, which is suspended above the seabed on steel legs and has a tube umbilically connecting it to the surface. The biggest obstacle to underwater living to date has been the difference in pressure: all of the habitats constructed over the last fifty years have been at ambient pressure. Under water, the pressure is much greater, which can cause gases in the bloodstream to dissolve. This in turn sometimes results in the feared condition known as the bends, which can cause intense pain and even death. The H2Ome is a real advance, however, as the interior pressure is identical to that on land. Unlike the other experiments, therefore, it presents for the first time a viable aquatic living environment.

Like space, the underwater world is an alien and potentially deadly environment for humans, and undersea structures can be problematic to build. "We manufacture in a dry dock," explained Jones, "after which the completed structures are floated out and sunk onto the ocean bed using a semi-submersible. We then build legs so that the structure stands above the sea floor: this is done for ecological reasons. Next, it is connected to an umbilical central column, via which oxygen is obtained. It is by means of this cylindrical column,

containing a spiral staircase connecting the home to the surface, that power is also supplied. This allows services such as heating, ventilation etc." Michael Schütte, a designer on the project, admits it is very costly, but affirms that when compared with prime waterfront real estate or the cost of a tropical island villa, the $10m or so is actually very reasonable.

Naturally, the structures have to be extraordinarily robust and built to withstand not only the immense water pressure but also storms and hurricanes. "Although we work on a 25-year lifespan, the reality is that the underwater structures will not decay as fast as they would if they were on the surface due to there being a lower level of oxygen", says Schütte. "You could either remove the pod and paint it after 10 years or just not keep it clean and encourage marine life to grow around it, which will serve to protect the structure too. It is ideal to be no more than 15 metres down because about 97 per cent of all life in the ocean is in the top 10 metres. It is possible to go as deep as 200 metres but extremely heavy-duty viewing ports would be required and it would be completely dark." Those viewing ports are the main point of the underwater home. Plexiglas has been identified as the ideal material. It performs extraordinarily well under the pressure of water, far better, in fact, even than steel.

It might seem somewhat fanciful to begin thinking about undersea colonies of the types envisaged in watery sci-fi films. After all, what would their inhabitants live on? What would they produce? But recent research into the hot streams of water which spew from undersea vents has revealed a rich and plentiful mix of minerals emerging from beneath the seabed which could be accessed far more easily than by traditional mining methods. In addition, aquaculture and the study of the processes and chemical transformations in undersea organisms could provide a rich seam of research for everything from medicine to fuel. And studies using algae are also producing extraordinary results. If algae were to be grown in special floating bags on the surface of the water, it could be photosynthesised and provide not only a rich source of biofuel but potentially, food too.

Writing (Task 1)

> I cannot think of anything that excites a greater sense of childlike wonder than to be in a country where you are ignorant of almost everything. Suddenly you are five years old again. You cannot read anything, you have only the most rudimentary sense of how things work; you cannot even reliably cross a street without endangering your life. Your whole existence becomes a series of interesting guesses.
>
> *Bill Bryson, Neither here nor there: Travels in Europe*

Lead-in

1   What do you think of the quote about living in a different country? What might be the most positive and negative aspects of living in another country? If you could live anywhere in the world, where would you choose and why?

Understand the task

➤ EXPERT WRITING page 195

2a   Look at the tables below. Which data would be best represented in a pie chart and which data would be best represented in a bar chart? Give reasons for your answer.

Cost of living by country, 2015	
Country	Consumer Price Index Score
Switzerland	126.03
Norway	118.59
Australia	99.32
New Zealand	93.71
Kuwait	92.97
UK	92.19
Spain	65.70
China	48.89
Poland	45.11

Most popular destinations of migrants from the UK, 2010–2014	
Australia	38,000
Spain	17,000
China	19,000
France	24,000
Poland	18,000
Other	174,000

b   In some cases you may have a bar and pie chart together in the same task. Look at the information in Exercise 2a and read the sentences below which compare and contrast the information. Which sentences are true?

1   A   The countries with the very highest costs of living were generally not popular destinations for UK migrants.
    B   The information presented shows that UK migrants prefer to immigrate to countries where the cost of living is higher.

2   A   There is only one country that was a popular destination despite its relatively high cost of living in comparison to the UK.
    B   There are only two countries that were popular immigration destinations which were less expensive than the UK.

3   A   Cost of living does not appear to play a large role in the choice of destination country for UK migrants, as can be seen in the variety of destination countries with wide-ranging living costs.
    B   Cost of living has a strong effect upon the choice of destination country, which can be seen by the fact that most people do not choose these countries as their choice of destination.

c   Add detail to the correct sentences in Exercise 2b to explain your answers.

Language and content

3 a Turn to page 190 and read the band descriptors for lexical resource. Work in pairs and discuss the differences between band 6 and band 7.

b Look at the list below and tick the sentences which you think are true for you.

- I always try to think of synonyms for key words in the data where possible.
- I can paraphrase by changing the word forms and word order of some short phrases.
- I know what collocations are and try to think about words that go together in my writing.
- I try to use less common vocabulary in my writing.
- I do not use informal vocabulary in my IELTS writing.

c Look at the charts below. What words could you use as synonyms and collocations to describe the data?

The two charts below outline the statistically most desirable countries in terms of quality of life and reasons for migration.

Summarise the information by selecting and reporting the main features and make comparisons where relevant.

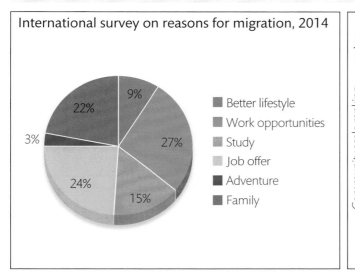

International survey on reasons for migration, 2014

- Better lifestyle
- Work opportunities
- Study
- Job offer
- Adventure
- Family

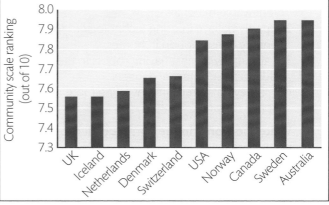

Rankings based on the categories of: housing, income, jobs, community, education, environment, health, life style, civic engagement and work-life balance.

Plan the task

4 Plan your answer. You should consider:

1 what information the two charts present.
2 the key features you can identify.
3 ways in which you can compare and contrast the two charts.
4 how paragraphs will be organised.
5 what the general overview of all the data will include.
6 accurate use of a range of grammar, vocabulary and cohesive devices.
7 any synonyms and collocations you can use in your answer.

Write your summary

5 Write your answer. You should write at least 150 words.

Assess and improve

6 a Work in pairs and compare your writing. Discuss the questions.

1 Does the summary contain all the key information from the charts?
2 Have some links been formed between the two charts?
3 Is there a clear overview at the end of the summary?
4 Is all the data included relevant and has it been accurately reported?
5 Have synonyms and collocations been used appropriately?

b Try to improve your answer with your partner, taking into account your answers to the discussion questions in Exercise 6a.

Review

1a Complete the text with the words below.

user-friendly state-of-the-art the majority accessible
automation versatile innovations

A sought-after feature of modern housing is extensive natural light. In order to transform older houses various 1 _____ have recently become available. For example, the use of glass bricks is now popular. They can be used in bathrooms, kitchens and as parts of internal walls too so they are very 2 _____ . However, the most 3 _____ invention is smart glass. This glass can change from being opaque to transparent in order to make light more 4 _____ . Smart glass can be controlled manually or it can be done via 5 _____ thanks to a simple timing system. 6 _____ of customers have described it as extremely 7 _____ .

b Decide if the sentences express a strong (S) or weak (W) opinion. Write S or W next to each sentence.

1 I am firmly in favour of building houses from renewable materials.
2 I partly believe in using technology to reduce energy consumption in homes.
3 I am utterly against having robots in the house due to their potential dangers.
4 I somewhat agree with investing more money in space research.

c Write the words in the correct order to make noun phrases.

1 gadget a cost-effective
2 heating the the floor under
3 life battery
4 less which energy device a uses

d Match the percentages (1–4) with the phrases with the same meanings (A–D).

1 25 percent
2 9 percent
3 68 percent
4 53 percent

A just over two-thirds
B approximately half
C exactly a quarter
D a little less than a tenth

2a Change the following comments into reported speech and use the reporting verbs in brackets.

1 'Too much money has been spent on building new houses in my neighbourhood. I want to see more public facilities.' (claim/said)

Cynthia _____ .

2 'I think that if you renovate your house, you will increase its value, David.' (tell)

Simon _____ .

3 'I am going to lend you my new camera for your holiday.' (promise)

Joanne _____ .

4 'It will be easy to use the laptop when you have installed the correct software.' (explain)

Jack _____ .

5 'I don't like the new office block which was built last year.' (complain)

Leah _____ .

6 'Mary, I think we'll need to move to a bigger house next year.' (tell/think)

Leah _____ .

b Choose the correct sentence to match the reporting structure.

Request
1 A My parents asked me if I could change bedrooms with my sister.
  B My parents asked to me I could change bedrooms with my sister.

Question-word questions
2 A The mayor asked people what they thought of the town's new spending policies.
  B The mayor asked if people thought of the town's new spending policies.

Order
3 A The company directed to its workers that hot-desk in order to reduce the size of the office.
  B The company directed its workers to hot-desk in order to reduce the size of the office.

Yes/No questions
4 A The government sent people a survey to find out if they wanted more green energy.
  B The government sent people a survey to find out that they wanted more green energy.

6 Law and order

6a Training

- **Reading:** Work out the meaning of unknown words (Flow chart completion; Sentence completion)
- **Vocabulary:** Verbs for argument and opinion; Academic words; Collocations for argument
- **Speaking:** Develop topic-specific vocabulary; Order your argument; Pronunciation: schwa /ə/ (Part 3)
- **Listening:** Understand attitude from tone and intonation (Section 4: Summary completion)
- **Language development:** Link ideas; *Both, neither, either*
- **Writing:** Structures to compare and contrast; Contrast your opinions (Task 2: Opinion essay)

6b Testing

- **Listening:** Section 4: Multiple choice; Summary completion
- **Language development and vocabulary:** Cleft sentences; Using *there* and *it*
- **Speaking:** Part 3: Discussing crime
- **Reading:** Flow chart completion; Sentence completion
- **Writing:** Task 2: Opinion essay

Lead-in

1   Look at the photos from film and TV. What do they all have in common? How accurately do you think these pictures portray scenes from real life? Why?

Reading (Flow chart completion; Sentence completion)

Before you read

1   If you could reduce criminal activity, which crimes would be your main priorities? Why?

Work out the meaning of unknown words

2   Read the title and subtitle of the reading passage, then skim the passage quickly. What is it about?

3a Work in pairs. Think of a synonym for the list of words from the first paragraph of the passage.

1	post-mortem	6	throwbacks
2	notorious	7	discredited
3	bandit	8	tainted
4	intrigued	9	discarded
5	rodents	10	discipline

 b Look at the same words in context in the first paragraph of the passage and answer the questions for each of them.

1   What part of speech are they: nouns/verbs, etc.?

2   What clues can you get from the word itself? For example, has it got a negative prefix such as *un-*?

Questions 1–5

Complete the flow chart below.

Choose **NO MORE THAN THREE WORDS** from the passage for each answer.

Nature or nurture?

19th century – Lombroso's view: only primitive people became criminals.
Evidence based on examination of a criminal's
1 _____ , said to resemble those belonging to other species.

20th century – sociological explanations for crime became fashionable.

End of 20th/21st century – The analysis of 2 _____ taken of killers enabled Raine to formulate a theory of criminal behaviour.

Raine's biological explanation for the causes of violent crime.
Inability to control 3 _____ due to malfunction in part of brain.
Area of brain known as the 4 _____ : responsible for spontaneous behaviour.
Inadequate 5 _____ found to be common amongst psychopaths.

Questions 6–9

Complete the sentences below.

Choose **NO MORE THAN THREE WORDS AND/OR A NUMBER** from the passage for each answer.

Gesch found that providing a source of 6 _____ to prisoners might help to reduce crime.
Raine identified insufficient 7 _____ in children as a sign of a potential criminal.
Raine believes recognition of genetic predisposition to crime could affect how the 8 _____ operates.
Raine asserts that the concept of 9 _____ does not apply to everyone.

Test practice

4a Work in pairs and discuss the questions.

1   Why do you need to read the instructions carefully?

2   Why is it useful to read the passage quickly before doing the task?

3   How will reading the words around each gap help?

4   What will help you to locate the relevant parts of the passage?

 b Read the strategies and complete the test tasks.

➤ **TEST STRATEGIES** page 170

 c Work in pairs and discuss your answers.

Task analysis

5a Why are these answers to the test tasks incorrect?

2   brains
4   pre-frontal cortex
6   fish oil
7   lack of anticipatory fear

 b To what extent did the strategies in Exercises 3a and 3b help you to deal with other new words you did not understand? Were there some words which is was not necessary to understand?

Arrested development

Are criminals victims of their environment or is there "a criminal brain"?

Scholarly interest in the criminal cranium is by no means new. In 1871 the Italian physician and intellectual Cesare Lombroso was performing a post-mortem on the body of a notorious bandit when he became intrigued by the shape of the skull, which reminded him of "apes, rodents and birds." He concluded that criminals were born bad; throwbacks to an earlier, more brutal stage of our evolution. His theories were soon discredited, and in the 20th century all attempts to link biology with criminal behaviour were tainted by association with *eugenics. Consequently, these theories were discarded and the new discipline of criminology became a branch of sociology, which, for the most part, it remains. When politicians debate "the causes of crime", they tend to refer to social factors such as poverty and unemployment.

Later in the 20th and early 21st century, however, thanks to major advances in neuroscience and genetics, attention has reverted to the profound influence exerted by physiology on human behaviour. Evidence of this is the fast-growing field of neurocriminality; its pioneer is Professor Adrian Raine from the University of Pennsylvania, a former prison psychologist who has been investigating the subtle relationship between criminal behaviour, the brain and the environment for many years. Through the study of prisoners' brain scans Raine has discovered that murderers, predominantly those who kill on impulse, are far more likely to have a poorly functioning pre-frontal cortex. This is the rational, decision-making section of the brain which acts as a neurological brake for the majority of people in that it helps to regulate the aggressive behaviour linked to the more unpredictable regions of the brain which comprise the limbic system.

In contrast, violent criminals may suffer from a deficit in their capacity for emotion. Raine and his collaborators performed brain scans on people whom they had previously diagnosed with psychopathic personalities. When presented with a scenario in which a shocking moral decision was required, the scans indicated that the level of activity produced in the emotion-regulating regions was far lower in psychopathic individuals as opposed to non-psychopathic people who undertook the same test.

Despite these findings, Raine does not simply wish to identify and understand the biological causes of violent crime: his aim is to discover effective ways to prevent it. In an experiment conducted by Bernard Gesch, prisoners convicted of violent offences were given a regular dose of omega-3 fatty acids, critical in facilitating brain function, in the form of fish oil pills. It was subsequently noted that amongst those who took these pills, the rate of offending in prison showed a significant decline.

However, Raine's real mission is to identify ways in which children can be discouraged from turning to crime in the first place. One of his studies involved 1,800 three-year-old children, who were tested for another form of emergency brake: fear. The children were played a neutral tone followed by an unpleasant-sounding one. This was repeated until each child recognised that no sooner did they hear the neutral tone than the disagreeable one would follow. For most, the first tone was sufficient to raise their pulse rate and cause them to perspire. However, a small minority of participants demonstrated little or no "anticipatory fear" at all. Twenty years on, it was discovered that those children who had been unafraid were significantly more likely to have acquired a criminal record.

Of course, not all children with poorly functioning fear responses will grow up to be criminals. Much depends on the circumstances of their upbringing. Research suggests that the causes of anti-social behaviour are approximately 50% genetic and 50% environmental, the latter including conditions in the womb and the child's earliest experiences. In Raine's view, if criminologists fail to consider the contribution of biological and genetic processes to the causes of crime, a crucial chapter of the story will be overlooked. Being afraid protects us from our own worst impulses, as do strong social networks and our capacity to reflect on our behaviour. Raine believes the absence of these checks normally indicates a problem and he aims to help identify children who lack such protections and who are therefore at greater risk of becoming involved in criminal activity.

Fundamentally, the principle that our understanding of (anti) social behaviour can be advanced through the study of the brain has become far more widely accepted. But neurocriminology is still somewhat restricted by what it can measure and the arguments over its implications have barely begun. The idea that we derive criminal inclinations from our parents and early childhood raises a whole host of complex ethical and social questions, particularly where the law is concerned. For example, Raine believes that the nature of an individual's brain ought to be seriously considered during the process of sentencing. "Free will is not as free as we believe," he says. For some people "the dice are loaded."

* eugenics: the study of methods to improve the mental and physical abilities of the human race by choosing who should become parents

Vocabulary

Verbs for argument and opinion

1a Match the verbs below with their definitions (1–6).

conclude   contribute   derive   facilitate   identify   involve

1 To give money, help or ideas to something that other people are also involved in.
2 To decide that something is true after considering all the information.
3 To get something, especially an advantage or a pleasant feeling, from something; (passive) to develop or come from something else.
4 To include or affect someone or something.
5 To recognise something or discover exactly what it is, what its nature or origin is.
6 To make it easier for a process or action to happen.

b Complete the text with the correct form of the words in Exercise 1a.

1 _____ why some cities have higher crime rates than others may seem difficult, however certain patterns do emerge. Places where people 2 _____ more taxes into a system which supports poorer people generally have lower crime. This might explain the causes to an extent. Some people claim that some crimes are 3 _____ from poverty, which would support the concept of societal improvements leading to a lower crime rate. However, reducing crime will 4 _____ much more than just tackling poverty. Governments need to ensure the police are adequately staffed and able to 5 _____ a rapid response so as to deter criminal behaviour. Many cities with a low crime rate are known to have a strong police force that works as an effective deterrent. Perhaps we can 6 _____ by stating that social support and deterrence are the key contributors to improving the safety of our cities.

Academic words

2a Choose the correct option in *italics* to complete the sentences.

1 Although there are now moves towards involving offenders in rehabilitation, it must not be forgotten that they have *fundamentally / idealistically* done wrong in the eyes of the law.
2 Whilst people could derive a lot of happiness from cities being completely safe, this is not a/an *feasible / appropriate* situation in today's world.
3 The involvement of offenders in educating people of the dangers of crime may be *inconsistent / perceived* depending on the offender's personality and intentions.

4 It is undeniable that the police contribute *integrally / rationally* to making our society a safer place.
5 Many people *reasonably / debatably* conclude that crime has a negative effect on people's sense of security.
6 It would be ideal to have a police presence in every neighbourhood at all times, but this idea might not be *integral / practical* in terms of manpower.

b Work in pairs and discuss the topics.

1 A fundamental contribution someone has made to your life.
2 A time when you made a positive contribution to your community.
3 A problem in your life that you have identified a solution for.
4 An activity which you derive a lot of joy from.

Collocations for argument

3a Choose an option (A, B or C) to complete the collocations.

1 _____ an argument = to put forward an argument
  A propose   B propel   C promise
2 _____ an argument = to dismiss an argument
  A repel   B refuse   C reject
3 _____ an argument = to agree with and back an argument
  A support   B supply   C suppose
4 _____ of argument = the reasoning of an argument
  A lane   B line   C level
5 both _____ of an argument = the pros and cons of an argument
  A shades   B sides   C symbols
6 _____ argument = an argument which is very good or strong
  A conniving   B conceding   C convincing
7 _____ argument = an argument with a major weakness
  A flared   B flaccid   C flawed

b Complete the sentences with the correct collocations from Exercise 3a.

1 Many judges _____ the argument for reducing the number of people sent to prison for minor offences because of the huge financial burden it places on society.
2 Psychologists believe that there is a _____ argument for having criminals meet their victims as studies have determined that the personalisation of a crime can significantly reduce the likelihood of someone reoffending.
3 Research has shown that the argument that prison is the most effective punishment is _____ . In fact, some results have suggested that prisons can foster further criminal activity in many inmates.

c Work in pairs and discuss your opinions on the topics in Exercise 3b.

Speaking (Part 3)

Lead-in

1 Look at the photos. What forms of monitoring do they show?

Develop topic-specific vocabulary

2a Match 1–5 with A–E to make collocations.

1	invasion of	A	a website
2	surveillance	B	theft
3	identity	C	data
4	hack	D	privacy
5	track	E	system

b Discuss the following issues. Try to use the collocations in Exercise 2a.

The benefits of CCTV.
The uses of online data.
The reasons for surveillance.
The balance between monitoring and privacy.
The safety of different websites.

Order your argument

3a 🔊 6.1 Listen to an excerpt from a Part 3 test. What is the question? What is the candidate's opinion?

b How did the speaker structure her answer? Number the elements below in the correct order.

counter argument   thesis   evaluation   reasons

c Match the phrases (1–4) with the functions in Exercise 3b. Can you think of any other words or phrases that could be used instead?

1 I think that …
2 In general …
3 Most people think that … but …
4 I think this because …

4a Plan your answer to the question below. Follow the structure in Exercise 3b and use some of the language from Exercise 3c. Try to structure your answer to show both sides of the argument.

What do you think about the growth of CCTV in public places?

b Work in pairs and take turns to give your answer to Exercise 4a. Check your partner follows the structure correctly.

Pronunciation: schwa /ə/

5a 🔊 6.2 Listen to the words and mark the stress.

newspaper   cameras   surveillance   monitor

b Listen again and mark on the words where you hear the schwa sound /ə/. Is it used for stressed or unstressed syllables?

newspaper   cameras   surveillance   monitor

c 🔊 6.3 Listen to the sentences and mark where you hear the schwa sound. Practise saying these words with a partner.

1 Many people have quite a strong opinion on what newspaper they read.
2 There are far more cameras in public places these days than there were a decade ago.
3 Surveillance is in some ways a necessary part of society these days.
4 I don't see a problem with the way our daily activities are monitored.

Test practice

➤ TEST STRATEGIES page 175

6a Read the questions below. Consider how you could include language and structures from this page in your answers.

1 Why might some people be worried about buying goods or services online?
2 How could monitoring undertaken by surveillance systems benefit modern society?
3 What do you believe are the potential dangers of sharing too much personal information online?

b Work in pairs and take turns to ask and answer the questions in Exercise 6a. Record your answers if possible.

Assess and improve

7 Work in pairs and discuss your answers. Did your partner give an extended response? How well were his/her answers structured?

Listening (Section 4)

Before you listen

1 In what ways might the objects in the photos help to prevent crime? Should people pay more attention to their own safety and the safety of their possessions? Why?

Understand attitude from tone and intonation

2a Match the opinions (1–3) with their meanings (A–C).

1 to be sceptical
2 to be enthusiastic
3 to be neutral

A to think that something is not true
B to have no strong opinion about something
C to show interest in something

b 🔊 6.4 Listen to a speaker read the sentences (1–3) using different intonation to express her attitude. Write the correct attitude, sceptical (S), neutral (N) or enthusiastic (E), next to each sentence.

1 They say this study on crime prevention is really innovative.
2 They say this study on crime prevention is really innovative.
3 They say this study on crime prevention is really innovative.

3a 🔊 6.5 Listen to the first part of a lecture on crime prevention and choose the correct answer (A, B or C).

1 What does the speaker think about the study of crime prevention?
   A evaluating forms of punishment is a better idea
   B it is not as effective as traditional forms of punishment
   C it is something which should be focused on more
2 The speaker believes that improvements in science have
   A brought beneficial effects to studying crime.
   B not improved the ways we punish criminals.
   C been a waste of time overall.

b 🔊 6.6 Listen to the next part of the lecture on crime prevention and complete the sentences. Write no more than two words.

1 Situational crime prevention is a _____ to reducing crime.
2 One aim is to eradicate crime by _____ .
3 It tries to make crime _____ to people.

c Can you reject any of the options in the multiple-choice questions in Exercise 3a based on the speaker's tone of voice or word stress? Why? How did the speaker's tone and intonation help you answer the questions in Exercise 3b?

Test practice

➤ TEST STRATEGIES page 168

4 🔊 6.7 Listen to the last part of the lecture and complete the test task.

Questions 1–3
Complete the summary below.
Use NO MORE THAN TWO WORDS AND/OR A NUMBER *for each answer.*

Rational choice theory explains how people choose to behave by thinking 1 _____ about their surroundings. This theory can be applied to understanding how to stop people from deciding to commit a crime. Criminals have to calculate the 2 _____ of arrest before deciding to perpetrate a crime. Studies have demonstrated that cameras which record traffic can discourage people from violating traffic rules due to the 3 _____ possibility of being caught.

Task analysis

5 Read audio script 6.7 on page 207 and listen again. Work in pairs and discuss how the speaker's tone of voice and word stress helped you answer the questions in Exercise 4.

Discussion

6 Which ideas presented in the lecture do you consider would be the most successful and which the least successful? Why? What other ways can you think of to tackle crime?

Language development

Link ideas

> **EXPERT GRAMMAR** page 179

1a Read the sentences below. Do the underlined words introduce agreement or contrast between the ideas?

1 Training in parenting skills has been shown to reduce the number of young offenders, <u>whereas</u> investment in education has not achieved the same level of success.

2 Online piracy is rapidly becoming one of the most widespread types of cybercrime. <u>Similarly</u>, online banking fraud has increased considerably and is now rather commonplace.

3 <u>Despite</u> increased implementation of measures to counter cybercrime, many governments have been incapable of effectively tackling the problem.

b Complete the rules with the underlined words in Exercise 1a.

1 Words like *likewise*, _____ and *conversely* can start sentences or clauses but they cannot connect clauses without a conjunction.

2 Words like _____ , *although* and *while* connect two clauses together in one sentence.

3 _____ must be followed by a noun or noun phrase.

2 Complete the text with the correct linking words below.

although   conversely   despite   similarly

Blue-collar crime is defined as crime which is unskilled and usually committed by people from poorer groups in society, and white-collar crime describes financial, non-violent crime most often committed by people of high social status in the course of their work in business or government. **1** _____ this distinction seems fairly obvious, the rise of crimes perpetuated over the internet is making the distinction more difficult. **2** _____ , identifying the perpetrators of white-collar crime is far more difficult than for blue-collar crime. Often white-collar crime goes completely undetected or at least unreported, **3** _____ costing companies and governments billions of dollars in losses all over the world. As a result, law-enforcement agencies have often claimed that white-collar crime is their priority. **4** _____ , fewer and fewer white-collar crimes have been brought to trial in recent years.

3 Complete the sentences with your own ideas.

1 Although the number of people in prisons has risen, _____ .

2 Despite _____ , internet piracy is still a big issue for many international artists.

3 People who commit crimes must be punished. Similarly, _____ .

4 There are many people who think that potential criminals have a socio-political profile, but conversely, _____ .

Both, neither, either

4a Complete the sentences with *both, neither* or *either*.

1 Fraud and insider trading are _____ typical examples of white-collar crime in the financial sector.

2 _____ the government nor the judiciary should have sole control over introducing new legislation. They should _____ share the responsibility.

3 Society can choose between _____ improving education to prevent crime or introducing harsher punishments.

4 Due to the government cuts people can have _____ safer streets or safer public transport.

5 Experts say that education and employment significantly reduce crime. Unfortunately, _____ of these has been proven in research.

6 _____ parents and teachers have the responsibility to help teenagers stay away from criminal gangs and activities.

b Complete the rules.

1 _____ describes two things; *this* and *that*.

2 _____ means *not this* and *not that*; it is negative and used with a singular verb.

3 _____ is used to express a choice between two or more things; it is used with a singular verb.

c Rewrite the sentences. Use *both, neither* or *either*.

1 Businesses are adversely affected by cybercrime and so are individuals.

2 There are two measures that could be implemented to increase safety on the streets. The first would be to increase street lighting at night. The second would be to install CCTV.

3 Some people assert that the current justice system fails to rehabilitate criminals, and at the same time, does nothing to help the victims of crime.

4 The burglars could have entered my house through an open top floor window. It could also have been possible to come in through the garage.

5 Patience is a key skill when training police dogs. Also, another important aspect is having a sense of authority.

6 Blue-collar workers are not sent to prison as often as white-collar workers. This is the same for company CEOs as well.

Writing (Task 2)

Lead-in

'Crime prevention is everybody's business.'

1 Read the quote above. What do you think it means? To what extent do you agree or disagree with the statement? Why?

Structures to compare and contrast

2a Look at the following issues. Make a list of the arguments for and against each option.

a REASONS FOR CRIME
People commit crime due to their personality.

FOR	AGAINST

People commit crime due to environmental factors.

FOR	AGAINST

b PREVENTING CRIME
Society is responsible for crime prevention.

FOR	AGAINST

Governments are responsible for crime prevention.

FOR	AGAINST

b Read the following paragraph. What sections in Exercise 2a are written about?

Everyone should play an active role in crime prevention. There are many societal issues that contribute to crime such as availability of opportunity or treatment within the community, and as such government and wider society should try and ensure inclusion and opportunity for all. The more caring a community is, the more valued the individuals within it feel. However, society can only do so much. If individuals choose to distance themselves from those around them, this does not mean that efforts should be reduced. Although societal involvement might not be an instant or easy solution, it may certainly help in curtailing some of the many causes of crime.

c Using the paragraph in Exercise 2b, order the stages of the paragraph. One stage can be used twice.

A Explanation of idea   C Contrasting idea
B First idea   D Contrastive evaluation

Contrast your opinions

3 Look at the sentences below. Which ones compare and contrast ideas correctly? Which ones compare and contrast incorrectly? What are the problems with the incorrect expressions and how could you correct them?

1 Although many people consider themselves to be law-abiding citizens, a large proportion of them do actually commit crimes such as speeding or littering.
2 Education programmes sometimes rehabilitate offenders. Conversely, some offenders do not undertake these programmes.
3 Whereas many people live in poverty, only a minority of them commit crimes.
4 Despite many governments tackling poverty, crime rates have still not decreased.

Test practice

> EXPERT WRITING page 196

4a Read the essay title and the essay introduction below. How has the writer structured the introduction? What content could go in the paragraphs that follow?

Improving living conditions within society is a far superior approach to crime prevention than the threat of punishment. To what extent do you agree with this statement and why?

Crime prevention is a major concern for many governments, who want to be able to offer their citizens a safe and pleasant life. However, preventing crime is a problematic and complicated task. Whilst both improving conditions and punishment can be effective deterrents, showing that crimes are punishable is still the most effective deterrent to date. This essay will argue this point by exploring why individuals from both favourable and less favourable environments commit crime, and outlining how a punishment-free society may negatively affect the crime rate.

b Plan the structure of the main body and conclusion for the introduction in Exercise 4a. You will need at least three paragraphs.

c Write the rest of the essay. Try to use language to compare and contrast from this page. Write at least 250 words.

Listening (Section 4)

Before you listen

A 'super recogniser' is someone who has an exceptional ability to recognise human faces.

1 How might the 'super recogniser' skill be used in real life? Do you think you might be a super recogniser?

Understand opinion from adjectives

2a Do the adjectives below have a positive or negative meaning?

convincing	fascinating	flawed	improbable
misleading	perceptive	remarkable	significant
superficial			

b Read the questions in Exercise 3a and underline any key words. Which questions might be based on the speaker's opinion and how might you recognise this?

3a 🔊 **6.8** Listen to the first part of a lecture on super recognisers and choose the correct letter (A, B or C).

1 According to the speaker, super recognisers have
   A an extraordinary ability to notice detail.
   B a skill which is interesting to study.
   C a significant advantage over other people.

2 What does the lecturer think about the police employing super recognisers?
   A It is a bad approach to policing.
   B It can increase their resources.
   C It has helped to solve more crimes.

b Read audio script 6.8 on page 207. Which adjectives does the speaker use to show his opinion for questions 1 and 2?

Test practice

> **TEST STRATEGIES** page 168

4 🔊 **6.9** Complete the test tasks.

Questions 1–4
*Choose the correct letter, **A**, **B** or **C**.*

1 Being a super recogniser is a skill which people
   A probably possess from birth.
   B have to be taught to do it well.
   C master in their teenage years.

2 What is particularly interesting about super recognisers?
   A They originate from the same ethnic group.
   B Their skill does not work with other racial groups.
   C They only recognise a limited number of people.

3 The results of the study at the University of Greenwich demonstrated that
   A police officers are more inclined to be super recognisers.
   B not all the officers assessed were super recognisers.
   C their results were more consistent than those from Harvard University.

4 Why are super recognisers so useful to the police?
   A They are more reliable than finger printing and DNA.
   B They are never inaccurate.
   C They conserve vital resources.

Questions 5–10
Complete the summary below.
*Write **NO MORE THAN TWO WORDS** for each answer.*

Computers are becoming far more sophisticated when it comes to facial recognition due to the developments in 5 _____ . Despite the fact that processing images should be a straightforward task for computers, it does become problematic if the images are of 6 _____ . Additionally, computers find it harder to process video as the images are always 7 _____ . Developing facial recognition software for computers is incredibly difficult because there is also a lack of certainty about how 8 _____ are able to do this. One difference is that people are accustomed to identifying faces 9 _____ . Technological advances in photographic equipment will result in improved 10 _____ and will enable computers to become more adept at facial recognition in years to come.

Language development and vocabulary

Cleft sentences

> **EXPERT GRAMMAR** page 179

1a Match the example sentences (1–2) with the correct structures (A–B). The underlined text is old information

Can you tell me what <u>was stolen from your office</u>?

1 It was my laptop that was stolen from my office. (*It* + *to be* + noun, relative pronoun + verb)
2 What was stolen from my office was my laptop. (*What* + verb + *to be* + noun)

A new information + old information
B old information + new information

b Rewrite the sentences using the words in brackets.

1 I enjoyed the plot of the Agatha Christie novel the most. (what)
2 The bank robbers were caught because of the security footage. (it)
3 Transporting food across borders is illegal due to possible contamination. (it)
4 We need a fairer way to conduct trials in this country. (what)
5 The police interviewed all the witnesses first. (what)
6 My brother had his wallet stolen while he was on holiday. (it)
7 I liked the special effects in the movie more than aspects such as the acting or the music. (what)
8 When I went on holiday to Scotland, the scenery impressed me more than anything else. (it)

c Work in pairs and talk about the following topics. Use *It* or *What* clauses.

1 An amazing thing that happened to you.
2 Something you would love to do.
3 An important day in your life.
4 A place you want to visit.

Using *there* and *it*

2a Choose the correct option in *italics* for the type of information.

1 to say where something is   *it / there*
2 time and dates   *it / there*
3 before opinion adjectives   *it / there*
4 quantities and numbers   *it / there*
5 the weather   *it / there*
6 to introduce a new topic   *it / there*
7 in passive constructions   *it / there*

b Decide if the sentences are correct or incorrect. Correct the incorrect sentences.

1 According to the graph it was a substantial number of burglaries in the countryside in 2015.
2 There has been an increase in the number of prisoners gaining academic qualifications during their sentences.
3 There is reasonable to assume that significant improvements will be made to IT security in the near future.
4 It has been suggested that juveniles suffer most from injustices within the criminal justice system.
5 There used to be a police station on this street when I was young.
6 There could be argued that crime has been steadily decreasing over the last 50 years.

c Complete the sentence with *it* or *there*.

1 _____ are a variety of tried and tested methods for assessing whether criminals are likely to reoffend after leaving prison.
2 _____ has been claimed that crime has decreased in London due to people having better relationships with the police.
3 _____ was a prison on this site during the last century, but it was transformed into a museum a few years ago.
4 _____ is interesting to note that urban areas with a strong sense of community tend to experience less crime.
5 _____ is a new law for protecting cybercrime victims. Hopefully, it will be effective.
6 Crimes committed in public places such as parks tend to increase when _____ is sunny because people are distracted.

d Write 10 sentences using *there* and *it*. Follow the rules in Exercise 2a.

Speaking (Part 3)

Vocabulary development

1 Complete the text with the words below.

data sources   drones   facial recognition   hotspots
prediction   social media   suspects

The future of crime; law enforcement is everywhere

Although solving crime has developed rapidly with the introduction of more scientific means of identifying and capturing **1** _____ , the future of crime fighting looks even more impressive.
2 _____ sites are already being used by police forces and this is only set to increase further. Police are posting messages to local communities to help locate individuals or inform them about crime **3** _____ , and many stolen goods and missing people have been found due to sites like Pinterest. However, other technological advances are even more impressive. The use of **4** _____ may completely revolutionise the police force as they can remotely film suspects or search for particular people using **5** _____ software. This has major implications regarding manpower, as local forces are no longer limited to only using officers. Additionally, although it is unlikely crimes of the future will be foreseen in the manner shown in films like *Minority Report*, crime **6** _____ is already here. Large technology companies, such as Hitachi, are now combining a huge variety of **7** _____ such as surveillance cameras, geographical crime areas, sensor systems and social media to predict when and where a crime is going to occur.

Focus on fluency and coherence

2 Turn to page 183 and read the descriptors for fluency and coherence. Decide whether the statements below are true or false.

1 To achieve either a band 6 or 7 you need to give short answers to the examiner's questions.
2 To achieve a band 7 your line of argument or thought must always be clear to the examiner.
3 To achieve a band 7 you need to use some connectors in your speech but they do not always have to be accurately used.
4 To achieve a band 6 or 7 you need to use some connectors and discourse markers in your speech.
5 To achieve a band 8 you should never need to search for vocabulary in your answer.
6 To achieve a band 8 all topics must be developed clearly and logically.

3a 🔊 6.10 Read the audio script on page 208 and listen to a candidate talking about the pros and cons of using drones. Work with a partner to improve the fluency and coherence of the answer. Consider the following:

- Extending answers
- Reducing hesitancy and improving flow
- Use of connectors and discourse markers

b 🔊 6.11 Listen to the candidate answer the question again. How has his fluency and coherence improved?

Test practice

> **TEST STRATEGIES** page 175

4a Read the questions below and think about your answers. Consider the following aspects:

- How to organise your answer and extend it.
- How to connect your ideas.
- The variety of vocabulary you can use.
- Creating a smooth flow with little hesitation.

1 How are the police better at solving crimes nowadays?
2 Do you believe that crime rates will be lower in the future?
3 What do you think are the pros and cons of crime-prediction techniques?
4 If the police commonly used drones and predictive data to tackle crime, could this have any negative effects?

b Work in pairs and take turns to ask and answer the questions in Exercise 4a.

Assess and improve

5a Think about your and your partner's answers to the questions in Exercise 4a. How well did you both do the following?

1 Give a full answer to each question
2 Connect ideas clearly using signposting and connectors
3 Use a variety of vocabulary
4 Create a smooth flow with little hesitation

b What advice could you give your partner to help him/her improve his/her responses?

Reading (Flow chart completion; Sentence completion)

Before you read

1 Work in groups and discuss the questions.

1 Do you ever watch crime programmes on television? Why do you think they are so popular?
2 What responsibilities might a crime scene investigator have?

Test practice

2 Read the strategies and complete the test tasks.

> **TEST STRATEGIES** page 170

Questions 1–6
Complete the flow chart below.
Choose NO MORE THAN THREE WORDS *from the passage for each answer.*

Stages in the investigation of a crime scene

Police response:
• potential **1** _____ not allowed at crime scene
• provision of **2** _____ to be signed by visitors to scene

⬇

CSI arrival: initial **3** _____ informs strategy

⬇

Documented evidence: detailed photographic record and written **4** _____ provided for those not present

⬇

Recreation of crime scene: CSI develops supported **5** _____ of scenario, including who was probably there and exactly where they were

⬇

Analysis: All objects and documentation taken to **6** _____

> **HELP**

1 Who was not allowed access to the crime scene?
3 On what basis does the CSI decide on what she will do next?
5 Find another verb meaning *support*.

Questions 7–10
Complete the sentences below.
Choose NO MORE THAN THREE WORDS *from the passage for each answer.*

7 Overview photographs are needed to show the various _____ relevant to the crime.
8 Detailed photographs, from a short distance, of injuries such as _____ are taken on site.
9 Although _____ of the crime scene are acceptable as long as they are correct, they may have to be done again at a later date.
10 An everyday object might be included in a photograph as a _____ in terms of size.

> **HELP**

7 Will this be a singular or plural noun? What is another word for *overview*?
8 Several injuries are mentioned: which are usually minor?
9 Look for a word for drawings which are not detailed or carefully done.

Task analysis

3 Work in pairs and discuss the questions.

1 Which of the following techniques helped you to guess the meanings of new words/phrases?
   • guessing from the formation of the word itself
   • looking for contextual clues
   • finding a similarity with another English word or a word in your own language
2 Find examples of paraphrases or synonyms which helped you to complete the tasks.

Discussion

4 Work in groups and discuss the questions.

1 What personal qualities might someone wishing to be a Crime Scene Investigator require? Why?
2 Why might this be a very difficult job to do and one which not everyone would be able to handle?
3 What might be the positive aspects of doing such a job?

Crime scene investigation:
how it operates

From the moment the first police officer arrives at the scene of a crime, a strict set of procedures must be adhered to: this is designed to protect everyone present and guard evidence against damage, contamination or loss. Following these procedures and maintaining control of the scene until the arrival of crime scene investigators offers the best chance of obtaining the evidence required to successfully identify and convict those responsible for perpetrating the crime.

At the heart of crime scene protection is Locard's Exchange Principle, which states that when any two people come into contact with each other, trace materials such as hair, fibres and prints can be exchanged or transferred. Every person who enters the crime scene can leave behind signs of their presence, remove crucial traces on their shoes, clothes or hands or otherwise damage or alter any evidence that remains. Thus, access to the scene must be restricted immediately and denied to everyone but those authorised to enter it, as police may be unsure of who potentially are witnesses or suspects.

The next stage is to cordon off and secure the crime scene, which will involve a requirement for all people authorised to be at the scene to sign their names upon arrival. This security log is essential for limiting the number of individuals to be examined in the event of finding stray fingerprints and shoeprints. If investigators can be eliminated, the print may well implicate the perpetrators.

As soon as the crime scene investigator (CSI) arrives she must first gain an understanding of what the investigation will entail and establish a systematic approach to collecting evidence. Therefore, her first task is a walk-through examination of the crime scene; the focus being on the bigger picture, nothing is touched at this point. The CSI also talks to the police or detectives who were first on the scene and may have already begun interviewing witnesses.

Having formulated a plan, the CSI then organises documentation of all the evidence, with the aim of creating a visual record which will enable the forensics laboratory, detectives and lawyers to gain an exact representation of the scene and surrounding area. A designated note-taker records all activities in and around the crime scene. This includes a description of the scene and an accurate list describing what each piece of evidence is, when, where and by whom it was found, and who was responsible for transporting it to the laboratory. Each photograph is also identified and commented on.

Photographs need to be taken promptly so that they show the scene preserved in an unaltered condition prior to any evidence being removed for analysis. The CSI takes general shots of all locations related to the crime scene such as rooms, the building and the area and mid-range photos of key pieces of evidence in context. For close-ups, good-quality photos are essential in providing the forensics laboratory with details from which to analyse the evidence. Any sign of physical harm to the body is critical: bruises and scratches can be photographed at the scene but knife wounds and gunshots generally have to wait until the victim is hospitalised. CSIs also create sketches to depict both the entire scene and particular aspects which will benefit from exact measurements; they need to be accurate in terms of the details presented but can be rough as they are frequently redrawn later for clarity. In photographs where it is important to see the size of the object being recorded, the photograph may include a point of reference such as a car key or ballpoint pen.

After the crime scene has been carefully documented, it is time for the CSI to collect all physical evidence that might serve to recreate the crime and identify the perpetrator in a manner that will hold in a court of law. Certain information may be critical in determining the truthfulness of a suspect or the reliability of a witness. The investigator focuses on the likely sequence of events and the locations and positions of everyone present when the crime occurred before looking at each piece of physical evidence to find out whether or not it endorses this hypothesis: anything that does not confirm this must be reconciled or must change. As a result, the reconstruction of a crime scene is constantly evolving as more evidence is disclosed. All of this evidence is included in the crime scene report and, together with the evidence recovered from the scene, is transferred to a forensic science laboratory to be analysed.

Writing (Task 2)

Lead-in

1 Look at the crime scene cartoon. What is the joke? What are the police officers missing? What clues help the police?

Understand the task

2a Look at the essay title below. Are the ideas (1–7) for or against the main argument?

Science is more useful than human judgement in stopping crime. To what extent do you agree?

1 Humans make errors.
2 There is no replacement for common sense.
3 Science cannot find out the motives or take testimonies.
4 DNA is 100 percent accurate.
5 Science is more objective.
6 Scientific evidence may be inconclusive.
7 DNA can be planted at a scene to incriminate someone who is innocent.

b Note down some more reasons to support each view and decide which opinion you agree with most and why.

Plan the task

3a Turn to page 190 and read the descriptors for task achievement. Decide which points (A or B) best describe what you need to do. In which part of the essay would you include these aspects?

1 A Answer the question.   B Write about the topic.
2 A Give an objective overview.   B Present a clear viewpoint.
3 A Present a list of ideas.   B Present a few developed ideas.
4 A Provide support for your ideas.   B Ask new questions about the topic.
5 A Answer all parts of the task.   B Select one part of the task that most appeals to you.

b Read the essay question in Exercise 2a again. Which of these plans is likely to score highest for task achievement, and why?

Structure 1

Introduction: Police are the main force to stop crime. My answer – The police are an effective tool to stop crime.

Main body 1: The police are on the streets every day. The police use judgement to catch criminals. They follow clues. The police have arrested many people.

Main body 2: The police now use lots of technology. They have helicopters, cameras and laboratories to help catch criminals.

Conclusion: The police are using science well.

Structure 2

Introduction: Both human judgement and science important. My answer – human judgement slightly more important.

Main body 1: Human judgement is necessary, e.g. humans can use logic to determine suspects from many DNA samples.

Main body 2: Counter – Science can offer more objective evidence than humans, e.g. DNA but it can be wrong, e.g. identical twins share DNA, DNA can be planted.

Conclusion: Both are essential, police officers can work without science, but science cannot work without the police.

c Using your ideas from Exercise 2b, discuss how you could follow the guidance in Exercises 3a and 3b to develop your essay structure and argument.

Language and content

4a Look at the aspects below. Which of these are important in a conclusion?

1 Summarise key argument/points
2 Include some new information
3 Restatement of your opinion
4 Give questions for the examiner
5 Develop a final main point

b Read the two conclusions below. Which one is better and why? What is the writer's opinion?

Conclusion A

In conclusion, science is a far more effective tool than human judgement. Although human judgement will never leave us, and is one of the cores of solving crime. Human judgement is one of the most fundamental elements of solving crime. People can trust in the law. Could you trust in science alone deciding your fate?

Conclusion B

In conclusion, although both elements are important in fighting crime, science is becoming more important. Not only is science highly reliable and more objective than pure human judgement, in a changing world, the progress that science makes helps us fight against crimes such as fraud in ways that humans cannot do alone.

Write your opinion essay

> **EXPERT WRITING** page 196

5a Make a plan to answer the essay question in Exercise 2a. Form your own argument and decide on key points. Think about:

- What the question is asking.
- How you can answer fully.
- Contrasting both human judgement and science.
- The organisation of your paragraphs.
- The development of your key points.
- Including a restatement and summary in your conclusion.

b Write your essay. You should write at least 250 words.

Assess and improve

6a Work in pairs and review each other's essays. Complete the checklist.

1 Is there an introduction, well-organised paragraphs and conclusion?
2 Is the writer's standpoint clear from the beginning?
3 Does the writer give clear reasons to defend their standpoint?
4 Is each main point introduced clearly with a topic sentence?
5 Are these main points developed and given support?
6 Does the writer contrast both science and human judgement?
7 Is there a well-structured conclusion?

b Work on improving your answer. Use the feedback from Exercise 6a to help you.

Review

1a Choose the correct option in *italics* to complete the text.

Most viewers **1** *contribute / derive* a lot of joy from watching detective shows on television. These kinds of shows tend to feature a detective and sidekick who **2** *identify / involve* clues and motives and then **3** *facilitate / conclude* who must be the perpetrator. However, in real life dealing with the repercussions of a crime **4** *involves / contributes* many different groups of people. It is not only the law enforcement agencies like the police who **5** *conclude / facilitate* the capture of criminals and reduction of crime on our streets, there are also a multitude of other agencies involved. The courts, hospitals and scientific teams also **6** *derive / contribute* enormously towards this.

b Complete the sentences with *it* or *there*.

1 _____ is reasonable to conclude that punishments do go some way to deterring crime.
2 _____ used to be more crime in certain areas which was reduced by safety measures like increased lighting and more police on the streets.
3 According to recent figures, _____ was a reduction in the number of white-collar crimes in the last year.
4 _____ could be argued that rehabilitation is a more holistic answer to crime than simply punishment.
5 _____ has been an increase in the amount of scientific evidence used in courts.
6 _____ has been claimed that criminal activity is something which certain people are genetically predisposed to, although most experts refute this claim.

c Match the collocations (1–5) with the definitions (A–E).

1 a line of argument
2 a flawed argument
3 to reject an argument
4 a convincing argument
5 to propose an argument

A an argument with a major weakness
B an argument which is very good or strong
C the reasoning of an argument
D to put forward an argument
E to dismiss an argument

2a Complete the sentences with the words below.

although   both   conversely   despite   neither
similarly

1 _____ harsh punishments, some individuals still commit crimes.
2 _____ the police nor the courts can completely eradicate all criminal acts.
3 Having police officers enter schools to educate young people on the dangers of crime has had beneficial effects on their safety. _____ , leaflets given to parents about keeping their children safe have also seen good results.
4 _____ some crimes are due to desperation in terms of financial or emotional turmoil, it cannot be denied that greed motivates some crimes too.
5 _____ science and technology play a vital role in solving crime nowadays.
6 Arrests have reduced a great deal in the last decade, but, _____ there has been no reduction in reported crime.

b Put the phrases in the correct order to make sentences.

1 the man over there / It was / committed the crime / in the motorbike helmet / that

_____

2 about people who commit crimes / is / I find most difficult to understand / what / how they live with the guilt

_____

3 the fingerprints on the glass / finally led them to the culprit / it was / that

_____

4 most people don't understand / the judicial processes involved in crime / is / what

_____

c Rewrite the sentences using *it* or *what*.

1 Of all the things that were stolen from my bag, I miss my perfume the most because it was a present.
_____ what _____ .
2 The weather was dark and stormy on the night when the murder was committed.
It _____ .
3 The politician predicted that there would be a reduction in the number of traffic accidents after the new roundabout was built.
What _____ .
4 According to the camera footage, it was a wild animal that stole my plants from my garden, not a person as I originally thought.
_____ it _____ .

 **7**

On the move

7a Training

- **Reading**: Link ideas; Paraphrase (Matching sentence endings; Summary completion)
- **Vocabulary**: Academic nouns; Word families; Collocations with *plan*
- **Speaking**: Develop topic-specific vocabulary; Speak more accurately (Part 1)
- **Listening**: Identify distractors (Section 1: Form completion; Multiple choice)
- **Language development**: Sentence fragments and run-on sentences; Punctuation
- **Writing**: Represent data clearly and accurately; Identify inaccuracies in writing (Task 1: Tables and charts)

7b Testing

- **Listening**: Section 1: Multiple choice; Form completion
- **Language development and vocabulary**: Improve grammatical accuracy; Prepositions
- **Speaking**: Part 1: Describe travel and transport
- **Reading**: Matching sentence endings; Summary completion
- **Writing**: Task 1: Describe tables and charts

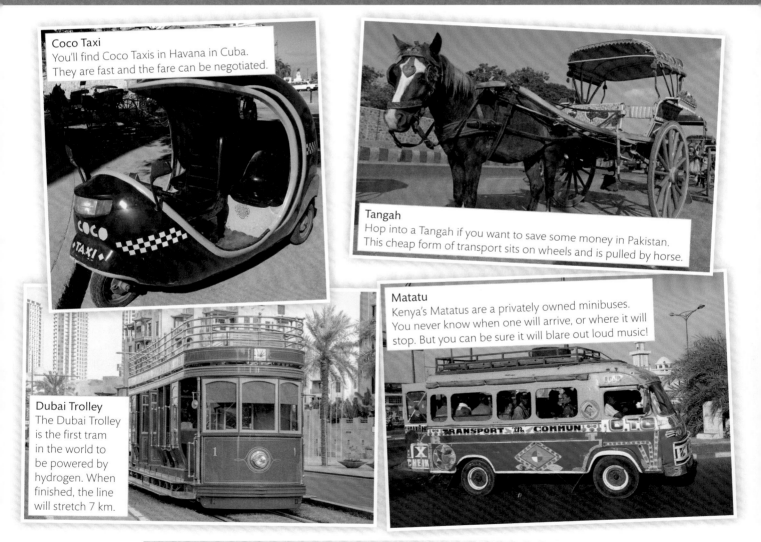

Coco Taxi
You'll find Coco Taxis in Havana in Cuba. They are fast and the fare can be negotiated.

Tangah
Hop into a Tangah if you want to save some money in Pakistan. This cheap form of transport sits on wheels and is pulled by horse.

Dubai Trolley
The Dubai Trolley is the first tram in the world to be powered by hydrogen. When finished, the line will stretch 7 km.

Matatu
Kenya's Matatus are a privately owned minibuses. You never know when one will arrive, or where it will stop. But you can be sure it will blare out loud music!

Lead-in

1   Read about the unique forms of transport above. Have you ever been on any of these forms of transport? Which one would you most like to go on? Why? How practical do you think these forms of transport are?

Reading (Matching sentence endings; Summary completion)

Before you read

1 What are the advantages and disadvantages of living in an urban environment?

Link ideas; Paraphrase

2a Look at the highlighted words in Question 1 of the test task and use them to locate the section of the passage which will give you the answer. Which of these options is the best summary of the section?

1 Bhatt was keen to continue with his project so that young people could benefit from travelling by bike.
2 Bhatt found it difficult to get his ideas accepted at first but he succeeded in the end.
3 Bhatt wanted to solve Gurgaon's traffic problem by banning cars permanently from the city centre.

b Which of the endings in the test task (A–G) is most similar to your summary? Identify the paraphrases in the options which helped you.

Test practice

3 Read the strategies and complete the test tasks.

> TEST STRATEGIES pages 170 and 172

Questions 1–5
Complete each sentence with the correct ending, A–G, below.

1 Amit Bhatt eventually obtained support for Raahgiri Day even though he
2 The concept for what became Raahgiri Day
3 As well as the desire to improve people's health, Gil Penalosa
4 Rather than having the stress of driving in the city, many people
5 Casey Neistat was fined because he

A drew attention to the dangers posed by motorists.
B ignored the rules of the road for pragmatic reasons.
C had to deal with initial resistance from the local authorities.
D hoped a traffic-free environment would develop a sense of community.
E had roots in a similar project in a different part of the world.
F would prefer to use an alternative method of transport.
G chose not to leave home unnecessarily at busy times.

Questions 6–9
Complete the summary using the list of words, A–I, below.

Cars in the city
The International Transport Forum is tackling the matter of traffic 6 _____ , now an issue in many of the world's cities even before the expected three-fold rise in the number of vehicles.

Disincentives, such as obligatory 7 _____ for driving in the city and restrictions on the number of available parking spaces, are already encouraging people to leave their cars at home.

However, the motivation for many people to change their commuting habits in and around the city is largely due to improvements aimed at 8 _____ traffic. It is hoped that by providing funding for more bike share and bike lane schemes, the 9 _____ of the average person will be extended.

A permits	B lifestyle	C safety
D congestion	E collisions	F assessing
G calming	H payment	I lifespan

Task analysis

4 Work in pairs and compare your answers. Discuss the questions.

1 In the first task, how did the first part of the sentence help you to locate the part of the passage you were looking for? Which linking words (e.g. *even though*) helped you to predict and choose the correct option?
2 In the second task, which paraphrases in the passage helped you choose the correct option? Which other words, if any, were you tempted by?

Discussion

5 Discuss the questions.

1 In what ways might it be a good idea to close a part of a city to traffic? Give examples of any places you know that do this and assess how successful it has been as an initiative.
2 To what extent is cycling in cities potentially dangerous? What could be done to encourage more people to cycle and how could accidents be prevented?

Streetwise

Since some cities have started to prioritise pedestrians and cyclists over motorists, it has made them healthier and more enjoyable places to live in.

Gurgaon, a city in northern India, has become ubiquitously associated with Raahgiri ("reclaim your streets") ever since its inception. In 2013, it first closed 4.5km of city streets to vehicles every Sunday in order to make them available to approximately 60,000 weekly revellers who now pack Gurgaon's streets: playing, walking and riding bicycles. Raahgiri has become a ground-breaking event in India, raising awareness about the benefits of non-motorised transport, and is also a model community occurrence to which other Indian cities can aspire.

During the preliminary stages of discussions on ways to resolve Gurgaon's traffic chaos and congestion, Amit Bhatt of EMBARQ, a green think-tank, advocated a focus on how to move people around rather than on the expansion of a vehicle-friendly system. However, from the outset, convincing officials of the effectiveness of this approach proved to be somewhat challenging: "This won't work here," one told Mr Bhatt when he proposed the Raahgiri and other alternatives to make Gurgaon's streets more pedestrian-friendly. Bhatt persisted in trying to convince them and finally succeeded after 200 schoolchildren cycled up to the city administration's headquarters to demonstrate public support.

The inspiration for Bhatt's idea stemmed from hearing about Bogota's "Ciclovía," during which Colombia's capital closes 120km of streets on Sundays and holidays. It was spear-headed by Gil Penalosa, the former parks commissioner in Bogota, who describes the implementation of the Ciclovía

Project as "a major initiative to encourage large numbers of the population to become more active and physically fit." Indeed, in a 2009 survey it was revealed that 42% of adults did as much exercise during a Bogota Ciclovía as the World Health Organization recommends in a week. A further goal was to create an urban centre where "thousands of people of all ages, levels of ability and ethnic, economic or social backgrounds enjoy the presence of each other and feel a sense of belonging." In the same way, Gurgaon, dominated by condominiums and extensive segregated private properties, uses Raahgiri Day to promote integration and provide residents with an opportunity to connect with other people in the area.

The International Transport Forum predicts that by 2050 the world's roads will be required to cope with 2.5 billion cars, three times as many as today, in urban areas which are already chronically overcrowded. In the face of growing concern, proposals have been submitted by transport planners to help resolve the issue: plans include converting city centres into pedestrian precincts, closing roads to cars at weekends and charging motorists a fee to take a car into town centres. Improvements to the public transport system, including rapid bus lanes and subways, have also played their part. However, it is the implementation of new regulations and measures to encourage safer and slower driving which has led to a significant proportion of people opting to walk or cycle in preference to using public transport or their own cars. Cost-benefit analyses for planned investment in new walking and cycling pathways have included a value for lives saved by the reduction in accidents and all lives prolonged through increased physical activity.

Cyclists and motorists have always resented sharing the road. Casey Neistat, a New York cyclist who was made to pay a $50 penalty for not riding in a cycle lane, produced a film of himself crashing into some of the thoughtlessly parked cars that so often make using the cycle lanes an impossibility. For cycling, Amsterdam sets the pace, with over half its residents using their bikes daily. Now other cities including London, New York and Paris are following in its footsteps, expanding their bike-share schemes and building new cycle lanes, some on quiet roads with more stringent speed limits implemented for cars, others running through central areas which separate cyclists from motorised traffic. Such schemes are particularly popular with women, who, transport planners say, are more apprehensive than men when it comes to sharing roads with roaring traffic and typically make up less than a quarter of urban cyclists. With the construction of an 80km network of separated two-way cycle lanes, their share of bicycle trips in the Spanish city of Seville rose from nearly zero to 7%. In Taipei, very few women cycled before the introduction of its YouBike share scheme which started six years ago; now around half of the city's cyclists are women.

It is all part of a movement which is accelerating around the world, providing opportunities for people to walk, cycle and play on their city streets. Activists are working hard to ensure past city planning mistakes are not repeated by lobbying for safe walking and cycling routes.

Vocabulary

Academic nouns

1a For each word (1–12), choose the closest meaning (A or B).

1 infrastructure:
  A a set of systems in place
  B a traditional method of building
2 implementation:
  A developing a plan
  B putting a plan into action
3 expansion:
  A a better version of something
  B an increase in size
4 parameter:
  A a set of fixed limits
  B something which is large
5 investment:
  A money given to improve something
  B training people to work as a team
6 distribution:
  A receiving something for free
  B sharing things in a planned way
7 integration:
  A combining things to work effectively
  B the fair division of resources
8 construction:
  A a modern approach to design
  B the process of building houses, roads, etc.
9 initiative:
  A a new approach to problem-solving
  B a controversial decision to delay an effect
10 maintenance:
  A repairs to keep things in a good condition
  B the movement of people in cities
11 co-ordination:
  A the flow of ideas between people
  B organising things or people
12 compensation:
  A money paid to someone for a loss
  B the feeling of sympathy for someone

b Choose the correct option in *italics* to complete the text.

The Brazilian city of Curitiba has one of the best Bus Rapid Transit (BRT) systems in the world. These bus systems are comparable to subways but operate above ground. They can be cost effective because they use the roads of the city. This means that little 1 *distribution / investment / compensation* is required from the government because the roads provide the 2 *infrastructure / construction / distribution*. In the case of Curitiba, the 3 *initiative / investment / implementation* of the BRT was gradual; the city planners avoided large-scale projects. In place of that the 4 *construction / initiative / maintenance* process of the BRT comprised several small improvements. The design of the system required the 5 *implementation /*

co-ordination / compensation of several departments of the city. This focus on small-scale developments and people working together, in effect, led to the 6 *distribution / parameter / expansion* of the BRT being a complete success.

Word families

2 Complete the table.

Noun	Verb
implementation	1 _____
investment	2 _____
distribution	3 _____
expansion	4 _____
maintenance	5 _____
compensation	6 _____

Collocations with *plan*

3 Complete the text with the correct form of the verbs below.

draw up go ahead oppose put forward unveil

The New York High Line is a park which has been constructed on a derelict elevated railway line. People can walk along the tracks high up in the city, completely surrounded by plants and flowers. The plans for this park were first 1 _____ by Joshua David and Robert Hammond, whose ambition was to create a park in the sky. Initially the plans were 2 _____ by local residents and businesses because their intention was to remove the tracks so as to improve the area's appearance. However, David and Hammond were so enthused by their idea that they enlisted the help of some local architects to help 3 _____ a more cohesive set of plans. When they finally 4 _____ the plans, the rail company that owned the tracks was so impressed that they agreed that the plans could 5 _____ . Now the park offers unrivalled views of this part of New York.

4 Match the collocations (1–6) with their meanings (A–F).

1 to draw up a plan
2 to put forward a plan
3 to unveil a plan
4 to go ahead with a plan
5 to shelve a plan
6 to oppose a plan

A to suggest a plan for consideration
B to start to implement a plan
C to disagree with a plan
D to postpone a plan until later
E to prepare a plan, usually in writing
F to show a plan to other people for the first time

Speaking (Part 1)

Lead-in

1 Look at the photos. Which is most similar to the place where you were born? What are the pros and cons of living in each place?

Develop topic-specific vocabulary

2 Complete the conversation with the idioms below.

a stone's throw away   home from home
hustle and bustle   live on top of each other   pace of life
run-down

Examiner: Where do you live?
Candidate: I live right in the centre of Shanghai, only **1** _____ from the Bund, actually, which can be incredibly hectic because there are always mountains of tourists. I love being amongst the **2** _____ of the city centre though; everyone going to work … people everywhere … it's great! I really thrive on the fast **3** _____ that city centres have, even if we all do have to **4** _____ . There's not that much space!
Examiner: Have you always lived there?
Candidate: No, I used to live in Hangzhou, which is roughly 200 kilometres south of Shanghai. In Hangzhou I lived in a pretty **5** _____ neighbourhood, but in Shanghai I live in a nicer area. Still, it's very much a **6** _____ for me because they are both coastal cities.

3 Work in pairs and discuss the topics.
   1 A place that is a home from home for you.
   2 The places that are a stone's throw away from where you live at the moment.
   3 What the pace of life is like where you live.

Speak more accurately

4a ◀) 7.1 Match the speakers (1–5) with the type of mistake they make (A–E).

   Speaker 1: _____   Speaker 2: _____
   Speaker 3: _____   Speaker 4: _____
   Speaker 5: _____

   A Word formation problems (e.g. *invest* instead of *investment*)
   B Lack of articles (e.g. *in south of city* instead of *in the south of the city*)
   C Problems with tense formation (e.g. *Last year I live in Saudi Arabia* instead of *Last year I lived …*)
   D No subject (e.g. *is hot here* instead of *it is hot here*)
   E Wrong choice of word (e.g. *I work far from house* instead of *I work far from home*).

 b Listen again and write down everything you hear in Exercise 4a. Correct the mistakes.

5a ◀) 7.2 Listen to two answers to the Part 1 test. Which version is less accurate? What kinds of mistakes does the speaker make?

 b Listen to the incorrect student in Exercise 5a again. In pairs, discuss some of the mistakes. Can you identify and correct them? What advice would you give the student to help him improve?

Test practice

➤ **TEST STRATEGIES** page 174

➤ **EXPERT SPEAKING** page 187

6a Read the questions and think about how best to answer them.

   1 Where do you live?
   2 What do you like about where you live?
   3 What would you change about it?
   4 How has it changed since you have lived there?
   5 What activities would you recommend to a visitor to your town?

 b Work in pairs and take turns to ask and answer the questions in Exercise 6a. Note down any inaccuracies your partner makes. Use the list in Exercise 4a for guidance. Record your answer if possible.

Assess and improve

7 Think about the answers your partner gave and answer the questions.
   1 What mistakes did you note down?
   2 Did your partner self-correct when speaking?
   3 Were there any words which were mispronounced?

Listening (Section 1)

Before you listen

1 The people in the photos belong to different clubs. What are they? Why do people join clubs? What clubs have you been part of?

Identify distractors

2a Read the question and options. Match the options (A, B and C) with the synonymous phrases (1, 2 and 3).

1 What does Karen want to know about the climbing club?
A if she needs protective clothing
B when and where they meet
C if she needs experience

1 whether beginners can join or not
2 what she should wear to be safe
3 the location and time of the club

b Read audio script 7.3 on page 208 and underline the correct answers in Exercise 2a, and also the distractors.

c Match the distractors in Exercise 2a with their type (1–2).

1 Word matching: The speaker uses the same words as in the answer option.
2 Similar choices: The distractor is similar to the correct answer, but the correct answer contains an extra detail.

d 🔊 7.3 Complete the test tasks.

Questions 1 and 2

*Choose the correct letter, **A**, **B** or **C**.*

1 What time do members arrive at the meeting place on Saturdays?
A 8.15   B 8.50   C 7.50
2 What benefits does the club offer members?
A individual training with the founder
B discounts on a climbing course
C coaching from other members

Question 3

Complete the form below.

*Write **NO MORE THAN ONE WORD AND/OR A NUMBER** for each answer.*

Name: Karen Whittaker
Mobile: 07865 322 475
Nearest locations: The city park, the river bridge
Membership cost: 3 £ _____

e Listen again and match the distractors in the recording in Exercise 2d with A–C.

A The speaker mentions all the options.
B The dialogue includes words which sound similar such as 'fifteen' and 'fifty'.
C Correcting information. The speaker revises the information they give.

Test practice

➤ TEST STRATEGIES page 168

3 🔊 7.4 Complete the test tasks.

Questions 1–4

Complete the form below.

*Write **NO MORE THAN THREE WORDS AND/OR A NUMBER** for each answer.*

Customer enquiry form: City Cycling Group
Reason for calling: 1 _____
Name: *Edward Simmons*
Address: 2 _____ , London, SW23 4GJ
Mobile: 3 07865 _____
Email: ed.simmons@mymail.com
Ability level: 4 _____

Question 5

*Choose the correct letter, **A**, **B** or **C**.*

5 Why does Anna think the Sunday club is not suitable for Edward?
A the members are old
B the routes are on flat roads
C the fees are expensive

Language development

Sentences fragments and run-on sentences

➤ **EXPERT GRAMMAR** page 179

1a Read the sentences below. Why are they incorrect?

1 Park full of exercise equipment and sports fields.
2 If this area received more investment.
3 Built some new apartments which have access to the river boat transport network.
4 This part of town is attractive it is a desirable place to live.

b Match the sentence fragments in Exercise 1a with the problems (A–D).

A add punctuation or a connecting word
B it is missing a verb
C it needs a subject
D there should be a second clause

c Rewrite the sentences in Exercise 1a so they are correct.

2a Read the sentences and decide if they are correct or not.

1 T'ai Chi is a popular community activity all across China many older people gather in their local parks to do the ancient exercises together.
2 The martial art is a combination of deep breathing and relaxation with a series of gentle movements.
3 Because it maintains physical health.
4 Recently 50,000 students to their local parks all over China to try to set a world record for the most people simultaneously practising T'ai Chi at once.
5 Residents took part in 15 different places across Henan Province.
6 In each location wore matching outfits in different colours and the displays could be seen from high vantage points around the areas.
7 Residents of the province are hopeful that the *Guinness Book of Records* will confirm the record.

b Correct the incorrect sentences in Exercise 2a.

Punctuation

3 Match the punctuation marks (1–7) with their uses (A–G).

Punctuation	Use
1 full stop .	A It is used to expand on the sentence by introducing a list or a second part of the same idea.
2 comma ,	B Used to show the exact words spoken by a person.
3 capital letter D	C This shows that a letter is missing in a contracted form, or shows possession.
4 colon :	D This marks the end of a sentence.
5 semi colon ;	E This shows the beginning of a sentence.
6 apostrophe '	F It separates clauses, phrases or words in a list.
7 quotation marks ' '	G This is between a full stop and a comma. It joins phrases and sentences which are linked, without having to use a conjunction.

4 Punctuate the text below.

Saving space and energy

car clubs are an excellent way for people to save space and energy in urban environments the premise is simple people register with a company which rents cars located in multiple locations all around the city after becoming a member customers are able to access an online members area to reserve a vehicle for a particular amount of time there are several reasons why people join car clubs cost convenience and attitude towards the environment joining international car companies also enables people to use these services while abroad

Writing (Task 1)

Lead-in

1 How do most people travel in the cities near you?

Represent data clearly and accurately

2 Look at the chart below. Discuss what the chart is about and what key features you can see.

Modes of transport in three major cities, 2014

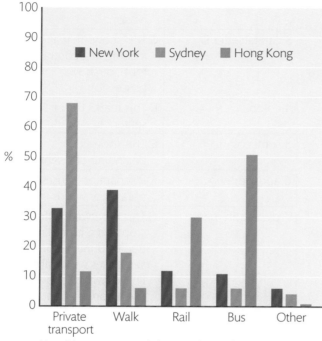

Note: Private transport includes privately owned vehicles and taxi use.

3 Look at the two opening paragraphs describing the chart in Exercise 2. Which is the best introduction? Why?

1 The bar chart outlines the share in modes of transport in 2014 of three cities: New York, Sydney and Hong Kong. The share is measured in percentage and the data is categorised into types of public transport.

2 There is a varied share of public transport in the three cities outlined in the graph: New York, Sydney and Hong Kong. While travelling by car is popular in Sydney, other forms of transport are more popular elsewhere.

4 Look at the two final summary overviews for the chart in Exercise 2. Which is the best summary overview? Why?

1 Overall, the data show that there are many forms of transport that can be used to travel. Private transport is most popular in Sydney, whereas bus is more popular in Hong Kong, and walking is the most popular in New York.

2 Overall, the data show that there is no one major form of transport for all cities, but rather popular transport modes vary depending on the city.

5 Complete the main body of the answer using the figures below.

5% 10% 30% 50%

Public transport, such as rail and bus services, were generally less popular in New York and Sydney. Both rail and bus had a share of approximately 1 _____ for the modes of transport given for New York. This figure was even lower in Sydney where these two forms of transport had about a 2 _____ share each. This is a significant contrast to Hong Kong, where public transport was the most popular mode of transport used (at 3 _____ and just over 4 _____ respectively).

6 Look at the table below. Make notes with a partner on what you could include in both the introduction and summary overview.

City transport mode shares in Asia, 2012

	Beijing	Delhi	Seoul
Private transport	33%	23%	23%
Rail	17%	4%	38%
Bus	27%	27%	27%
Walk	1%	35%	3%
Taxi	6%	0%	5%
Cycle	14%	6%	1%
Other	2%	5%	3%

Identify inaccuracies in writing

7 Match the types of mistakes below with the underlined sections of the sentences.

adverb placement   article use   incorrect preposition
passive formation   spelling   subject/verb agreement
tense formation   word formation

Transport in Asia

1 <u>Private transport, rail transport and taking the bus was</u> generally popular in all three cities, with <u>the except of</u> Delhi, where rail travel was not so popular.

2 Rather, travelling on foot <u>especially was popular</u> in Delhi (with around a 35% share in travellers).

3 In these cities, between 23% and 30% of <u>people are using</u> private means of transport <u>such as the cars</u>.

4 Conversely, taking a taxi was relatively <u>unpopular on all three</u> cities.

5 Taxis had a maximum of 6% total transport <u>shaire</u>.

6 <u>Cycling be found to be</u> quite a popular mode of transport in Beijing.

Test practice

> EXPERT WRITING page 197

8a Write your report for the table in Exercise 6. Write at least 150 words.

b When you have finished, check your work for meaning and grammatical accuracy.

7b Infrastructures

Listening (Section 1)

Before you listen

1 What types of problems do people experience when travelling to other countries?

Positive and negative language

2a ◀)) 7.5 Listen and tick the sentence you hear.
1 A Travelling by plane hasn't got much better since the early flights of the 1950s.
 B Travelling by plane has got much better since the early flights of the 1950s.
2 A Cruise ships are the best way to travel if you want to mix with like-minded passengers.
 B Cruise ships aren't the best way to travel if you want to mix with like-minded passengers.

b Read the questions below and change the answers (A–C) into the opposite form (negative to positive or positive to negative).
1 What happened on the bus journey?
 A the driver was not polite
 B the doors did not work
 C the bus broke down
2 At the end of the bus journey the passengers
 A felt relieved. B were tired. C complained.

c ◀)) 7.6 Listen and answer the questions in Exercise 2b.

Test practice

➤ TEST STRATEGIES page 168

3 ◀)) 7.7 Complete the test tasks.

Questions 1–4.
Choose the correct letter A, B or C.

1 What does Silvia want the train company to do?
 A to tell her why the tickets have increased in price
 B to officially record her complaint about the train service
 C to grant her some form of compensation
2 What time was the train supposed to arrive?
 A 8.15 B 8.50 C 9.15
3 What made Silvia's journey worse?
 A the ticket was so expensive
 B there were too many people on the train
 C it was over an hour late
4 How does Silvia think the train company could improve its service?
 A by increasing the number of employees
 B by reducing the number of passengers
 C by having larger carriages with more capacity

Questions 5–10
Complete the form below.
Write **NO MORE THAN TWO WORDS AND/OR A NUMBER** for each answer.

Customer complaint form
Name: Silvia 5 _____
Mobile number: 07865 6 _____
Email: silvia2000@fastmail.com
Journey details: service London to 7 _____
Ticket type: Standard class
Date: 8 _____
Issue: service delayed by over 30 minutes
Refund by: 9 _____
Preferred contact method: phone
Ticket price: 10 £ _____

Task analysis

4a Check your answers and then compare with a partner.

b Read audio script 7.7 on page 209. Did you answer any of the questions incorrectly? How does reading the audio script help you understand why your answers were correct or incorrect?

c What do you need to focus on for Section 1 of the IELTS Listening paper? How are you going to improve your performance in this area? Make a list of ways you could improve and discuss them with your partner. Ask your partner for their ideas.

Discussion

5 Discuss the questions.
1 Why do you think some people find travelling so stressful?
2 How could transportation companies improve the experience for their passengers?
3 Do you think travelling will be less stressful in the future when it is more automated? Why/Why not?

Language development and vocabulary

Improve grammatical accuracy

➤ **EXPERT GRAMMAR** page 180

1a Choose the correct option in *italics* to complete the text.

Greyhound **travel**

One of **1** *a / the* most ubiquitous travel logos in the USA **2** *is / are* that of the coach company Greyhound Lines. Greyhound Lines **3** *was / were* established in 1914 and **4** *are / is* still in operation today serving over 2,700 destinations across **5** *the / a* country. There are only a handful of people who **6** *do not / does not* know of the company and most Americans **7** *use / uses* it at some point in their lives. Greyhound buses **8** *has / have* featured in several famous films including *Breakfast at Tiffany's*. In addition, many singers included **9** *the / a* word Greyhound in their songs specifically to refer to the name of the celebrated bus company. For these reasons, it is likely to have **10** *the / a* prominent place in history, of cultural as well as commercial significance.

b Work in pairs and discuss your choices in Exercise 1a.

2 Correct the errors in the sentences.

1 A number of passengers choosing to travel internationally by train are increasing.
2 Neither the train service nor the bus service are operating today.
3 The main shipping route across both the Atlantic the Pacific have become rather crowded.
4 Recent data from airlines suggests that passengers are becoming more dissatisfied with waiting times.
5 Both children travels free with a package holiday deal.
6 The convenient way to travel across a continent of South America are by overnight coach.

Prepositions

3a What is the difference in meaning between the sentences below?

1 The number of people who flew to their holiday destination rose by 10 percent in 2015.
2 The number of people who flew to their holiday destination rose to 10 percent in 2015.

b Match the sentences in Exercise 3a with the meanings below.

A The final figure was 10 percent.
B The increase was 10 percent more than before.

4 Complete the text with the prepositions below.

at   by (x3)   on   over   through   to

The **train travel** of the future could be here soon!

The Hyperloop is a high-speed train system proposed **1**_____ the entrepreneur Elon Musk. It consists of tubes with capsules carrying passengers that travel **2**_____ them. The Hyperloop will operate **3**_____ sending capsules through a tube made from steel. In the plans, the capsules float **4**_____ a cushion of air and might be able to travel **5**_____ speeds of over 700mph. This means that travelling times could be reduced **6**_____ a much lower level. In addition, because the capsules are powered **7**_____ electricity, the Hyperloop is likely to bring many environmental advantages **8**_____ air travel because it will use less fuel.

5 Work in pairs and discuss how the prepositions in the sentences change the meaning of what is being said.

1 There are three categories of transport *among / besides* those most commonly used by commuters.
2 The findings were corroborated *by / with* the research council.
3 The cost of transport increased *from / by* $2.50 in 2010.

Speaking (Part 1)

Vocabulary development

1 Look at the photo above. Would you like to travel in this way? Why/Why not? What are the most popular ways to travel in your country?

2a Complete the sentences with the words below.

connection expedition getaway idyll road trip
stopover trek voyage

1 Some people just want a complete _____ when they go on holiday. Away from all the hustle and bustle of life ... some kind of rural _____ , but that's not for me, I prefer going to places with plenty of life.

2 I love flying, but I cannot bear it when I have to change planes. I always fear that I'll miss my _____ . This is why I prefer to have a _____ for a night or two near the airport.

3 I'm quite a fan of cruise liners. I've always dreamt of going on a long _____ somewhere remote or maybe even going on an _____ somewhere exotic and discover new experiences.

4 It's such a _____ to work. I drive, then take a train, then walk. It usually takes over two and a half hours each way! I don't appreciate that kind of travelling at all. I'm a fan of driving though. I'd love to go on a _____ ... preferably somewhere with very little traffic!

b Read the sentences in Exercise 2a again. Write a Part 1 question for each sentence.

3 Work in pairs and take turns to ask and answer the questions.

1 What kinds of journeys do you find stressful?
2 What type of trip would you like to take next?
3 Have you had any particularly exciting trips? Where?
4 Which form of transport do you prefer using in your daily life? Why?

Focus on grammatical range and accuracy

4a Turn to page 183 and read the descriptors for band 7. Which descriptors focus on accuracy?

b Think about your own speech and tick the aspects below which apply to you. If possible, use a recording you have made.

- I answer questions fully and develop my answer.
- I can easily continue speaking for more than 10 seconds.
- I do not generally hesitate or pause for long amounts of time when talking about myself.
- If I notice I make a mistake in language or pronunciation, I correct it.
- I know my errors in pronunciation and try to improve them.
- I generally speak clearly.
- If I use unusual vocabulary, I make sure I know how it can be used.
- I do not make many grammatical mistakes.
- I know my errors in grammar and try to improve them.

c Work in pairs. Look at your lists in Exercise 4b and discuss what you could both do to improve your accuracy in speaking.

Test practice

> **TEST STRATEGIES** page 174

5 Work in pairs and take turns to ask and answer the questions. Record your answers if possible.

1 How did you get here today?
2 How do you prefer to travel?
3 What is your favourite form of transport? Why?
4 Would you say you are a well-travelled person? Why/Why not?
5 Do you enjoy long-distance travel? Why/Why not?
6 Are you planning any journeys at the moment? How will you get there?

Assess and improve

6 Look again at the list in Exercise 4b and discuss your partner's performance in these areas. Which areas did he/she do well at and which ones need improving?

7a 🔊 7.8 Listen to a candidate answering questions 1–4 in Exercise 5. Compare your performance with the candidate's.

b With reference to the speaker in Exercise 7a, discuss how you and your partner could improve your answers.

Reading (Matching sentence endings; Summary completion)

Before you read

1 Discuss the questions.

    1 How might technology affect transport in the future?

    2 In what ways will cars differ from the ones we have today? Do you think they will ever become truly autonomous? If they do, how could this help us?

Test practice

2a Which of these strategies can help you with the following tasks: a) matching sentence endings b) summary completion c) both?

    1 reading the subtitle and skimming the passage quickly looking for topic sentences

    2 predicting what comes next

    3 using clues to find the relevant place in the passage

    4 scanning the passage

    5 looking for paraphrases

  b Read the strategies and complete the test tasks.

> TEST STRATEGIES pages 170 and 172

Questions 1–5

Complete each sentence with the correct ending, A–G, below.

    1 According to car makers, self-driving vehicles

    2 If Google's prototypes are typical, the design of futuristic cars

    3 Having fewer private cars in urban centres

    4 Car manufacturers of the future

    5 The impact of a move towards driverless cars

    A will create opportunities for the new giants of the technology world.

    B will be disruptive for some businesses.

    C will involve a restriction on people's personal freedom.

    D will be introduced at the high-end of the market.

    E will need to prioritise computer programmes over machinery and equipment.

    F will probably bear little resemblance to the models we know today.

    G will enable a higher number of new homes to be built.

> HELP

1 Is '*According to car makers …*' a fact or an opinion?

2 Are the Google self-driving cars similar to or different in design from modern cars?

Questions 6–10

Complete the summary using the list of words, A–I, below.

The advantages of self-driving cars

One major advantage of driverless cars would be far fewer 6 _____ on the road. It is probable that when autonomous cars become more common, there will be 7 _____ which will discourage cars with drivers from using the roads at all.

A further advantage is that road 8 _____ would increase and delays decrease as it became less crucial for cars to keep so much distance between them.

The 9 _____ would also gain from increased output as commuters make constructive use of the time they previously spent sitting behind the wheel.

Finally, autonomous cars would facilitate a greater degree of 10 _____ for vulnerable members of society.

A capacity	F speed
B car manufacturers	G regulations
C vehicles	H protection
D independence	I economy
E casualties	

> HELP

6 Look for an option which means *people who are killed or injured*.

7 If something is banned, how is this done?

Task analysis

3 Work in pairs and discuss the questions.

    1 Which of the two task types do you find easier? Why?

    2 Give examples from both tasks of paraphrases in the passage which helped you to locate the answers.

    3 Give an example from both tasks of how predicting the type of word you were looking for helped.

Discussion

4 Work in groups and discuss the questions.

    1 In which ways has technology influenced transport in the last 50 years?

    2 Do you think most people would want to share the road with robots? Why/Why not?

    3 What potential problems might arise from the use of completely autonomous cars?

If autonomous vehicles rule the world

Self-driving cars promise to be as disruptive and transformative a technology as the mobile phone.

The world's automobile manufacturers envisage the future of self-driving technology as features like "piloted driving". Initially such driver assistance will be installed in luxury vehicles but will gradually become a common feature of mass-market cars, just as electric windows and power steering had done beforehand. Autonomous driving will, from this viewpoint, make motoring less stressful but people will still buy and own cars much as they do today.

However, a visit to a "pod parking" area at Heathrow airport gives a contrasting view of self-driving technology. Transfers between the car park and the terminal are provided by driverless electric pods moving on dedicated elevated roadways. Using a touch-screen kiosk, a pod is summoned and your destination specified. A pod pulls up, parks itself and drives you to your destination, avoiding other pods and neatly parking itself on arrival.

The spread of Advanced Driver Assistance Systems will be gradual over the next few years but self-driving vehicles that can be summoned and dismissed at will, such as the ones described above, could do more than make driving easier: they promise to redefine urban life as we know it. Making existing cars suddenly appear as outmoded as steam engines and landline telephones. Like the very first motor cars, which facilitated suburbanisation and became symbols of self-definition, a driverless means of transport will also have unexpected impacts. Cars need look nothing like existing ones: already, Google's futuristic pods are on the public roads of California and some concept designs, liberated from the need to have steering wheels and pedals, have seats facing each other around a table.

Autonomous vehicles will also challenge the very notion of car ownership. The idea that they will be owned and used just as cars are today is a "tenuous assumption", according to Luis Martinez, of the International Transport Forum. Fleets of self-driving vehicles could, he says, replace all car, taxi and bus trips in a city, providing the same level of mobility with far fewer vehicles and reducing urban vehicle numbers by as much as 90%. With cars in constant use, much less parking space would be needed and by liberating space wasted on parking, autonomous vehicles could allow more people to live in city centres.

All of this would be transformational for car makers, who would be in a situation where rather than selling autonomous vehicles to individual drivers they would be selling them to fleet operators. The value in car making would shift from hardware to software and from products to services, says Mr Martinez. This would have the same negative impact on existing car makers that smartphones had on Nokia and Kodak. Already, hi-tech newcomers such as Google, Uber and Tesla are vying for control of the new technology.

Car insurance – worth $198 billion a year in America alone – is also likely to experience major upheavals as cover switches from millions of consumers to a mere handful of fleet operators. Automation would be far from popular news too for firms selling spare parts and taxi drivers, among others. For example, America's 3.5 million truck-drivers sustain workers in businesses such as motels and restaurants, which will be in jeopardy now the first self-driving truck has taken to the road.

But self-driving cars would also have enormous benefits. According to the World Health Organization, approximately 1.2 million people are killed on the road each year with 94% of road accidents reputedly being the result of human error, the main causes being drink-driving, speeding or distracted driving. However, as driverless cars cannot drink alcohol, break the speed limit or get distracted by a text message, accidents should be dramatically reduced, if not eradicated. In fact, once self-driving cars do become more widely available, it is highly likely that some places will consider banning ordinary cars on the grounds of safety.

As well as being far less dangerous, self-driving vehicles would make traffic flow more smoothly because they would not brake erratically, could be routed to avoid congestion and could travel closer together in order to increase the volume of traffic on the road. In addition, riders in these vehicles would be able to use their journey more effectively. Financial services company Morgan Stanley calculates that the resulting productivity gains could be worth an incredible $5.6 trillion worldwide. Moreover, as illustrated in one of Google's videos showing a blind man doing errands in an autonomous car, self-sufficiency would be within the reach of children, the elderly and the disabled.

Some car-lovers will doubtless mourn the passing of machines that, in the 20th century, became icons of self-determination. But this independence is purely illusory: the empty roads seen in car adverts are far from most people's experience of driving. Ironically, in a driverless future, people will doubtless be incredulous as to why such a high rate of road deaths was tolerated for so long and why so much money was spent on machines that largely sat unused.

Writing (Task 1)

Lead-in

1a Look at the photo. If you were getting on the plane, where would you like to fly to and why?

b What are the most popular destinations to fly to from your country? Why are they so popular and what type of people tend to go to these places the most?

Understand the task

2a Look at the chart below. What does it show?

World air passengers, by country, 2014–2034

Passenger numbers '000s

2014 2024 2034

Canada USA Brazil Mexico UK France China Saudi Arabia

b Answer the questions about the chart in Exercise 2a.

1 How is the data measured?
2 How is the chart categorised?
3 What is the timeframe for the chart?
4 Is the information definite or not? How could this change the language you use to describe it?
5 What tense or forms will you use to write your answer?

c Work in pairs and discuss a summary overview for this chart. Use ideas from page 110 to help you.

Plan the task

3 Turn to page 190 and read all the descriptors for bands 7 and 8. Discuss where they focus on the accurate representation of data and where they focus on accurate language.

4a Read the sentences below and tick the ones which are true for you.

Accurately representing data
• I always read the chart carefully and analyse what is being shown.
• I consider the categories and measurements carefully.
• I look at the timescales and decide which tense(s) should be used.
• I identify any general trends in the data.
• I look for similarities and differences within the data.
• I check my writing when completed to ensure the data is accurately represented.

Accurate language
- I think about how I can express the figures in the diagrams.
- I consider carefully the grammar I need to use and how to formulate this correctly.
- I am aware of my main errors and carefully consider these when writing.
- I proofread my writing when I finish and correct any grammatical or vocabulary errors I spot.
- I proofread for mistakes that I commonly make and think about these sections carefully.

b Considering your answers in Exercise 4a, look at the chart in Exercise 2a and decide how you can accurately represent the data and which tenses and vocabulary are appropriate.

c Plan your answer to the chart in Exercise 2a. Before you start writing, consider the following.
- What the chart means
- How you can best group the main trends or features
- How you can support these with data
- How you can give an effective summary overview
- What language you need to use

Language and content

5a Underline the expressions in the sentences which indicate future possibility.
1 It is predicted that Canada will remain the country with the highest number of air passengers.
2 Numbers of airline passengers in the South American countries shown may only increase by a small amount.
3 The number of people travelling by plane is expected to rise in all countries.
4 It is estimated that China and Saudi Arabia will see considerable growth in numbers of airline passengers.
5 It is likely that the USA will have the most airline passengers in 2034.
6 Air passenger numbers could possibly double in all the countries over the next 20 years.

b Which of the sentences in Exercise 5a accurately reflect the data in Exercise 2a? Which do not? Correct these sentences.

c Look again at the words you underlined in Exercise 5a and discuss with a partner the key trends and features of the chart.

Write your report

> EXPERT WRITING page 197

6a Write your answer to the chart in Exercise 2a. Write at least 150 words.

b Edit your work. Read your answer and check
1 that your information is an accurate reflection of what is shown in the chart.
2 for any mistakes in grammar or spelling. If you see any, correct them.

Assess and improve

7a Exchange your report with a partner. Check each other's work using the points in Exercise 6b and discuss the strengths and weaknesses of each other's report.

b Do you notice any consistent mistakes being made? Make a note of them to help your partner improve the accuracy of his/her writing.

Review

1a Complete the sentences with the correct form of the words below.

compensate   distribute   expand   implement   invest
maintain

1 It is very advantageous to have areas of natural beauty for people to visit, but these must be _____ by ensuring there are rules to protect these areas.
2 Although sometimes it is necessary to use parks and woodland to make way for new housing, there is little _____ for the loss of green spaces for existing residents in the area.
3 Although _____ promotional material about local services may be of use to residents, it is more important that these services are run well.
4 The infrastructure at present cannot cope with the numbers of commuters, and therefore the _____ of rail and bus networks is an essential concern.
5 Some tourist attractions will _____ e-ticketing in order to facilitate a smoother booking and payment process and reduce queues.
6 The more money is _____ into keeping the area nice, the happier the residents will be.

b Choose the correct preposition, A, B or C.

1 _____ 20 percent of those surveyed had complained about the train service.
   A on   B at   C over
2 The number of passengers that travelled to work by bus has increased _____ 10 percent this year.
   A by   B on   C through
3 Most of those surveyed agreed _____ the need for a tram system.
   A over   B by   C on
4 _____ the end of the year, the number of people walking to work had reduced significantly.
   A through   B at   C to
5 The number of people commuting long distances had risen _____ the highest number seen for a decade.
   A by   B to   C on

c Complete the sentences with the phrases below.

shelve their plan   oppose the plan   unveiled their plan
go ahead with the plan

1 The city bus company _____ for a new terminal in the city centre in a press conference yesterday.
2 After a lot of discussion, the school decided to _____ of redesigning the access from the car park to the main school building.
3 The government is going to _____ to invest in transport infrastructure until after the election.
4 Local residents _____ to build a motorway around the edge of the town due to the potential noise pollution.

2a Add the necessary punctuation to the text below.

The Rise of the Segway

segways also known as hover boards might be considered as a futuristic form of transport yet they are readily available to buy in most countries today in fact you can see pictures online of many celebrities riding them and they might not even be an unusual sight in city parks however in some countries riding a Segway on the streets is illegal this is largely because they are not deemed safe to be amongst traffic so before you consider buying a segway just remember they may be fun but you can't use them as an everyday as a form of transport

b Correct the errors in the sentences.

1 Neither passenger leave the train until this dispute is over.
2 A number of trains along this route is increasing.
3 The latest data recommends that people always book their tickets in advance.
4 The final destination of both flights TE223 and BA115 are Istanbul.
5 This steam train holds the particular place in history as one of the earliest of its kind.

c The following sentences are sentence fragments. Rewrite them so they are correct. You may need to separate them into two sentences.

1 The new flats built on the university campus excellent in terms of value for money and quality.
2 Is a tranquil park near my house which I often go to when I need to destress and relax after work.
3 Although the city is generally considered to be a safe place to live.
4 Has become more attractive for couples with young children to move to since the new shopping centre and restaurant complex was constructed.

d The text below contains two kinds of mistakes: word formation and preposition use. Find and correct the mistakes.

Both the bus and car were popular forms of transport in Beijing, Delhi and Seoul at 2008. Other forms of transport showed larger differents between the three countries. Rail was a high used form of transport in Seoul, whereas travelling by foot was extreme popularity in Delhi. Other forms of transport, such for cycling or taking taxis, were not used as much.

8 Social networks

8a Training

- **Reading:** Identify the writer's views/claims (*Yes/No/Not given*; Multiple choice: select two answers)
- **Vocabulary:** Vocabulary related to community; Academic collocations; Describe emotions
- **Speaking:** Develop topic-specific vocabulary; Real and hypothetical situations and reactions; Pronunciation – connected speech 2 (Part 2)
- **Listening:** Follow lines of argument (Section 2: Matching; Table completion)
- **Language development:** Review of future forms; Speculate on the future
- **Writing:** Understand situations, causes and effects; Develop a situation, cause and effect paragraph (Task 2)

8b Testing

- **Listening:** Section 2: Matching; Note completion; Multiple choice
- **Language development and vocabulary:** Cause and effect linking words; Noun phrases 2
- **Speaking:** Part 2: Describe a famous person
- **Reading:** *Yes/No/Not given*; Multiple choice
- **Writing:** Task 2: Cause and effect essay

'A community is like a ship; everyone ought to be prepared to take the helm.'
Henrik Ibsen

Lead-in

1 What do you think this quote means? To what extent do you agree with it and why? Why is community important? What kind of roles do you play in your community?

Reading (*Yes/No/Not given*; Multiple choice: select two answers)

Before you read

1 Work in groups and discuss the questions.

    1 How helpful are people generally in your country towards those in need of assistance? Give reasons.

    2 Do you think people today are more or less altruistic than they were in the past? What makes you think this?

Identify the writer's views/claims

2 Read the passage to get an idea of the content and structure. Is the passage mainly factual, argumentative or descriptive?

3a Look at these phrases from the passage. Which ones express a fact (F) and which an opinion (O)?

    1 Against the odds, both survived.

    2 Autrey's good deed could be interpreted as heroic.

    3 … it might lead us to draw quite the opposite conclusion …

    4 Various theories have been proposed …

    5 Wilson maintains that this view is now generally accepted …

    6 Wilson is dismissive of such speculation, maintaining that …

    7 Pfaff … is convinced that …

    8 All of which suggests to Pfaff that …

    9 Some of the extra neurons gained are most likely …

    10 According to Pfaff, …

    11 Wilson has also conducted research, …

    12 … their evidence suggests that …

    13 The encouraging message is …

b Underline the words which indicate that they are opinions (e.g. *could be interpreted*).

c Which of the opinions are NOT those of the writer?

4 It is possible to understand the writer's opinion from the language used. Are words below from the passage adjectives or nouns? Are they generally considered to be positive (+), negative (-) or both, depending on the context (+/-)?

cohesive co-operative coward daring dismissive
empathy exceptional heroic indifference influential
ordinary plausible ruthless sceptic selfishness
selflessness self-sacrificing spontaneous

Test practice

5a Read the strategies and complete the test tasks.

> **TEST STRATEGIES** pages 171 and 172

Questions 1–5

Do the following statements agree with the views/claims of the writer? Write

YES   *if the statement agrees with the views/claims of the writer*

NO   *if the statement contradicts the views/claims of the writer*

NOT GIVEN   *if it is impossible to say what the writer thinks about this*

    1 What Autrey did was representative of how most humans would react.

    2 The importance of altruism for human survival is widely acknowledged.

    3 Most biologists are cynical about the existence of genuine altruism.

    4 Pfaff's neuroscientific explanation for altruism is credible.

    5 Humans have the potential to show altruism if they feel supported.

Questions 6–7

*Choose **TWO** letters, **A–E**.*

*Which **TWO** of the following factors will encourage altruism?*

    A faith in the goodness of human beings

    B financial support from government

    C awareness-raising in schools

    D confidence in our intuitive reactions

    E strong community relationships

b Work in pairs and discuss your answers.

Task analysis

6 Work in pairs and compare your answers. Discuss the questions.

    1 Justify why you chose the answers you did. Which parts of the passage helped you to decide?

    2 Which, if any, of the vocabulary did you find difficult? How did you deal with this?

How to be good

Scientists offer different answers on how to help altruism flourish.

One day, an ordinary New Yorker jumped in front of an approaching train to rescue a young man who had had a seizure and fallen on to the subway tracks. This ordinary New Yorker, Wesley Autrey, rolled them both into a drainage ditch and covered the stranger with his body as the train passed over them. Against the odds, both survived.

Autrey, who has been fêted round the world as a hero, showed a selflessness which should restore our faith in human nature. However, although Autrey's good deed could be interpreted as heroic, it might lead us to draw quite the opposite conclusion about the behaviour of human beings. It is not because his action was ordinary that Autrey has since been proclaimed as one of the most influential men of the year by *Time* magazine, but rather because it was so exceptional. Amid the grim-faced indifference of city life, his self-sacrifice is striking. His case simultaneously draws attention to the possibility of genuine altruism and highlights its everyday absence. Indeed, how we might have evolved to be self-sacrificing has long been a challenge for Darwinism since those who renounce their lives to save their community do not transmit their genes. Even less extreme acts of kindness, such as sharing food with a sick friend, could disadvantage someone in the ruthless race to survive.

Various theories have been proposed to resolve this puzzle. David Sloan Wilson, Professor of Biology and Anthropology and author of *Does Altruism Exist?* has long been an advocate of one particular theory which is called group selection. The reasoning behind this theory is that groups of altruistic individuals can flourish because they outperform groups of cowards. Competition within a group, he asserts, tends to make us selfish individualists, whereas competition between groups turns us into co-operative, self-sacrificing team players. However, although Wilson maintains that this view is now generally accepted, it is a claim which many biologists would disagree with. In any case, a sceptic could argue that supporting others on the assumption that this will improve our collective strength would imply we were not truly altruistic. Nonetheless, Wilson is dismissive of such speculation, maintaining that the beliefs or thoughts are immaterial; the resulting actions should be sufficient.

In contrast, neuroscientist Donald Pfaff, in *The Altruistic Brain: How We Are Naturally Good*, is convinced that our altruistic deeds are as selfless as they seem: they are not, for example, simply careful cost-benefit analyses couched in moral language. He points to studies which confirm that helpful instincts emerge naturally in even very young children and to the spontaneous nature of many altruistic acts. Heroic feats of bravery are often split-second decisions or indeed barely decisions at all, but more like impulses because there is often little time to weigh the pros and cons before acting. All of which suggests to Pfaff that the wiring of our brains makes such actions natural. This is a plausible hypothesis since the human brain increased in size very rapidly at a time in our evolutionary history when the benefits of co-operation were becoming evident. Consequently, some of the extra neurons gained are most likely dedicated to making us better team players. According to Pfaff, the process begins when we visualize someone and then link this image with our own self-image in our minds. Having identified with the person, we are much more inclined to try and save him. In other words, we are hard-wired to act on empathy.

Both Wilson and Pfaff feel certain that a better understanding of the science of altruism will help us to foster it. Though they have faith in our moral instincts, they are not oblivious to the fact that these instincts frequently founder. Pfaff maintains that many human interactions are concerned with trust and we need to assume that other people are not intent on exploiting us. Where trust fails, relationships and ultimately whole communities disintegrate. If, on the other hand, people become aware that everyone is fundamentally altruistic, a basis will be provided on which trust can be established. Wilson has also conducted research supporting this idea. Having acquired data on the level of altruistic inclination of high-school students in Binghamton, he overlaid this on a map of the town. What this revealed was that where residents were surrounded by caring neighbours, they professed themselves willing to help, whereas selfish neighbours bred selfishness. Like Pfaff, Wilson therefore advocates grass roots schemes to improve neighbourhoods and support social networks in order to maximise people's potential.

Wilson and Pfaff are right in that we are more likely to promote goodwill through careful study of the conditions that foster it and their evidence suggests that people are more altruistic when they are part of cohesive, flourishing environments. The encouraging message is that we do have the resources to be better, as long as we believe in the kindness of others. Therefore, reading these powerful new books on the existence of altruism could be the first step to making the world a much more pleasant place.

Vocabulary

Vocabulary related to community

1a Match the words below with the words with a similar meaning (1–6).

division guidelines inhabitant neighbourhood
project structure

1 community	3 scheme	5 policy
2 resident	4 network	6 sector

b Choose the correct option in *italics* to complete the sentences.

1 The local government has introduced a new *policy / structure* on the provision of open spaces.
2 In the *neighbourhood / scheme* where I live, there are several ways to get involved with town planning.
3 Last year people started working on a *network / project* to provide assistance to elderly people.
4 People who move into the apartment block are asked to respect other *residents / communities* and ensure the cleanliness of communal areas.
5 We have a *sector / scheme* to enable new residents to integrate into the village.
6 If you intend to join the local community centre, please follow the membership *networks / guidelines* on our website.

Academic collocations

2a Complete the collocations with the words below.

ethnic local rural virtual wider

Community

1 _____ community: a group of people that share an environment
2 _____ community: a group of people who live in the countryside
3 _____ community: a group that includes more than a small number of people immediately concerned by an issue
4 _____ community: a group of people who identify with each other based on common ancestral, social, cultural or national experience
5 _____ community: a network of people who interact through social media, potentially crossing geographical boundaries in order to pursue mutual interests or goals

current economic key national social

Policy

1 _____ policy: the ideas and guidelines that governments have about their citizens' lives and how to improve them
2 _____ policy: a very important policy
3 _____ policy: the policy that is being used now

4 _____ policy: the actions that governments take regarding money, taxation, budgets and other financial aspects of the country
5 _____ policy: the actions a government implements in order to achieve its objectives for the country as a whole

b Complete the text with the collocations in Exercise 2a.

Stoneville:
A great place to live

The residents of Stoneville report a high level of satisfaction with where they live. There are two main 1 _____ communities; Brazilians and South Islanders, but the 2 _____ community consists of a variety of people from many different countries. Many people moved there from the 3 _____ communities of the countryside in order to find employment and live in a place with better services and facilities. As the town flourished, the government became aware of the need for substantial investment in infrastructure. It introduced a series of 4 _____ policies a few years ago to set the standards for healthcare and education. The 5 _____ policy aimed to effectively integrate new citizens into the community. Overall, it has been a great success and as a result, people enjoy living in Stoneville.

c Write a description of your community. Use the vocabulary in this section.

Describe emotions

3 Complete the sentences with the correct adjective A, B or C.

1 The mayor was _____ with the positive reaction from the local community to her ideas for developing the town.
   A delighted   B devoted   C supportive
2 It is important to be _____ when someone goes out of their way to help you with something.
   A liberal   B overwhelmed   C appreciative
3 The secretary was _____ by the gifts and messages she received on her retirement day.
   A supportive   B sympathetic   C overwhelmed
4 The inhabitants of the town were _____ when the park was sold to an apartment construction company.
   A devoted   B outraged   C dreadful
5 Most people on the committee feel that the decision to stop the funding for the youth club was a _____ mistake.
   A dreadful   B liberal   C disgruntled

Speaking (Part 2)

Lead-in

1 What kinds of activities do people in your community share?

Develop topic-specific vocabulary

2a Discuss what you think the words below mean. Can you think of their opposites?

attentive   conscientious   generous   modest   sensitive
tolerant   warm-hearted

b Choose the correct option in *italics* to complete the two descriptions.

My neighbour's such a **1** *generous / tolerant* woman; she's always volunteering to help the families on our street. For example, she offers to babysit so that the parents can spend an evening in peace. She's extremely **2** *conscientious / tolerant* of young children, even when they are naughty. I'd imagine that it's because she used to be a teacher, so she's **3** *modest / sensitive* to the needs of children. Anyway, people are very grateful for her efforts, but she's so **4** *warm-hearted / modest*. She thinks her help is nothing special.

I think my grandfather is a very **5** *conscientious / attentive* person because he's always available to listen to people and he doesn't interrupt. He's also a **6** *tolerant / warm-hearted* man. I think this could be because he lived in different countries so he would have got used to integrating with people from a variety of backgrounds. I've learnt to be more **7** *sensitive / conscientious* in my studies from him because he believes in doing things properly.

c 🔊 8.1 Listen and check your answers.

Real and hypothetical situations and reactions

3a Read the sentences below. Which sentence relates to a real situation and which one relates to a hypothetical situation?

1 By being part of my local community youth club, I would really make a difference.
2 By being part of my local community youth club, I really made a difference.

b 🔊 8.2 Listen to the sentences and decide if the speaker is talking about a real (R) or a hypothetical (H) situation or reaction.

1 R/H   2 R/H   3 R/H   4 R/H   5 R/H   6 R/H

c Read audio script 8.2 on page 210 and discuss which language helped you identify the real and hypothetical sentences.

Pronunciation – connected speech 2

4a 🔊 8.3 Read and listen to the language examples (A–D). Match them with the type of connected speech (1–4).

A my train/might rain   C the best part
B I'd like to help you.   D Would you help me?

1 Sounds which disappear when a word is contracted.
2 Words which are difficult to separate because there is more than one way to separate them.
3 When the last sound of the first word and the first sound of the following word both change to a new sound.
4 When /t/ and /d/ sounds are between two consonants they disappear.

b Listen again and repeat phrases A–D. How do the sounds change?

c Which of these pronunciation features do you find the most difficult to achieve in fluent speech? How could you improve them?

Test practice

> **TEST STRATEGIES** page 174
> **EXPERT SPEAKING** page 188

5a Read the task card. You have 1 minute to prepare your answer.

Describe someone who has done something nice for you. You should say:
who this person is
what kind of person they are
what they did for you
and say how you could do something nice for them in return.

b Work in pairs and take turns to talk about the task card in Exercise 5a. Try to speak for two minutes. If possible, record your answers. Time your partner when he/she speaks and note any examples of:
• adjectives for personal qualities.
• language for real and hypothetical situations.
• the pronunciation features above.

Task analysis

6 Work in pairs. Review your and your partner's responses and discuss the questions.

1 How many adjectives for personal qualities did you use and were they used correctly?
2 How well did you use language to distinguish between real and hypothetical situations?
3 How fluent and connected was your speech?
4 How could you improve in these areas?

Listening (Section 2)

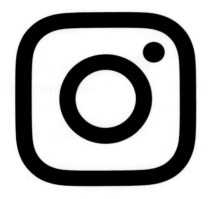

Before you listen

1 Can you name the websites from the images above? Which ones do you use? How do they help people? How are they connected to community?

Follow lines of argument

2a Read the test tasks in Exercise 3a. Decide on the order in which you expect to hear the following topics. What other topics might you hear?

Benefits of SoPals   Drawbacks of EverywhereUs
Single people   Benefits of EverywhereUs
The elderly   Teenagers   Future of SoPals
Drawbacks of Sweet

b Discuss the questions about the test tasks in Exercise 3a.

1 What type of talk do you think it will be (e.g. presentation, tour, etc.)? Why?
2 What synonyms can you think of for words within the questions?

c 🔊 8.4 Listen to the talk. Were your predictions from Exercises 2a and 2b correct?

Test practice

> TEST STRATEGIES pages 168 and 169

3a Listen again and complete the test tasks.

Questions 1–4
Look at the following reasons why different groups use social networks.
*Match each group with the correct reason, **A–E**.*
*Write the correct letter, **A–E**.*

1 The elderly
2 Teenagers
3 Mothers
4 Single people

List of reasons
A Loneliness
B Popularity
C Reconnecting
D Entertainment
E Reassurance

Questions 5–10
Complete the table below.
*Write **NO MORE THAN THREE WORDS** for each answer.*

Social networking site	Pros	Cons	Future
SoPals	5 _____ Popular in different countries	Harvests data on users	Moving into 6 _____ postings
EverywhereUs	A network for 7 _____	8 _____ is poor	Continue to grow
Sweet	Targeted at 9 _____ Most media supported	Childish design No app	Expand to other 10 _____

b Work in pairs and discuss how analysing the questions can help you follow the order information is given in.

Task analysis

4a Read audio script 8.4 on page 210 and mark where the topics change.

b With a partner, discuss the language used to indicate a change in topic.

Language development

Review of future forms

➤ EXPERT GRAMMAR page 180

1a Read the article and match the underlined future forms (1–9) with the structures (A–I).

New University Maker Space to open

The university **1** is creating a new space on the main campus for arts and innovation. The aim is that by the time our students graduate, **2** they will have been practising transferable skills for the creative industries for some time, which should improve their career prospects. The head of the Art School **3** will be opening this new 'maker space' area at 4p.m. on Friday. The centre **4** was going to open next month, but the area was ready earlier than expected.

A maker space is an area for a group of people to collaborate. While usually a public phenomenon, the Arts department has embraced this concept to enhance the students' creativity and is set to offer a range of activities from needlework to games design. Hopefully, all participants **5** will have made something new by the end of term. The university claims that this innovation **6** is going to be of great benefit to everyone. Students **7** will be able to meet a wider network of people and discover more about activities that **8** are on offer. Practice sessions **9** will also be provided for new crafts or skills.

A present simple	F future passive
B present continuous	G future perfect simple
C *going to*	H future perfect continuous
D future with *will*	I future in the past
E future continuous	

b Using the text in Exercise 1a, write the structures used for each future form.

c Complete the sentences using the correct form of the verbs in brackets. There may be more than one possible answer.

1 The community centre for retired people _____ (build) by next summer.
2 The council meeting _____ (hold) on Saturday evening.
3 By September, I _____ (help) with my friends' street cleaning project for a year.
4 The town _____ (receive) substantial investment to improve services for residents.
5 The advertising campaign _____ (focus) on promoting our local businesses.
6 The leisure centre _____ (start) offering parenting classes, but there was little demand from the local community.

d Work in pairs and discuss the questions.

1 What are you doing later today?
2 What are you going to do tomorrow?
3 Where will you go this weekend?
4 What will you be doing this time next week?
5 How do you think your life will have changed in five years' time?

Speculate on the future

2a Match the sentences (1–4) with the speaker's perspective (A–B).

1 Next year we might be living in a new country.
2 Next year we will be living in a new country.
3 Next year we are likely to be living in a new country.
4 Next year we are bound to be living in a new country.

A The speaker expresses a strong degree of certainty about a future event/situation occurring and has strong evidence to support his/her view.
B The speaker is speculating on the possibility of a future event/situation occurring and although he/she has some evidence of future possibility, the evidence is not strong enough to be sure.

b For the speculative sentences in Exercise 2a, which structures are stronger or weaker in their prediction?

c Rewrite the text below to make it more speculative.

The Rise of the YouTube influencer

According to an online magazine, the top five most influential figures for 13-18-year-old Americans are all young adult YouTube stars. The magazine predicts that this trend will continue for the foreseeable future because of the way young people use the internet. It has been suggested that the 'traditional celebrity' is going to disappear because the YouTube stars are more in touch with the lives of young adults. These internet stars have created a community which is very attractive for young people seeking to demonstrate their self-expression. Some sources estimate that in five years' time YouTube will have taken over as the main channel for cultivating a celebrity image, and communities of followers will be created for a plethora of celebrity types from niche writers to product advertisers to fashion advisors. In the not too distant future people will be finding their heroes online.

Writing (Task 2)

Lead-in

1 Why do people do volunteer work? What are the benefits of helping others in your community?

Understand situations, causes and effects

2a Read the paragraph below and identify:
- the situation • the cause • the effect

1 Modern lifestyles have undergone significant change recently. 2 In some countries, such as Japan, the number of people who live alone has risen to over 25 percent. 3 Many reasons have been suggested to account for this increase. One such reason, which applies to several nations, is that the family structure is of demonstrably less importance to individuals these days than it had been previously, and more citizens are interested in career development rather than the creation of a family unit. 4 However, those countries where living alone is more prevalent might start to see its downsides. 5 For example, property prices may rise as more and more people require a property for sole occupancy in preference to sharing. More worrying than this is the loss of community that could arise from living alone. Although living alone may not necessarily be lonely, integration in a community often originates from being part of a unit.

b Read the essay tasks (A–C) and answer the questions.

A *It would be of great benefit if all citizens undertook voluntary work within their own communities. Discuss the effects of such voluntary activities.*

B *The traditional sense of community is fragmenting as more people interact online rather than with actual people in their local environments. What are the reasons for this, and what are the effects?*

C *Despite living in urban environments, people are more isolated than ever before. Outline the reasons for this situation.*

1 Which task mostly deals with causes? What are the causes?
2 Which task mostly deals with effects? What are the effects?
3 Which task deals with both? What are the causes and effects?

c Discuss the causes and effects of the following. Write a list for each topic.
1 Declining community spirit
2 Lack of affordable housing
3 Increased production of waste

Develop a situation, cause and effect paragraph

3a Read the paragraph in Exercise 2a and match the functions below with the numbered sections (1–5) in the paragraph.

Topic sentence
Transition sentence from reason to result
Reason   Result   Explanation of situation

b Put the sentences below in the most logical order to form a cohesive paragraph.

A Not only do these groups meet in local halls, but there are now also social events for mothers in local cafes and restaurants.
B When more children are born, there are more mothers to accommodate, which in turn necessitates an increase in the number of groups.
C As well as reducing social isolation, these groups enhance community spirit.
D There has recently been an increase in the number of mother's groups in the local area.
E This could be the result of the sharp rise in the birth rate over the last year.
F These groups are considered by many as a much-needed part of society.
G However, some say that these groups are preventing others from using cafes and restaurants and should be confined to community halls.

Writing practice

➤ EXPERT WRITING page 198

4a Make an essay plan for one of the tasks in Exercise 2b. Outline the causes and/or effects and decide how you would organise your ideas into clear paragraphs.

b Write the essay for your chosen task. Try to write it in 40 minutes. Write at least 250 words.

Listening (Section 2)

Before you listen

1 Look at the following book titles. What are the titles in your language? Have you read them? Do you know the plot? What do they all have in common?

Cause and effect

2a Match the causes and effects, putting the cause first and the effect second.

The popularity of certain books
The creation of life-like special effects
The development of sound in film
The development of CGI
The disappearance of silent film
The development of film versions

b Work in pairs and use the linking words below to connect some of the ideas in Exercise 2a. Write five sentences.

was a key reason for   was as a result of
was the cause of   led to   was due to
was as a consequence

c 🔊 8.5 Listen to three people talking about the subjects in Exercise 2a and write down any words or phrases they use to talk about cause and effect.

Test practice

> TEST STRATEGIES page 168 and 169

3a Work in pairs. Look at the test tasks in Exercise 3b and discuss the questions (1–4).
1 What kind of talk might you hear?
2 What is the main subject?
3 What areas will be talked about? In which order?
4 In questions 5–9, what kinds of words are you looking for?

b 🔊 8.6 Complete the test tasks.

Questions 1–4

Look at the following reviewer's opinions about different books.

Match each book with the correct opinion, A–E.

Write the correct letter, A–E.

1 Wuthering Heights
2 The Life of Pi
3 The Girl with the Dragon Tattoo
4 The Maze Runner

List of opinions

A Puzzling   D Bland
B Stunning   E Emotional
C Disappointing

Questions 5–9

Complete the notes below.

*Write **NO MORE THAN THREE WORDS** for each answer.*

The Making of *The Shadow Thief*

5 *The Shadow Thief* was _____ in 1951.
6 The story explores the _____ of the Russian Revolution.
7 The film gives a _____ portrayal of one main character.
8 The film was delayed due to a difference of opinion with the _____ .
9 The film has been _____ the most this year.

Question 10

Choose the correct letter, A, B or C.

10 The reviewer thinks *The Shadow Thief* is
A overrated.
B fantastic.
C doomed.

Task analysis

4 Work in pairs. Think about your answers and discuss the questions.
1 Did you manage to follow the talk and answer all the questions?
2 Which questions were easier? Which were more difficult?

Language development and vocabulary

Cause and effect linking words

> **EXPERT GRAMMAR** page 181

1a Read the two sentences below. Which is correct and which is incorrect? Why?

    A Languages were developed as a result of the need to communicate.

    B Languages were developed as a result the need to communicate.

b Choose the correct linking words or phrases in *italics* to complete the text.

The Development of Morse Code:
changing communication in the 19th century

Morse Code was invented by an American called Samuel Finley Breese Morse. Before his invention, written notes were hand-delivered by messengers. **1** *As a result, / As a result of* the information could only be delivered as quickly as the fastest horse. Other ways of communicating included using flags, smoke signals and semaphore telegraphs. **2** *Because of / Because* the necessity for visual proximity between both parties, these forms could not be used in low visibility or at night. This was very problematic and limited their effectiveness. Samuel Morse created a telegraph device which transmitted messages using a special code which represented each letter of the alphabet. These were sent electronically as well as via light and radio waves and **3** *due to / therefore* the issues relating to other forms of sending messages quickly disappeared. **4** *Consequently, / As a result of* Morse's system began to be used all over the world for long-distance communication. Although nowadays other forms of communication such as satellites have become more widespread, it is still used by the Navy and in aviation.

c Using the text in Exercise 1b as a model, complete the sentences with either 'clause' or 'noun/noun phrase'.

    1 *Because* is followed by a _____ but *because of* is followed by a _____ .

    2 The words *as, since* and *because* all have the same meaning and are followed by a _____ .

    3 *As a result of* must be followed by a _____ .

    4 *Due to* is followed by a _____ .

    5 *Consequently* and *as a result* are followed by a comma and then a _____ .

    6 *Therefore* introduces a result and is followed by a _____ .

d Complete the sentences with a correct linking word or phrase from Exercise 1b. There may be more than one possibility.

    1 These days, people often feel stressed _____ the sheer quantity of emails they receive.

    2 Many older people now have started to use social media to communicate _____ they want to stay in touch with younger members of their family as well as those living abroad.

    3 Communicating online is far more convenient than talking by phone. _____ there is an increasing number of 'talking' apps being created.

    4 There is a wide array of communication options available nowadays _____ the fact that the breadth and complexity of technology has developed so rapidly.

    5 People now write fewer letters by hand. _____ , some historians worry that a valuable source of cultural understanding could be lost.

Noun phrases 2

2a Which of the underlined nouns in the noun phrase below is general and which is specific?

    The <u>problem</u> with <u>face-to-face meetings</u> is they are incredibly time-consuming compared to online forms of communication.

b Read the sentences and identify the noun phrases which follow the structure in Exercise 2a. Underline the general and specific nouns.

Teenage communication

    1 The issue of teen-adult communication has been a concern for many parents all over the world.

    2 Although the majority of parents think it is mainly related to mood swings and the lack of desire to communicate with adults, this is not entirely true.

    3 The main problem of adult and child misunderstanding concerns vocabulary and language choice.

    4 The use of a specific set of vocabulary enables young people to bond and start to develop their adult identity while simultaneously distancing themselves from more parental language.

    5 However, the true impact of this linguistic disparity is not fully explored in research.

c Complete the sentences in your own words.

    1 The issue of _____ is the most important challenge for all new students.

    2 The results of _____ could be catastrophic for the environment.

    3 The question of _____ needs to be considered carefully when visiting another country.

    4 The cause of _____ might well be associated with lifestyle factors.

Speaking (Part 2)

Vocabulary development

1a How do we form our opinions of other people's personalities? What do you think the people in the photo might be like in terms of their personality? What makes you think that?

b Complete the sentences with the words below.

earth   eye   life   nature   tongue

1 I've always wanted to meet Barack Obama. He doesn't seem self-important. In fact, he comes across as really down to _____ , just like everyday people.
2 With his oversized glasses and fancy costumes, Elton John always appears larger than _____ .
3 If I ever met my hero, I imagine I'd be so surprised that I'd become _____ -tied instantly.
4 I don't think it's good to meet the celebrities you admire as they're probably different from how you've imagined them and you might not see eye to _____ on issues.
5 I admire successful businessmen such as Steve Jobs. I'd imagine they'd have to be quite a force of _____ to achieve what they have.

c Match the phrases in Exercise 1b with their meanings (A–E).

A to be friendly and reasonable
B someone who is very determined
C to agree with someone
D to become unable to express yourself
E someone who is more exciting than most people

d Think of two people you know well and describe them, using some of the phrases above.

Focus on grammatical range and accuracy

2a Turn to page 183 and read the descriptors for bands 7 and 8. What is the difference between the bands in relation to the words below?

limited   frequent   complex   error-free

b Which of the grammatical structures below do you think are more complex?

Conditionals
Past simple
Present perfect continuous
Comparatives
Cleft sentences
Non-defining relative clauses

c Discuss the questions below. Try to use the appropriate structures from Exercise 2b.

1 If you were going to meet your hero, what would you say to them?
2 Which musician, author or artist do you admire the most and why?
3 How would you describe your favourite celebrity?

Test practice

➤ TEST STRATEGIES page 174

3a Work in pairs. Read the task card and discuss what kinds of structures you could use in your answer.

> *Describe a famous person you would like to meet. You should say:*
>
> *who this person is*
>
> *why you would like to meet them*
>
> *what you think they would be like*
>
> *and explain what you would say to them if you ever met them.*

b Prepare to speak about this topic. You have 1 minute to make notes.

c Work in pairs and take turns to speak for 2 minutes. Record your answers if possible.

d 🔊 8.7 Listen to a student's answer and compare it with yours.

Assess and improve

4 Work in pairs. Listen to your answers and analyse them, using the list below.

- Write a list of the grammatical structures you used.
- Did you use a range of grammar?
- Did you use any complex structures?
- Can you identify and correct any mistakes?

Reading (*Yes/No/Not given*; Multiple choice)

Before you read

1 Work in groups and discuss the questions.

1 Do you keep or would you like to keep pets or working animals? Why?

2 Think of ways in which humans in your country co-operate or work with animals.

2 Skim the passage. What is the main argument?

1 Our ties with animals are weakening as we place more importance on technology than the outdoors.

2 Animals have been a key influence in shaping how the human species has developed.

Test practice

3 Read the strategies and complete the test tasks.

> TEST STRATEGIES pages 171 and 172

Questions 1–5

Do the following statements agree with the views/ claims given in the passage? Write

YES *if the statement agrees with the views/ claims given in the passage*

NO *if the statement contradicts the views/ claims given in the passage*

NOT GIVEN *if there is no information on this*

1 Complex tools were invented so that ape men could kill large prey.

2 Developing communication skills enabled humans to compete with animals for food.

3 The main significance of the cave paintings is the high standard of the art.

4 Cave paintings portrayed more males than females on the hunt.

5 The relationship between dogs and humans in prehistoric times was mutually beneficial.

> HELP

1 Why did our ancestors learn to make tools from rocks?

2 Are there any examples in the passage of these communication skills?

3 They may have been of a high standard but was this the main significance?

Questions 6–7

*Choose **TWO** letters, **A–E**.*

*In which **TWO** of these ways did our ancestors benefit from domesticating animals?*

A evolving superior practical skills

B developing an understanding of emotional and nonverbal skills

C acquiring a means of companionship in the home

D expanding the range of supplies available

E obtaining an important new source of nutrition

> HELP

C This may well be true, but does the passage actually say this?

E Is there an example of this?

Task analysis

4 Work in pairs and discuss the questions.

1 Which of the strategies suggested for the *Yes/No/ Not given* task did you use? Which did you find most helpful?

2 In the multiple-choice task, why did you decide against the options that you did not choose?

Discussion

5 Discuss the questions.

1 In what ways do domesticated animals and humans communicate with each other? Are some animals more successful than others?

2 To what extent do you agree with Shipman's comment 'Our links to the animal world are precious and shouldn't be taken for granted?' In which ways are domestic animals still important in our current lifestyles? Give reasons and examples.

Theanimalconnection

Professor of anthropology Pat Shipman believes that when our prehistoric ancestors began to interact with animals, there were adaptive consequences.

Humans became masters of the planet for a startling reason: our love of animals gave us unsurpassed power over nature. This is the claim of Dr Pat Shipman, of Pennsylvania State University, who says in her book *The Animal Connection* that our prehistoric ancestors' intense relationship with other creatures propelled the human race towards global domination.

Shipman traces humanity's animal connection to the period 2.5 million years ago when our hominid ancestors first made tools. These crafted pieces of stone still litter sites in eastern Africa and bear testimony to the mental transformation in our ancestors' brains. According to Shipman, the ape men had a mental image of the kind of implements they needed for a specific purpose and created them by chipping away at a large piece of stone until they achieved their desired result, which were tools for dissecting carcasses. Rather than using them as weapons to kill animals or to fell trees, their primary use was to process dead animals that had already been brought down by other carnivores such as leopards and cheetahs. Until that point we had been a prey species, but the development of these devices transformed hominids from predominantly plant-eating apes into predators, who began by scavenging for meat before going on to hunt on their own behalf.

It was at this crucial point that our special relationship with the animal kingdom began. Meat provided our ancestors with a wonderful, rich and nutritious sort of sustenance but left them in a vulnerable position and in danger of being consumed themselves. To survive, they had to improve their observational skills and learn about the behaviour of a vast number of different species, not only the ones they wanted to kill but also the ones they wanted to avoid. The ability to make judgements about what other animals would do next was most likely as important to obtaining food as was the knowledge of how to manufacture stone tools. In the end, this expertise would have become crucial to human survival; in fact, the necessity for collaboration and the sharing of knowledge about how prey animals and predators behaved was to become a driving force behind the development of symbols and language some 200,000 years ago.

This is well illustrated in the paintings created by humans 20,000 to 30,000 years ago and discovered in caves in France and other locations, which demonstrate that after 2 million years of evolution, humans had become utterly fixated by animals as a result of our own dependency on them for our own survival. In these artistic creations, there are no landscapes and only a handful of poorly executed depictions of humans. There are, however, stunningly beautiful and superbly crafted artistic depictions of lions, stags, horses, bulls and many other animals which have been painted on walls, sculpted out of clay or rock and even carved out of wood.

Interestingly, dogs are rarely depicted in cave art which suggests that cave painters may have regarded them not so much as the game animals they tended to depict, but more as fellow-travellers. As it was, not long after the paintings were created, the dog became a domesticated animal. Sometime later, for different reasons, so too did the horse, sheep, goat and other animals. Shipman believes that the common explanation – food – is unlikely, since killing an animal in the wild would have had the same outcome without the need to wait. A more likely explanation, in her view, is that, rather than merely being a source of food, animals were transformed into renewable resources, providing milk, wool and opportunities for the production of tools and clothing. This transition to using animals as living tools was to give humans a decisive edge in adapting to new environments and gaining an evolutionary shortcut. The development was also crucial because humans had to learn to put themselves in the mind of these creatures in order to get them to do their bidding, thereby enhancing their ability to empathise, both with animals and with members of their own species

Shipman speculates that the affinity between humans and dogs manifested itself mainly in the hunt. Dogs would help humans to identify their prey, but they would also work, the theory goes, as beasts of burden, being fed and cared for in return. Since transporting animal carcasses is an energy-intensive task, getting dogs to do this work would mean that humans could concentrate their energy on more productive work: hunting, gathering, reproducing. Shipman argues that because of this co-operation, humans and their canine friends got stronger together over time.

Looking at the situation today, our special relationship with animals is revealed through our desire to have pets. "No other creature on Earth would waste resources on a member of another family, let alone a member of another species," asserts Shipman. It is a unique human attribute because we have evolved such close ties with specific animals over the millennia and because we are adapted to empathise with other creatures. However, as society becomes increasingly urbanised those ties are being stretched and broken "Our links to the animal world are precious and shouldn't be taken for granted," says Shipman.

Writing (Task 2)

Lead-in

1 Look at the ways of communicating. How has communication in your country changed over the last 20 years? What positive and negative effects do you think this has had on society?

Understand the task

> EXPERT WRITING page 198

2a Read the essay task. What kinds of effect could the writer write about?

> Spending time online has affected the communication skills of young people both positively and negatively.
>
> Discuss the effects of increased online activity on communication skills.

b Read the plan for the essay in Exercise 2a. What effects does the writer mention in his/her plan?

> Para 1: ANSWER: More positive than negative effects
> WHY? Still talk with people/More flexible communicators
>
> Para 2: Young people still talk face-to-face with others, e.g. at school, out, with family. Internet use not stopped this although maybe they do it less.
>
> Para 3: More flexible communicators. Internet means that young people communicate in new and diff. ways. They can speak, text, message, Facebook post, blog and face-to-face with Skype. Maybe even better communicators really?
>
> Para 4: Conc. Online time has positive effects on communication skills of young people.

c Write your plan for the essay in Exercise 2a. Use your own ideas.

d Work in pairs and compare your plans. Answer the questions below.

1 How well have you answered the question?
2 What improvements can you make?
3 Are your arguments logically ordered?
4 Is the paragraph structure clear?
5 Have you used linking words/phrases effectively?
6 Have you provided supporting information for your main arguments?

Plan the task

3a Turn to page 190 and read the descriptors for lexical resource. Work in pairs and discuss the differences between bands 7 and 8.

b Read the list of good practice for lexical resource below and add your own ideas.

1 Try to vary vocabulary.
2 Avoid repetitive use of words/phrases.
3 Check word forms are correct.

c Write some sentences you could use in the essay task in Exercise 2a using the words below.

---

adolescence   ameliorate   communicative ability   deficit   deteriorate
isolated   linguistic   socialisation   technological   verbal

---

Language and content

4a Complete the sentences with collocations.

1 Teenagers might use social media as an extension of
   r_____-l_____ relationships.
2 Interacting f_____ - to-f_____ is still a popular method of communication.
3 Teenagers overwhelmingly use texting as their main m_____ of communicating.
4 Many young people prefer using c_____ rooms to using the telephone.
5 Facebook is probably the world's most popular tool for staying in c_____ with friends.
6 There are many disadvantages to m_____ in person compared to simply getting in t_____ online.

b Read the paragraph below. Correct the five underlined mistakes.

> Teenagers communicate differently from many other groups. Not only do they <u>pass</u> more time online, but their online conversations tend to be short back and <u>forward</u> dialogues with a variety of friends. This kind of communication can last for hours and many teenagers do this while <u>simultaneous</u> playing computer games. This means that meaningful communication is lost while <u>distraction</u> communication becomes the <u>normal</u>.

c Discuss what other words the writer of the text in Exercise 4b could have used to describe how teenagers communicate.

Write your essay

5a Read your plan from Exercise 2c. Make a list of words and collocations you could use in your essay. Work in pairs and discuss your ideas.

b Write your answer to the essay task. Write at least 250 words.

Assess and improve

6a Underline any unusual items of vocabulary you have tried to use. Work in pairs and discuss whether you think these words have been used correctly or not.

b Improve the lexis in your answer. Use comments from Exercise 6a as a guide.

Review

1a Match the sentence beginnings (1–5) with the endings (A–E).

1 There is an event in the local community
2 The council implemented a new residents' parking
3 In order to claim discounts on the town's attractions, proof that you are a
4 In every community it is important to have a support
5 Although governments have control over national issues,

A scheme which has reduced congestion in many areas.
B network for those who are disadvantaged or vulnerable.
C policy can also be set at a local level by local government.
D centre to raise funds for local children.
E resident in the local area will be required.

b Use TWO words below to complete the sentences.

benefits   cause   diversity   impact   issue   migration
overcrowding   poverty

1 The _____ of _____ includes lack of jobs, lack of education and a fragile economy.
2 The _____ of _____ can be both positive and negative for a receiving country.
3 The _____ of _____ is becoming more and more salient as increasing numbers of citizens move to large cities.
4 The _____ of _____ are numerous and range from new tastes and music to new beliefs and attitudes.

c Complete the sentences with the correct word or phrase below.

because of   due   as a result   therefore

1 It is often difficult to understand young children's reactions to situations _____ their inability to express themselves clearly at a young age.
2 More and more teenagers are becoming interested in reading _____ to the popularity of books such as the Harry Potter series.
3 Online communication brings a certain number of risks for the younger generation _____ laws should be introduced to combat these risks.
4 Our local community has organised a series of parties in the neighbourhood. _____ , people have been able to meet each other more.

2a Choose the correct option in *italics* to complete the sentences.

1 The school *is to build / was going to build* a sports centre here, but they couldn't secure funding for it.
2 A new local government representative *will appoint / will have been appointed* by next summer.
3 This city *is going to receive / is receiving* a $200 million investment in transport next year.
4 Next summer, we *will be celebrating / will have celebrated* the 200-year anniversary of this village and there will be parades and parties all summer.
5 Next year, students *will provide / will be provided* with pens and books for school in the first semester.
6 Due to having received a promotion, *I'll be moving / I will have moved* to the company's New York office next year.
7 The library *was going to open / is going to open* its new wing this month, but this has been postponed due to problems with the roof.
8 The winning city in the bid to host the next Olympic Games *is announcing / will be announced* next month.

b Correct the errors in the sentences.

1 The students couldn't study abroad that summer because of the university couldn't fund the places.
2 The carnival was cancelled at the last minute as rain.
3 As a result the rise in house prices, many people struggled to buy a property in the area.
4 The student won a scholarship due to she had excellent results.
5 Many people gathered in the town square to celebrate therefore crowded.

c Put the words/phrases in the correct order to make sentences.

1 a lack of / The cause of / teenagers / may / loneliness amongst / 'real' friendships. / well be

_____

2 underestimated. / of / The issue / cyber-bullying / must not be

_____

3 needs to be / online personal security / further addressed. / The question of

_____

4 tired eyes. / spending / online / The result of / is often / headaches and / too much time

_____

5 is that / with online communication / The problem / it is impersonal.

_____

9 Being successful

9a Training

- **Reading**: Infer meaning and attitude (Multiple choice; *Yes/No/Not given*)
- **Vocabulary**: Vocabulary related to talent; Collocations for success and talent; Describe personal qualities
- **Speaking**: Develop topic-specific vocabulary; Create thinking time (Part 3)
- **Listening**: General and specific language (Section 3: Sentence completion)
- **Language development**: Explain how something works; Describe what something looks like
- **Writing**: Work with unknown vocabulary; Write about unknown processes (Task 1: Diagrams)

9b Testing

- **Listening**: Section 3: Sentence completion; Multiple choice
- **Language development and vocabulary**: Estimation and indication; Replace *thing*
- **Speaking**: Part 3: Discuss work and skills
- **Reading**: Multiple choice; *Yes/No/Not given*
- **Writing**: Task 1: Describe changes over time

Successful People

- Are grateful
- Give compliments
- Admit when they fail
- Congratulate others on their victories
- Are forgiving
- Read regularly
- Keep a diary
- Share information
- Want others to be successful
- Are happy
- Share ideas
- Are always learning
- Are not afraid of change
- Keep a 'to-do' list
- Have life goals

Lead-in

1   What do you think of the infographic above? To what extent do you agree that these points define a successful person? What points would you add/remove? Why?

Reading (Multiple choice; *Yes/No/Not given*)

Before you read

1 What is the meaning of *multitasking* and why has it become common in the 21st century?

Infer meaning and attitude

2a Look at the underlined words in the reading passage and answer the questions.

1 What is a 'click-hole'? Do you think the writer approves of task switching?
2 What does 'porous' mean? Is *porous* positive or negative in the context?

b Look at these phrases in the context of the passage and answer the questions.

1 Of course, there is much to be said for "focus", but there is much to be said for immaculate handwriting too. ... the world has moved on. (line 55–57)
Does the writer think that focus is essential? Why?
2 For those who insist that great work can only be achieved through superhuman focus, think long and hard on this discovery. (line 90–92)
What does 'this discovery' refer to? What point is the writer making?

Test practice

3 Read the strategies and complete the test tasks.

> **TEST STRATEGIES** pages 171 and 172

Questions 1–5
Choose the correct letter A, B, C or D.

1 What does the writer say about the impact of multitasking in the modern world?
   A Job applicants who can do several things at the same time have a big advantage.
   B Achieving a satisfactory work-life balance can be stressful.
   C Being able to do what you want when you want is a great pleasure.
   D Technology has a bad effect on children's performance at school.

2 What did David Strayer's study reveal?
   A It is more dangerous to speak on a mobile phone while driving than to have drunk alcohol.
   B It is safe to drive while talking on a mobile if you have both hands on the steering wheel.
   C A driver's reaction time is slower when speaking on a mobile phone.
   D Most people do not accept that total concentration is required when driving.

3 What was unexpected about Carson's laboratory tests?
   A Being required to switch tasks made participants more creative.
   B The original ideas produced by participants bore little relation to genuine creativity.
   C Switching attention between different tasks led to higher levels of achievement overall.
   D An ability to switch tasks is a common feature of writers and artists.

4 What is the advantage of low latent inhibition?
   A It encourages us to ignore extraneous information.
   B It prompts us to abandon an activity which has become time-consuming.
   C It prevents us from becoming overstressed about what we are doing.
   D It gives us the opportunity to view a situation from a different angle.

5 What is the writer's main purpose in the passage?
   A to explain the differences between multitasking and task switching
   B to highlight the dangers of working on multiple projects at the same time
   C to warn readers about the potential pressures of modern life
   D to increase awareness of the benefits of successful multitasking

Questions 6–9
Do the following statements agree with the views/claims of the writer? Write

YES   *if the statement agrees with the views/claims of the writer*

NO   *if the statement contradicts the views/claims of the writer*

NOT GIVEN *if it is impossible to say what the writer thinks about this*

6 Real multitasking requires one or both of the tasks to be done almost automatically.
7 Task switching is a way of coping with underlying anxiety about uncompleted work.
8 Paying attention to just one activity at a time should be a realistic goal in the modern world.
9 Simultaneous involvement in different office tasks means very few are completed on time.

Multitasking: how to survive in the 21st century

Modern life now forces us to do a multitude of things at once – but can we? Should we?

The superpower we all want is the capacity to do several things at once. However, unlike other superpowers, being able to multitask is now taken for granted and widely regarded as a basic requirement for employability. Fuelled by technology and social change, the boundaries between work and play have become somewhat blurred. Because you can do your weekly shop whilst sitting at your desk and handle a work query while queuing at the supermarket, time once wasted is now productive.

Nevertheless, it is perhaps only now that we are starting to concede that the blessings of a multitasking life are not unmitigated. The majority of people living in more industrialised countries feel overwhelmed by the sheer number of activities in which they might plausibly be engaged at any one time. Equally, teenagers do their homework whilst simultaneously listening to music, watching TV and chatting on their mobiles. Whilst youngsters might believe that they are deftly managing all these inputs concurrently, various studies suggest otherwise.

Indeed, there is overwhelming evidence in favour of the proposition that we should only focus on one activity at any one time. Consider a study led by Professor of Cognition and Neural Science, David Strayer, who used a high-fidelity driving simulator to assess the performance of drivers who were speaking on a mobile phone. While these drivers did not adopt the aggressive, risk-taking style of drunk drivers, they were found to take much longer to respond to events outside the car and also failed to notice many of the visual cues around them. Strayer's infamous conclusion: driving while using a mobile phone is as dangerous as driving while under the influence.

Less famous was Strayer's finding that it made no difference whether the driver was using a hand-held or hands-free phone. The problem, it seems, with talking while driving is a shortage of mental bandwidth rather than a shortage of hands. Yet this discovery has made little impression either on public opinion or, surprisingly, the law. In the UK, for example, it is an offence to use a hand-held phone when driving but perfectly legal to use a hands-free device.

However, before concluding that multitasking is wholly negative, it is probably useful to define our terms. There are at least four different practices which fit under the label "multitasking". One is genuine multitasking, such as playing the piano and singing or patting your head while rubbing your stomach. It is possible but at least one of the tasks needs to be so practised as to be done without conscious thought. Then there is the challenge of creating a presentation while also fielding phone calls and monitoring your email. A better term for this would be task switching,

as our attention flits between the different tasks. We do this because we can't forget about all our unfinished tasks. It is the overlapping possibilities that take the mental toll as our subconscious keeps reminding us that the task needs attention. Of course, there is much to be said for "focus", but there is much to be said for immaculate handwriting too. People are not perfect and the world has moved on. Whilst there is something rather appealing about blocking internet access, it is also somewhat futile.

Task switching is often confused with a third, quite different activity, the guilty pleasure of becoming distracted and disappearing down an unending click-hole of celebrity gossip and social media updates. The final type of multitasking is simply the condition of having a lot of things to do, which can in fact be highly productive. Coordinating multiple projects is not the same as doing them all at once, and not necessarily a stumbling block to getting things done by the deadline. In fact, when a team of psychologists interviewed almost 100 exceptionally creative people, every one made a practice of keeping several projects going simultaneously.

Moreover, even frenetic flipping between Facebook, email and a document can be beneficial. When psychologist Shelley Carson recruited subjects for a test of rapid task switching, each individual was given a pair of tasks to do online: solve a set of anagrams and read an article from an academic journal. Half the participants were presented with the tasks sequentially but the other half had to switch between the two tasks every few minutes. As predicted, task switching delayed the subjects and confused their thinking, leading to a poor performance. However, the involuntary multitaskers produced a greater number and variety of answers and showed more originality on tests of "divergent" thinking, such as listing all the consequences of a world in which everyone has three arms. One might reasonably object that these tasks are trivial measures of innovative thinking but it appears that scores on these laboratory tests for divergent thinking correlate with substantial creative achievements, such as creating an award-winning piece of visual art. For those who insist that great work can only be achieved through superhuman focus, think long and hard on this discovery.

Carson and colleagues have also found an association between significant creative achievement and a trait which psychologists term "low latent inhibition". Latent inhibition is the subconscious filter that allows us to ignore apparently irrelevant stimuli and prevents us from being overwhelmed by them. Yet people whose filters are a bit porous have a big creative edge. "The act of switching back and forth can grease the wheels of thought," says psychologist John Kounios. He suggests that doing something totally new can help us abandon bad ideas that we are fixated on, leaving us free to solve the problem in another way.

It would seem that in an age where we face constant distraction, people who are particularly prone to being distracted are in fact flourishing creatively.

Vocabulary

Vocabulary related to talent

1a Choose the correct definition of the words (1–6).

1 achievement: *a goal that you succeed in achieving / a competition that you win*
2 investment: *a technique for making something / the time and energy spent on doing something*
3 motivation: *the eagerness / the pressure* to do something
4 commitment: a *promise / desire* to do something or behave in a particular way
5 capability: *the natural ability to do something / the approach to a difficult task*
6 coordination: the organisation of people or things so they *produce better results / work well together*

b Complete the text with the correct form of words from Exercise 1a.

Talented people can be found in a variety of professions ranging from those involved in entertainment to more mundane roles in commercial organisations. However, they all share some fundamental characteristics. One of which is making a 1 _____ to themselves to perform a particular task, despite the possibility of this being challenging or time-consuming. Although they may possess the requisite 2 _____ to achieve this, they still need to have a high level of 3 _____ in order to fulfil such challenges. Without this, there is a tendency to abandon the task due to a lack of desire. The 4 _____ of talented people result from the presence of these characteristics combined with considerable hard work.

c Work in groups and discuss the topics.

1 An achievement you are incredibly proud of
2 Something you invested a lot of time and effort in
3 Your motivation to study English
4 A time when you showed commitment to something
5 A unusual skill or capability you possess

Collocations for success and talent

2a Choose the correct option in *italics* to complete the definitions.

1 *transferable / changing* skill: a skill developed in one situation which can be used in another
2 *wanted / desired* outcome: the result that someone wants from a situation
3 *broad / ranging* spectrum: possessing a large number of something
4 *driving / pushing* force: the power or energy which sets something or someone in motion
5 *overriding / pivotal* role: something or someone important for the success of something else
6 *mutual / concerted* effort: a serious attempt to do or achieve something

b Complete the sentences with the collocations in Exercise 2a.

1 The team's coach played a _____ in us winning the championship last year.
2 Problem-solving is an example of a _____ which improves employment prospects.
3 Polymaths are people who have a _____ of expertise and knowledge.
4 The director of the company has been the _____ behind its recent success.
5 Being selected to represent their country is the _____ for most sportspeople.
6 Inventors have to make a _____ to continue their work after every failure.

c Write five questions of your own using the collocations in Exercise 2a. Work in pairs and take turns to ask and answer your questions.

Describe personal qualities

3a Complete the definitions with the words below.

accomplished   expressive   innovative   inspirational
single-minded   tenacious

1 A _____ person has one clear aim and works very hard to achieve it without deviating from this goal.
2 Someone who is _____ provides encouragement or fosters motivation in others.
3 A _____ individual is unwilling to stop trying even when there are setbacks.
4 Someone who is _____ tends to show very clearly what they think or feel.
5 An _____ person uses or creates methods and techniques that are new, different and superior to those that existed before.
6 An _____ individual is very skilful or very successful in the area in which they work.

b Choose the correct option in *italics* to complete the text.

Bill Gates' considerable financial success demonstrates that he is clearly an 1 *accomplished / expressive / innovative* businessperson and his decision to use his wealth to fund the Bill and Melinda Gates Foundation is an 2 *expressive / inspirational / accomplished* model for ethically minded businesspeople. One example of the foundation's work includes its 3 *innovative / tenacious / expressive* determination to rid the developing world of polio despite many hurdles such as geographical and cultural barriers to vaccination. At present, another of the charity's objectives is finding 4 *single-minded / expressive / innovative* ways of handling money in countries that do not have a traditional banking structure.

Speaking (Part 3)

Lead-in

1 What does the metaphor about success mean? What personal qualities would you say great achievements are based on?

Develop topic-specific vocabulary

2a Complete the text with the idioms below. You may need to change the form of the idiom and/or pronouns. There is one idiom you do not need.

be a cut above   go to great lengths
have a hidden talent   put your mind to
set your sights on   stand out from the crowd

During the first decade of the 21st century, talent shows such as *The X Factor*, *American Idol* and *The Voice* became an extremely popular genre of television. In these shows, the contestants usually perform songs in an attempt to try to capture the judges' attention by 1 _____ . In order to win, the contestants have to 2 _____ the other performers. Many of them have 3 _____ to take part in the contest and have been practising for many years. Some have even given up their jobs for this once-in-a-lifetime opportunity. These talent shows are an absolutely fascinating example of the psychology behind the quest for success in the music industry as those who win these talent shows often state that they had 4 _____ becoming a successful performer from an early age. Sometimes there are unexpected winners and it is not always the case that the people with the best voices win. This demonstrates that winning can be more about 5 _____ achieving success rather than actual talent.

b Write six questions using each of the idioms in Exercise 2a. Ask them to the class.

Create thinking time

3a 🔊 9.1 Listen to a candidate's answer and read audio script 9.1 on page 211. Underline the phrases the candidate uses to get some 'thinking time' and to deal with unknown words.

b How does the candidate use his voice to signal thinking time and when he is unsure of a specific word?

c Read the phrases below (1–8) and match them with the functions (A–D).

1 That's an interesting question ...
2 What I'm trying to say is ...
3 Success and society? Well, ...
4 You want to know my feelings on ...
5 I've not thought much about this before, but ...
6 So, you're asking whether I think ...
7 I'm not sure if this is the right way to put it, but ...
8 Talent and its importance ...

A Select keywords and repeat
B Reformulate the question
C Use a thinking-time phrase
D Signal an explanation

d Work in pairs and discuss the topics. Use the techniques in Exercises 3b and 3c to create thinking time.

1 Talent is natural and cannot be learnt.
2 Everyone is talented in more than one area.
3 Children should be taught that making an effort is more important than success.

Test practice

➤ **TEST STRATEGIES** page 175

➤ **EXPERT SPEAKING** page 189

4a Read the discussion questions below. Think of some words in your language which you do not know in English but would be useful when answering the questions.

1 Which personality traits would you say are the main contributors to being successful?

2 What do you think about teaching children and young people that success is something they should always aim for?

3 How can the pressure to be successful be damaging for individuals?

b Work in pairs and take turns to ask and answer the questions in Exercise 4a using the techniques A–D in Exercise 3c.

Task analysis

5 Work in pairs and analyse your responses. Check you used some of the techniques in Exercise 3c.

Listening (Section 3)

Before you listen

1a Look at the photos of world record breakers. What records do you think they broke?

b What characteristics do you think people need to possess to break a world record?

General and specific language

2a Read the sentences. Which one is general and which one is specific? Why?

1 To break a land speed record, it is essential to have bravery, great skill and determination.
2 There are many qualities needed to be a record breaker.

b Make the underlined words more specific by adding the words below before them.

long-term financial   personality   pivotal   quality of successful tech

1 Commitment plays a <u>role</u> in being successful.
2 Financial success can improve the <u>life</u> that people have.
3 Many entrepreneurs have created <u>start-ups</u> in the last 20 years.
4 Success is largely down to the <u>traits</u> of an individual.
5 If you want to be successful in business, you must think about the <u>goals</u>.

c Read the sentences in Exercise 2b. How does the meaning of each sentence change with the added words?

3a You are going to hear a group of students discussing success. Which of the subjects below do you think might be more abstract?

1 Characteristics of record breakers
2 Examples of new records
3 The first records set
4 Ideas on how record-breaking inspires others
5 Theories about the characteristics of successful people

b 🔊 9.2 Listen to the students discussing their presentation. Which of the topics in Exercise 3a do they mention?

Test practice

> **TEST STRATEGIES** page 168

4a Listen again and complete the test task.

Questions 1–5
Complete the sentences below.
Write **NO MORE THAN THREE** *words for each answer.*

1 The group is going to use _____ to identify what it takes to be successful.
2 They will try to identify _____ of the individuals they focus on.
3 By moving from examples to theory, they are taking an _____ .
4 The female who has the _____ is discussed as an example.
5 Penny thinks that their _____ will ensure their work is taken seriously.

b Work in pairs and compare your answers. Have you used the same amount of detail?

Task analysis

5a With a partner, discuss which words in the answers are general and which are more specific.

b Read audio script 9.2 on page 211 and find other examples of phrases containing general and specific nouns.

Discussion

6 What do you think drives individuals to accomplish these kinds of achievements? How do these individuals do this? Do you think it is through luck, hard work, natural ability or a combination of all three factors?

Language development

Explain how something works

> **EXPERT GRAMMAR** page 181

1a Match the phrases (1–4) with the grammatical structures (A–D).

1 the part which makes
2 the thing which is used
3 the bit that you use to move
4 what you use to make

A noun + relative pronoun + present simple passive
B relative pronoun + present simple + infinitive
C noun + relative pronoun + present simple
D noun + relative pronoun + present simple + infinitive

b Match the sentence beginnings (1–4) with the endings (A–D).

1 It is what people use
2 This is the thing that
3 They are what you
4 It is the part which is

A used to change the settings.
B to measure their temperature.
C makes climbing up mountains easier.
D use to control the air flow.

2 Read the text and underline the language which explains how bionic limbs work.

Prosthetic body parts have been in existence for centuries but today, bionic arms and legs are so highly developed that they can enable disabled athletes to achieve outstanding results. Modern limb technology is complex in its design with each element providing a specific function. For example, at the top of a bionic leg is the socket which joins the artificial element to its host's body. Then there is the pylon. It is the section which is used to provide support. This element is much like a metal pole which acts as a substitute for the actual leg. Lastly, the bionic leg needs a suspension system. This is the part that surgeons use to attach the limb to the body and it is usually a belt or set of straps. Some bionic limbs even have small motors. They are what people use to control the prosthetic device so that it moves in a more natural fashion.

Describe what something looks like

3a Match the sentences (1–4) with what they are describing (A–D).

1 The majority of these types of traditional buildings are constructed from brick and stone.
2 This fitness device consists of a small computer and a battery.
3 The new stadium is shaped like a long oval.
4 Many internal medical devices are millimetres in diameter.

A structure
B size
C material
D form

b Underline the descriptive language used in the sentences in Exercise 3a.

c Complete the sentences using similar phrases to those in Exercise 3a. Use no more than three words.

1 His new diet predominantly _____ protein to build muscle strength.
2 The durability of the building was due to it having _____ flexible glass and modern plastics.
3 Our new tracking sensor is only a few _____ .
4 Some new running shoes have a heel _____ disc for extra comfort.
5 The new rowing machine _____ lightweight materials in order to improve performance.
6 The bicycle repair kit _____ some glue and a selection of plastic strips.

d Look at the photos of objects from Module 5. Choose one object and describe it to your partner using language from this section.

e Choose another object and write a description of it using language from this section. Compare your descriptions in pairs.

Writing (Task 1)

Lead-in

1 What famous modern cities can you name? What factors make cities famous nowadays?

Work with unknown vocabulary

2a Look at the following diagram. How did this kind of city design keep the inhabitants safe?

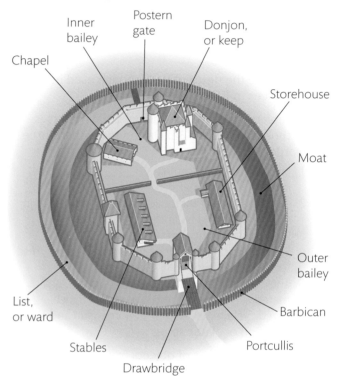

b Use visual clues in the diagram to match the words below with their descriptions.

> drawbridge   keep   moat

1 The _____ is the circle of water surrounding the city walls.
2 The large gate that lowers to allow people entrance is known as the _____ .
3 One of the buildings in the walled city was a _____ , which is the largest building.

c Now write one explanatory sentence for another word in the diagram that you are unsure of.

Write about unknown processes

3a Look at the diagram of the Roman and modern aqueducts above. Work in pairs and discuss:
1 what the overall process is.
2 how familiar you are with the two processes.
3 where the diagrams start and finish.
4 what the differences are between the two diagrams.
5 what each word given might mean.
6 the type of words used.

Water supply: Roman Aqueduct

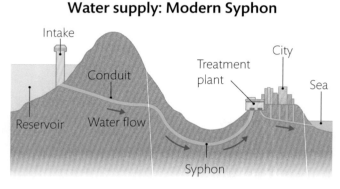

Water supply: Modern Syphon

b Whether the nouns are known or unknown to you, think of the verbs that describe the activity shown. Read the sentences below. Choose the correct verb in *italics* in each case.

1 The reservoir *adds / supplies / begins* the city's water.
2 The water *collects / inserts / enters* through the intake in the reservoir.
3 The water *pushes / flows / falls* though the conduit.
4 The treatment plant *adds / forces / sanitises* water for the city.

c Read the sentences about the aqueduct and put them in a logical order.

1 The water enters the system from the intake and then flows through the conduit.
2 This entire system works due to gravity, as the entire flow of the water is downhill.
3 When the land reaches a low point, an aqueduct, which is similar to a bridge-like structure, carries the water across this area.
4 Finally, the water reaches its destination.
5 Water from the reservoir is supplied to the city via an aqueduct.
6 The water is drawn from a reservoir, which is a large body of water similar to a lake.

Test practice

4a Write an explanatory paragraph about the syphon system in Exercise 3a. Think about which verbs you can use and a logical order for your paragraph.

b Write an overview sentence which explains the difference between the two diagrams in Exercise 3a.

Listening (Section 3)

Before you listen

1 What job would you most like to do? Why?

Deal with abstract ideas

➤ **TEST STRATEGIES** page 168

2a 🔊 9.3 You are going to listen to four people talking about different working environments. Match the speakers (1–4) with the environments (A–D).

Speaker 1	A forward-thinking workplaces
Speaker 2	B hectic workplaces
Speaker 3	C home working
Speaker 4	D lone working

b Listen again and note down the key points each speaker makes.

	Positive points	Negative points	Overall opinion
Speaker 1			
Speaker 2			
Speaker 3			
Speaker 4			

c Read the questions and select your answers based on your notes.

1 Speaker 1 believes busy environments are
   A exciting.   B tiring.   C unpleasant.

2 Speaker 2 thinks productivity
   A fluctuates with working environments.
   B is hard to measure.
   C is only one part of work.

3 Speaker 3 believes that creativity
   A is more abundant these days.
   B needs fresh environments.
   C relies on technology.

4 Speaker 4 is
   A not convinced he can work alone.
   B a reflective worker.
   C good at dealing with other people.

Test practice

3a You are going to listen to two students and their supervisor discussing their research into working environments. Read the questions in the test tasks and think about:

1 how information might be paraphrased.
2 possible answers.

b 🔊 9.4 Complete the test tasks.

Questions 1–6
Complete the sentences below.
Write **NO MORE THAN THREE WORDS AND/OR A NUMBER** for each answer.

1 Charlotte's research mainly focuses on _____ .
2 Professor Hickey wants Jim to _____ .
3 Jim has _____ of his research to finish.
4 Both students agree that _____ aids productivity.
5 Jim has found that it is not _____ to increase workspace.
6 Professor Hickey warns Jim that he might not _____ .

Questions 7–10
*Choose the correct letter, **A**, **B** or **C**.*

7 Charlotte is _____ her findings.
   A unsure about
   B confident of
   C surprised by

8 Jim thinks his and Charlotte's research is _____ .
   A complimentary
   B contradictory
   C unconnected

9 Charlotte _____ Jim's conclusions.
   A is sceptical of
   B agrees with
   C misunderstands

10 Professor Hickey thinks Charlotte _____ .
   A has designed her research well
   B should think more critically
   C needs to return in a week

Task analysis

4a Work in pairs and discuss your answers. Which ones are you most sure of? Why? Were any questions or answers more abstract? What made them abstract?

b Check your answers in audio script 9.4 on page 212 and think about why you got certain answers incorrect.

Language development and vocabulary

Estimation and indication

> EXPERT GRAMMAR page 181

1a Read the two paragraphs below. In what part of the IELTS test might you find this type of language?

A These days it can be difficult for employers to choose their employees because many people have <u>more or less</u> the same qualifications. In the past, fewer people went to university, but now approximately 50 percent of young people have a degree. Also, there is less diversity … many people study the same <u>kinds of</u> subjects such as economics, business, marketing <u>and so on</u>.

B The diagrams show that the factory size has <u>approximately</u> doubled in a ten-year period. It can also be seen that while the overall size has grown, the <u>types of</u> jobs done have changed. In 1995 there were <u>about</u> 10 managers, however, this grew to <u>around</u> 15 in 2005.

b Look at the underlined words in Exercise 1a and complete the sentences.

1 _____ are used before numbers and quantities to give an approximate size.
2 _____ indicates that there are further examples.
3 _____ is used before a noun to show an approximation.
4 _____ are used before a noun to refer to a category which is similar.

c Complete the sentences using the words and phrases below. You need to use some words/phrases more than once.

about   and so on   kinds of   more or less

1 Honesty, loyalty, kindness … In my experience, it is really people with these _____ qualities that make the best friends.
2 There has been a significant change in the amount of money the creative industries have invested in new technology. Now, _____ 15 percent of turnover is spent in this area, indicating that these _____ companies are embracing new techniques.
3 It shows that, rather than learning new skills in leisure time, people prefer to be entertained by activities such as going to the cinema, watching TV _____ .
4 I am not sure if we will see a great change in art forms in my lifetime. I think art has pushed most of the boundaries it can and I suspect, although we may see great new artists, wonderful and innovative installations, paintings _____ , the actual forms art takes will remain _____ the same.

d Discuss the questions below using language of estimation and indication.

1 How has industry changed in your country in the last 20 years?
2 What kinds of people tend to be most successful in business?
3 Where do you see yourself working in ten years' time?

Replace *thing*

2a Read the two paragraphs below. Which is a better example of academic writing? Why?

A There are many things to consider when thinking about changes in the workplace. Firstly, things such as flexible working have become more common in some places. These help some people do more essential things in their lives like care for children while they are still in employment.

B There are many factors to consider when thinking about changes in the workplace. Firstly, benefits such as flexible working have become more common in some workplaces. These help some employees do more essential activities in their lives like care for children while they are still in employment.

b Consider the topic of work and complete the table below with relevant vocabulary.

1 Thing	*factors,*
2 Person	*employee,*
3 Place	*workplace,*

c Complete the sentences with a more specific alternative to the underlined word. Make any other necessary changes.

1 One of the biggest <u>things</u> that employers have to cope with is ensuring they can pay their employees their wages each month.
2 Whereas doing training can be a valuable experience, <u>these people</u> often do not receive any pay.
3 <u>People</u> need to ensure that their staff feel valued and respected at work if they want to get the best from their employees.
4 Insurance for builders can be extremely high. The <u>places they work in</u> are often quite hazardous despite regulations to protect their safety.
5 Many academics have claimed that the most significant <u>thing</u> in our working lives in the last 50 years is the incorporation of new technology.

Speaking (Part 3)

Vocabulary development

1a Look at the picture. Which do you think employers value most when it comes to recruiting staff: qualifications or experience? Why might that be? What qualities, skills and knowledge do you think will be important in the job market of the future and why?

b Complete the sentences using the words below. There are three words you do not need to use.

apprentice corporation entrepreneur incentive industry lucrative monopoly overheads redundant turnover worth

1 Whilst there are many benefits of being an _____, setting up a business on your own can also be rather risky.

2 The employees were given an _____ of $500 each to complete the project in advance of the deadline.

3 In many countries a single company has the _____ on the provision of telecommunication services.

4 Companies based in central New York have extremely high _____ due to the tremendous running costs they incur for their premium location.

5 One of the consequences of the global financial crash was that many companies were forced to make many employees _____ so as to reduce costs and stay afloat.

6 The current _____ of technology companies is increasing dramatically compared to those involved in manufacturing, which is good news for their shareholders.

7 Some people argue that the rise of the _____ has been hugely detrimental to both the global economy as well as small businesses, which face stiffer competition than ever.

8 Having grown up in poverty, she chose to pursue a _____ career in the field of banking.

c Work in pairs and discuss the questions.

1 Would you rather work for a corporation or become an entrepreneur? What challenges might you face in each situation?

2 What kind of incentives do you think are motivating for employees? Why?

3 Which industries and types of company do you think will be lucrative in 50 years' time?

Focus on Pronunciation

2 🔊 9.5 Listen to two candidates answering a Part 3 question. Turn to page 183 and read the descriptors for pronunciation. Discuss their performance.

Test practice

➤ **TEST STRATEGIES** page 175

3a Before answering the questions below, discuss what features of pronunciation you could use to increase your overall speaking score.

b Work in pairs and take turns to ask and answer the questions. Record your answers if possible.

1 How has technology impacted the way people now work?

2 What skills would you consider to be essential in the modern workplace? Which workplace skills from the past have retained their importance? Why?

3 Which jobs are most valued in your society? Why is this? How likely is it that this will change in the future?

4 How do you think the workplace and offices of the future are going to change?

Assess and improve

4a Work in pairs and analyse your responses. Discuss the questions below.

1 What are your strengths and weaknesses in pronunciation?

2 What aspects do you need to practise?

3 How could you improve them?

b Repeat the test task in Exercise 3b and try to work on these aspects.

Reading (Multiple choice; *Yes/No/Not given*)

Before you read

1   In what ways do you think the world of work is changing? Can people expect more or less job security these days? Why?

Test practice

2   Read the strategies and complete the test task.

> TEST STRATEGIES page 172

Questions 1–5
Choose the correct letter A, B, C or D

1   Why does the writer mention BlaBlaCar?
   A   It has been the most financially successful new small business.
   B   It is representative of the new approach to earning money.
   C   It recruits employees from countries all over the world.
   D   It was the first example of an internet 'sharing platform'.

2   Why does the writer say the 'sharing economy' is a possible solution to the current employment crisis?
   A   It has the potential to be more efficient than old ways of trading.
   B   It could eventually guarantee people a more predictable source of income.
   C   It promises to provide better working conditions for many employees.
   D   It might open up different kinds of work to the unemployed.

3   What is Carl Frey's opinion of the 'sharing' economy?
   A   It may have a negative effect on people who are still in traditional jobs.
   B   It will become popular because of the savings to be made in the work force.
   C   It may compensate for the inevitable loss of jobs to scientific progress.
   D   It will benefit the economy to have people working independently with different companies.

4   Jeremy Rifkin believes that
   A   there is still a chance that new inventions will generate employment.
   B   most young people are reluctant to work for established businesses.
   C   young people are already accustomed to working in a variety of different ways.
   D   governments have a responsibility to decide on a policy for future job losses.

5   In the last paragraph, Rifkin makes the point that
   A   freedom is no longer something to be valued in the way it once was.
   B   there has been a change in perception about what it means to feel free.
   C   younger people need to learn to disconnect from one another if they are to feel free.
   D   there is now less freedom for the younger generation to choose what they want to do.

> HELP

1   Be careful not to be distracted by similar words in the passage. Read the question carefully.

3   What might the 'negative effect' in 3A be?

Test practice

3a   Read the instructions and answer these questions about the *Yes/No/Not given* task.
   1   Whose opinions are you looking for?
   2   How will you find the correct place in the passage?
   3   Are the statements in the same order as the passage?

b   Read the strategies and complete the test task.

> TEST STRATEGIES page 171

Questions 6–9
Do the following statements agree with the views/ claims of the writer? Write

YES   if the statement agrees with the views/ claims of the writer

NO   if the statement contradicts the views/ claims of the writer

NOT GIVEN   if it is impossible to say what the writer thinks about this

6   A combination of circumstances contributed towards BlaBlaCar's breakthrough.

7   BlaBlaCar is regarded as a threat to an established business.

8   Many people choose to leave their permanent jobs in order to sell their services online.

9   The sharing economy is already having a dramatic effect on the economy.

> HELP

6   What prevented Mazzella from launching his idea in 2003?

8   This seems possible but is there evidence for this in the passage?

The sharing economy

In the 'gig' or 'sharing' economy, say the experts, we will do lots of different jobs as technology releases us from a nine-to-five working day. But will it be all good?

Although the idea for the 'ride-sharing platform' BlaBlaCar was first conceived in 2003, it was not until much later that it could be put into practice. Apart from the technological changes, – Facebook and smartphones – external factors, such as the financial crash, made a huge contribution to its success. Thus demonstrating to the generation seeking work for the first time, both the fragility of capitalism and the necessity to investigate new revenue streams. The other key factor enabling success was the 2010 ash cloud, which gave BlaBlaCar the traction of publicity as a smart solution for people stranded far from home. In the years since then, Frédéric Mazzella's concept of being able to rent spare seats in cars has become a multimillion-euro success story.

While BlaBlaCar has little infrastructure and fewer than 300 employees in territories all around the world, its internet platform finds seats for more than 2 million journeys a month and the chief executive of the French rail operator SNCF recently cited the ride-sharing business as his company's most significant competitor. While SNCF has thousands of miles of track and untold rolling stock to maintain and renew as well as thousands of employees to reward, BlaBlaCar's infrastructure and organisation is provided free of charge by its 10 million active members.

BlaBlaCar is a perfect example of the possibilities of the emerging "sharing economy" which finds spaces for employment in the inefficiencies of capitalism and exploits them through the sheer scale of the "sharing platform" on the internet. Being a member of BlaBlaCar, working as a cab driver for a few hours for Uber, or selling knickknacks on Etsy are activities which are increasingly part of the working profile of large numbers of people these days. All of which exploit spare capacity in assets or under-utilised skills, using the reach of technology to find a market. At a time when full-time jobs in traditional industries are disappearing, these multiple micro-businesses are an enticing source of potential revenue.

Indeed, the novelty of these models has convinced some policy-makers that freelancing over digital platforms might be something of a panacea* to depressed and stagnating economies, and a portfolio of such interests may even represent the future world of work. So far, they are probably less economically consequential than the hype suggests, but, as BlaBlaCar shows, zero-marginal-cost ideas can grow exponentially at a rapid pace. Even so, if this patchwork of employment and shared services represents the future, it will certainly not involve secure salaried careers from hierarchical employers and may well include low wages and weak collective bargaining rights. Despite these reservations, it might also be an opportunity and perhaps a necessity.

Way back in the 1930s, John Maynard Keynes prophesied that the term "technological unemployment" would become a familiar part of the language. Or, in other words, the way that computers and robots would soon replace the workforce. A 2013 study,

undertaken by the Oxford economists Carl Frey and Michael Osborne, compiled a list of the occupations most under threat and, of 702 occupations, almost half fell into the high-risk category of "potentially automatable". Asked if he thought the gig technology of sharing platforms might mitigate those effects, Frey said that although people remained very attached to payroll, the rise of sharing platforms is giving people opportunities to establish a market to utilise their skills. He suggested that one result of doing this would be more pressure on the wages of the full-time employed and a reduction in protected working conditions. He does not, however, believe that because technology disrupts labour markets in one sphere it will automatically provide the solutions in another. "My reading of the evidence so far is that there will be less job creation and ever-greater labour savings. It is not necessarily true that we will have a jobless future. But I struggle to see which industries will emerge to balance the loss of jobs."

The writer and economist Jeremy Rifkin has been predicting a shift since 1995. "At that time, standard economic theory argued that new technologies would create more jobs than they destroy. I didn't believe that." Rifkin believes that conventional capitalism is already over and he is advising governments and corporations how to deal with the fallout. One key component of a possible solution he believes will be the sharing economy, which he calls the "collaborative commons". "We are in an age of new communications technology, new sources of energy and new modes of transportation. When these three merge then you get a fundamental change in how people work."

That shift is already the reality in the "millennial" generation, he believes. "They already exist in a hybrid economic system. Part of the day they may be in capitalist markets, buying and selling and producing goods and services that are sold at margins to produce profits, and they will continue to do this. At the same time, they will be producing virtual goods at near zero costs and sharing them for free, as with music".

A lot of the change, he suggests, connects with a transformed idea of freedom. When the older generation considers freedom, it imagines it as autonomy, self-sufficiency, personal choice and exclusivity. However, when the younger generation think about the meaning of this word, it is no longer about exclusivity, it is about inclusivity. "For them, the more networks they belong to, the more social capital they establish, the freer they feel," he says. "It's about expanding the network. This is the sharing economy."

*something that people think will make everything better and solve all their problems

Writing (Task 1)

Lead-in 1 Look at the photos. How do you think workplaces have changed over time? How might these changes have contributed to workplace productivity? How important is the working environment to work efficiency? Why?

Understand the task 2a Look at the plans below of a UK office and discuss the questions.
1 What do the diagrams show?
2 What similarities are there between the two diagrams?
3 What differences do you notice between the diagrams?
4 What tense(s) would you use to write about these diagrams?

Office plan 1975   **Office plan 2015**

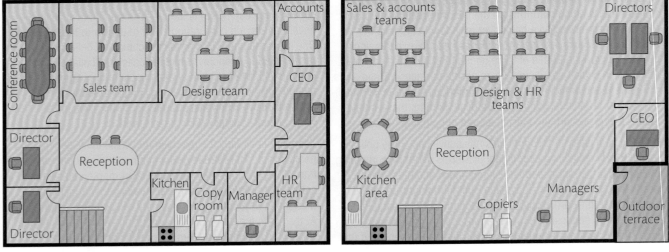

b Complete the sentences about the diagrams in Exercise 2a using the phrases below.

---

were able to use   were changes   were organised

---

1 There _____ in the working environment of some companies.
2 Departments and employees _____ in separate spaces in 1975.
3 In 2015, employees _____ some additional space for relaxation.

c Work in pairs and discuss the details from the diagrams that support the statements in Exercise 2b.

Plan the task

3a Turn to page 190 and read the descriptors for task achievement. Answer the questions.

1 Which band describes key features well, but could be more thorough?
2 Which band presents a clear overview of the main stages or trends?
3 Which band describes and explains key features very well?
4 Which band covers all of the task requirements thoroughly?

b Read the test task instructions below. What are you required to do? Underline the key words that show the requirements.

> *The diagrams below show the floor plans for a UK office in 1975 and then in 2015.*
>
> *Summarise the information by selecting and reporting the main features, and make comparisons where relevant.*
>
> *Write at least 150 words.*

c Look at the office plans in Exercise 2a. With a partner, discuss how you can fulfil the requirements using information from the diagrams.

Language and content

4a Match the words that can be used to describe workplaces below with the definitions (1–6).

contemporary   functional   hierarchical   open-plan   integration   partition

1 _____ (n): the act or process of joining parts or elements into a whole
2 _____ (adj): belonging to the present time/modern
3 _____ (adj): if a system, organisation, etc. is like this people or things are divided into levels of importance
4 _____ (n): a structure that divides a space into separate areas, usually a wall
5 _____ (adj): designed to be useful rather than simply visually appealing
6 _____ (adj): having a large space not separated by many walls

b Work in pairs and use the terms (1–6) to make comparisons about the diagrams in Exercise 2a.

1 open-plan layout
2 contemporary design
3 integration of teams
4 functional appearance
5 hierarchical design
6 partitioned areas

Write your report

> EXPERT WRITING page 199

5a Plan your description of the diagrams in Exercise 2a and make notes. Make sure your plan fulfils the task requirements.

b Write your report. Write at least 150 words.

Assess and improve

6a Work in pairs. Review your reports and discuss the questions.

1 Have you covered all of the requirements of the task?
2 Have you given an overview and summarised key changes and comparisons?
3 Do the main body paragraphs detail key comparisons and changes?
4 Which information did you take from the diagrams to develop your answer?

b Work in pairs to improve your reports. Use the feedback in Exercise 6a to help you.

Review

1a Complete the sentences with the words below.

broad   concerted   desired   driving   pivotal   transferable

1 A leader is someone who is a _____ force behind the motivation of their team.
2 It is important to learn _____ skills as they give a candidate the ability to be employed in different sectors.
3 There is a _____ spectrum of ways in which an individual can show ability.
4 If people work hard enough, then it is often conceivable that they will achieve the _____ outcome.
5 A project co-ordinator plays a _____ role in any large-scale development.
6 Nobody can do well based on ability alone. Most success requires a _____ effort.

b Match the phrases in the columns to make sentences.

Most new trainers	consist of	rubber or synthetic material.
Most memory sticks	were the size of	a small highlighter pen.
The earliest computers	are made from	a small car.
Top-of-the-range laptops	are shaped like	glare-free screens and a very long battery life.

c Replace the underlined words with a more specific word below. You may need to change the form of the word. Make any other necessary changes.

factor   employee   manager   issue   country

1 It is important that <u>people</u> are treated well in the workplace and that their rights are respected.
2 There are many <u>things</u> that are important when looking for a new job such as working hours and conditions and opportunities for advancement.
3 The right to paid maternity leave is applied to all in some countries, but it is a <u>thing</u> which can leave small businesses in financial trouble.
4 There are lots of skills necessary for <u>people who run things</u> such as the ability to motivate and enthuse staff and delegate effectively.
5 Lots of <u>places</u> have different laws that apply to their workers and their businesses. Some of these protect workers, while others boost company productivity and profit.

2a Put the phrases in the correct order to make sentences. Can you guess what they describe?

1 when travelling overseas / the thing / this is / people need
_____
2 to control the temperature / the thing that / it is / can be used
_____
3 which stops / this is / the liquid / the car overheating
_____
4 keep cool / what people use / it is / help them / to
_____
5 what you / to help you / see in the dark / they are / eat
_____
6 what you use / these are / when skiing / to help you balance
_____
7 hot drinks / to make / this is / boils water / the thing that
_____
8 when watching TV / it is / to change channel / use / what people
_____

b Write a definition for the following words.

1 functional: _____   3 partitioned: _____
2 open-plan: _____   4 contemporary: _____

c Match the words in Exercise 2b with a word below to make compound nouns.

layout   design   appearance   areas

d Write a paragraph describing your classroom, office or a room in your house using the words above.

e Choose the correct option in *italics* to complete the text.

Changes in entrepreneurship

There are essential qualities that all entrepreneurs have such as the tenacity to never give up, inspiration, creativity and effort. Without these **1** *kinds of / more or less* characteristics, there is little room for success. Over the last 20 years the number of entrepreneurs has risen, partly due to the ability to set up a business online. In fact, the growth of small online businesses has risen by **2** *approximately / variously* 50 percent in this time. However, some business experts claim the online market is **3** *more or less / about* saturated now. This remains to be seen as technology is constantly changing, but with the advent of new technologies and ways of social networking, such as smart glasses, YikYak and **4** *so on / go on*, we don't see an end to the online business bubble.

10 Cutting edge

10a Training

- **Reading:** Paraphrase ideas (Matching sentence endings; Multiple choice)
- **Vocabulary:** Nouns for hypothesising; Academic collocations; Phrases for speculation
- **Speaking:** Develop topic-specific vocabulary; Use speculation in your answers (Part 2; Part 3)
- **Listening:** Metaphors and similes in lectures (Section 4: Note completion)
- **Language development:** Unreal conditionals, *wish* and *if only*; Other hypothetical forms
- **Writing:** Write about hypothetical alternatives; Develop a coherent argument (Task 2)

10b Testing

- **Listening:** Section 4: Table completion; Note completion
- **Language development and vocabulary:** Past modal verbs; Verb patterns
- **Speaking:** Part 3: Discuss inventions
- **Reading:** Matching sentence endings; *Yes/No/Not given*
- **Writing:** Task 2: Opinion essay

Tim Berners-Lee

Momofuku Ando

Hedy Lamarr

Lead-in

1   Can you match the people in the photos above with their inventions? What do you think makes a great inventor? Is it more important to be creative or knowledgeable to be an inventor? Why?

instant noodles   radio guidance technology   world wide web

Reading (Matching sentence endings; Multiple choice)

Before you read

1 What do you think makes someone creative? How would you define creativity?

Paraphrase ideas

2a Read the title and subtitle, then skim the reading passage to find out how the argument develops.

b Work in pairs and look at the highlighted words in the first part of question 1 in the test task below. Follow steps 1–3.

1 Brainstorm paraphrases of the words/idea.
2 Scan the passage and underline the part which paraphrases question 1.
3 Choose the best option (A–G) to complete the sentence. How is this expressed in the passage?

Test practice

3 Follow the same strategy as in Exercise 2b and complete the test task.

➤ TEST STRATEGIES page 172

Questions 1–5
Complete each sentence with the correct ending, **A–G**, below.
Write the correct letter **A–G**.

1 A test which evaluates the ability to be rational
2 A typical indication of a high IQ
3 The proven link between better food intake and higher intelligence
4 Visualising the brain as a division into 'rational' and 'emotional' halves
5 The complexity involved in the creative process

A can be obtained by trying to drive brain rhythms more directly.
B is now recognised as an over-simplistic interpretation.
C is the speed at which someone can handle information.
D gives a good indication of how successful a person might be in the future.
E involves different parts of the brain interacting together perfectly.
F is the correlation between the logical and creative hemispheres of the brain.
G demonstrates that genetic factors are not the only consideration.

Test practice

4 Read the strategies and complete the test task.

➤ TEST STRATEGIES page 172

Questions 6–9
Choose the correct letter **A**, **B**, **C** or **D**.

6 What does the writer say about the process experienced by creative people?
A It is often the case that it leads to a form of mental illness.
B The initial phase can be extremely time-consuming.
C The most common way to find a solution to a problem is when asleep.
D It is always a struggle to transfer ideas from the brain to the written word.

7 By studying how to become more creative we learn that it is important to
A take risks with the way that you approach ideas.
B take every opportunity to rest your mind.
C be organised and methodical in the way you work.
D clarify your ideas by speaking to other people.

8 The writer says that the urban myth he refers to
A is scientifically improbable.
B is completely and utterly false.
C provides him with daily encouragement.
D explains why creativity is innate rather than acquired.

9 What point does the writer make in the last paragraph?
A Schools fail to encourage the development of creativity.
B Students whose right and left-brain thinking is imbalanced fail to achieve academic success.
C Schools are exclusively focused on skills useful for technology.
D It is essential for the modern age that creativity is nurtured at school.

Task analysis

5 What helped you indentify the parts of the passage and choose the correct options?

Discussion

6 Would you describe yourself more as a rational or a creative person? Why?

The science of imagination

Are creative people's brains different from other people's? Professor John Stein explains what creativity looks like from a neuroscientific perspective.

How do you quantify creativity? Is it different from intelligence? Among academics there is no agreement about what intelligence is, yet IQ* measures of aptitude in memory, logic and comprehension seem to capture something useful about the brain's processing ability that is a good predictor of both academic and other types of achievement. The speed of this explains why different intelligence subtests, such as verbal and nonverbal reasoning, correlate with each other fairly well. Thus "g", the general intelligence factor believed by Charles Spearman in the 1920s to underlie all other intellectual attributes, is most likely explained by the speed and effective exchange of data between the front and back, and left and right hemispheres of an individual's brain.

The efficiency of this interchange, which is mediated by synchronisation of the rhythms of the brain, is a product of both genetic and environmental aspects. Temporal processing seems to be even more heritable than intelligence itself but environmental factors play just as important a role in intelligence. For example, the specialised neurons which mediate the synchronising rhythms are especially vulnerable to dietary deficiencies, particularly during childhood. General improvement in diet is one explanation for the "Flynn effect": the increase in the average IQ in all developed countries by 30 points over the past century.

It is widely agreed that intelligence tests only capture verbal and spatial reasoning and other 'left-hemisphere' traits, such as linear and 'convergent' thinking. In order to include other attributes, such as emotional, holistic, lateral and imaginative thinking, generally deemed to be characteristic of right-hemisphere processing, Spearman used a factor "s". This assumed difference is, however, misleading as in reality both hemispheres work collectively in dealing with any one task. Whilst differing kinds of thinking do involve activity in diverging parts of the brain, they do not do so in the clearly compartmentalised way envisaged by early phrenologists*. Even simple thought processes tend to involve several parts of the brain and the intricate nature of the systems involved in creative thought range widely over both hemispheres. Creative people are those who have the ability to think unexpected new thoughts and produce innovative concepts. They are highly likely to be the fortunate ones and to have both inherited and developed methods which enable their brains' two hemispheres to work optimally together.

Where highly creative people are concerned, four different stages in their pattern of work can be discerned. For which preparation, namely immersion in the problem, can take many years. Often, preparation involves deliberately instigating crazy ideas so as to provide the raw material for the mind to then work on. This is why creative people tend to be highly impulsive and possess a more easily activated right prefrontal cortex: the part of the brain involved in divergent open-ended thinking. Incubation, when a problem is deliberately set aside to allow for imaginings and ideas to interweave subconsciously, with luck will naturally lead to the third stage, whereby insight and illumination will burst forth in your mind with wonderful clarity. In the case of Mendeleev, sleep gave rise to his imagination, logically ordering all the

Coco Chanel

chemical elements into what we now refer to as the periodic table. The fourth and final stage, that of recording ideas on paper, requires the left hemisphere's strengths. Mozart said 'It rarely differs on paper from what it was in my imagination." Others are not so lucky; Einstein spent huge amounts of time attempting to capture in symbolic form the visuo-spatial intuitions that had come to him in a flash.

We can all profit from our perception of the creative process by consciously facilitating each of these stages: deliberately giving our imagination free rein, brain-storming, allowing lateral thinking by free association and then sleeping on the new ideas or changing task completely. It is surprising how often ideas will arrange themselves into coherent plans and how a flash of insight will make clear how to convey the information so others can understand it. A widely believed urban myth claims only 10% of our brain is generally in use and suggests that if we used more, we could all aspire to be a Leonardo da Vinci. However, Nature would not allow us to expend 20% of all the energy generated by the body on the brain (which is 2% of our body weight) if 90% of it is likely to be wasted. But this conjecture has a grain of truth: if we could learn – as we can through practice – to optimise the connections between the different parts of our brains to increase its efficiency, we can only speculate how much more creativity would be released.

Meanwhile, ensuring that our educational systems foster rather than stifle creativity is vital. Modern education quite properly stresses the importance of developing reasoning, verbal and literacy skills, which are of supreme importance in this technological age. However, the non-verbal, holistic, emotional right hemisphere is necessary if we are to generate any new concepts or innovative ideas, as will be required if we are to cope with the rapid pace of change in the 21st century. It has been found that creative people are quite often deficient in logical, literate left-brain skills, but superior in holistic, visuo-spatial right-brain ones. A disproportionate number of creative artists, engineers and architects fall into this category. The implication of this is that we must create space for arts, fantasy and imagination – our future may well depend on it.

*IQ (intelligence quotient) - your level of intelligence, as measured by standardised tests *phrenology: 19th-century practice of studying the shape of people's heads

Vocabulary

Nouns for hypothesising

1a Match the words (1–6) with the correct definitions (A–F).

1 assumption
2 concept
3 implication
4 insight
5 speculation
6 inference

A a possible future effect or result of an action, event or decision
B an abstract idea of how something is
C when you guess about the possible causes or effects of something without knowing all the facts
D something that you believe is true although you have no definite proof
E a conclusion formed on information that you have
F a deep understanding of something, especially a complicated situation or idea

b Write the verb forms for the nouns 1–6 in Exercise 1a. Which noun does not have a verb form?

2 Choose the correct option in *italics* to complete the text.

Creativity is for everyone

Many people **1** *speculate / assume* that creativity is something that humans are born with or without. However, this is actually conjecture and not based on actual evidence. Recent academic studies have shown that creativity is present in everyone, but that most people cannot **2** *conceive / infer* of it in themselves. A study of 300 elderly people at George Washington University found that creative activities slowed the aging process. There are several positive **3** *insights / implications* of this study including fewer hospital visits and improved mental health in the elderly. Experts suggest we need to expand our **4** *concept / inference* of creativity. As neurologist Richard Restak says, 'Creativity is critical to solving problems in all parts of our lives.'

3 Work in groups and discuss the questions.

1 What assumptions do you have about creative people?
2 Why do people like to speculate on artists' inspiration?
3 What are the implications of removing creative subjects from the school curriculum?

Academic collocations

4a Choose the correct adjectives (A–C) to complete the sentences below.

1 Innovation is good, but some advances have _____ implications for society, such as nuclear power.
A underlying B wider C abstract
2 The _____ perception of modern art varies from appreciation to disdain.
A intense B abstract C public
3 There has been _____ speculation about the provenance of the newly discovered painting.
A heavy B underlying C intense
4 There is an _____ assumption that creating art is a compulsive action for many creative people.
A underlying B everlasting C omnipotent
5 Communicating _____ concepts to young children can be very challenging.
A public B abstract C straightforward

b Complete the text with the correct form of the collocations in Exercise 4a.

Creativity – the force of the future

Forbes magazine recently conducted a survey on creativity among business leaders with some intriguing results. Many respondents cited the abstract **1** _____ of creativity as critical to the success of the global economy. Although the public **2** _____ of creativity concentrates on the traditional art forms, business leaders see things differently. Many businesses have evidence that creativity has enhanced production in their organisations. There is certainly an underlying **3** _____ that the 'imagination' economy will be responsible for creating new solutions to many of the world's problems. The manner in which the world of business harnesses creativity to foster new ideas will have wider **4** _____ for problems such as climate change and disease.

Phrases for speculation

5 Complete the sentences with the correct words below.

chances confident guess impression likelihood surprised

1 I get the _____ that it is difficult for creative people to predict how successful their work will be.
2 I would not be _____ if many cultures lost some of their traditional artistic practices.
3 The _____ are that everyone can find something creative that they can do competently.
4 I am _____ that creativity in children can be fully developed if they are given encouragement.
5 In all _____ , music will only be available electronically in the future.
6 My _____ is that in the future, science-fiction novels will become a thing of the past.

Speaking (Part 2; Part 3)

Lead-in

1 Read the definitions of creativity in the poster. Which one(s) do you agree and disagree with? Discuss your ideas in groups.

Develop topic-specific vocabulary

2a Match the phrases (1–5) with their definitions (A–E).

1 to waste your talent
2 to have a vivid imagination
3 to stifle creativity
4 to have artistic flair
5 to think laterally

A to have a way of doing things that is interesting and shows imagination
B to stop creativity from happening or developing
C to use your imagination to see relationships between things that are not normally thought of together
D to have the ability to imagine unlikely situations very clearly
E to have ability which you do not put to good use

b 🔊 10.1 Listen to five speakers. Complete each of their sentences with phrases from Exercise 2a. You may need to change the form of the language used. Use no more than three words.

c Work in groups and discuss the topics.

1 A time when you were creative
2 A talent you had as a child
3 A problem you solved in an unusual way

Use speculation in your answers

3a Read the task card and make some notes for your answer. Where could you use your imagination to answer the prompt?

Describe something you made that did not go as planned. You should say:
  what you made
  what problems you had
  how you tried to solve the problems
and explain how you would do things differently if you tried to make the same thing again.

b 🔊 10.2 Listen to Jing answering the task in Exercise 3a. Make notes on her answer.

c Read audio script 10.2 on page 213 and underline the parts where Jing speculates on events. What grammatical structures does she use to speculate?

d Read your notes in Exercise 3a again. Add some ideas which speculate on events.

Test practice

➤ TEST STRATEGIES pages 174 and 175

4a Read the Part 2 task card and the Part 3 discussion questions below it and prepare some ideas.

Part 2

Describe a creative project you were involved in. You should say:
    what your role was
    what the project was aimed at creating
    what you learnt from the project
and explain how you felt about the finished item.

Part 3

In what ways is creativity valued and rewarded in society?

What opportunities for creativity does modern life provide?

In what ways would you expect to find creativity in the workplace nowadays?

How can more creativity be brought into our everyday lives?

b Work in pairs and take turns to ask and answer the questions for Parts 2 and 3.

Listening (Section 4)

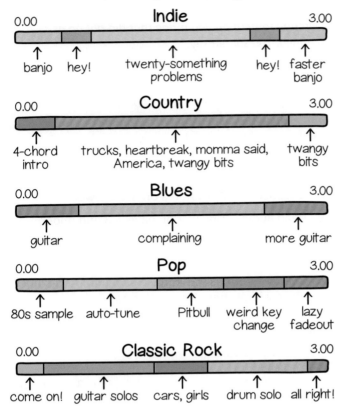

anatomy of songs

Indie
0.00   3.00

↑ banjo   ↑ hey!   ↑ twenty-something problems   ↑ hey!   ↑ faster banjo

Country
0.00   3.00

↑ 4-chord intro   ↑ trucks, heartbreak, momma said, America, twangy bits   ↑ twangy bits

Blues
0.00   3.00

↑ guitar   ↑ complaining   ↑ more guitar

Pop
0.00   3.00

↑ 80s sample   ↑ auto-tune   ↑ Pitbull   ↑ weird key change   ↑ lazy fadeout

Classic Rock
0.00   3.00

↑ come on!   ↑ guitar solos   ↑ cars, girls   ↑ drum solo   ↑ all right!

Before you listen

1 Look at the infographic for songs. Do you think there is any element of truth in this infographic? Do you think songs tend to require a lot of creativity or do you think they follow a formula? Why/Why not?

Metaphors and similes in lectures

2a Read the definitions and examples of metaphor and simile from song lyrics. Decide which definition and example is A) a metaphor and B) a simile.

   1 A figure of speech that identifies something as being the same as another unrelated thing and therefore highlighting relevant similarities between these two things.

   2 A figure of speech which is a direct comparison of one thing with another thing of a different kind, using words such as *like* or *as*.

   A   My love is like a bridge to your soul.

   B   You're the tower in my life.

b 🔊 10.3 Listen to two people talking about music. What is the subject discussed by each speaker? What is the metaphor or simile they are using?

c Read what Speaker 2 says below. What is the comparison that the speaker is making? Why is it appropriate?

> Of course, music has changed a great deal in the last hundred years. In one way the diversity of music has changed, and as this has happened our taste in music has become more diverse. We the listeners are sponges, soaking up everything around us, no matter what it may be. So, nowadays we cannot simply say 'I'm a jazz buff' or 'I'm into rock', generally we are into many different musical genres, and this can depend entirely on mood.

Test practice

> **TEST STRATEGIES** page 168

3a 🔊 10.4 You are going to hear a lecture on robotic music making. Listen and put the topics (A–E) in the order you hear them.

   A Sampling music
   B Cultural importance of songs
   C Music created by the masses
   D Reverse-engineering songs
   E Robotic pop stars

b Listen again and make a note of the metaphors or similes you hear. Discuss your ideas in pairs.

4a Read the notes in the test task below. Think about what the missing words might be and discuss your ideas in pairs.

b Listen again and complete the test task.

> *Complete the notes below.*
> *Write **NO MORE THAN THREE WORDS** for each answer.*
>
> **Can music be created by computer?**
> Against:
> John Covach: Songs need cultural relevance to appeal to the 1 _____
> Compares writing a good song to 2 _____ – conditions key
> For:
> Susan Schmidt-Horning: Many songs reassembled in the way a 3 _____ might be
> Sampling: This is using 4 _____ of an older song. For some, this is seen as 5 _____ , but it is often allowed.
> Hatsune Miku: Not 6 _____ but very popular music star.
> But is a 7 _____ of her followers (plays their music).
> Summary:
> The 8 _____ for a great song is both social and musical.

Language development

Unreal conditionals, *wish* and *if only*

> **EXPERT GRAMMAR** page 181

1a Read the sentences. Which describe an event that happened and which describe an event that did not happen?

1 A I wish I had studied a more arts-based subject at university.
   B I am glad I studied a more arts-based subject at university.
2 A If only I had more time, I would do something creative.
   B I would often do creative things if I had the time.
3 A Studying an arts-based subject has lead me to an inspiring job.
   B If I had studied a more arts-based subject at university, I might have found a more inspiring job.

b Underline the sections in Exercise 1a that show past hypotheticals.

c Answer the questions below.
1 Are *I wish* and *if only* used to express regrets or future desires?
2 What tense is used after *wish* and *if only* to talk about the present?
3 What tense is used after *wish* and *if only* to talk about the past?

2 Decide if the sentences are correct or incorrect. Correct the incorrect sentences.
1 If only more people will take up some kind of craft hobby, I think stress levels could fall dramatically.
2 If I had grown up in a city, I would have been exposed to a wider variety of people and experiences.
3 Teachers often wish the school curriculum is more creative so that their teaching could be more inspiring.
4 If she had followed her heart and gone to design school, she would be a graphic designer now.
5 Many adults wish their jobs are involving more opportunities to be creative.
6 I might not started building websites if I had not taken that short evening class last year.

3 Work in groups and discuss the topics. Use hypothetical structures from this lesson.
1 Explain a situation in your past which you would like to be different.
2 Imagine how an aspect of your life could be different now.
3 Describe a regret you have.

Other hypothetical forms

4a Read the sentences and underline the phrase which is used for hypothesising.
1 Suppose we hadn't met James. We wouldn't have such a great creative team for the project.
2 Let's transport the musical equipment by car in case something gets damaged.
3 It's time the company started adding some more innovative ideas to its range of kitchenware products.
4 What if you'd been born in California? How would your life have been different?

b Decide if the sentences in Exercise 4a are describing the present or the past.

c What verb forms are used after the hypothetical forms in Exercise 4a? Why are they used?

d Complete the text using the correct form of the verbs in brackets.

Why is being creative so hard?

Scientists have suggested that our own brains could be sabotaging our chances of creativity. This is in part due to cognitive bias, which means that we are influenced a lot by our patterns of thinking. Supposing someone 1 _____ (think of) a great, but unconventional idea at work. It is likely that that person would not discuss their idea in case their colleagues 2 _____ (disagree). This is a form of cognitive bias which affects our thinking patterns. But what if people 3 _____ (create) new patterns of thinking? Some scientists argue that people can retrain their thinking patterns to foster more creativity. Perhaps it is time people 4 _____ (begin) to take control of cognitive bias and reduce its effects.

Writing (Task 2)

goodbye

Lead-in

1a Look at the visual representation of a phrase in English. Work in pairs and try to work out what it means.

b What kinds of skill do you need to solve these kinds of problems? How can these skills be used in other areas of life?

Write about hypothetical alternatives

2a Giving hypothetical alternatives can be done with past, present and future situations. Match the sentence beginnings (1–5) with the endings (A–E). Which are past, present and future?

1 If children were taught more creative skills at school,
2 Without creative thinkers like Leonardo Da Vinci,
3 It may well be possible to envisage a world without creativity,
4 If we did not invest in creativity,
5 If humans had not used simple creative problem-solving skills,

A the sciences and arts would not be the thriving arenas that they are today.
B but it would be an uninspiring place with little to engage the mind.
C they would never have invented things like the wheel, boats or aeroplanes.
D they may gain more skills needed to solve the problems our planet may face in the future.
E there would be far less progress in science and the arts.

b Read the paragraph below and underline any hypothetical situations mentioned.

Creativity is an ability that should be encouraged in schools. Many schools nowadays are more focused on exams and maths and language skills. However, if this continues, it might not develop a child fully enough. Without having their creativity fostered, children may only grow up to deal with logical tasks, but not think creatively about what they can do with their lives and for the world. This could mean that the world would be a less innovative place.

c Read the statements below. How could you develop them using hypothetical situations?

1 Learning art and music as a child is less important than learning maths and sciences.
2 Scientists are also creative but in different ways to musicians and artists.
3 Creativity has changed the world in a number of ways.

Develop a coherent argument

3a Complete the text with the sentences (A–D) to make a logical, coherent argument.

Teamwork is a key factor in innovation. Developing new ideas or projects involves many skills. **1** _____ It is unlikely that these abilities can be found in one single person. **2** _____ Nowadays, large projects are often undertaken by a group of people. **3** _____ This requires architects, builders, surveyors and many other people, all of whom bring a different skill set to the project. **4** _____ Therefore, in order to innovate and develop society to the best of our abilities, collaboration must be seen as a key tool.

A As a result, working in a team can offer many advantages as team members can possess a range of different skills and talents.
B These skills include those such as creativity, perseverance and logic.
C If buildings were solely in the hands of builders, then they may be structurally sound but they might lack the design and functionality that more creative people can bring to them.
D An example of this is the construction of a building.

b Read the statement below. Plan your points to support the statement. Make sure they are ordered coherently.

Everybody is capable of some kind of creativity.

c Work in pairs and share your ideas from Exercise 3b.

Test practice

> EXPERT WRITING page 200

4a Read the following essay question and make a plan of your answer. Focus on the aspects given below.

Creativity is the key to problem-solving. To what extent do you agree with this statement? Give reasons to support your answers.

- Ensuring you answer the question
- Your main points
- Support for your main points
- Presenting some hypothetical alternatives to support your argument
- The order of your paragraphs
- The logical order of information within your paragraphs
- What to include in your introduction and conclusion

b Write the main body paragraphs of the essay. Focus on making the argument coherent. Use the feedback from Exercise 3c to help improve your answer.

c Work in pairs and share your paragraphs. Discuss the points in Exercise 3c.

Listening (Section 4)

Before you listen

1 What do you think is the most important medical advance in history? Why?

Hypothesising

2a Read the statements below. Which statement is hypothetical and which is not?

 1 Let's ask ourselves where we would be without penicillin. Well, we would not be able to fight infection. We would probably have a much shorter life expectancy and be more susceptible to all sorts of diseases.

 2 Leeches were used for thousands of years for treatment of a variety of illnesses. They also had a resurgence in popularity for medical use in the 1980s, when they were used to reduce swelling and promote healing.

 b Underline the language of hypothesis in the statements in Exercise 2a.

3a 🔊 10.5 Listen to four people hypothesising and match each speaker to the question they are answering (A–D).

Speaker 1 _____   Speaker 3 _____
Speaker 2 _____   Speaker 4 _____

 A Do you think people will commonly live to be a 100 years old in the future? Why/Why not?
 B What kind of medical innovations do you think the world will see in the next 50 years?
 C What do you think the world would look like without doctors or hospitals?
 D What would have happened if painkillers had not been developed?

 b Read audio script 10.5 on page 213 and underline further examples of language used to hypothesise.

Test practice

> **TEST STRATEGIES** page 168

4 🔊 10.6 Complete the test tasks.

Questions 1–8
Complete the table below.
Write **NO MORE THAN THREE WORDS AND/OR A NUMBER** for each answer.

21st-century Medical Innovations

Innovation	Pros/Cons	Implications
fMRI (brain scan)	+ provides information on language and memory + detects illness + helps 1 _____ in their work	Ability to assess how drugs 2 _____
Artificial kidneys and livers	+ have already been developed	May reduce existing 3 _____
4 _____ transplant	+ helps people who suffer trauma - problem of 5 _____ (loss of self)	
Gene 6 _____ (most significant breakthrough)	+ tells us about ourselves + possibility of 7 _____ medications + helps us understand how we evolved - could be used to 8 _____ against individuals	As yet undetermined

Questions 9–10
Complete the notes below.
Write **NO MORE THAN THREE WORDS** for each answer.

 9 Other issue: Who views data? e.g. A _____ may be chosen on genetic strength.
 10 Homework: Prepare _____ .

Task analysis

5 Work in pairs and discuss your answers.

Language development and vocabulary

Past modal verbs

> EXPERT GRAMMAR page 182

1 Match the phrases (1–3) with their functions (A–C).

1 Medical science could have found a cure for the common cold if there was more interest in the topic.
2 The government should have invested more in engineering companies to encourage innovation.
3 The attempt to fly a hot air balloon across the Atlantic would have been successful if the burner had not failed.

A to say that a different action in the past was recommended
B to talk about other possibilities if something in the past had been different
C to imagine an alternative result if something in the past had been different

2 Complete the text with the words below.

could (x2)   may   should   would not

Innovation under the sea

Jacques Cousteau's television programmes captured the hearts of many as they followed his quest to understand the underwater world. However, his life **1** _____ have been very different. In 1933 Cousteau had a serious car accident which almost took his life. During his rehabilitation he took up swimming and became fascinated by the sea. If he had not had the accident, he **2** _____ not have become so interested in the sea. Later in life Cousteau served in the French Resistance movement during the Second World War. His life **3** _____ have been cut short by this dangerous work, but he survived and went back to his underwater research. His work was expensive and at times Cousteau struggled to finance his expeditions. He realised that he **4** _____ have used the media to generate attention and he started writing books, films and TV programmes. It could be argued that if Cousteau had not dedicated himself so thoroughly to his work, we **5** _____ have furthered our knowledge of the sea nearly so quickly.

3 Work in pairs and discuss the topics.

1 Choose an event in your past and imagine an alternative outcome.
2 Think of a decision you have made recently and imagine making a different decision.
3 Imagine a different outcome to a recent world event.

Verb patterns

4a Are the verbs below followed by the infinitive or the gerund?

afford   avoid   deny   involve   manage   promise   risk   suggest

b Complete the sentences with the correct form of the verbs in brackets.

1 Many parents cannot _____ (afford/pay) for their children to go to medical school.
2 Driving innovation forward _____ (involve/ensure) that there are plenty of opportunities for people to express their ideas.
3 Potential inventors should _____ (avoid/spend) too much time on social media or the internet if they want to develop their ideas fully.
4 The government _____ (deny/subsidise) the technology industries more than they subsidised the engineering industries.
5 Last year my teacher _____ (suggest/participate) in a design competition.
6 Several well-known actors have _____ (promise/invest) in a new organisation for young people to get involved in design and technology.

c Work in pairs and take turns to ask and answer the questions below, using suitable verbs.

1 What would you recommend to someone who has lots of ideas for inventions?
2 What kinds of things have you made? What did the process involve?
3 How would you encourage someone to be more inventive?
4 What would you suggest doing if someone you knew had a great idea for a product?

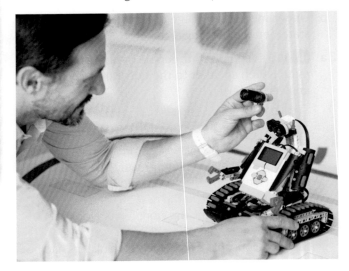

Speaking (Part 3)

Alexander Graham Bell invented the telephone in the late 19th century.

Steve Jobs made the iPhone into a desirable object and a cultural icon of its time.

Vocabulary development

1 What do the photos above illustrate? What do you think the difference is? Is the difference important? Why/Why not?

2 Choose the correct option in *italics* to complete the sentences.

1 Last year's *best-selling / state-of-the-art* gadget was the tablet, which outperformed mobile phone and laptop sales by 20 percent.
2 Honda is considered to be the automobile company which does the most *pioneering / life-enhancing* research into robotics and design.
3 An example of *best-selling / cutting-edge* technology in medical science is nanotechnology.
4 The company only uses *state-of-the-art / world-leading* chairs to ensure their employees suffer less from back problems.
5 Philips is a *world-leading / cutting-edge* company in the consumer electronics industry.
6 Nowadays surgeons can change people's lives with operations to give patients new, *pioneering / life-changing* replacement limbs.

3 Complete the text with words below.

instigated   laid the groundwork   launched
spearheaded   took the lead

Alibaba is an excellent example of innovation. The company was 1 _____ in China in 1999 and was 2 _____ by Jack Ma, businessman and philanthropist. Alibaba is an e-commerce company and it is the world's largest online business-to-business trading platform for small businesses. People see it as a mix of eBay, Amazon and PayPal and as such it 3 _____ on the idea of one company diversifying into a range of industries rather than the more traditional approach of focusing on one industry. The company has become so powerful that in 2009 it 4 _____ a new sales holiday. Called 'Singles Day', it is a kind of anti-Valentine's Day where people organise parties to meet friends, generating enormous sales for Alibaba each year. Perhaps Alibaba has 5 _____ for other organisations to adopt, or even adapt, their model.

Focus on lexical resource

4a Turn to page 183 and read the band descriptors for lexical resource. Discuss the differences between band 7 and 8.

b 🔊 10.7 Listen to a candidate answering a Part 3 discussion question. Discuss her use of lexis and make notes of any examples of high-level vocabulary.

Test practice

> **TEST STRATEGIES** page 175

5a Read the Part 3 discussion questions and make notes on some vocabulary you could use to achieve a high score. Use language from the unit to help you.

1 Why is invention vital for the development of society?
2 What do you think it is that might drive people to invent?
3 How have recent technological inventions or discoveries changed the world?
4 What would you say have been the most useful inventions?

b Work in pairs and take turns to ask and answer the questions in Exercise 5a. Record your answers if possible.

Assess and improve

6a Analyse your use of vocabulary in Exercise 5b with a partner.

b Work in pairs and discuss how you could both improve your vocabulary. If possible, listen to your recorded answers first.

Reading (Matching sentence endings; *Yes/No/Not given*)

Before you read

1 Which scientific ideas or innovations do you think are the most extraordinary? Why?

2a Read the title and subtitle and then skim the reading passage to get an idea of the argument.

b Which of the following advice is appropriate for these tasks? Write A (matching sentence endings), B (*Yes/No/Not given*) or C (both).

1 Highlight the key words/ideas in the question or stem and use these to find the place you need in the passage.

2 Underline paraphrases in the passage which have the same meaning as the options.

3 You are identifying the opinions or claims of the writer.

4 The questions follow the same order as the information in the passage.

5 Predict how the stem of the sentence might end.

Test practice

3 Read the strategies and complete the test tasks.

> **TEST STRATEGIES** pages 171 and 172

Questions 1–4

*Complete each sentence with the correct ending, **A–F**, below.*

*Write the correct letter, **A–F**.*

1 The delay in scientific advances has been blamed by some scientists on

2 Science historians view new hypotheses in relation to

3 It is believed by some science historians that all new ideas should be given

4 The Quine-Duhem thesis states that any scientific investigation is open to

A an equal amount of respect irrespective of their intrinsic merit.

B the dangers of fellow scientists attacking a proposal on principle.

C multiple interpretations, depending on how the issues is approached.

D the acceptance of established theories that were faulty.

E the problems entailed in having to prove a thesis was incorrect.

F the period in which people live and the way in which society has developed.

> **HELP**

1 Look at the second paragraph for why better ideas were delayed.

2 The passage says they were looking at theories 'in the context of their times'. What is another way of saying this?

Questions 5–9

Do the following statements agree with the view/ claims of the writer? Write

YES   *if the statement agrees with the views/ claims of the writer*

NO   *if the statement contradicts the views/ claims of the writer*

NOT GIVEN *if it is impossible to say what the writer thinks about this*

5 People will consciously reject a new theory if it is contrary to their own prejudices and beliefs.

6 Ptolemy's Earth-centric view of cosmology was an acceptable theory for hundreds of years.

7 The people responsible for testing Galileo's theory were at fault for refusing to examine his evidence.

8 Experiments are becoming a less common way of verifying a scientific theory.

9 An awareness of good science will reveal itself over time.

> **HELP**

5 Did people know it was wrong when they rejected it?

6 It was later rejected but was there a reason why it lasted for centuries?

Task analysis

4 Work in groups. Compare your answers and answer the questions.

1 How easy did you find it to skim the passage for the main ideas? Which strategies did you use?

2 What strategies did you use to deal with unfamiliar words? For example, which words did you ignore? Did you use the context or prefixes/ suffixes to help you?

3 How confident were you of your answers to the questions? What did you find particularly difficult to do? In which areas do you think you have most improved?

Discussion

5 In which areas do you think we are most likely to see scientific progress over the next 50 years?

The nature of scientific progress

If "wrong" scientific ideas had not been so widely accepted, might "right" ideas have arrived sooner? Philip Ball argues it is just not that simple.

If you believe in scientific progress, you will agree that the fate of all theories is to be replaced with updated and improved ones. Newton's theory of gravitation was good; Einstein's improved on it; some day we will find another one that is better still, and so on. But does this mean that the best theories are actually impeded by inferior ones?

Some eminent scientists think so. The cosmologist Joe Silk argued that Copernicus's Sun-centred universe was "held back" by Ptolemy's Earth-centric version. According to the physicist Steven Weinberg, meanwhile, Ptolemy himself suffered from similar issues: the ancient astronomer allowed his scientific acuity to be clouded by the "bad theory" of astrology. Weinberg also argues that the 14th-century French polymath Nicole Oresme was on the threshold of discovering heliocentrism* before he "finally surrendered" to the misconceived Ptolemaic orthodoxy – the good idea crowded out by a bad one.

Historians of science tend to be much more relaxed about "wrong" ideas. Their task, after all, is not to adjudicate on science but to explain how ideas evolved. This requires them to understand theories in the context of their times: to examine how people thought as they did rather than to decide on the best one. At its worst, however, this position has at times led to the suggestion that there is no right and wrong in the history of science. In this extreme "relativist" view, modern science is no more valid than medieval philosophies, and today's theories have gained acceptance solely because of social and political factors, not because they are objectively any better.

Plenty of scientists and historians have rejected extreme relativism and accepted that science develops ever-more-reliable theories about the world, but I believe the idea that better theories are inhibited by worse ones should be resisted, not so much because it makes for bad history but rather because it denies the realities of how science is done. After all, no-one adheres to a wrong theory in the face of a better one, knowing that it is unsound. We do so because we are human and stubborn, attached to our own ideas and also because we are prone to confirmation bias, seeing only what suits our preconceptions. Moreover, we also believe the old theory provides a better account of the situation as it is.

What is more, theories are not only (or even) classed as good because they are eventually proved 'right' but when they offer an adequate account of the reasons for the current situation, without too many arbitrary assumptions. They should be both consistent with and motivated by observations, and ideally they should also have a degree of predictive power. Ptolemy's cosmology largely met those conditions for centuries as did Newton's theory of gravity. In contrast, Max Planck's proposed quantum fell short, at least initially. Taken at face value, quanta undermined the Newtonian physics that was otherwise so successful, without (at that point) any compelling reason to do so.

Whilst we love to deride people who dismissed an idea that proved to be right, sometimes they had good grounds for doing so. There was no widely accepted empirical evidence for quantization as a fundamental property until Einstein's work on the specific heat of solids in 1907. A similar defence can even be made for those who allegedly refused to look through Galileo's telescope to confirm his claims with their own eyes. After all, the telescope was a new invention of unproven reliability and without some practice it was far from simple to use or to interpret what one saw.

So, how can we distinguish "good" theories from "bad" ones? When we are taught the scientific method at school, the answer is usually to do an experiment. Unfortunately, the notion that experiments can be trusted to deliver a clear verdict on the rights and wrongs of theories is simplistic. Defending conclusions against rival interpretations in peer review means that a clean, decisive experimental result quickly becomes a battle against potential confounding factors and alternative explanations. If you have ever experienced that yourself, you will have encountered something called the Quine-Duhem thesis, which says, in essence, that there is always more than one way to read the data. (More strictly, the thesis is that no scientific hypothesis can make predictions independently from other hypotheses). The Quine-Duhem thesis deserves to be much more widely recognised among working scientists; the fantasy that experiments resolve everything looks increasingly threadbare.

Indeed, some famous scientists have explicitly refused to accept experimentation as the ultimate authority. If observations of the 1919 solar eclipse had failed to support general relativity, Einstein averred that he would still have insisted his theory was correct. If a theory were discarded the instant an experimental result seemed to contradict it, progress would be nigh on impossible.

Ultimately, science does appear to be capable of developing ever more dependable, more accurate, more predictive theories. But this in itself does not mean that we should imagine that bad theories or ideas prevent the progress of good ones. To do so is to put the cart before the horse, or to suppose that history has a goal. Instead, further detailed exploration into how science evolves is needed: as David Wootton argues in his book *The Invention of Science*, to understand how reliable knowledge and scientific progress can and do result from a "flawed, profoundly contingent, culturally relative and all-too-human process".

* heliocentrism: an astronomical model in which the Earth and planets revolve around the Sun at the centre of the solar system

Writing (Task 2)

Lead-in

1 Look at the inventions in the photos. What are they? What are the positive or negative effects of these inventions?

Understand the task

2a Work in pairs. Read the essay question and discuss the questions below. Make notes.

> *Scientific innovation is always a positive thing and should be encouraged. To what extent do you agree with this statement? Give reasons for your answer and include any relevant examples from your knowledge or experience.*

1 What does the question mean?
2 What is your opinion/answer?
3 What might your main points be?

b Read some opinions about the essay question in Exercise 2a. Are they for or against innovation, or could any be both for and against depending on how the paragraph was developed?

1 Despite the negative effects of some innovation, we should encourage it in all its forms as the benefits outweigh the drawbacks.
2 Innovation is absolutely essential to the development of humanity.
3 Innovation is a part of development but we must remember the importance of restricting and regulating how innovation is undertaken.
4 Some innovations have had detrimental effects on the natural world.
5 Innovation is unstoppable and we must live with the consequences.

c Read the hypothetical statements (A–E) and match them with the points in Exercise 2b (1–5).

A If we continue making weapons, we might be in the situation where we have no planet to care for.
B Imagining a world without electricity or medicine is arguably worse than imagining a world without more negative innovations like surveillance technology.
C People innovate on their own, in small ways, and as such it would be impossible for it to be curbed by the state.
D A world without innovation would mean that we would be susceptible to illness and disease and have a far more difficult life without today's necessities such as artificial heating and lighting.
E If factory farming had not been developed, many animals would have had much happier lives.

d Work in pairs and discuss whether you could incorporate any of the ideas in Exercises 2b and 2c into your own notes for the essay.

Plan the task

3 a Turn to page 190 and read the descriptors for coherence and cohesion. Discuss the questions below.

1 Why should you always plan an essay before writing?
2 How do you organise your paragraphs?
3 In which part(s) of the essay do you state your answer?
4 What do you include in your main body paragraphs?
5 How do you sequence your ideas in a paragraph?
6 How do you link ideas together?

b Look back at your ideas in Exercise 2a and make a plan for your essay. Ensure you think about the questions above.

Language and content

4 Read the list of innovations below and discuss both their positive and negative effects.

1 cars   3 money   5 plastic
2 fertiliser   4 nuclear energy   6 the internet

5 a Complete the sentences with the words below.

culture   form of transport   lack of activity   material   process   products

1 Money has stimulated a _____ of consumerism which promotes the idea that people need to constantly update and have the best of everything and dispose of the old.
2 Excessive use of the internet can lead to _____ which can have negative effects on the mental health of individuals.
3 Nuclear energy may be undesirable but is necessary. This _____ is one of the cleanest ways of producing sustainable energy.
4 Fertilizers are common in arable farming. These _____ help crops grow bigger and faster.
5 Plastic is not good for the environment. This _____ is not biodegradable and is difficult to recycle.
6 Cars have given everyone a great deal of convenience. This _____ has made it possible for us to travel more easily and save time.

b Work in pairs and discuss how you could extend sentences 1–6 in Exercise 5a using the discourse markers below.

although   as a result   consequently   however   in addition   in turn

Write your essay
➤ **EXPERT WRITING** page 200

6 Write your answer to the essay question in Exercise 2a. Write at least 250 words.

Assess and improve

7 a Work in pairs and review each other's essays, using the checklist below.

Argument quality	Does the writer explain his/her point of view in the introduction? Is each point valid and well developed?
Logical ordering	Has the writer organised his/her points well? Are there explanations and examples following the main points?
Clarity of points	Are connections between ideas clear? Are there any points of argument that are not expressed clearly?
Paragraphing	Is there a clear introduction and conclusion? Is there one clear point for each of the body paragraphs? Is the content arranged logically within the paragraphs?

b Using ideas from Exercise 7a, work together to improve each other's essays.

Review

1a Complete the text with words below.

wider implications   speculate   concept
in all likelihood   assume   public perception

At the end of the twentieth century the self-help industry started to grow substantially and nowadays it is estimated to be worth billions of dollars. The **1** _____ of the self-help industry is for people to improve their lives by implementing ideas and techniques which will change their lives for the better. Many people **2** _____ that the industry has been built on solid scientific principles; the **3** _____ of the self-help industry is that it is organised and run by expert academics and doctors. This has **4** _____ for society because if people believe they can solve their own problems, they may not seek professional help. Psychologists **5** _____ that people could be doing more damage than good by using self-help programmes, books and online resources. **6** _____ , there are probably both benefits and drawbacks depending on the individual.

b Choose the correct option in *italics* to complete the sentences.

1 The government promised to *invest / investing* more in the development of space probes.
2 The company managed *expand / to expand* its range of innovative products.
3 Becoming a concert musician involves *practising / to practise* for many hours per day.
4 People who want to push their boundaries should avoid *becoming / to become* negative after setbacks.
5 Athletes who take chances risk *losing / to lose* matches, but it is often worth trying.

c Choose the correct phrase in *italics* to complete the sentences.

1 It is only when we think about a situation deeply and from many different angles that we can begin to develop a useful *insight / concept*.
2 *I get the impression / I would not be surprised* if my son studies biology later in life; he's always examining insects and birds in the garden.
3 Due to the way the workplace is changing nowadays, *the chances are / my guess* we would recognise very few jobs of the future.
4 From observing modern graduates *I am confident / I get the impression* that job satisfaction could be as important as salary and career progression for them.
5 When the interviewer thanked me for coming there was an *assumption / inference* in his tone of voice which suggested that I had been successful.
6 *My guess / In all likelihood* is that our approach to success will have to change significantly in the future.

2a Complete the sentences with the correct form of the verbs in brackets.

1 The directors of the organisation wished that they _____ (invest) more in staff training.
2 If only the education system _____ (include) more creative activities for teenagers.
3 If I had studied harder at high school, I _____ (gone) to medical school.
4 Suppose the internet hadn't been invented. We _____ (be) able to communicate in such a global way.
5 It's time scientists _____ (focus) more on finding life on other planets.
6 What if people hadn't invented mobile phones? How _____ your life _____ ? (change)

b Complete the sentences with the correct past modal forms below, to match the meanings in bold.

could have   would have   should have

1 The number of people suffering from malaria _____ been significantly reduced by using specially designed mosquito nets.
= this expresses a **possible** alternative if something in the past had been different
2 The government _____ consulted some technology experts to help them before they changed their policy on online fraud.
= this suggests a different past action was **recommended**
3 The Philae probe _____ provided more data if it had not broken down on the surface of a comet.
= this imagines an **alternative result** if something in the past had been different

c What is the difference in meaning between the pairs of sentences?

1 A Air conditioning systems should have been designed to be more environmentally friendly.
  B Air conditioning systems could have been designed to be more environmentally friendly.
2 A If inventors in the past had been better at showing off their inventions, more young people would have chosen to study science subjects at university.
  B Inventors in the past should have been better at showing off their inventions in order to inspire more young people to study science subjects at university.
3 A The internet would have been less innovative if it had been managed by national security agencies.
  B The internet could have been less innovative if it had been managed by national security agencies.

Expert reference

Listening paper

The **Listening paper** tests your ability to understand spoken English. The test itself is approximately 30 minutes, after which you will be given 10 minutes to transfer your answers from the question paper to the answer sheet. There are four different recordings with ten questions each. There will be more than one task type for each recording. Each recording is played just once. You must write your answers in pencil. Incorrectly spelt words are marked as incorrect.

General advice

Before you listen
- Read the instructions carefully so you know the number of words required or if any answers could be a number.
- Read the questions to help you predict the topic, the order you will hear the information and the possible answers. This will help you focus when you listen to the recording.
- Think about what synonyms and paraphrases you might hear in the recording.

While listening
- Listen carefully to the introduction because it will give you information about the recordings.
- Note down your answers quickly – do not worry about spelling at this stage.
- Do not panic if you miss an answer. Just move on to the next question.
- Pay attention to signposting language – this will help you move on to the next question.
- Use the time between the recordings to read ahead. Read the next set of questions and predict the content of the next recording.
- Remember that the answers must be the exact word forms from the recordings.

After listening
- Make sure you transfer your answers to the answer sheet carefully and check they match the question numbers.
- Check your spelling. You must spell answers correctly and use capital letters where necessary.
- If you have any gaps on your answer sheet, have a guess and write something.

Gap-fill tasks (form/note/table/sentence/ summary completion) and short-answer questions

In the Listening Paper you will often see completion questions. For this question type you will see a form, sentences, a summary, a table or some notes with some gaps that you need to complete with words or numbers. For the short-answer questions, you have to answer a question with words from the recording. All the completion questions will be in the order you hear the information.

Before you listen
- Read the instructions and notice how many words you can use for each answer or whether the answer will be a number. If the instructions say 'up to THREE words and/or a number', you can use one, two or three words or a number.
- Skim-read the questions to give you an idea of the content of the recording.
- Think about the part of speech you will need for the answer (e.g. noun, verb, adjective).
- Try to predict how the answers may be paraphrased in the recording.
- For table questions, check how the information is organised and for short-answer questions, pay attention to the question words (these will tell you what kind of answer you need) and the most unusual words (these often help you know when the answer is coming).

While you listen
- Listen for any corrections. Sometimes the speakers will change what they say and this could be an answer so be ready to change your answer.
- Remember your answers MUST be taken directly from the recording so listen carefully and write down exactly what the speakers say.

After you listen
- Check your answers carefully. Review the number of words, the spelling and the form of the word. Remember that your answers MUST be grammatically correct.

Multiple choice

In a listening multiple-choice task, you will see a question or statement followed by some options. There are three types. One type is a question or prompt followed by three options (A–C) where you have to choose the correct option. Another type has a question and multiple options from which you have to choose more than one correct answer. All the multiple-choice questions will be in order, but you may hear the options in a different order.

Before you listen
- Look at all the multiple-choice questions. Can you see the flow of the topic? How do the questions progress? Asking yourself these questions can help you understand the progress of the recording.
- Look at each question or statement. What key words can you listen for? These are often the most unusual words or numbers (e.g. *Florida*, *ten thousand*). Think of how the question or statement might be said differently as you are unlikely to hear this information in exactly the same way.
- Look at the answer options and try to think of synonyms or synonymous phrases for each option.

While you listen

- Try to keep up with the recording. Eliminate incorrect answers to help you choose the correct answer. Remember, even if you hear the same word in the recording as you see in an option it does not necessarily make it correct. Listen for details and check.
- Circle the option you think is correct on your answer paper and strike through options you believe are wrong.

After you listen

- When transferring your answers, make sure you write the letter down (A, B or C) and NOT the answer in word form.
- If you are unsure of an answer, but have discounted one or two answers from that question, take an educated guess. You cannot lose points for guessing.

Matching/Classification (information, features, sentence endings)

Matching/classification questions involve matching a set of items from the recording to a set of options or categories. There are many varieties of information that you may be asked to match or classify. For example, you may have to match people to their opinions or places to their descriptions. You may also have to match sentence halves to form complete sentences.

Before you listen

- Skim read the questions and think about what you are going to hear on the recording.
- Read the questions and matching categories in more detail. Notice what you are matching or classifying. Remember that the information on the recording will be in the same order as the questions.
- Underline key words in the questions.
- Think about how the information in the questions could be paraphrased in the recording.

While you listen

- Listen for different speakers if you are matching names of people to opinions or actions.
- Pay attention to key words and paraphrases in the questions.
- If you are not 100 percent sure of the answer, note down the possible answers and then eliminate the wrong possibilities at the end of the recording.
- If you are listening to more than one speaker, be prepared for speakers to change what they say. If this happens, you may need to change your initial answer.

After you listen

- Check that you have an answer for every question and whether or not you can use one of the options more than once. If not, make sure you have a different option for each answer.
- Transfer your answers onto the answer sheet. Make sure you follow the correct format for your answers. Usually this means you must write the letter (A, B, C, etc.) and not the words in the list of options.

Label a map/plan, diagram or flow chart

Sometimes you will be asked to label a map, plan or diagram or to complete a flow chart. In this type of question, you may have words next to the image that you need to add to the correct place (there will be a letter for each word), or you may be required to write the words. You will hear the answers in order.

Before you listen

- Read the instructions carefully. Do you have options to choose from or do you need to complete spaces?
- Look at the visual information. From what perspective is it shown? (Above, front view, etc.) What order will you hear the information? Look at the question numbers and think about how you can describe the visual information in that order.
- Look at any words given in the visual. You will hear these words so think about how they relate to the answer spaces.

While you listen

- Try to follow the map carefully. You will be given a starting point. You can use your pencil to follow along as you go.
- Note down the answers as you hear them. (Write the letters if you have options or the words if there are no options given.)

After you listen

- Make sure you transfer your answers carefully. Remember to use the correct format (letters or numbers), the correct word form (noun, verb, adjective) and check your spelling. If your spelling is not correct, your answer will be marked as incorrect.

Reading paper

The **Academic reading paper** tests your ability to understand written English in an academic environment. The total time for the test is 60 minutes, and there are 40 questions you need to answer. In total, the passages are 2,000–2,750 words long and this is spread over three different passages. There are a variety of question types, and you will have up to 4 question types for each text.

Note In the Reading test you MUST write your answers on the answer sheet during the 60-minute time limit. No extra time is given at the end of the test to transfer them. Write your answers next to the correct number, and pay extra attention if you leave an answer blank. Where possible try to take a guess and fill any gaps.

General advice

DO allocate the right amount of time for each set of questions – you have 40 questions and only 60 minutes. Spend about 20 minutes on each passage.

DO start with Part 1 and work through, as the passages become increasingly difficult.

DO move on if you cannot find an answer in 2 minutes.

DO start by reading the questions. These are often written in easier language and you can get a feel for the main ideas in the text from the questions.

DO check you have written answers in the correct form as given in the rubric and have not exceeded any word restrictions.

DO double-check the spelling of your answers. US or UK spelling is fine. If you make a mistake, put a line through the old answer and rewrite the new answer clearly beside it.

DON'T go back and change answers unless you are sure. Studies show test takers more often change correct answers to the wrong answers.

DON'T read everything. Even native speakers cannot read all 2,750 words carefully and complete the tasks. Scan to locate information, then read carefully for the answer.

Completion tasks

1 Notes, tables, flow charts (Section 1), summaries, sentences (Section 2)

In these reading tasks, you are looking for details or the main information in a passage which is usually factual. You have a summary of part of the passage and have to complete it, using words from the passage. You will not need to, or have the time to, read the whole text; you need to scan the passage to find the parts you need to read in order to do the task. You might have incomplete notes, a table, a chart, sentences or a piece of continuous text – a summary – to complete with a maximum given number of words from the passage. The answers usually come from one part of the passage but the answers to the notes and summary may not come in the same order as the passage.

Before you read

• Read the instructions so that you know the maximum number of words/numbers you are allowed to use.

• Read the task and the title of the task (if there is one) to get a good idea of what information you are looking for. Remember that if the information is in note form, there will probably not be articles, pronouns, etc. Sentences are different and a summary consists of complete sentences which are connected together grammatically.

• Underline the key words. These will be the 'content words' such as nouns, adjectives and verbs which carry meaning, and they will help you to locate the information you need to find.

• Predict what kind of information you are looking for by reading the words around the gaps. Think about the grammatical function (noun, verb, etc.) as well as the kind of meaning.

While you read

• Locate the section in the passage which gives you the answer. If there are subheadings, these may help you to find the correct section.

• Read the relevant part carefully. Underline the answer you need.

• Copy the words exactly as they are spelt in the passage. Be careful not to change the words in any way.

After you read

• Make sure the spelling is correct or you will lose marks.

• Check that you have not written more than the maximum number of words stated in the instructions or you will lose marks. Numbers can be written either as figures (e.g. 30) or words (thirty). Hyphenated words count as one word and contracted words are not used.

• Make sure you have not repeated words from either side of the gap.

• Read what you have written carefully to make sure it makes sense in terms of meaning and that it fits grammatically (e.g. Do you need singular or plural words?).

2 Diagram labelling (Section 1)

In this task, you have to complete labels on a diagram. The diagram is based on a description from the passage and you have to relate it to information in the passage. A word limit is given. The answers may not come in the same order as the passage but are usually from one or two paragraphs. Follow the strategies for other completion activities.

3 Objective summary completion (Section 3)

In this task, you have to complete a summary by using the words in a box, NOT words from the passage. There are always more words in the box than there are gaps in the summary.

Follow the strategies for other completion activities.

True/False/Not given (Section 1)

In this reading task, you are reading to identify specific information and the passage is generally factual/descriptive. You are given statements; you will have to decide whether the information in the passage agrees with the statement (True), says the opposite of what is stated (False) or whether the information is not mentioned in the passage (Not given). It is very important to base your answers on what you read in the passage and not on what you consider to be the correct answer from personal knowledge. If you think the answer is *True* but cannot find it mentioned in the passage, the answer is *Not given*.

The statements follow the order of the information in the passage but may appear in different parts of the passage. There may be some paragraphs which do not relate to any of the questions.

Before you read

• Read each statement carefully so that you know what information you are looking for. Underline the words which will help you to find the relevant section in the passage.

• Read the title and subheading then skim the passage (use topic sentences to help you read faster) or skim the first and last paragraphs so that you know what the passage will be about. If you skim efficiently, it will be easier to find where in the passage the answer is located. Do not worry about understanding every word.

While you read

- Scan the passage to find the relevant information for the first question. Look for paraphrases or synonyms of the statements: they will probably not be written in the same way.
- Read the information carefully and decide on what it is saying. Does it match the statement or contradict it? (Make sure that both parts agree or disagree in more complex statements). It may be that the idea may seem to belong in the passage but there is no information on this actually stated, in which case it is *Not given*.

  Check words which qualify a statement, e.g. frequency adverbs such as *rarely*, *sometimes*, quantifiers such as *most*, *few* or verbs such as *refuse*, *suggest*, *believe*, *confirm*, *deny*.
- Do the same for the other questions.

After you read

- Make sure you have written *True/False/Not given* in the format stated in the instructions (i.e. not *T/F/NG*).

Yes/No/Not given (Section 3)

In this reading task, the passage is mainly argumentative. You are given a number of statements and asked whether they agree with the views or claims of the writer. You have to write *Yes*, *No* or *Not given*, based on evidence or lack of evidence from the passage. This type of question tests your ability to recognise opinions and/or claims stated by the writer.

Follow the strategies for *True/False/Not given*.

Short-answer questions (Section 1)

In this reading task, you will have to scan the passage for specific information and then give a short answer in no more than the number of words stated, using words or numbers from the passage. The questions follow the order of the text.

Before you read

- Read the instructions so that you know how many words you are allowed to use.
- Read the questions/statements and underline the words which will help you to locate the answers in the passage.

While you read

- Scan the passage to find the relevant paragraph. The questions will follow the same order as the information in the passage. Look for paraphrases of the words in the questions/statements.
- Underline the information you need.

After you read

- Make sure you have kept to the word limit, otherwise your answer will be marked wrong. Numbers can be written as words or figures; hyphenated words count as one word.
- Check you have copied the words correctly as they appear in the passage.
- Check that the answers fit grammatically with the questions/statements.

Matching tasks (Section 2)

1 Matching headings

In this reading task, you will have a passage divided into paragraphs or sections (i.e. with more than one paragraph) and lettered A, B, C, etc. You are given a list of headings with Roman numerals (i, ii, iii, iv, etc.); each heading summarises one of the sections. The questions are testing your ability to identify the main idea of a paragraph or section and to recognise the main idea and supporting details.

There are more headings than sections so not every heading is used. Headings cannot be used more than once and it is also possible that not every section will have a heading. With this task type, you have to match each heading to a section of the passage.

In this part of the test, the list of headings always come before the passage.

Before you read

- Read the instructions.
- Read the title and subheading of the passage so that you know what it will be about.
- Always read the headings before you read the passage so that you know what you are looking for, and underline the key words. Think of one or two questions that you would expect a paragraph with this heading to answer.
- Cross out any headings which are definitely not connected.

While you read

- Skim each paragraph or section to identify the main topic or idea. You will do this faster if you can identify the topic sentence and see how each paragraph is organised. Focus on the main idea, not on matching words with the same meanings.
- Choose the heading which summarises the general topic of each paragraph. If you are unsure, match the other headings first and leave this one until last. Remember that there are always extra headings which you will not need to use.

After you read

- Check that the extra headings could not fit with any of the sections.

2 Matching information

In this reading task you have a passage divided into paragraphs or sections lettered A, B, C, etc. and a list of questions containing information which relates to one of the paragraphs or sections. The information is not in the same order as it appears in the reading passage. You have to match this information to one of the paragraphs. If a paragraph can be used more than once, the instructions will tell you this. A paragraph may not have a question.

You are tested on your ability to scan a text to find specific information, such as detail, reasons, examples, etc.

Before you read

- Read the title and subheading of the passage to get an idea of what it is about.

- Read the questions and underline the type of information that you are looking for, such as descriptions, problems, causes, etc.

While you read

- Read the passage quickly to get an idea of what it is about.
- Read each paragraph and decide whether it contains any of the information in the questions. Look for paraphrases of the key ideas that you underlined. There may be more than one piece of information in a paragraph, or none at all.

After you read

- Check that the answer you choose has exactly the same information as the paragraph.

3 Matching features

In this reading task you have to match a list of statements or information to a list of options in a box, lettered A, B, C, etc. The options could be a range of features from the passage such as names of people, places, dates, etc. Options may not be used and some may be used more than once. If they are to be used more than once, the instructions will tell you this. The focus of this part is to skim and scan to recognise opinions, etc. and make connections before reading for more detail. The 'features' are listed in the same order as they appear in the reading passage but they may appear more than once in different parts of the passage.

Before you read

- Read the instructions.
- Read the list of features and list of statements.
- Underline key ideas in the statements.

While you read

- Scan the passage and underline all references in the passage to the options in the box (e.g. *the people*).
- Find the relevant parts for each name or date, etc. and read it carefully. Look for paraphrases of what is said in the statements.
- Match each statement to an option.

Multiple-choice questions: selecting more than one answer (Section 2)

In this reading task you have to choose two options from a list of five. You are given a question and a number of statements. You may need to complete a 'stem' (the first part of the sentence) or select the best response to a question. You may have to choose the best two answers from five alternatives (A–E) or the best three answers from seven alternatives (A–G). The answers may come from one part or different parts of the passage and the questions are in the same order as the information in the passage. The questions may test understanding of main ideas, specific information or details. They may focus on facts or opinions.

Before you read

- Read the instructions carefully so that you know how many options to choose.

- Underline the key ideas in the question or stem; they will help you choose the right place in the passage.

While you read

- Scan the passage to find the place where the information is located.
- Underline the relevant part and read the options carefully to see which one of them matches each stem or answers the question.
- Write down the options you choose making sure you have chosen the correct number.

After you read

- Check that the options you have not chosen do not link to any information in the passage.

Multiple choice (Section 3)

In this reading task, you may have a question with four possible answers or the first half of a sentence with four possible sentence endings. You have to choose one possible answer (A, B, C or D). The questions are in the same order as the information is given in the passage. The questions are testing main points, specific information or detail.

Before you read

- Skim the passage first to get a general idea of what it is about.
- Read each question/incomplete statement and mark the key words.

While you read

- Locate the relevant part of the passage and read it carefully.
- Predict what the answer might be. Try to answer in your own words.
- Read all four options carefully and eliminate any options which you think are incorrect.
- Choose the one which is closest to your answer.

After you read

- If none of the options seem correct, go back and read the relevant section again, comparing each option to what you read.

Matching sentence endings (Section 3)

In this reading task you are given one part of the sentence, the stem, (numbered) which is based on information in the passage and you have to choose the best ending for the sentence from a series of options (lettered). There are extra options which you do not use. The sentences are in the same order as the information in the passage and each option can be used only once.

Before you read

- Underline key information in the stem which might help you to locate where it comes from in the passage.

While you read

- Predict how the first stem might end, using any linking words to help you.

- Use any names or key words to find the part of the passage that you need to focus on.
- Read the options and find the one which paraphrases the ideas/language in the passage.
- Cross out the options you choose as you go through the task. Leave any that you cannot do for the moment and go back to them later when you have fewer choices. Be careful not to be distracted by similar information or language from the passage (it is more likely to be paraphrased).

After you read

- Read the completed sentences to make sure they are coherent and factually correct.

Writing paper

The **Academic writing paper** tests your ability to write academic texts. You will be required to interpret and describe visual information in Task 1 and write an essay in Task 2. The paper is one hour long, with 20 minutes recommended for Task 1 and 40 minutes recommended for Task 2. You can write in either pen or pencil.

General advice

- Read the questions carefully and make sure you understand exactly what you are being asked to write about.
- Plan each task to make sure you answer all parts of the question and organise your ideas clearly and logically.
- Spend about five minutes doing this for Task 1 and no more than ten minutes doing this for Task 2.
- Write your answer once only – you do not have enough time to write two versions.
- Remember to write in paragraphs and connect your ideas with signposting words.
- Include a variety of grammatical structures, including complex ones, and make sure your vocabulary is specific to the topic.
- Remember to use a formal register for both tasks and try to avoid using features such as contractions.
- Leave some time to check and edit your writing. Read it once to check it makes sense. Then, read it again and check for accurate usage of language, punctuation and spelling.

Task 1: Factual description

Task 1 is a factual description of some visual information. You might be asked to describe a chart, diagram or map/plan. There may also be more than one chart or image on a connected theme. You must write at least 150 words. You are not required to give your opinion in this task.

Before you write

- Look carefully at the image(s) and the title so you understand what information is being shown in the chart, diagram or map/plan.
- Notice the way the information is organised and any labels, keys or categories.
- Look for any connections or relationships in the information and also for anything that stands out as different.
- Identify an overview. This means understanding the general purpose and/or message presented by the data or image(s).

While you write

- Start with an introduction which describes the visual information in general. Try to use synonyms or paraphrase the title wherever possible.
- Describe the main trends shown in the visual information.
- Select some facts and numbers to illustrate your main points, remembering to describe them accurately.
- Finish with an overview which explains the overall purpose of the information.
- Do not include your opinion or comment on the reasons for the information.
- Use signposting words to show the relationship between the information such as similarities, differences and trends.
- Write clearly and write at least 150 words, otherwise you will lose marks.

After you write

- Read your description and check that you have described the information accurately and organised your answer logically.
- Correct any errors in grammar, spelling and punctuation. Cross out any changes neatly and write the correction clearly above or below the word or section which has been crossed out.

Task 2: Essay

Task 2 is an academic essay and there a variety of forms. You may be asked to discuss an opinion, provide solutions to a problem, compare and contrast or explain the causes and/or effects of something. There may be two parts to the question and you must make sure you address both parts in the essay. You must write at least 250 words.

Before you write

- Carefully read the question, focusing on the key words. Identify the type of essay and exactly what you are required to write about.
- Note down your ideas and organise them into a logical order.
- Note down some topic-specific vocabulary which you could use in your essay.
- Think about some high-level grammatical structures which would be appropriate for the essay.

While you write

- Write an introduction which provides some background information to the essay question and clearly states your answer. Remember to paraphrase the essay question where possible.
- Write a topic sentence at the beginning of each paragraph, then add supporting points by including explanations, reasons or examples.
- Summarise the main points in the conclusion. Do not introduce any new ideas in the conclusion.
- Write clearly and write at least 250 words or you will lose marks.

After you write

- Read your essay and check that you have organised your ideas logically in paragraphs and expressed them using high-level grammatical structures and topic-specific vocabulary.
- Correct any errors in grammar, spelling and punctuation. Cross out any changes neatly and write the correction clearly above or below the word or section which has been crossed out.

Speaking paper

The **Speaking paper** is a test of your ability to communicate information and ideas in English on a variety of topics. The test lasts for 11–14 minutes and is divided into three parts. Part 1 lasts for 4–5 minutes and consists of general questions on familiar lifestyle topics such as family, hobbies and studies. Part 2 is the 'long turn' and requires you to speak for 2 minutes about a topic given to you by the examiner. Part 3 is a discussion on a topic related to that in Part 2 at a more abstract and conceptual level.

See page 183 for the assessment criteria for the speaking paper.

General advice

- Speak as much as you can. You have 11–14 minutes to show the examiner the extent of your linguistic skills.
- Make sure you expand your answers by giving examples, descriptions and reasons wherever possible.
- Speak clearly and confidently and remember to smile at the examiner.
- Try to sound interested in the topics and questions.
- Demonstrate both the range and accuracy of your linguistic skills.

Part 1: Introduction and general questions

Part 1 focuses on general questions about the candidate and lasts 4–5 minutes. The examiner will ask the candidate to introduce themselves and will then ask further questions on a range of familiar topics.

Before you speak

- Listen carefully to the questions and notice the tense the examiner uses.
- If you do not hear the question fully, ask the examiner to repeat it.

While you speak

- Use expressions such as *That's an interesting question* or *Let me see* to give yourself some thinking time before you answer.
- Answer the question directly and then give some additional information to expand on your answer. Use this additional information to show your range of language, both lexically and grammatically.
- Speak fluently, but not too fast. You should speak without too much hesitation, and use features of pronunciation and intonation to respond appropriately and communicate nuances of meaning.
- Remember to be as accurate as possible; self-correct if you make a mistake.
- Use linking words to show how your ideas relate to each other.

Part 2: Individual long turn

In **Part 2**, the candidate is given a task card which has a topic and specifically four points to talk about. Three of these points usually focus on describing something and the final point asks for reasons for something. The candidate is given exactly one minute to prepare and should then aim to talk for 2 minutes. During the one-minute preparation time candidates can make notes and will be given a piece of paper and a pencil to do so.

After your talk, the examiner might ask one or two more questions on the topic.

Before you speak

- Read the task card carefully and notice exactly what you are being asked to talk about.
- Think about some grammatical structures and topic-specific vocabulary which will be useful for your answer.
- Write down key words and ideas to help you; do not try to write whole sentences as there is not enough time.
- Make sure you use all the one-minute preparation time to plan what you want to say and order your ideas logically.

While you speak

- Follow the prompts on the card to make sure you talk about all of the things on the card, using your notes to help you.
- Expand on each point to make sure that you are able to speak for the full 2 minutes. You can do this by including descriptions, reasons, examples and contrasts.
- Use a range of grammatical structures and topic-specific vocabulary in your answer.
- Listen carefully to any follow-up questions that the examiner might ask before moving onto Part 3. Give yourself time to think with phrases such as *I'm not sure about that* or *That's a good question*.

Part 3: Two-way discussion

In **Part 3**, the examiner asks the candidate some more abstract and conceptual questions on the topic in Part 2. This part is 4–5 minutes. Although it is a two-way discussion, the candidate is expected to talk more than the examiner and to take the lead in the discussion.

Before you speak

- Listen carefully to the questions so that you are clear about what you are being asked. Remember that the questions in Part 3 are likely to be longer and more complex than the questions in Part 1.
- If you do not understand a question, ask the examiner to repeat it, speak more slowly or explain a word. The examiner can help you with this in Part 3.

While you speak

- Use thinking-time expressions such as *That's an interesting question* or *Let me see* in the same way as in Part 1.
- Give thorough answers as much as possible by giving reasons, contrasts and examples wherever you can.
- Be prepared for the examiner to ask you to explain or justify your ideas.
- Do not speak for too long on one question. The examiner will ask you follow-up questions to help you keep talking.
- Speak fluently and clearly, but do not rush. The questions in Part 3 require some thought, as well as a range of grammatical structures and vocabulary.
- Be as accurate as you can and remember to self-correct if you hear yourself make a mistake.
- Use linking words to show how your ideas relate to each other.

Expert grammar

Module 1

Synonyms, prefixes, word formation (page 13)

Synonyms (words of a similar meaning)

Using the internet can improve your pace of learning.
*Using the internet can improve your **rate** of learning.*

Prefixes (initial letters before words)

If you don't check the instructions, you won't understand.
*If you don't check the instructions, you'll **mis**understand.*

Word formation (changing nouns, verbs, etc.)

Sometimes watching video instructions can make a task simpler.
*Sometimes watching video instructions can **simplify** a task.*

Tense review (page 16)

1 Simple tenses, e.g. present simple, past simple

Use the simple form of the verb and the auxiliary *do* or *did* for negative and question forms.

***Do** you **go** to school every day?*
*I **didn't do** my homework yesterday.*

2 Continuous tenses, e.g. present continuous, past continuous

Use the *-ing* form of the verb and the auxiliary *be*.

*I'm **learning** to speak Hindi.*
*Ahmet **wasn't having** lunch at 2p.m. yesterday.*

3 Perfect tenses, e.g. present perfect, past perfect

Use the past participle of the verb and the auxiliary *have* or *had*.

*Huan **hasn't seen** the teacher yet.*
*I **hadn't learnt** any Greek words before I arrived in Athens.*

4 Tenses that are a combination of continuous and perfect, e.g. present perfect continuous, past perfect continuous

Use *had/have + been + -ing* form of the verb.

*Daniel **hasn't been studying** very much, so he probably won't pass.*
*Mariella **had been studying** a lot, and she got a good grade.*

5 Future forms

There are three common future forms: present continuous, *be + going to + simple verb*, future simple (*will/won't + simple verb*).

*Bella **is sitting** a music exam tonight.*
*Yasmin **is going to study** English in Australia.*
*One day, people **will study** in any country they want.*

The future simple has continuous, perfect and mixed forms that follow the patterns above.

*In 2070, we **will be studying** on Mars.*
*By this time next year, my class **will have graduated**.*
*My teacher **will have been teaching** here for 50 years in January!*

Further ways of expressing the future include: present simple, *about to, expect to* and modals such as *could* or *might*.

Module 2

Present simple, past simple and present perfect passive (page 29)

1 We use the passive to change the focus of a sentence. We can move the object of the verb to the subject position to change the emphasis of a sentence.

*This is an interesting report. It **was written** by our manager.*

*The majority of the world's rice **is grown** in Asian countries.*

In these sentences the active forms are possible (*Our manager wrote it/The Asian countries grow the majority of the world's rice*), but the writer has chosen to use the passive to change the focus and emphasis in the sentence.

2 We also use the passive when we don't know who did an action or when the person who did an action is not important or when it's not necessary to mention who was responsible. This is often the situation in academic English which describes processes or procedures, such as IELTS Writing Task 1. So, the passive form is often used in this type of academic English task.

*The patient **was asked** to fill out the form with their personal details.* (It is not important who asked the patient to fill out the form.)

*A long pipe **is connected** to the turbine.* (Who connected the pipe is not important.)

*This window **has been left** open.* (We don't know who left the window open.)

3 We form the passive by using the verb *be* + past participle.

Present simple	*The report **is written**.*
Past simple	*The report **was written**.*
Present continuous	*The report **is being written**.*
Present perfect	*The report **has been written**.*
Past continuous	*The report **was being written**.*
Past perfect	*The report **had been written**.*
Future simple	*The report **will be written**.*
Modal	*The report **should be written**.*

4 We often use the passive with impersonal *it* constructions.

It is claimed that feedback is the most important part of a teacher's role.

5 Adverbs follow the same rules as with the active; before the subject or after the verb *be*.

Research is usually done by academics and students.

6 We can introduce the person who did the action by adding *by* to a passive sentence.

The best presentation was done by the last group of students.

Relative clauses (page 32)

Relative clauses give extra information about something in a sentence and begin with words such as *which*, *who* or *that*. There are two types of relative clause; *defining* and *non-defining*.

1 Defining relative clauses are part of the description of something in a sentence. They give us specific details about the subject or object in the sentence.

This is the book which is the most useful for your essay. Susan Jones is the person who would be suitable for this position.

- Defining relative clauses do not have commas around them.
- We can replace the relative pronouns *who* and *which* with *that*.
- We cannot remove defining clauses from the sentence.

2 Non-defining relative clauses give us extra details about something in a sentence. These details are not essential to the description of the subject or object of the sentence.

The project, which has cost more than predicted, will finish this week.
Your final grades, which were agreed by two tutors, are available on the university's intranet.

- Non-defining relative clauses must have commas around them.
- We CANNOT replace the relative pronouns *who* and *which* with *that*.
- Non-defining relative clauses can be removed from sentences because they are not essential to the meaning.

3 Both forms of relative clauses (defining and non-defining) are often reduced to a shorter form. This does not change the meaning. When the clause is formed of *be* + adverb, adjective or adverbial phrase, we can remove the relative pronoun.

The director is the person who is able to make that decision. = The director is the person able to make that decision.

We can reduce the clause when the form is an *-ing* or past participle.

The reason which was given for the factory closure was the rising cost of electricity. = The reason given for the factory closure was the rising cost of electricity.

Sometimes we can replace the relative clause with an infinitive form.

The person who you should talk to is the librarian. = The person to talk to is the librarian.

Module 3

Real and unreal conditionals review (page 45)

Conditional sentences have two clauses; an *if* clause and a main clause. The *if* clause proposes a situation and the main clause explains the consequences of the *if* clause. Conditional forms describe real and unreal situations.

1 Real conditionals describe situations which are true, those which happen often or regularly, or situations which are likely to happen.

When I study, I listen to classical music.
If I finish my work early, I go home.
I won't be able to afford to move if I don't save money every month.

2 Unreal conditionals describe situations which are less likely to happen, impossible or imaginary according to the speaker.

If the government wanted to improve education, they would invest more heavily in teacher training. (the speaker thinks this is unlikely or impossible)
If I understood more about economics, I'd be able to contribute to the discussion. (the speaker is imagining a situation)

3 The clauses in both real and unreal conditional sentences can be connected with other words such as *provided that*, *otherwise*, *unless* and *supposing*. It is important to use these words to introduce the correct clause (main or *if*) and use the correct positive or negative form of the verb.

Unless something is done to protect the world's rainforests, they will disappear.
Universities need to adapt their curricula otherwise students won't be equipped for the jobs of the future.
Supposing we all started using public transport, the world would be very different.
Medical research is valuable provided that it does not cost too much money.

Modal forms; Degrees of certainty (page 48)

We use modal forms to express how sure we are about something. We use them to express possibility, speculation (guessing) and deduction (using clues to say how certain we are about something).

Expert grammar

1 We use *must* when we are sure about something.

*Scientists **must** be close to finding a cure for heart diseases by now based on the latest reports from the World Health Organization.*

2 We use *could*, *may*, *might* if we are not sure about something, but we think there is a possibility that it will happen or is true.

*I **might** get an interview for the job because I have the right qualifications even though I don't have any experience.*

3 We use *mustn't* and *can't* when we are sure that something is not true or won't happen.

*We **can't** rely on traditional fuel sources to provide the energy we will need in the future as they are rapidly running out.*

Module 4

Form clauses (page 61)

1 Clauses need to contain a subject and a verb and can also have an object.

The sun always rises.
Many people like technology.

2 Some sentences contain two clauses; a main clause and a subordinate clause. These can be connected using coordinating conjunctions such as *and*, *but* or *so*, or by using a subordinating conjunction such as *whereas*, *although* or *as*.

*There are many spelling rules in English, **but** they are not impossible to learn.*
*Some people plan their meals and don't waste anything **while** other people end up throwing their food away.*
***Although** skiing looks difficult, it can be mastered after just a few lessons.*

Note: When the subordinating conjunction is in the middle of the sentence there is no comma. This is different from co-ordinating conjunctions.

3 *That* clauses are a type of subordinating clause which means that they cannot exist alone and they must be subordinate to a main clause. We can use *that* clauses to express opinions.

*Many experts **agree that** sugar poses a serious threat to our health.*
*The students **thought that** the exam was fair.*

Pronoun referencing (page 64)

We use pronouns such as: *it*, *this*, *their*, *those* to refer to nouns within and across sentences in order to avoid repeating nouns.

1 Personal pronouns such as *he*, *her*, *their*, *our* replace people.

*There are five regional managers in the company and **they** have a lot of experience.*

2 *It*, *this* and *that* can replace singular nouns, phrases or whole ideas.

*Social networking is a modern phenomenon which has spread all over the world. **It** has become popular with people of all ages.*

3 *These* and *those* can replace plural nouns and people, as well as longer phrases and ideas.

*There are some arguments against climate change, but **these** have mostly been discredited.*

4 *Which* can replace objects, phrases and whole ideas, *who* can replace people and *where* can replace places.

*The internet has become a research tool **which** most people cannot live without.*

Module 5

Reported speech patterns (page 77)

1 Reported speech (also known as indirect speech) is used when we want to report something that was said earlier.

Aunt: 'I've never been on a plane before.'
My aunt said that she had never been on a plane before.

To turn direct speech into reported speech there often needs to be a pronoun change and a tense change. The tense should reflect that time has passed since the words were spoken. The pronoun reflects who was the original speaker.

2 In some cases the tense or pronoun however, does not need to change.

'I don't want to go.'
I told him that I didn't want to go. (The pronoun does not change as the speaker is the same).
Karen: 'I'll be able to retire in 2050.'
Karen said she'll be able to retire in 2050. (The tense does not change because the speech is still true or has not happened yet.)

Some modals (*should*, *would*, *might*, *could*, *needn't*) are not moved back in tense.

3 There are also many reported verb structures, some of which are outlined below:

Subject + reported verb + *that* + clause.

She denied that she had changed the date of our meeting.

Subject + reported verb + *to* + object + (*that*) + clause OR + infinitive verb

The manager explained to me that the offer had expired.

Subject + reported verb + object + (*that*) + clause OR + infinitive verb

Many people told me to go and study abroad.

Noun phrases 1 (page 80)

1 Noun phrases are used to give more detail to the noun. There are many ways to structure a noun phrase. Four ways are outlined below:

a Noun + relative clause
Houses + which are in low land

Houses which are in low land *are more susceptible to flooding.*

b Adjective + noun
prominent + positions

Prominent positions *are held by a range of people in business and politics.*

c Noun + noun
database + designer

A **database designer** *is a role that is sought after by many large companies.*

d Noun + prepositional phrase
people + in the study

The people in the study *were asked several questions.*

2 Noun phrases can also be used for quantities:

A (fraction) + of + (category).

A fifth of homeowners.

A fifth of homeowners *wanted to move house.*

The/A (majority/minority) of (category).

The majority of young adults.

The majority of young adults *wish to work overseas.*

Module 6

Link ideas; *Both, neither, either* (page 93)

1 An adverb can be used to begin a new sentence that connects ideas between two sentences.

Multinational companies are important to countries. **Similarly,** *they also promote trans-national networks.*

An adverb can also be used with a connecting conjunction between clauses.

Multinational companies are powerful **and similarly** *they also promote trans-national networks.*

Note: If the point is the same but the agents are different, *so* can be used.

Multinational companies are incredible powerful. **Similarly, so** *are governments.*

2 A conjunction can be used to connect two ideas together in the same sentence.

Multinational companies are powerful **although** *they still need to abide by the laws of governments.*

3 *Both/and, neither/nor* and *either/or* can be used to write about two subjects or objects.

Both can be used to say that two things are similar. A plural verb must be used.

Both *the manager* **and** *his assistant enjoy training events.* (The two subjects like these events.)

Neither can be used to say *not this* and *not that*. A singular verb must be used.

Neither *the manager* **nor** *his assistant enjoys training events.* (The two subjects do not like these events.)

Either can be used to give options between two things. A singular verb must be used.

Either *the manager* **or** *his assistant should have attended the event.* (One of the subjects should have gone.)

You can also use *both* + object pronoun when the subjects are clear and involve two people or groups.

Both of them *attended the training event.* **Neither of them** *attended the training event.* **Either of them** *should have attended the event.*

Cleft sentences (page 96)

Cleft sentences are used to connect something which is already understood with new information. They also serve to stress new information. Two forms of cleft sentence are:

1 The *it* clause

It + to be + noun, relative pronoun + verb

It was in France that I learnt how to sail.

The new information is contained in the *it* part of the sentence.

2 The *what* clause

What + verb + *to be* + noun.

What I need to focus on is my listening skills.

The new information is contained in the final noun.

Other question words such as *how/why/when/where* can be used but are more unusual.

How he managed to get that job, I'll never know.

Module 7

Sentence fragments and run-on sentences (page 109)

A sentence fragment is an incomplete sentence. When you write sentences in English they must have a subject and a verb. Some sentences also need other parts such as an object or two clauses, depending on the grammatical structure and meaning. A run-on sentence is two sentences written as one. It needs to be separated by punctuation or a conjunction.

If the government invested more money. This needs a second clause because the first clause depends on another piece of information.

I play football at weekends I like it a lot. This sentence needs a conjunction (*and*) between *weekends* and/OR a full stop.

The university a variety of courses at undergraduate and postgraduate levels. The sentence needs a verb after university (has).
Discovered an ancient burial site during their last expedition. The sentence needs a subject before the verb *discovered* such as *They/The archaeologists*.

Punctuation (page 109)

Punctuation is required in writing to help the reader follow the flow of writing easily. All punctuation marks have specific uses as follows:

Capital letter (G): All words at the beginning of a sentence must start with a capital letter. There are other capital letter rules too such as the names of countries, days of the week and months always begin with a capital letter.

Full stop (.): It is a point that marks the end of a sentence or the short form of a word.

Question mark (?): It is the mark that is used at the end of a question in writing.

Exclamation mark (!): This is the mark that you write after a sentence or word that expresses surprise, anger or excitement.

Comma (,): It is the mark which is used in writing to show a short pause, separate clauses or separate items in a list.

Semi-colon (;): This expands on the sentence by introducing a list or a second part of the same idea.

Colon (:): This separates clauses or phrases in a sentence OR items in a list.

Apostrophe: It is the sign (') that is used in writing to show that numbers or letters have been left out in contracted forms, as in *don't* OR to show possession as in *Fred's car*.

Quotation marks (' ') or (" "): They are one of a pair of marks that are used in writing to show that you are recording what someone has said. They are also known as speech marks or inverted commas.

Prepositions (page 112)

Prepositions are words such as *in, to, for, above*, which show the relationship between a noun or pronoun and the other parts of a sentence or phrase. They have a variety of functions in English such as to express position or location, time or direction and can also appear in prepositional phrases.

There are some common relationships which prepositions describe. These are as follows:

Comparison: *like, as*
Direction: *through, towards, into*
Place: *on, near, at*
Possession: *of*
Purpose: *to, for*
Time: *before, at*
Agency: *by*
Source: *from*

Module 8

Review of future forms (page 125)

1 Present simple

Use the present simple form of the verb and the auxiliary *do* for negative and question forms.

*The meeting **is** on Tuesday afternoon next week.*
*I **have** a tennis class tomorrow.*

2 Present continuous

Use the *-ing* form of the verb and the auxiliary *be*.

*My parents **are visiting** next weekend.*
*I'**m studying** for my exam tonight.*

3 *going to*

Use *be + going to* + bare infinitive.

*I'**m going to study** French at university.*
*We'**re going to fly** to Mexico for our holiday.*

4 future with *will*

Use *will* + bare infinitive.

*I'**ll send** you an email about the party.*
*Sarah thinks she'**ll do** well in the test.*

5 future continuous

Use *will + be + -ing* verb.

*We'**ll be waiting** for you when you arrive at the station.*
*Next week, he'**ll be staying** at the Hotel Intercontinental.*

6 future passive

Use *will + be* + past participle

*You'**ll be given** your next assignment in class tomorrow.*
*A new airport **will be built** in the city.*

7 future perfect simple

Use *will + have* + past participle

*This time next year, I **will have finished** my course.*
*Michael **will have found** a new job soon.*

8 future perfect continuous

Use *will + has/have + been + -ing* verb

*Next month Susan **will have been working** here for ten years.*
*By the time you get here, I'**ll have been waiting** for over an hour.*

9 future in the past

Use *would* + bare infinitive OR *was/were going to* + bare infinitive

*She thought she **would take** the job, but then changed her mind.*
*They **were going to go** to Paris. In the end, it was too expensive.*

Other future forms

1 We use modals *may*, *might* and *could* to speculate about the future when we are unsure.

   *We **might** go to the cinema at the weekend.*
   *James **could** arrive at any moment – he didn't say when he was coming.*

2 We can use *be + likely/bound to + bare infinitive* to talk about events and situations that we think are probably going to occur.

   *The cost of living in London **is likely to increase** in the near future.*
   *We're **bound to enjoy** the film – it's had such great reviews.*

Cause and effect linking words (page 128)

Linking words are used to show the relationship of ideas in and across sentences. They have specific functions and also fixed grammatical structures.

1 *Because/as/since* + clause, *because of* + noun

   We're studying English because/as/since it is important for our future.
   We're studying English because of its importance for our future.

2 *As a result/consequently* + clause, *as a result of* + noun

   I practised a lot before my driving test. As I result/ Consequently, I passed.
   As a result of a lot of practice, I passed my driving test.

3 *Due to* + noun, *due to the fact that* + clause

   Due to her kindness, she was always popular at school.
   Due to the fact that she was kind, she was always popular at school.

4 *Therefore* + clause

   I wanted to work in the fashion industry therefore I applied to do an internship at a famous store.
   The weather was good therefore Bill decided to go for a walk.

Module 9

Explain how something works (page 141)

There are many structures which can be used to describe how something works. These often involve using defining relative clauses.

The part The device The element The area	which that	is used to … engineers manipulate to … makes …

Describe what something looks like

There are many terms that can be used to describe what something looks like. Some of these terms can be found below.

Structure – *consists of, includes, incorporates, comprises*
Size – *in diameter, in height, in width, in depth, to scale, magnified, elongated, reduced, minimised*
Material – *constructed from, made of, formed by, constituted*
Form – *shaped like, resembles, the appearance of*

Estimation and indication (page 144)

Phrases that estimate or indicate types of examples can be useful for Task 1 writing and Part 3 speaking. Sometimes Task 1 requires more abstract language if there are not specific numbers or details on the visual information. In Part 3, when you are referring to something that is an unknown quantity or idea, you might need to estimate or indicate rather than sound too certain.

Approximately/about/around can be used before numbers or quantities to give an approximate size.

And so on indicates that there are further examples.

More or less can be used before a noun to show approximation.

Kinds of/types of can be used before a noun to refer to a category.

Module 10

Unreal conditionals, *wish* and *if only* (page 157)

The third conditional is often used to explain the results of something that did not happen. It is often used to express regret. It is formed in the following way: *If + past perfect + would have + past participle.*

If I had taken more time to consider my options, I would have continued my education. (In this case, the person thinks they did not consider their options enough and now believes education was a better option.)

Note: The third conditional can also express the result of something that **did** happen.

If I hadn't studied so hard, I wouldn't have passed the test. (The student passed the test.)

There are also many other terms which can be used to express hypothetical **past situations**:

I wish + past perfect (*I wish I'd gone home earlier.*)
If only + past perfect (*If only I'd gone home earlier.*)
Suppose + past perfect (*Suppose I'd gone home earlier …*)
What if + past perfect (*What if I'd gone home earlier?*)

These terms can also be used to express hypothetical **present situations**:

I wish + past simple (*I wish I had more money.*)
If only + past simple (*If only I had more money.*)
Suppose + past simple (*Suppose I had more money ...*)
What if + past simple (*What if I had more money?*)

Other phrases can also be used to express hypothetical situations:

In case can be used to say *in the chance that the situation becomes true* and also *if it is true.*

Take an umbrella **in case** *it rains.*
In case *you don't understand the instructions, I'll explain again.*

It's time ... can be used to say something does not happen but that it should happen.

It's time *they change the enrolment procedures. (They should change the enrolment procedures.)*

Past modal verbs (page 160)

Past modal verbs are constituted of modal verb + *have* + past participle, and these modal verbs can be used for many different purposes.

1 A recommendation about a past action (*should have*).

  You **should have seen** *that programme.* (It was a good idea.)

2 To imagine a hypothetical result (*would have*).

  I **would have been** *happier if my team had won.* (I was not happy.)

3 To imagine a possible hypothetical result (*might have*).

  I **might have been** *on time if the bus were quicker.* (It is possible I would have been on time.)

4 To express hypothetical possibilities (*could have*).

  We **could have gone** *to France if we'd had enough money.* (It was not possible.)

Speaking assessment criteria

Band	Fluency and coherence	Lexical resource	Grammatical range and accuracy	Pronunciation
9	• speaks fluently with only rare repetition or self correction; any hesitation is content related rather than to find words or grammar • speaks coherently with fully appropriate cohesive features • develops topics fully and appropriately	• uses vocabulary with full flexibility and precision in all topics • uses idiomatic language naturally and accurately	• uses a full range of structures naturally and appropriately • produces consistently accurate structures apart from 'slips' characteristic of native speaker speech	• uses a full range of pronunciation features with precision and subtlety • sustains flexible use of features throughout • is effortless to understand
8	• speaks fluently with only occasional repetition or self-correction; hesitation is usually content-related and only rarely to search for language • develops topics coherently and appropriately	• uses a wide vocabulary resource readily and flexibly to convey precise meaning • uses less common and idiomatic vocabulary skilfully, with occasional inaccuracies • uses paraphrase effectively as required	• uses a wide range of structures flexibly • produces a majority of error-free sentences with only very occasional inappropriacies or basic/non-systematic errors	• uses a wide range of pronunciation features • sustains flexible use of features, with only occasional lapses • is easy to understand throughout; L1 accent has minimal effect on intelligibility
7	• speaks at length without noticeable effort or loss of coherence • may demonstrate language-related hesitation at times, or some repetition and/or self-correction • uses a range of connectives and discourse markers with some flexibility	• uses vocabulary resource flexibly to discuss a variety of topics • uses some less common and idiomatic vocabulary and shows some awareness of style and collocation, with some inappropriate choices • uses paraphrase effectively	• uses a range of complex structures with some flexibility • frequently produces error-free sentences, though some grammatical mistakes persist	• shows all the positive features of Band 6 and some, but not all, of the positive features of Band 8
6	• is willing to speak at length, though may lose coherence at times due to occasional repetition, self-correction or hesitation • uses a range of connectives and discourse markers but not always appropriately	• has a wide enough vocabulary to discuss topics at length and make meaning clear in spite of inappropriacies • generally paraphrases successfully	• uses a mix of simple and complex structures, but with limited flexibility • may make frequent mistakes with complex structures, though these rarely cause comprehension problems	• uses a range of pronunciation features with mixed control • shows some effective use of features but this is not sustained • can generally be understood throughout, though mispronunciation of individual words or sounds reduces clarity at times
5	• usually maintains flow of speech but uses repetition, self-correction and/or slow speech to keep going • may over-use certain connectives and discourse markers • produces simple speech fluently, but more complex communication causes fluency problems	• manages to talk about familiar and unfamiliar topics but uses vocabulary with limited flexibility • attempts to use paraphrase but with mixed success	• produces basic sentence forms with reasonable accuracy • uses a limited range of more complex structures, but these usually contain errors and may cause some comprehension problems	• shows all the positive features of Band 4 and some, but not all, of the positive features of Band 6
4	• cannot respond without noticeable pauses and may speak slowly, with frequent repetition and self-correction • links basic sentences but with repetitious use of simple connectives and some breakdowns in coherence	• is able to talk about familiar topics but can only convey basic meaning on unfamiliar topics and makes frequent errors in word choice • rarely attempts paraphrase	• produces basic sentence forms and some correct simple sentences but subordinate structures are rare • errors are frequent and may lead to misunderstanding	• uses a limited range of pronunciation features • attempts to control features but lapses are frequent • mispronunciations are frequent and cause some difficulty for the listener
3	• speaks with long pauses • has limited ability to link simple sentences • gives only simple responses and is frequently unable to convey basic message	• uses simple vocabulary to convey personal information • has insufficient vocabulary for less familiar topics	• attempts basic sentence forms but with limited success, or relies on apparently memorised utterances • makes numerous errors except in memorised expressions	• shows some of the features of Band 2 and some, but not all, of the positive features of Band 4
2	• pauses lengthily before most words • little communication possible	• only produces isolated words or memorised utterances	• cannot produce basic sentence forms	• speech is often unintelligible
1	• no communication possible • no rateable language			
0	• does not attend			

Reproduced with permission of Cambridge English Language Assessment ©UCLES 2016

Test 1 (Part 1)

Before you watch

1a Look at the sentences below. Are they True or False? Correct any false statements.

   1 The IELTS speaking test lasts for 18–20 minutes.
   2 There are three parts to the IELTS speaking test.
   3 The first part is a short interview with personal questions.
   4 The second part is a prepared speech on a topic of your choice.
   5 The third part is a discussion about the Part 2 topic.

b Work in pairs and discuss the questions.

   1 What kinds of answers is the examiner looking for in each section?
   2 On what areas are candidates marked?
   3 What distinguishes a band 7-score from a band 5-score candidate?

c ▶ 1.1 Now watch the examiner describe the test. Were your answers to Exercises 1a and 1b similar?

2 You are going to watch a candidate, Filippo, answer Part 1 of his speaking test. In pairs, discuss what kinds of questions and answers you might hear for the following subjects:

   • Studying English   • Entertainment

While you watch

3a ▶ 1.2 Watch Filippo answer Part 1 of his speaking test. Were your predictions in Exercise 2 correct?

b Watch again and make notes on the questions below.

   1 What will Filippo's new English course help him do?
   2 Why does Filippo think a teacher is useful when learning English?
   3 Why does Filippo enjoy writing?
   4 Why does Filippo like Jim Morrison?
   5 Why does Filippo think entertainment is important?

c Read the list below and then watch Part 1 a third time. Decide what were the stronger and weaker areas of Filippo's performance before discussing your answers in pairs.

Fullness of answer
Grammatical and lexical range
Fluency
Grammatical and lexical accuracy
Pronunciation

d ▶ 1.3 Watch the examiner talking about Filippo's performance. Note down what the examiner says are the positive and negative aspects of his performance. Are they similar to your ideas?

After you watch

4a Look at the excerpt below. How does Filippo's answer help him extend his speech?

   Examiner: Do you think entertainment is important?
   Filippo: Yes, it is because we need …

b Use the phrases below to extend your ideas on the following topics.

The reason I started …   This is largely due to …
What I particularly like about it is …
What I particularly enjoy is …

   1 Your favourite film
   2 How long you have been learning English
   3 Reading books
   4 Your favourite thing about English

c Look at the Part 1 questions below. What kind of tenses and other grammatical structures could you use to answer these questions?

Part 1

I'm going to ask you some questions about studying English.

   1 When did you start studying English?
   2 What is the most enjoyable part of learning English for you?
   3 Do you think English is more difficult to learn than other languages?
   4 Why is English important to you?

Now let's talk about entertainment.

   5 What forms of entertainment do you prefer?
   6 Is entertainment important to you?
   7 Have you ever been to a music concert?

d Work in pairs and take turns to ask and answer the questions in Exercise 4c. Extend your answers by giving reasons where possible.

Test 1 (Part 2)

Before you watch

1a What happens in Part 2 of the IELTS Speaking Test? Number the activities (A–E) in the correct order.

    A The candidate tries to speak for two minutes.
    B The candidate is given a prompt with some instructions.
    C The examiner may ask follow-up questions.
    D The candidate is given a minute to make notes.
    E The candidate is also given a pen/pencil and a piece of paper.

b Look at steps 1–9 for doing Part 2. Write G for good advice and B for bad advice. Improve any bad advice given.

    1 Think about what you will talk about.
    2 Start making notes as soon as you get given the card.
    3 Write on the card you are given.
    4 Check what the three points you must talk about are.
    5 Write exactly what you will say.
    6 Consider which tense(s) forms you might use.
    7 Start talking when you are asked to.
    8 Ask the examiner questions during your talk.
    9 Keep talking until you are asked to stop.

While you watch

2a ▶ 1.4 Read Filippo's task card below. Watch Filippo complete Part 2 of the test and answer the questions below.

> *Part 2*
>
> Describe a memory from your childhood.
> You should say:
>   what the memory is
>   where you were
>   who was involved
> and what is significant about it.

    1 Did Filippo speak for the correct length of time?
    2 Did he speak about all of the points?
    3 Was there a lot of hesitation?
    4 How could Filippo improve his answer?

b Look at the notes below. Complete them with Filippo's answers.

A *what memory is*	B _____ 6 years old
C _____ Father and family	D *why significant*

c Work in pairs and discuss Filippo's performance. What were his strengths and weaknesses? Use the list below to help you.

Task achievement
Cohesion
Grammatical and lexical range
Fluency
Grammatical and lexical accuracy
Pronunciation

d ▶ 1.5 Watch the examiner talking about Filippo's performance. What does the examiner say about:

    1 the organisation?
    2 the amount of time he speaks for?
    3 the relevance of his answer?

After you watch

3a Match the strategies (1–4) with the phrases (A–D).

    1 Self-correction
    2 Signposting
    3 Creating thinking time
    4 Linking to other statements

    A Firstly, Secondly
    B As I explained before
    C How can I say …
    D didn't see for four years … I mean, I haven't seen …

b Now look at the strategies below. Discuss how Filippo could have used them to improve his answer.

Hypothetical statements, e.g. *If I could go back, I would …*
Phrases for being vague, e.g. *I'm not sure exactly …*
Phrases for adding description, e.g. *I think it looked …*
Phrases for adding feelings/impressions, e.g. *It reminded me of …*

c Make your own notes on Filippo's task card in Exercise 2a. Create notes in a grid similar to Filippo's and try to include 2–3 bullet points in each box so you can extend your answer.

d Work in pairs and take turns to give your answers. If possible, time yourself and record your performance so that you can listen back to it.

e Work in pairs and discuss your performances. In what areas are you better than Filippo? In what areas was Filippo better than you?

Test 1 (Part 3)

Before you watch

1a Look at the list (1–4). Which of these things do you need to do in Part 3 of the Speaking Test?

1 describe your own life
2 describe everyday things around you
3 offer an opinion on a wide range of more abstract issues
4 justify opinions in an academic way

b Filippo is going to answer questions connected to his Part 2 task card on memories. In pairs, make notes on possible questions he might be asked.

While you watch

2a ▶ 1.6 Now watch Filippo doing Part 3. Make a note of the questions asked. Are yours similar?

b Watch again and read the views below. Choose the view that Filippo expresses.

1 People tend to remember happy events and forget unhappy ones. / People remember significant events no matter whether they are happy or sad.
2 Society can only develop by learning about historical development. / History has a tendency to occur again in the same kind of way.
3 Social media has made the concept of memory less important. / Social media has forced people to share their memories more.
4 The renaissance was unique. / The renaissance was revolutionary.

c How well did Filippo do? Tick the areas below which you think he could improve on.

Answering the questions directly
Giving additional information
Using a range of expressions
Giving fluent responses with little hesitation
Producing sentences with very few errors
Intelligibility

d ▶ 1.7 Watch the examiner's feedback and compare it with your ideas.

After you watch

3a Look at the questions below and Filippo's answers. Match his answers (1–3) with the techniques for extending answers (A–C).

1 Do you think most people remember happy or unhappy memories?

> Basically, as far as I know, people remember, uh good moment. Um, I came across different articles that say that um, memory delete or erase uh, bad moment of our live-, of our life.

2 In your opinion, is it important to remember past world events?

> Um, yes of course, um, I like history and sometimes when I look at the present I understand the that, uh things keep repeating itself, and there's a saying that history keeps repeating itself – so I totally agree with that.

3 Do you think it's a good thing that many memories today are permanently recorded on social media?

> Hmm. Basically, you know, I remember when I was um, younger, um my mother used to keep all the photo-, picture of myself and she used to show it to other people, and now there's social media, uh we don't give much importance to certain picture or certain moment of our life, that's what I think.

A Give an explanation of an opinion.
B Relate the question to your own experience.
C Talk about an article/something you have read.

b Work in pairs and practise asking and answering the questions (1–3). Use your own ideas and extend your answers using the techniques in Exercise 3a.

c What three tips would you give another student answering Speaking Part 3?

Test 2 (Part 1)

Before you watch

1a The examiner is going to ask a candidate, Gonzalo, questions about places and food. Work in pairs and write down at least three questions the examiner could ask on each topic.

b Work in pairs and discuss which of the statements about fluency and coherence are True and which are False.

1 Candidates must speak quickly.
2 It is better to use common vocabulary than to hesitate while searching for higher-level vocabulary.
3 You should correct yourself if you make a mistake.
4 Candidates should try to connect their ideas using linking words.
5 You should keep talking until the examiner interrupts you.
6 Repeating words will result in a lower score.

While you watch

2a ▶ 2.1 Watch Part 1 of the test and assess Gonzalo's fluency and coherence. Answer the questions below.

1 Does Gonzalo speak at length to answer the examiner's questions?
2 Does he repeat any words or phrases?
3 Does Gonzalo correct himself during Part 1?
4 What linking words and phrases does he use?

b ▶ 2.2 Watch the second section of Part 1 and complete Gonzalo's answers.

1 _____ that I love Mediterranean food.
2 _____ we have lots of them popular in my country.
3 _____ it's quite interesting.
4 _____ one of them, probably I will go for Spanish tapas.
5 _____ you need to have a huge quality food.

c ▶ 2.3 Listen to the examiner's assessment. What positive points does she make about Gonzalo's performance for fluency and coherence? What does she say could be improved?

After you watch

3a Improve the coherence of Gonzalo's answer below by increasing the variety of linking words and phrases, and limiting the use of the word *different* through the use of synonyms.

Well, I'm really fascinated about the fact that you can learn so many things about different people, different places, and you –, it's –, it's good as well just to see different type of things as well, just going outside your comfort zone. And I have to say that they were really fascinating because you know different things and you start learning different ways of thinking, and that's –, I think that that's the main point.

b Compare your new answer with a partner. Whose answer is better and why?

4 Work in pairs and take turns to ask and answer the Part 1 questions below. Record your answers if possible, then listen and evaluate each other's performance for range and accuracy of grammar and vocabulary.

Part 1

1 What interesting places have you visited?
2 Why were they interesting?
3 What country would you most like to visit? Why?
4 Do you prefer the countryside or the city?
5 Let's move on to food. What kind of food do you prefer?
6 What kinds of food are popular in your country?
7 What is the most important thing for you when you go to a restaurant?

Test 2 (Part 2)

Before you watch

1a You are going to watch Gonzalo complete Part 2 of the IELTS Speaking Test. In terms of lexical resource and grammatical range and accuracy, which of the following should candidates do to achieve a high score?

1 Use lots of idioms in their answers.
2 Be 100 percent accurate with grammatical structures.
3 Use specific vocabulary to communicate meaning precisely.
4 Show that they can easily use a wide variety of grammatical structures.
5 Demonstrate linguistic flexibility through paraphrasing the examiner's questions.
6 Only use the grammar they feel they know well.

b Read the Part 2 task card and make some notes. You have 1 minute.

Part 2

Describe an adventure you would like to go on.
You should say:

what it is

who you would take with you

what skills/abilities/equipment you might need

and why this adventure appeals to you.

While you watch

2a ▶ 2.4 Watch Gonzalo making notes for Part 2 and answer the questions.

1 What is the first thing he does before writing any notes? Why?
2 Does he write a lot? Why/Why not?
3 How does Gonzalo's approach to note-taking compare with your own?

b ▶ 2.5 Watch Part 2 and tick the words and grammatical structures you hear.

1 conditionals   6 simple passive
2 *equipment*   7 modal verbs
3 present perfect   8 *integrating*
4 future with *will*   9 past continuous
5 *unique*   10 *to broaden the mind*

c ▶ 2.5 Watch Part 2 again and assess Gonzalo's lexical resource and grammatical range and accuracy. Answer the questions below.

1 Does Gonzalo use a wide variety of grammatical structures?
2 Is his grammar usually accurate?
3 Does Gonzalo demonstrate he knows some less common vocabulary?
4 Does he use any idioms or collocation-based phrases?

d ▶ 2.6 Listen to the examiner's assessment. According to the examiner, what are Gonzalo's strengths and weaknesses in terms of lexical and grammatical resource?

After you watch

3a Read an excerpt from Gonzalo's Part 2 response. Rewrite the content to improve the lexical resource and grammatical range and accuracy. Use the examiner's feedback in Exercise 2d to help you.

Probably we don't need that big equipment or skills or abilities, because it's just like normal travelling, it's just knowing the culture, it's just mixing with local people. I think that that's the best thing that you can do to really know the culture and really know the country.

So I will say that the only thing that you need it's a bag, so we'll be backpacking. It's really interesting. And I would say that the most important thing is just to understand the way they think. Just to see why they do things, why they do that type of sushi, why they love that food, is something that really makes the whole experience something unique and different.

And actually that's the thing that later you can tell your friends, like, 'I know Japan. I don't –, I know all the tourist place, but I know as well the little village near by the sea where no-one have ever been, just the local people.' And I think that that's the magic of travelling, and that's the magic of seeing different things.

b Work in pairs and compare your answers.

4 Work in pairs and take turns to do the Part 2 task in Exercise 1b. Speak for 2 minutes and record your answer if possible. The 'examiner' will time the 'candidate' and stop them speaking after 2 minutes. Listen and evaluate each other's performance for lexical and grammatical resource.

Test 2 (Part 3)

Before you watch

1 a In Part 2, Gonzalo spoke about an adventure. Write a list of three questions that the examiner could ask him in Part 3.

b In pairs, ask and answer your questions. As you listen, note some good examples of grammar or vocabulary your partner used.

While you watch

2 a ▶ **2.7** Watch Gonzalo answering the questions in Part 3 and answer the questions about his pronunciation and use of linking words.

1 Is Gonzalo's pronunciation clear throughout? Why/Why not?
2 Are there any sounds which are unclear in his speech?
3 Does he use the features of connected speech?
4 Does Gonzalo use intonation to communicate his meaning?

b ▶ **2.8** Watch an excerpt of Part 3 and read the text. How could Gonzalo improve his pronunciation in the underlined sections?

Coz I <u>think</u> that it's a good way to break with everything, it's a good way to either learn more about yourself and learn more about <u>the world that you are living in</u>, so I think that it's really good coz it –, <u>first of all you mature</u> with all that, you go to another country that they don't speak –, m –, they may don't speak English, they may not speak your own language, so I think that it push yourself to a way where you need to have something, you need to be –, <u>you need to express yourself</u>, so it really helps you becoming a new person.

c ▶ **2.9** Watch the following excerpt from Part 3 and read the text. How could Gonzalo link his ideas better?

Well, I think that you don't need to have a special personality, I think that it is just a matter of really looking forward to learn something new. I think that everybody can be adventurous, you just need to, as I say, you just need to break that routine and you need to go out of your comfort zone.

And you start realising there is a lot of things out there. Sometimes when you are just in a city and you know that bar that you like and you go all the time to that certain supermarket, and you go out and you see that there is different food, there is different type of things, they are different type of people, you start getting that feeling of being adventurous, and you –, you are all the time willing to have more and more all the time.

d ▶ **2.7** Read the list of aspects below then watch Gonzalo answer all the questions in Part 3 of the test. Circle *Good/Satisfactory* or *Needs improvement* for each aspect.

1 Answers the questions fully
Good / Satisfactory / Needs improvement
2 Uses complex grammatical structures
Good / Satisfactory / Needs improvement
3 Uses some idiomatic language
Good / Satisfactory / Needs improvement
4 Speaks fluently and coherently
Good / Satisfactory / Needs improvement
5 Has some phrases to increase his thinking time
Good / Satisfactory / Needs improvement
6 Uses his voice to express finer shades of meaning
Good / Satisfactory / Needs improvement
7 Is grammatically accurate most of the time
Good / Satisfactory / Needs improvement
8 Develops his answers with details, examples, etc.
Good / Satisfactory / Needs improvement

e ▶ **2.10** Watch the examiner talking about Gonzalo's performance in Part 3. How does she evaluate it? Based on her evaluation what score do you think Gonzalo is likely to achieve?

After you watch

3 Rewrite Gonzalo's answer below using higher-level language. Make sure the ideas are linked well.

Coz I think that it's a good way to break with everything, it's a good way to either learn more about yourself and learn more about the world that you are living in, so I think that it's really good coz it –, first of all you mature with all that, you go to another country that they don't speak –, m –, they may don't speak English, they may not speak your own language, so I think that it push yourself to a way where you need to have something, you need to be –, you need to express yourself, so it really helps you becoming a new person.

4 a Work in pairs. Take turns to answer the Part 3 questions above. Record your answers if possible. Listen and evaluate each other's performances for fluency and coherence, lexical resource, grammatical resource and pronunciation.

b Work in pairs. Discuss the areas you need to improve and make suggestions on how you could both do this.

Writing assessment criteria

TASK 1

Band	Task achievement	Coherence and cohesion	Lexical resource	Grammatical range and accuracy
8	• covers all requirements of the task sufficiently • presents, highlights and illustrates key features/bullet points clearly and appropriately	• sequences information and ideas logically • manages all aspects of cohesion well • uses paragraphing sufficiently and appropriately	• uses a wide range of vocabulary fluently and flexibly to convey precise meanings • skilfully uses uncommon lexical items but there may be occasional inaccuracies in word choice and collocation • produces rare errors in spelling and/or word formation	• uses a wide range of structures • the majority of sentences are error-free • makes only very occasional errors or inappropriacies
7	• covers the requirements of the task • (Academic) presents a clear overview of main trends, differences or stages • (General Training) presents a clear purpose, with the tone consistent and appropriate • clearly presents and highlights key features/bullet points but could be more fully extended	• logically organises information and ideas; there is clear progression throughout • uses a range of cohesive devices appropriately although there may be some under-/over-use	• uses a sufficient range of vocabulary to allow some flexibility and precision • uses less common lexical items with some awareness of style and collocation • may produce occasional errors in word choice, spelling and/or word formation	• uses a variety of complex structures • produces frequent error-free sentences • has good control of grammar and punctuation but may make a few errors
6	• addresses the requirements of the task • (Academic) presents an overview with information appropriately selected • (General Training) presents a purpose that is generally clear; there may be inconsistencies in tone • presents and adequately highlights key features/bullet points but details may be irrelevant, inappropriate or inaccurate	• arranges information and ideas coherently and there is a clear overall progression • uses cohesive devices effectively, but cohesion within and/or between sentences may be faulty or mechanical • may not always use referencing clearly or appropriately	• uses an adequate range of vocabulary for the task • attempts to use less common vocabulary but with some inaccuracy • makes some errors in spelling and/or word formation, but they do not impede communication	• uses a mix of simple and complex sentence forms • makes some errors in grammar and punctuation but they rarely reduce communication

TASK 2

Band	Task achievement	Coherence and cohesion	Lexical resource	Grammatical range and accuracy
8	• sufficiently addresses all parts of the task • presents a well-developed response to the question with relevant, extended and supported ideas	• sequences information and ideas logically • manages all aspects of cohesion well • uses paragraphing sufficiently and appropriately	• uses a wide range of vocabulary fluently and flexibly to convey precise meanings • skilfully uses uncommon lexical items but there may be occasional inaccuracies in word choice and collocation • produces rare errors in spelling and/or word formation	• uses a wide range of structures • the majority of sentences are error-free • makes only very occasional errors or inappropriacies
7	• addresses all parts of the task • presents a clear position throughout the response • presents, extends and supports main ideas, but there may be a tendency to overgeneralise and/or supporting ideas may lack focus	• logically organises information and ideas; there is clear progression throughout • uses a range of cohesive devices appropriately although there may be some under-/over-use • presents a clear central topic within each paragraph	• uses a sufficient range of vocabulary to allow some flexibility and precision • uses less common lexical items with some awareness of style and collocation • may produce occasional errors in word choice, spelling and/or word formation	• uses a variety of complex structures • produces frequent error-free sentences • has good control of grammar and punctuation but may make a few errors
6	• addresses all parts of the task although some parts may be more fully covered than others • presents a relevant position although the conclusions may become unclear or repetitive • presents relevant main ideas but some may be inadequately developed/unclear	• arranges information and ideas coherently and there is a clear overall progression • uses cohesive devices effectively, but cohesion within and/or between sentences may be faulty or mechanical • may not always use referencing clearly or appropriately • uses paragraphing, but not always logically	• uses an adequate range of vocabulary for the task • attempts to use less common vocabulary but with some inaccuracy • makes some errors in spelling and/or word formation, but they do not impede communication	• uses a mix of simple and complex sentence forms • makes some errors in grammar and punctuation but they rarely reduce communication

Module 1

Task 1: Describe a line graph

Task

The chart below shows the changes in wage levels of full-time U.S. male workers by education for 1964–2012.

Summarise the information by selecting and reporting the main features, and make comparisons where relevant.

Write at least 150 words.

Changes in Wage Levels of Full-Time U.S. Male Workers by Education, 1964–2012

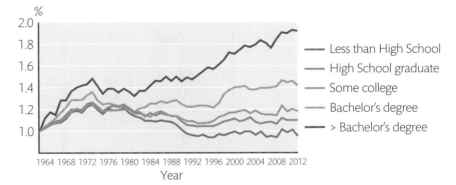

Model answer

Introductory sentence to explain the graph.	The line graph shows how the salaries of male full-time workers in the USA have changed from 1964 to 2012 by type of education.
Description of the main trend shown in the graph.	The graph shows that during the 1960s and 1970s the percentage rise in wages and the difference in wage levels by education were reasonably small. Although men with higher than a Bachelor's degree earned more than men with lower education levels, the difference was less than 0.2 percent.
Explanation of the most important feature.	This trend started to change during the 1980s. From this point in time, it can be seen that the wages for men with less education started to decrease and those for men with a postgraduate qualification increased significantly.
Data to support the feature.	Between 1984 and 2012 the latter group experienced an increase from 1.4 percent to almost 2.0 percent. On the other hand, those men with the two lowest levels of education experienced a reduction in their wage level. At the end of the period, they were being paid 0.5 percent less than they were in 1964.
Overview to summarise the main message in the graph.	Overall, it can clearly be seen that differences in salaries for men in full-time employment in the USA have become more pronounced relative to qualification levels.

Another feature with data for support.

Module 2

Task 1: Describe a process

Task

The diagram below shows how energy is produced from household waste.
Summarise the information by selecting and reporting the main features, and make comparisons where relevant.
Write at least 150 words.

Recovering energy from waste

Energy production from household waste materials

1 Collect waste

2 Transport to factory

3 Pre-sort waste –
   check for leftover recyclables

4 Incinerator. Insert waste.
   Temperature 850 degrees C.

5 Boiler. Heat enters –
   steam produced

6 Steam powers turbine –
   electricity for homes

7 Excess electricity used in
   power plant

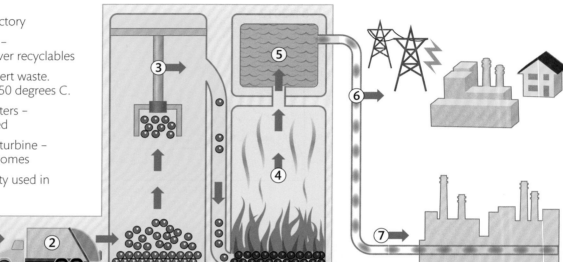

Model answer

Introduction to describe the process and the number of stages.	The diagram shows the process of energy production from waste materials which have been collected from households. There are seven stages in the process from collection through to the production of electricity which will be outlined below.
Explanation of the first stage of the process.	Firstly, waste <u>is collected</u> from households and transported to the energy production plant. At the plant, the material is pre-sorted before it is processed. This is to check for any leftover recyclable materials which, if found, are removed. Next, the waste is inserted into the incinerator for burning. The temperature of the incinerator is 850 degrees Celsius. <u>The following part</u> of the process is where the heat enters the boiler and is then turned into steam. The steam produced in the boiler is used to power a turbine and this generates electricity for use in homes. The process can produce excess electricity which is then used to power the plant.
Next part of the process (and subsequent parts in a logical order).	
Overview of the process in general.	Overall, the process of producing energy from household waste involves burning it to power an electricity turbine.

Example of the passive.

Linking phrase to introduce the next part of the process.

Module 3

Task 2: Problem and solution essay

Task

Since the beginning of the twentieth century, child obesity has been increasing in many countries around the world.

What problems are associated with this issue and what are some possible solutions?

Write at least 250 words.

Model answer

Obesity in human beings is one of the most serious health issues facing the world today. There has been an unprecedented increase in the number of overweight people in recent years, and this includes children. This essay will outline the problems connected to obesity in children and present some solutions.

| Presentation of the first problem. |
| Discussion of the effects of the problem. |

One of the main problems associated with child obesity is that of the pressure that will be put on future healthcare provision. Obesity in childhood is likely to result in a variety of health issues in adulthood; many of which could be expensive to treat, such as heart problems. It could be argued that the cost of managing this high level of obesity may become prohibitive for many governments in the near future.

| Presentation of a solution. |

One solution could be the introduction of legislation for unhealthy food products or at least changes to how food is marketed to children in order to prevent further rises in child obesity.

| Presentation of the second problem. |
| Extra detail for the second problem. |

Secondly, sustained levels of child obesity could have a significant effect on the future workforces of the world. Even though many professions nowadays revolve around technology and sedentary desk work, there are still a significant amount of jobs which require a good level of physical fitness.

| Presentation and discussion of a solution. |

Therefore schools should take far more responsibility in ensuring children receive a sufficient quantity of physical activity to counteract other bad habits which can contribute to obesity, such as long periods of time on the internet. Schools must also be encouraged to include sports and games in the school day as much as possible and also to provide healthy school meals.

In conclusion, there are some serious problems connected to child obesity including those related to healthcare and employment. However, there are plenty of possible solutions which could be implemented to mitigate and improve the current situation.

Module 4

Task 2: Opinion essay

Task

The growth of consumerism has led to a 'throw-away' culture where people are more concerned with acquiring material possessions than protecting the environment.

To what extent do you agree or disagree with this opinion?

Write at least 250 words.

Model answer

The twentieth century has seen a rapid rise in consumerism all over the globe, primarily due to the increased access to markets generated by globalisation. As a result, there has been a real shift in people's desire to own and replace their possessions more often. I believe that this has had an extremely detrimental effect on how the protection of the environment is viewed.

First of all, the rise of global brands means that more people than ever before have access to material wealth. In my opinion, these global brands have become so ubiquitous that they have produced trends and consumer groups that the majority of people would like to belong to. For example, many people would like to be in possession of an iPhone and the company which makes this product makes sure that it updates its products regularly in order to ensure consumers keep replacing their phones every couple of years. However, these days, the fact that the materials required to make these phones require complex processes which damage the environment is often lost on the average consumer.

On the other hand, it can be argued that consumerism has created many positive aspects. For example, the rise of entrepreneurship which allows people to start small businesses and gives them more control over their income and subsequently their lives. Having said this, I firmly believe that protecting the environment should take priority because too much damage to the environment will reduce the opportunities for economic growth for everyone.

In conclusion, despite some of the perceived benefits, I still believe that consumerism has taken over in people's consciousness and that the state of the environment is suffering as a result.

Writer's opinion in the introduction.

The main idea in paragraph 1.

Explanation of the effects of the main idea.

Example to support the main idea.

Explanation of the effects of the main idea.

Presentation of a counter argument as the main idea for paragraph 2.

Example to support the main idea.

Opposition to the counter argument.

Conclusion restating the writer's opinion.

Module 5

Task 1: Describe a chart

Task

The charts below show results of an international student survey carried out in New Zealand in 2004.

Summarise the information by selecting and reporting the main features, and make comparisons where relevant.

Write at least 150 words.

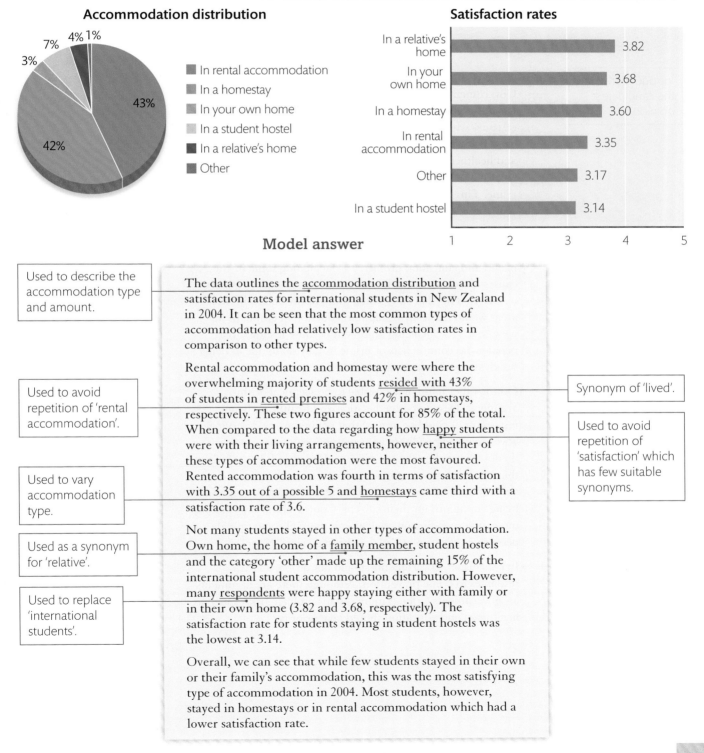

Accommodation distribution

7% 4% 1%
3%
43%
42%

- In rental accommodation
- In a homestay
- In your own home
- In a student hostel
- In a relative's home
- Other

Satisfaction rates

In a relative's home	3.82
In your own home	3.68
In a homestay	3.60
In rental accommodation	3.35
Other	3.17
In a student hostel	3.14

1   2   3   4   5

Model answer

Used to describe the accommodation type and amount.

The data outlines the <u>accommodation distribution</u> and satisfaction rates for international students in New Zealand in 2004. It can be seen that the most common types of accommodation had relatively low satisfaction rates in comparison to other types.

Used to avoid repetition of 'rental accommodation'.

Rental accommodation and homestay were where the overwhelming majority of students <u>resided</u> with 43% of students in <u>rented premises</u> and 42% in homestays, respectively. These two figures account for 85% of the total. When compared to the data regarding how <u>happy</u> students were with their living arrangements, however, neither of these types of accommodation were the most favoured. Rented accommodation was fourth in terms of satisfaction with 3.35 out of a possible 5 and <u>homestays</u> came third with a satisfaction rate of 3.6.

Synonym of 'lived'.

Used to avoid repetition of 'satisfaction' which has few suitable synonyms.

Used to vary accommodation type.

Used as a synonym for 'relative'.

Not many students stayed in other types of accommodation. Own home, the home of a <u>family member</u>, student hostels and the category 'other' made up the remaining 15% of the international student accommodation distribution. However, many <u>respondents</u> were happy staying either with family or in their own home (3.82 and 3.68, respectively). The satisfaction rate for students staying in student hostels was the lowest at 3.14.

Used to replace 'international students'.

Overall, we can see that while few students stayed in their own or their family's accommodation, this was the most satisfying type of accommodation in 2004. Most students, however, stayed in homestays or in rental accommodation which had a lower satisfaction rate.

Module 6

Task 2: Opinion essay

Task

Governments should focus more on preventing crime than on other issues such as healthcare and education. To what extent do you agree with this statement and why?

Give reasons for your answer and include any relevant examples from your knowledge or experience.

Write at least 250 words.

Model answer

Introduction stating the candidate's opinion.

Governments are responsible for deciding the best way in which to spend taxpayers' money and there are a variety of issues which could be considered as necessary. Some of these involve the provision of services such as education and healthcare, whereas others are more connected to the environment such as controlling pollution or preventing crime. This essay will argue that governments should focus more on education and healthcare than preventing crime.

First main idea.

First of all, high crime rates are often associated with a lack of education or poor healthcare. Many experts have identified health and education problems as facilitating some of the causes of crime, especially among poorer groups of people in society. They have suggested that improvements in these areas would naturally result in a reduction in crime. In my view, this is a convincing argument because it shows that people who commit acts of crime usually do so due to being disadvantaged in some way.

Sentences to support the main idea.

Introduction to the counter argument.

Second main idea - counter argument.

On the other hand, it is possible to be sceptical of this argument. Despite both education and healthcare being important, it could be argued that neither are as deserving of government expenditure as crime prevention because they do not ensure the safety of citizens. However, I do not believe that by spending a significant amount of money on crime prevention governments would be able to radically improve living conditions for their citizens. Conversely, in my opinion, increasing spending on education is more likely to provide people with alternatives to committing crime.

Evaluation of counter argument.

Restating the opinion.

In conclusion, governments should not devote all their resources to crime prevention. Although there are arguments for governments to focus more on this problem, issues such as healthcare and education should take priority.

Summary of main idea.

Module 7

Task 1: Describe tables and charts

Task

The table below gives information about changes in the European cruise market by main passenger country between 2011 and 2014.

Summarise the information by selecting and reporting the main features, and make comparisons where relevant.

Write at least 150 words.

European cruise market, by main passenger country, 2011–2014

Passengers (000s)	2011	2012	2013	2014
Germany	1,388	1,544	1,687	1,771
UK and Ireland	1,700	1,701	1,726	1,644
Italy	923	835	869	842
France	441	441	522	593
Spain	703	576	475	454
Scandinavia (incl. Finland)	306	324	289	305
Other*	224	270	325	327
Total	5,684	5,731	5,893	5,936

*Other European markets and those not specified
Source: CLIA Europe/IRN Research

Model answer

The table shows the passenger share in the European cruise industry. The data gives yearly passenger numbers (in thousands) for the period 2011 to 2014 and focuses on those countries which have large cruise markets.

It can be seen that over the period, the greatest numbers of passengers come from the UK and Ireland and Germany. In 2011, these countries accounted for 1.70 million and 1.39 million passengers, respectively. In 2014, Germany had taken over as the biggest cruising nation (with 1.77 million passengers to 1.64 million in the UK and Ireland). Both of these countries have double the amount of passengers than the next largest cruising country, Italy (923,000 passengers in 2011 and 842,000 passengers in 2014).

Whilst cruising was not as popular with the French, Spanish or in Scandinavia, the table shows the passenger numbers for France did increase from 441,000 in 2011 to nearly 600,000 in 2014 but that the opposite trend was observed for Spain and Scandinavia, which both experienced a decrease over the period.

In conclusion, we can see that Germany and the UK and Ireland are by far the largest European cruise markets and that, although there are both increases and decreases in the popularity of cruising within individual countries, overall there is a slight increase over the period.

Respectively is used to attribute figures to their particular country.

Identify differences in data that enable countries to be separated into different groups.

Give a clear overview which accurately represents the data and the main body of your answer. Do not include details in this section as it represents the whole, rather than a specific point.

Present figures in their millions to 2 decimal places (which is clearer than writing 1,388,000). Where necessary, use rounded figures.

The past perfect is used for a change before a certain date in the past (2014).

Identify contrasting trends.

Module 8

Task 2: Cause and effect essay

Task

Nowadays, the 'sense of community' is weakening in many countries. Why might this be? What are the effects of lack of community feeling? Write at least 250 words.

Model answer

> An example of a near synonym to indicate a form of change, which is a common and unavoidable theme in the essay. Other nouns and adjectives used are *variance, diverse, wide-ranging* and *variation.*

The concept of community in its many forms has been in existence for centuries. From tribal bonds to online social networks, feelings of community have given people a sense of belonging. Yet, community is a changing concept and some claim this is weakening. This essay will explore why this might be and what effects it may cause.

> Used to mean 'a feeling that people are a part of a group'.

Overwhelmingly, variance in feelings of community spirit are related to how an individual relates to the community surrounding them, as well as their sense of self. Firstly, lack of shared characteristics may mean that people do not bond with the community they are in. As communities become more diverse, in for example language or values, then people may feel different to the group. Then those particular individuals may become isolated and in turn shun the wider community. Secondly, the reduction in community spirit may just be caused by an increase in selfishness. Perhaps more people want to focus only on themselves or their families but have little or no desire to help others.

> Used to mean 'connect'.

> Used to mean 'turn away from'.

The effects of a reduction in community spirit may be profound, however. Community has been a part of society for millennia, yet if some individuals decide not to take part in the community, this could lead to other people feeling resentful. Perhaps it could be argued that community is actually transforming rather than lessening and that a new form of pluralised community is developing; online, in peer groups, by modern cultural interests. However, a worst case scenario could be the fragmentation of local communities or groups.

> Used to signify 'a long time'.

> Used to mean 'separated into smaller parts'.

> Used to mean 'break up'.

> Used to mean 'situation'.

In conclusion, community may be lessening in some areas and the effects of this could be wide-ranging, from a more pluralistic community sense to a disintegration of some local physical communities.

Module 9

Task 1: Describe changes over time

Task

The maps below show the planned changes to the town of Peterford in a 20-year period.

Summarise the information by selecting and reporting the main features, and make comparisons where relevant.

Write at least 150 words.

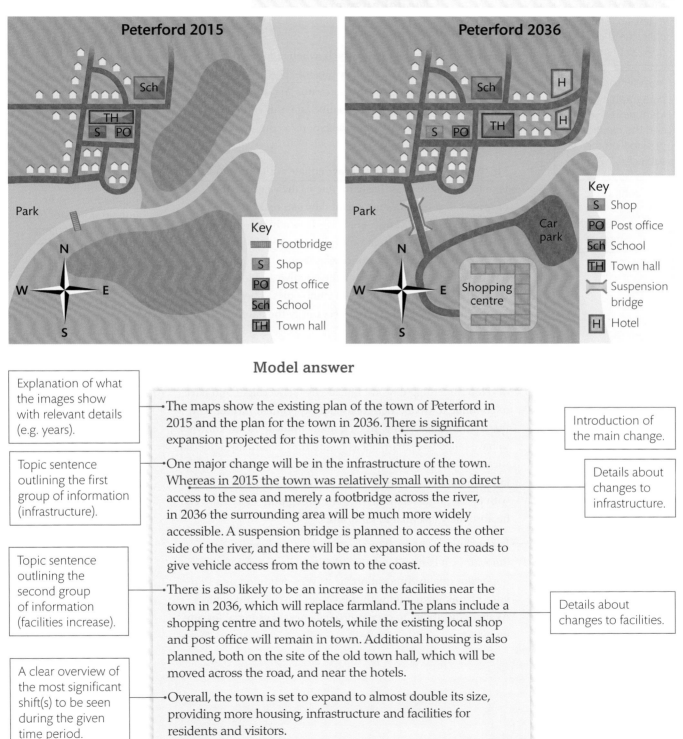

Model answer

Explanation of what the images show with relevant details (e.g. years).

→ The maps show the existing plan of the town of Peterford in 2015 and the plan for the town in 2036. There is significant expansion projected for this town within this period.

Introduction of the main change.

Topic sentence outlining the first group of information (infrastructure).

→ One major change will be in the infrastructure of the town. Whereas in 2015 the town was relatively small with no direct access to the sea and merely a footbridge across the river, in 2036 the surrounding area will be much more widely accessible. A suspension bridge is planned to access the other side of the river, and there will be an expansion of the roads to give vehicle access from the town to the coast.

Details about changes to infrastructure.

Topic sentence outlining the second group of information (facilities increase).

→ There is also likely to be an increase in the facilities near the town in 2036, which will replace farmland. The plans include a shopping centre and two hotels, while the existing local shop and post office will remain in town. Additional housing is also planned, both on the site of the old town hall, which will be moved across the road, and near the hotels.

Details about changes to facilities.

A clear overview of the most significant shift(s) to be seen during the given time period.

→ Overall, the town is set to expand to almost double its size, providing more housing, infrastructure and facilities for residents and visitors.

Module 10

Task 2: Opinion essay

Task

In order to truly innovate, continued hard work is more important than intelligence. To what extent do you agree with this statement and why? Write at least 250 words.

Model answer

Metaphor used to talk about the characteristics needed to innovate.

Introductory paragraph clearly identifies the issues and the candidate's position on the subject.

Two contrastive sentences. One using 'but' and the other using 'yet'.

Signpost that the second main point is going to be introduced.

Used to show the result of the argument.

Signpost for the conclusion.

Linking phrase to signify an example of a characteristic.

Used to signify a contrast regarding the importance of intelligence.

Clear signpost to introduce the first main point, followed by a topic sentence.

Used to show the result of the argument.

Used to strengthen the previous sentence (with some factual information, in this case, an example).

Overall, the essay follows a rigid structure. There is some parallel in argument development between both main body paragraphs, but the writer has used different signposts in developing these paragraphs. The conclusion and introduction agree and reinforce the main body paragraphs.

There are many ingredients which, when combined, create a recipe for innovation or success. One of these is undoubtedly the intellectual abilities of the innovator. Yet, for all the intelligence required in order to innovate, this cannot be superseded by the drive and motivation to continue in endeavours.

Firstly, knowledge does not always equate with innovation. People may be seen as 'brilliant' due to their knowledge or grades, but this does not mean they can make advances in the way we live. Many people study to a high level and get excellent grades, yet go on to chase money rather than develop knowledge and technologies. Some traditionally intelligent people may also lack the creative and logical skills needed to develop new ideas or technologies. Therefore, intelligence or brilliance is not necessarily the natural precursor to innovation.

Secondly, the ability to deal with failure and overcome hurdles is a key part of innovative change. Often people who want to develop something new are not successful overnight and have to continue to tweak their ideas and experiment further with them before succeeding. In fact, many innovators are known to have failed with many ideas before they eventually achieved success. One such innovator was Henry Ford, who initially failed in business. Consequently, the ability to be able to cope with failure, understand what went wrong and solve issues can be absolutely essential to innovators.

In conclusion, although intellectual skills are beneficial to innovators, it cannot be denied that tenacity is a far more important quality. Innovation, by its very definition, is a step into the unknown, and with this comes barriers and failures. As such, the ability to overcome challenges is essential for any innovator.

Audio scripts

Module 1

1.1

E = Examiner   Z = Zeyna

E: What did you want to be when you were younger?

Z: I always wanted to be a writer when I was younger. I was inspired by people like J.K. Rowling. I was really dedicated and used to write short stories in my spare time. I remember once I'd sent a story to a publisher, and got a letter from them but it was a rejection. I was really disheartened by this. I was thinking about giving up, but then I decided to learn more about writing.

E: How are you going to do that?

Z: I've decided to go to university and study literature. I'm really eager to learn more about this. I think I'm really lucky actually. So many people are uncertain about what they want to do when they're older.

1.4

N = Narrator   F = Felicity Moore

N: You are going to hear a librarian giving a talk to some students. Listen and answer the questions.

F: Hello everyone. My name's Felicity Moore and I'm the head of library services here at the university. During the summer, some changes have been made to make the library even better for you all. We've always had some of the best IT services around, and now you'll find these on the 2nd instead of the 3rd floor. We've also added a more informal area in front of the study spaces on the ground floor. Here you'll be able to chat with your friends, have a coffee and take a break from your hard work.

Now, you'll be getting your library card later today, but before that I'm just going to talk you through the facilities we have here. We have three floors of books and if we don't have what you want, we're happy to get it in for you from another library. Now, usually you'll need your card when taking out books, but we understand the pressure of deadlines. As long as you have your student number, and some ID, that'll do. But, you'll be unable to use the automatic machines; you'll need to come to the desk. We also have a range of journals which can be accessed; the most up-to-date ones are just past the reception desk. However, if you want older versions, they're on the top floor and you'll have to swipe your library card to get into the room. All the PCs are on the second floor, just log in with the email and password you were given by IT services. When you want to print, you just pay directly on the printer. It'll store any work you send, just access it via the screens on the printer and there's a payment slot. We used to have a system where payment would go through your library card, but this didn't work as smoothly as we liked. Just make sure you have change! Now, your library card's still important as it can access a lot of services for you. It can be used to reserve an appointment with a learning tutor. These are absolutely free and are available every morning between 10.00 and 12.00. Not every library has this, so please do take advantage of it. Also, you'll have to use your card to book one of the quiet rooms for when you want to work without distraction. These are all on the third floor at the back. Any questions so far?

1.5

N = Narrator   P = Presenter   E = Eleanor

N: You are going to listen to someone talking about learning apps. Listen and answer the question.

P: So, today on *Teaching Matters* we're talking about learning apps. Eleanor Jenkins is with us today to talk us through the latest apps. Hello, Eleanor.

E: Hello, John.

P: Welcome to the programme.

E: It's good to be here.

P: Now, Eleanor, you have a vast experience of these apps, don't you?

E: Absolutely. I used to use a lot of apps when I was teaching and got so interested in their use that I left my job and set up my own consultancy in educational app development. I now advise on learning objectives and work with schools and tech companies to help develop apps with real learning benefits.

1.6

N = Narrator   P = Presenter   E = Eleanor

N: You are going to listen to someone talking about learning apps. Listen and answer the questions.

P: Well, tell us what apps we should be downloading.

E: There are an awful lot of apps on the market at the moment covering every subject imaginable. Some are paid for and some are free. However, the free apps are rarely as effective as the paid apps, but there are a couple of exceptions which I think are really invaluable educational tools. These are *Dictable* and *Soundwave*. *Dictable* is an app that lets you search for words and gives you meanings, pronunciations, synonyms. *Soundwave* is an app that lets you create music. It's for younger children, and once they make music on the app they can then see the notes they've played. This is quite useful in developing music reading skills. Another app which is paid for, but well worth the money, is *Mathword*. This is an app for university students which writes equations from verbal input. I think it costs about $6.99 but for people studying maths, it can save a lot of time usually spent formatting these kinds of things. The app is also user-friendly. You could even give it to your grandmother to use! Another paid-for app that is invaluable is *Bodies*. This is an app which children can use to learn about parts of the body. It's got a great design and gives useful information not just about what parts of the body do, but basic health too. I'd recommend this for seven-to-ten year-olds particularly.

P: Very useful. Do you think the educational app market is still growing?

E: Absolutely. The number of educational apps on the market is almost doubling year on year. But not all topics are equally catered for. Most apps are based around maths or English. In fact, the choice can be quite bewildering for these categories. But there isn't a lot for subjects which require more creativity. For those who for example are interested in design, there's not a lot of choice. It might be worth developers looking into this, as the competition is not fierce. The same can be said of music. Although *Soundwave* is a great app, it's really only one of a handful in this area. People still have to hit the books to learn about it, which seems strange in such a forward-thinking industry. I mean, so much music is now made with technology. I do think though this is likely to change. We'll see more apps in all areas in future. And I think they'll be of better quality as consumers become more demanding.

1.7

E = Examiner   ML = Mei Ling

E: Now in this first part, I'd like to ask you some questions about yourself. Let's talk about education. What was your school like?

ML: My school was very nice. It was a big building, in the countryside. My teachers were nice and I was a very good student. I did well.

E: Why did you decide to come and study in Australia?

ML: Well, I came top of the class in an English test at my school. For me English was difficult, so I studied it very hard. It was a nice feeling. You know, being the top. This was in maybe the fourth year. Then I became more interested in English. So I decided that I'll go to Australia to study. To hear and talk more in English.

E: What would you like to achieve with English?

ML: For me English is an important subject. I think it helps you get a good job and also when you travel … English is important because there are many people who speak English. I want to be able to speak English like a native speaker. I want to go to university here in Australia, but I also want to be able to talk in English without problems. This is my goal.

E: How will you achieve this?

ML: As I said, I chose to come and study in the Australia. I thought maybe of other countries, but Australia is better for me I think. I study every day. I go to an English class, and my teacher's very nice and helpful. I watch a lot of movies, in English, and I have some friends online. I talk to lots of them in English. English is cool in China, which is where I am from, and it's fun to speak English online. I do need to study it more though.

Module 2

2.1

S1: The old building that I like is the town hall in the city where I live. The town hall's very old, maybe two or three hundred years, and many people who live in the city go there to get lots of different types of information for living in the city. You can find out about all the services in the city, for example, about car parking places and prices, information about buses and trains … and other transport and other things which are necessary for people's daily lives. It's a large building. It's made out of stone and has a tower in the middle of it, and there are many floors and lots of rooms inside. A lot of people work there too. They do many different types of jobs to help the people who live in the city. The building has changed a lot over the years. When I was a child it was brown and looked boring, but a few years ago the town hall was painted white. I think it looks much better now because it's bright and more attractive. It's much more like the traditional style of the other government buildings in the city, so we can notice the government buildings more easily. I like this building a lot because it shows the history of the city. When I go inside I can feel the history and imagine being a worker in the town hall in the past. For me it's important that people know about the history of the place where they live. Nowadays there's a small museum inside which I think is very interesting for people. I think that not many tourists visit the museum, but schoolchildren go there to learn about why the town hall was important in the past and why it is still important now. Also, the gardens outside are a nice place to have lunch or take a rest. Many office workers go there to eat lunch or walk around to relax in the gardens.

S2: My favourite old building is the old railway station which is near my house and is now a museum. It's an amazing old building and I'm always really impressed whenever I walk past it. It dates from the last century and is an excellent example of the local architectural style of public buildings. If you walk around the town, you will notice other public buildings constructed in the same style, and they give the town a kind of architectural theme which is quite nice. It's made from stone and oak from the surrounding region with carvings in the roof. I think that the carvings represent scenes from the history of the town. This is a traditional building design of my area, and it's very ornate. The builders were highly skilled stone carvers and they carved all the designs by hand. The region where I live has quite a lot of stations constructed in the same way. The station's located in the historical part of the city … this is towards the north-east and nowadays attracts a lot of tourists primarily due to the station and the other ornate buildings. The station itself is on the main square opposite the town hall. It's had a few different uses over its lifetime. After the station was closed some years ago, it was turned into a hotel for a few years, although it was not very successful … and then it was turned into a museum of local history. It shows us our architectural heritage and the importance of maintaining the condition of old buildings. The museum has collected items such as furniture and clothing and tools and the main function of the exhibitions is to educate people and show what life was like in the town when the station was in operation. The main reason I like it is because it represents what life in the town was like in the past … and I think it's really important for us to maintain links with our past.

2.2

N = Narrator   R = Robert   F = Filipo

N: You will hear two people talking about their walks.

R: I began my walk on the edge of the forest and walked past the cabin and along the river. After a while I saw the campsite on the other side. I noticed a picnic area next to the campsite and decided to have lunch there, so I went back along the river to the bridge so I could cross over. I could see the lake in the distance and it looked so inviting, so I changed my plans and went straight there. I had to go through the field to get to the lake. I thought the cows were going to chase me!

F: I got out of my tent early this morning as I wanted to make the most of the day. I planned to go to the forest, so I walked past all the picnic benches to the bridge. I started to walk over the bridge, but then I saw the mountain and it looked like a really good walk. So, I walked along the river and climbed up the bottom part of the mountain. It was a pretty hot day, so I thought about a swim afterwards. I managed to avoid the cows by walking around where they were and took a dip in the lake.

2.3

N = Narrator   R = Receptionist   J = John

N: You will hear a visitor talking to a receptionist at a campsite.

R: Hello and welcome to Camp Horizon. So, I'm just going to use this map to talk you through the layout of the camp so you know where everything is for your stay.

J: That would be great, thanks.

R: So, we're currently here at the reception block. If you take the path immediately on the right from where we are now and follow it to the end, you'll be at the campsite. We're literally at that fork in the path here now.

J: OK, and what about the activities? Where can I find those?

R: They can mostly be found near the centre of the camp. See, just beyond the reception block is the swimming pool which is located on your left, and you can find the play area directly opposite that. Just beyond the play area, there are two paths. One leads to an archery range. At the end of the other path is where the barbecue area is situated, but if you don't go all the way down that path, you'll see the craft cabin.

J: OK, I see. My friend came here last year and told me that you have a skate park. Where's that?

R: Oh actually, we don't have that anymore. It's now a bike park because that's more popular. I think you'll like it because it's been built recently and it's really big.

J: That sounds great.

R: It's quite near Horizon beach too. Just take a left as you head towards the beach.

J: That's really helpful. I think I'm going to have a great time.

2.4

N = Narrator   C = Customer   R = Receptionist

N: You will hear a receptionist talking to a customer. Listen and answer the questions.

C: Hello, I'm here to check in.

R: Welcome. Could you give me your name and I'll find your details on the system.

C: My name's Cindy Philips.

R: OK, just let me have a look. Is that Philips, P-H-I-L-I-P-S?

C: Yes, that's right.

R: Thank you. Here you are. I've got your telephone number as 09669 343123. Is that right?

C: Yes, that's right.

R: And you're from the USA?

C: No, I'm Canadian.

R: Oh, a lovely part of the world. Can I just check how long you've booked for?

C: One week. I wanted to stay for two but I haven't got enough time off work. I really need to relax.

R: Oh, I'm sure you'll relax just fine during your stay with us here. Most people find the camp a great way to de-stress after being here for a couple of days.

C: Great!

R: I've got your accommodation listed as standard cabin.

C: Actually, I was wondering if I could upgrade to a superior?

R: Let me have a look … Yes, that's fine, we've got one superior cabin available. Now, I just need to take your credit card number. We won't charge you until you check out though.

C: That's fine. It's a Visa card, number 4458 6974 double 231.

R: Let me read that back to you to check. It's 4458 6974 231.

C: No, it's double 2 31 at the end. Oh, and do you want the expiry date?

R: Yes, please.

C: It's October 2020.

R: Thank you. One last thing. Do you have any special requirements?

C: I don' think so. Oh, actually, I don't eat meat.

R: OK, I'll make a note that you're a vegetarian and let the kitchen know. Now, let me tell you a bit more about the camp … So, here's a map so you can see where everything is. I'll just talk you through it. So, obviously we're here at the reception, and the reforestation project is surrounded by the camp. Adjacent to us here we've got the main lodge. This is where all meals are served.

C: Oh, what time is breakfast?

R: Between 7.00 and 9.00. All the meal times are written on the back of the map. I should say that opposite reception is where the emergency point can be found. From here just go up to the main circular path and you'll see it.

C: That sounds confusing!

R: Don't worry, it's signposted, so it's easy to find. Right, at the top of the map you can see the main path. It's this circular one. Just beyond this, right at the top here, is Turtle Bay. This is where our turtle-watching trips take place. You'll see a small road opposite Turtle Bay. Half way down this road is a picnic area and at the end of that road is our spa.

C: Oh, lovely. And how do I find my accommodation?

R: Well, we're at reception now. So, just go up until you reach the main circular path, turn right onto this path and follow it round. You'll go past a large viewing point on your left. Just carry on and you'll reach the standard cabins. The superior cabins are located just after them. It's not that far – only about five minutes to walk.

C: OK. I'm really looking forward to using the pool. Where can I find that?

R: Easy, it's just behind reception and it's open from eight in the morning till eight in the evening.

C: Thanks.

2.5

N = Narrator   C = Carmen

N: You will hear a student talking about an important place in their country.

C: A place that is important in my country is the Sagrada Família. It's a famous church which is located in Barcelona in northern Spain. It's really impress, impressive. The architectural style is from the famous architect Gaudí, who built many interesting buildings in Barcelona, and this is one of the reasons why it's so important. Gaudí's style of designing buildings was … err … unique and extremely, extremely modern. He is quite controversial – many people hate his style, whereas others think he is a … a genius. Um, … He used a lot of bright colours which are very impressive and, and so for the people of Barcelona his buildings are a strong part of our … mmm … of our cultural heritage. It's taken many years to build the Sagrada Família. This is something that people have strong feelings about because many people think that it should be finished already. When I was a child it was uncom … incomplete and we couldn't see the church towers, but over the last decade they've been doing a lot of construction work, so now the towers are vis … visible from different areas in the city … I think it's one of the most impressive buildings in Spain and in my opinion I think that everyone must … should visit it sometime. It's really stunning. It's very tall and when I walked up the towers to view the city for the first time it made me feel very proud of Barcelona and its history and its architecture. The views from the top show you how amazing a lot of the architecture in Barcelona is and how the city has changed over time. After visiting it I always feel happy that I live in such a great place.

Module 3

3.1

For me the main thing that influences positive thinking is a person's attitude. People who are pessimistic are much less likely to demonstrate positive thinking. A positive attitude can be personal or it can come from specific things in life like work or family. It's all about how you conceptualise positivity and this is different for everyone. For some people it involves being cheerful or grateful for aspects of their lives, whereas for others it's more connected to understanding what you find inspiring. I find spending time with my children therapeutic – their positive approach to life really makes a difference to my outlook.

3.2

1

E = Examiner   A = Anya

E: Why is positive thinking important in our daily lives?

A: Well, I think we have to think positively to maintain a healthy outlook on life. If we're always pessimistic about life, we'll probably achieve less. For instance, people who don't think positively don't learn as much. This is because they're afraid of failing, so they don't try to learn new things.

2

E = Examiner   K = Keigo

E: Why is positive thinking important in our daily lives?

K: In my opinion, positive thinking helps us to make progress in everything we do and be happy more often. I think that when we're positive, it helps us to learn more and improve our lives. For me being positive is really important and I think everyone should be more positive.

3.3

Jing Lee

I think that it depends. I mean, for some people being surrounded by loving and supportive friends and family generates a sense of optimism about life. For others, it's more a case of achieving personal success such as having a fulfilling career or learning new skills. There are also those that feel more positive when they hear stories in the news about inspiring events in the world.

Mario

For me it's more about self-awareness and small acts of kindness. For example, it's true that people who are generous towards others often appear to be positive thinkers. I think we should encourage people to connect with others more so they can improve their outlook.

Susanna

That's an interesting question. As far as I'm concerned, people have a better outlook on life when they're engaged in doing things they really enjoy. If you have a hobby that you love, it'll make you feel fantastic when you do it. Afterwards these positive feelings will spill over into other aspects of your life.

Heidi

In my view, culture is often a really important factor. We can see that some nationalities tend to be more positive than others. People who live in hot countries usually appear happier than those who live in colder climates, especially during the winter months.

Mahmoud

Well, I firmly believe that it's different for each individual because there are so many things that change in our lives. Because each person's life is unique, we wouldn't give exactly the same advice to everyone about how to improve their outlook on life.

3.4

N = Narrator   Dr G = Dr Gregson

N: You are going to listen to part of a lecture on the health benefits of meditation. Listen and answer the questions.

Dr G: Now, when we think of meditation, some of us may just consider that it's a new-age or alternative concept, one which is focused on relaxing and centering yourself. But in today's lecture we're going to explore meditation in a completely new light and focus on the wide range of health benefits meditation can provide. Although there haven't been many large-scale trials focused on the effects of meditation in the scientific community, there have been many smaller studies which have shown some very positive results. The effects noted include not only psychological benefits, but physical ones too. There is even evidence to indicate that meditation can boost our gene activity. So, let's review some of these studies and their findings.

Firstly, research which was undertaken at the University of Sheffield strongly suggests that meditation, in combination with other techniques such as relaxation sessions, clearly has an effect and that it helps improve problems such as skin disorders. By skin disorders, I refer to eczema or acne. The researchers combined data from over 900 participants in 22 studies and found that psychological treatment, which included meditation, helped reduce the physical symptoms of these skin disorders. Also, it seems quite plausible that meditation can slow down the rate of aging. The University of California recently undertook a study which revealed that meditation has the capacity to lengthen telomeres. These are basically a key part of our DNA which naturally shorten and in effect, drive the aging process of our bodies. The study itself examined two groups, a control group and another one whose members attended a three-month meditation course. Their findings clearly demonstrated that the group who had been doing meditation had strengthened telomeres.

3.5

N = Narrator   Dr G = Gr Gregson

N: You are going to listen to the second part of a lecture on the health benefits of meditation. Listen and answer the questions.

Dr G: So, the benefits of simply meditating could be much more extensive than initially considered by much of the medical community. These health benefits need to be studied in larger numbers before anything conclusive can be claimed such as that meditation can maintain our youth and heal our skin. However, there are also what I would call the 'knock-on effects' of meditation. This is where meditation has more incidental effects on our health. Studies show that people who start meditating are often more predisposed to giving up smoking, if of course they smoke in the first place. This knock-on effect is of great interest in terms of improving overall public health in populations. In addition to this, and possibly inspired by the practice, many frequent meditators also start to change their relationship with food and begin eating more healthily. Now, both of these activities have definite health benefits. These kinds of changes in lifestyle undoubtedly come from the fact that meditation improves our psychological health, and this is the area where there is the most research.

Psychologically, meditation can cause a person to become more energetic, more alert, happier and less stressed. Now, stress and meditation is one area where many studies have been undertaken. There is actually quite clear evidence that an individual can see quite a marked change in their ability to deal with stressful situations with just 10 minutes a day of meditation. However, although it is undeniable that meditation is good for us, we shouldn't believe that it is a comprehensive cure. While meditation can be beneficial, it cannot and shouldn't be used in the place of medical intervention when mental or physical problems are marked within an individual. In fact, this might be considered the point where meditation might actually be harmful if it prevents an individual from seeking more traditional help. Perhaps meditation should be thought of as a compliment rather than an answer. There are some newer studies which suggest that this may be …

3.6

Hello, everyone. Please take your seats. So, today, in this introductory lecture, I'm going to give you an overview of different kinds of medical treatments, and how these are perceived here in the UK. Firstly, it's quite important for us to define some key terms at the start as some definitions have multiple meanings. The idea of 'traditional' medicine, for example, could refer to medicine which has a strong scientific base and has passed a series of vigorous trials to check safety and effectiveness, alternatively it could refer to medicines which are created through mixing herbs or which use relaxation techniques. So the term can be quite unclear. For the purpose of this lecture, however, we'll not use the word 'traditional', but will refer to medicine that has developed as a result of scientific research in the West as 'scientific' medicine … such as antibiotics or vaccines. We'll use the term 'alternative' medicine to apply to natural-based remedies, such as herbs or acupuncture.

So, let's explore scientific medicine … there are many who argue that science has been used in the field of medicine since the middle ages, but I would consider pinpointing the start at just over 250 years ago, with scientists such as Louis Pasteur and Edward Jenner and the invention of treatments such as vaccines and antibiotics.

These treatments remain popular today and we'll examine these scientific developments in more detail during the second half of today's lecture. It might surprise you to learn that scientific medicine isn't the most popular form of medicine. You may be under the impression that the support for alternative medicine is low … maybe you would estimate it at perhaps less than 20 percent? Well, this would be incorrect. Actually, it has been estimated that over 50 percent of people in the Western world still favour alternative methods of treatment while in the East, what we might consider to be alternative medicines are in fact commonplace and widely used. Additionally, these forms of medicines are growing in popularity in the West and in fact, have a far longer history than scientific medicine. However, there is an argument … and I think this generally comes from the scientific community in the West … that much of this kind of treatment is deemed as ineffective when dealing with many illnesses. So, let's explore the truth of this assertion.

Firstly, acupuncture … the practice of inserting fine needles into specific locations in the body … has been popular for centuries in Asia and is becoming increasingly used in Western countries … the list of ailments it's used to treat is extensive. However, support of the effectiveness of acupuncture varies. Much Western research questions the benefits of acupuncture when used to help someone, for example, give up smoking or gain allergy relief. However, there does seem to be some evidence that it can help to relieve back pain … a 2009 study by the National Institute of Clinical Excellence in the UK showed that there were improvements here … especially regarding pain in the lower back or lumbar region. There is also evidence which demonstrates that acupuncture can reduce headaches, both in their number and severity, in some cases. However, this evidence is constantly questioned in the West and there are very much two schools of thought; that acupuncture works and that acupuncture doesn't work.

Secondly, I'd like to briefly discuss herbal medicines. As you might know, a great number of scientific drugs are derived from or use natural ingredients. For example, in Ancient Greece Hippocrates developed a treatment for headaches incorporating a particular tree bark that was eventually used in the development of aspirin, now a popular painkiller. Medicine with natural ingredients can be ingested in many forms, such as in teas or treatments which are rubbed onto the skin. Fish oils are one such form of medication. These oils are believed to enhance concentration so much so that many parents give them to their children in order to try and help them perform better at school. In the UK this was even recommended by the government! Such oils can also help to protect the heart, which I'm sure you'll agree is invaluable. However, it might be that a change in diet to just simply eating more oily fish could be just as effective as taking fish oil supplements. Other traditional herbal cures like ginger or rosemary have also been used for centuries …

3.7

1

E = Examiner   F = Fatima

E: Do you think that the government should control what people do in terms of their own health?

F: Well, I'm not sure. I think the government should stop the smokers. Maybe they can just smoke in a place for smokers only. Not smoking in the street, or near children, or near the public. I also think maybe alcohol shouldn't be drunk in the street. Perhaps the government could introduce a law against this too. They should also try to limit how much people drink and say 'you can only drink three drinks a day'. But I think people should choose how much they exercise or what they eat though. But some people are unhealthy. It's fine. But it's not OK to make other people unhealthy for this.

2

E = Examiner   G = Gao

E: Do you think that the government should control what people do in terms of their own health?

G: In some respects, yes. The government … I think … has a duty to protect wider society. So, any activity which harms other people should have restrictions. Take for example the issue of smoking. This habit can pose a real threat to those around the smoker, you know, the passive smokers. So this needs to be restricted and in many countries I think it is. But there are other activities which are perhaps a thornier issue. Obesity can be a real problem in some societies, yet this does not harm anyone else. So, in my view, you have to let people get on with it and not interfere. I don't think there are any quick fixes for these kind of problems anyway. I mean, even if we were to raise taxes on unhealthy food, I don't think this would stop people from eating it.

Module 4

4.1

N = Narrator   S = Simon

N: Listen to the talk about upcycling workshops and answer the questions.

S: Welcome everyone to our community upcycling project, which is going to start next month. First of all, I'll go over the workshops, then some of the requirements and finally, sign-up procedures. So, basically this project aims to equip local residents with the fundamentals of upcycling skills. Upcycling is the process of revitalising old objects to give them a new lease of life or to repurpose them rather than sending them to landfill. Be aware that it's not the same as recycling, which is an industrial process. Upcycling is about repurposing objects by doing it yourself. Here's a slide listing all the workshops. As you can see the first one is about remodelling chairs and tables and so on. In our view it's going to be extremely well attended, if not oversubscribed, which is why we decided to offer this weekly on Mondays. People are under the illusion that furniture restoration is a skill reserved for experts, whereas it's actually fairly straightforward. You'll learn some techniques for the upkeep and maintenance of wood and metal, as well as fabric repair.

Now, the next one will demonstrate how to fashion useful household items from leftover rubbish that's lying around, like packaging. This class takes place on Tuesdays from two o'clock in the afternoon until six, but only at the beginning and end of the month … in other words, the first and last Tuesdays. It'll focus on techniques for using craft tools, and methods for joining materials with glue and screws and so on. OK, the next workshop is highly likely to attract fashionistas more than anyone else. It'll concentrate on bringing new life to tired old garments in your wardrobe, you know, the things you should have thrown out years ago, but can't bear to part with. This workshop is going to be on Tuesday and Thursday mornings, but only once a month. We're thinking of introducing more of these, but it will depend on the uptake as some previous sewing experience is needed to successfully participate. Lastly, we're offering something for those looking to make unique gifts for their loved ones, like trinket or jewellery boxes, or wall hangings. It'll be on Friday mornings and will teach you basic carving techniques along with suggestions for embellishments or ornamentation.

Right, so now let's talk about the registration process and key points, starting with 'How to reuse your furniture and make stylish pieces.' Now, as I said, this course isn't nearly as complicated as it sounds. While we do accept people who have done this before, it's not necessary for you to have any specialist knowledge of making furniture. However, one thing to note is that you'll be working on your own chairs or tables or whatever it is you bring, so you must be able to get them here using your own transport. This class will obviously be using chemical substances so it's important that you state on the application form if you have any allergies to paint or something that you think we should be aware of. As you can imagine, given the nature of the chemicals and techniques you'll be working with, we need to make sure you're safe during this class, so we insist that you bring something appropriate to change into. It's vital that you wear protective clothing made from heavy-duty material to cover your arms and legs in order to protect them against spillages. OK, now, I want to talk about the next course.

4.2

N = Narrator   I = Interviewer   B = Belinda

N: You are going to listen to an interview about buying presents for people at work. Listen and answer the questions.

I: So, Belinda, thank you for coming on today's show to talk to us about the thorny issue of buying gifts for people that we work with here in the USA.

B: Thank you. Well, let's go through some of the issues and possible solutions. Firstly, it's vital not to spend too much. Workplaces are often hierarchical, in other words there are managers and subordinates. Purchasing high-value gifts may sound like a good idea to impress someone and this may happen. On the other hand, it can also disturb the power balance in a work situation. Since you don't want to cause offence, it's worth thinking about the price of the gift. This means it's better to think about a more modest gift, which reflects the relationship between you and the receiver. There's nothing wrong with paying a reasonable amount of money since this demonstrates that you've put some thought into the gift. Another thing to focus on is the style of gift. Instead of focusing on what you think the tastes of the person might be, opt for something which is classic. Although there is a common belief that personalisation is better, this is often untrue. A classic gift avoids any offence, whereas something out of the ordinary can be considered inappropriate. Remember though, it's important not to go too far the other way. A gift that is too traditional may be interpreted as if the buyer was just going through the motions as well as being thought of as unoriginal.

Another point that I'd like to talk about is the gifts that mark the stages of employment and what usually happens in a typical workplace here in the USA. Now in some cultures, new employees are given a gift when they join a company. This is not true for everywhere and usually it is more of a token of acceptance than a meaningful gift, however, it does have some symbolic value rather than monetary value. More common though are gifts which function as a way of marking out periods of time, so people may receive something after ten or twenty years' service. A longer time period is usually reflected by a higher-value gift, so it's important to bear that in mind if you have to source such a gift. These gifts are designed essentially to reward employees for their loyalty and hard work over long periods of time and show how much the company thinks highly of them. They also have an additional role in terms of motivating other staff members by acting as an incentive to remain working in the organisation for longer. Lastly, I want to mention those gifts that we give people who are leaving a company. This can either happen when someone changes job voluntarily or when they retire. Leaving dos are very common nowadays and usually involve a party and a gift which other employees contribute money to. This may be everyone in a small company, or in a larger company, people who work in the same department, but remember that people don't have to give a lot of money. These gifts are usually given on the employee's final day at the company and the party is often held at a restaurant. This process is quite similar to the other type of leaving gift, that which marks a person's retirement. However, a retirement gift is likely to be more expensive, especially if the employee has put in many years of service to the company. Sometimes there is a speech from the head of the company or a senior manager too. This is to mark the significance of the event and ensure that the person has been thanked for their work appropriately. Well, I think that's about all I have to say.

4.4

E = Examiner   J = Jean Paul

E: Do you think people try to acquire too many new possessions these days?

J: Yes, I think so. I mean, you always hear of different sales and people buying all sorts of things both online and in the shops. Sometimes on the news you can see pictures of people racing and fighting to get hold of the latest deals. And there's always some new gadget coming out which everyone must have. I don't think it's a very good situation. For example, if people don't have a lot of money, seeing people buying lots of things is probably really depressing. It would be much better for everyone if people just bought what they needed, instead of being driven by the latest trends.

E = Examiner   N = Nisha

E: Do you think people try to acquire too many new possessions these days?

N: Yes, I think so. I mean, you always hear of different sales and people buying all sorts of things both online and in the shops. Sometimes on the news you can see pictures of people racing and fighting to get hold of the latest deals. And there's always some new gadget coming out which everyone must have. I don't think it's a very good situation. For example, if people don't have a lot of money, seeing people buying lots of things is probably really depressing. It would be much better for everyone if people just bought what they needed, instead of being driven by the latest trends.

Module 5

5.1

S = Scott   C = Charlotte

1

C: These LED slippers are a great idea! I think they'll make things easier for us. No need to turn the lights on anymore!

S: I think you've got a point there. People can get up in the night without bumping into things or totally waking themselves up. You know, sometimes you can turn on the main lights and it's so bright you just can't get back to sleep again.

2

S: These picnic pants are a terrible invention. Can you imagine people wandering around the park and trying to eat with them? Once they put their food down they won't be able to move!

C: Oooh, I hadn't thought of that. I see what you mean. It could actually be dangerous if you were eating something hot.

5.2

B = Ben   D = Debbie   P = Phillip

B: I'm so glad we're nearly done on this project. It's been so hard!

D: I know what you mean, Ben. But we're halfway there now. I think we've got a really great idea. We should be pleased with ourselves. What do you think, Phillip?

P: Well, I think what we're doing now is much better than our first idea. That was absolutely terrible!

B: Oooh, it wasn't that bad!

D: Well, that doesn't matter now we've got this design for a body umbrella! This is such a good idea. Normal umbrellas never keep people totally dry!

B: I completely agree.

D: And I think we've made it look really futuristic too. Don't you think so, Ben?

B: Well, I'm not sure about that. I think some of it is a bit too complicated. If a factory wanted to make a batch of them, it would be pretty expensive!

P: I think the design is actually the best thing about it! But still, I'm pretty glad we don't have to build a prototype to show people!

D: What do you mean, Phillip? We do! Look, it's in the instructions.

P: Oh no! We're bound to fail now. We'll never get it finished in time!

D: Of course we will, Phillip! There are no classes next week so we've got time.

P: Oh yes, you've got a point there. Maybe we'll do OK.

D: OK?! I think we're going to do really well. It's a great invention after all.

B: I'm glad you're feeling confident. I'm not so sure myself. Maybe it'll be more impressive once it's been made.

5.3

N = Narrator   M = Mick

N: You are going to listen to a description of a spaceship. Listen and answer questions one to four.

M: The *Spaceship Two* is quite an incredible feat of engineering. Designed to transport up to six passengers and two pilots, the aim is for it to become one of the world's first commercial space travel vehicles. The *Spaceship Two* is designed with practicality and comfort in mind. The pivoting wings on each side of the ship are used to guide the ship back into the atmosphere at many angles, keeping the flight as smooth as possible. There's also a thermal layer that protects the ship from the heat of re-entry, which is a scorching 1,650 degrees Centigrade! The devices that control the roll of the ship are the thrusters, and there's one of these on each wing tip. These thrusters work by keeping the ship from overly rotating on its axis, and thus help the ship maintain a steady trajectory. Lastly, one of the most impressive elements of the design is the engine. The engine of the *Spaceship Two* consists of a hybrid rocket, which uses both solid and liquid fuel, to power the ship forwards.

5.4

N = Narrator   S = Susie   B = Brad   Dr K = Dr Kaye

N: You are going to listen to two students discussing their project with a tutor. Listen and answer questions one to ten.

S: Hi, Brad; Hi, Dr Kaye.

B: Hi, Susie.

Dr K: OK, now you're both here let's get started. Can you start by telling me about your initial decisions regarding your design project ... What are you going to focus on?

B: Well, we were going to design a floating hotel, but Dr Walters told us that it would be too difficult to calculate the costs of the building materials. She warned us not to take on something which is overly complicated otherwise we might not be able to meet the deadline. The thing is though, we really wanted to do it because it's something that we've been really fascinated by, and we'd done some of the designs already.

Dr K: Oh yes? And what do you think about abandoning this idea, Susie?

S: I wanted to do it too, but I suppose we should probably do what Dr Walters says. We haven't studied building materials in that much depth yet I suppose, so maybe it's wiser to stick to something that we can calculate.

Dr K: Well, I think you'll be able to do it. You could make a hypothetical model without costings but with types of materials that could be used ... then give your presentation on this and ask other students what they think. It would be a really good opportunity to get feedback and also improve your critical thinking.

S: I hadn't thought about that. I was just looking at it from the point of view of financial practicality instead of physical design. Do you think we should go back to our original idea, Brad?

B: One hundred percent! Dr Kaye is right – It would be amazing presenting just our practical thoughts without having to worry about the costs. I think that would make a great presentation, because it would allow us to be a lot more imaginative in our presentation and design.

Dr: Think about it anyway. It seems a good way forwards. Now, show me these initial drawings you mentioned. Mmm, interesting. What do you think of this first attempt?

S: Well, I like the design, but I'm not sure the scale is at all accurate.

B: You've got a point there Susie, but we can always revisit that later. I think the concept and the design are crystal clear and really innovative.

Dr K: I'm inclined to agree with Brad here. Now, how are you going to develop these plans?

B: Well, we need to consider what kinds of clientele the hotel is going to attract. This will probably lead us onto the issue of the hotel style – you know, boutique, classic, traditional, modern.

S: Actually, Dr Kaye, do you think that approach might be a bit too focused on face-value issues? In my view, we should focus more on the experience and sustainability rather than attracting a certain type of customer.

Dr K: I thoroughly agree with that as an approach as it'll definitely offer a different perspective to other students. Now, can you talk me through the diagram you have here? ... OK, so let's start by your telling me what the different parts of the floating hotel are and explaining how certain components work.

B: Well, you told us in last week's lecture how it would be more challenging to have a range of different accommodation because this would test our design skills more thoroughly.

Dr K: That's great, Brad. I'm glad you took my suggestion on board. Now, can we work our way round the hotel from the left?

B: OK. Well, over here there are two pools. One is a swimming pool and the other is to be used as an aquarium. There'll be a range of marine wildlife for people to observe.

Dr K: I see. And the accommodation here all consists of chalets?

S: Yes, it does. The hotel works by placing different types of accommodation in zones. The chalets are aimed at families on a tighter budget and the pools are near them, whereas, over here, above the standard accommodation, is where the luxury accommodation will be situated. In this zone there are also a series of multifunctional spaces.

B: One of them is here – the sun terrace, which can be used by our guests in many different ways, such as sunbathing or simply enjoying the view.

Dr K: That's a good use of space. And this area on the right of the main building ... it looks like there's another zone, is that right?

B: Yes. This zone is more about entertainment. The central area is what we've called the event plaza, which is used for shows and performances. In our Business module, Professor Harris highlighted the importance of interactive features of modern architecture so we wanted to have an integral performance space rather than the typical hotel dance hall.

S: And we found a study which claimed that a large number of people like their accommodation to be near to any entertainment so we decided to situate the cottages here.

Dr K: I like the way you've balanced the design with some of the business aspects in this initial plan. OK, so now let's talk about ...

5.5

I don't know whether it'll be possible in my lifetime, but one of the places where I've always wanted to live is the Moon! I imagine you weren't expecting me to say that! Obviously, there would be many fundamental lifestyle differences compared to living on Earth ... I mean, if I lived on the Moon, I'd no doubt need to get used to living indoors because of the lack of breathable air in the atmosphere outside, and this would very likely have a major impact on the way in which people, including myself, managed their communal living spaces. I imagine people living in such an environment would have to co-operate far more to ensure their survival and we'd probably have to take responsibility for doing everything ourselves ... you know, from producing energy to growing our own food, although I'm not sure how we'd do that. I'm ashamed to say I'd probably miss TV, but you never know, in the not-so-distant future, it could become possible to watch shows in space as well as live there. You might think that my choice sounds quite strange but the world is becoming more and more overcrowded so as a species, we may need to look elsewhere for viable living options in the future. And imagine being part of the group that first starts that civilisation and makes it a thriving community. It would be absolutely amazing! Obviously, I've not heard much from other people about what the Moon is actually like and the realities involved in terms of adapting to living there ... it's only been visited by a very small number of people ... but the astronauts have enthused about how magical it is to be on the Moon looking back down to Earth. I don't know how I'd handle living in such a place but I would definitely like to try it if there's ever the possibility to. It'd definitely be much more exciting than just changing towns or cities – swapping one crowded street for another!

Module 6

6.1

E = Examiner   B = Babara

E: How safe do you think people feel about using websites?

B: I think people generally feel pretty safe. I think this because, well … most people I know have a good idea of which sites they should use and which are perhaps just trying to get your data … you know, more dubious websites. I think these kinds of sites are quite obvious. I know that some people say that there are perhaps more vulnerable groups in society who might not know the difference between these kinds of websites and the safer ones but I think these people are in the minority. In general, I think these days the majority of people have a good idea of what they're doing when they're using the internet.

6.5

N = Narrator   L = Lecturer

N: You are going to listen to a lecture on crime prevention. Listen and answer questions one to two.

L: Crime prevention is now a far more important part of the study of criminality virtually all over the world. Although most people are somewhat unsure of the effectiveness of researching and implementing crime-prevention methods, there is growing evidence to suggest that more attention should be paid to this than the traditional forms of punishment focused on in the past. One of the main reasons for this is the development of psychology and medical technology. The advances in these two areas have allowed us to study the brain more comprehensively and, as a result, people's behaviour in far more depth than we ever imagined possible 50 years ago. As such we are now much more interested in how to prevent people from becoming criminals than seeking more effective ways to punish them.

6.6

N = Narrator   L = Lecturer

N: Listen to the next part of the lecture on crime prevention and complete the sentences. Write no more than two words.

L: In addition, criminologists have become interested in an approach to crime prevention which is called situational crime prevention. This unusual and modern approach focuses on ways in which the opportunities for crime to take place can be reduced. So, how does this work in practice? Well, it aims to understand more about the circumstances which allow specific crimes to occur – you know, things such as fragmented communities or poor street lighting, then it attempts to explore measures which will have an effect by changing environments so that the crimes do not occur. This is actually a really interesting way of tackling this kind of problem. The goal is to make committing a crime less appealing to people in order to reduce the instances of crimes happening in the first place.

6.7

N = Narrator   L = Lecturer

N: Listen to the last part of the lecture and complete the test task.

L: The way in which this is done is by using the theory of rational choice. Everyone has to make choices all the time and we use information around us to feed into how we make these choices. The theory is about how human beings assess a situation logically and then make a decision on how to act. It applies to all forms of social behaviour and that, of course, includes criminal behaviour. As a result, it means criminologists can start to better understand how to demotivate people from committing crimes. Let me explain this further. Criminals will evaluate the likelihood of being caught when weighing up the decision to commit a crime in any given situation. An example of how this works in practice is automatic traffic systems such as speed cameras or cameras installed at road junctions. Research has shown that these systems work really well in reducing speeding and running red light offences because people know that the chance of being caught is extremely high.

6.8

N = Narrator   S = Sam

N: You are going to listen to a lecture on super recognisers. Listen and answer questions one to two.

S: Modern policing methods have changed considerably in recent years. One of these changes is the use of super recognisers to help solve crimes. Super recognisers are people who can recognise faces more easily and reliably than other people. According to research done in a variety of studies, most of us can recall the features of the faces of people we see approximately 20 percent of the time, whereas super recognisers can do this an amazing 80 percent of the time, sometimes even up to 95 percent. This is a significant difference and one which the police are using to their advantage. Nowadays the police are using these people to help them solve crimes. The reason these super recognisers are so useful is because they can identify faces of people in distorted or blurred CCTV footage or photographs. Identifying criminals using 'normal' police officers is time consuming and expensive, as is the development of sophisticated technology to do this. Therefore, employing these super recognisers can have a significant impact on the different types of methods to fight crime which are available to the police.

6.9

N = Narrator   S = Sam

N: Now listen and answer questions one to ten.

S: So, let's look at super recognisers in more detail and explore the ways in which these people work with law enforcement agencies. Firstly, it's important to note that only a very small percentage of the population are super recognisers – about 1 or 2 percent. Although science currently doesn't know much about why some people are super recognisers, it's believed to be an innate quality. That's to say people are born with this skill and it cannot be taught. There is also some evidence which suggests that it tends to appear in people who are in their twenties or thirties. So far there haven't been any teenagers discovered with this ability. The other point to make here, which is particularly fascinating, is the cross-race effect. This is a specific and strangely inexplicable limitation of the skill. What it means is that super recognisers are not very good at recognising people from another race. This can be crucial in terms of recruitment for law enforcement agencies who should focus on recruiting super recognisers from the same ethnic groups as the people who live in certain areas.

Research has been conducted into super recognition at Harvard University in the USA and at the University of Greenwich in the UK. A team of psychologists from the University of Greenwich tested some police officers from the London Metropolitan police force who seemed to be exceptionally good at recognising people in CCTV footage to determine if they had super-recognition abilities. The results showed that some of these officers did indeed possess this remarkable ability. It should be noted here that the researchers at Greenwich were using methods consistent with those used at Harvard.

The thing that was also interesting about the research was that it highlighted that super recognisers are excellent at knowing when they have not seen a face. This is important because it means that these people are far less likely to provide the police with false leads. In the process of identifying potential criminals this is extremely useful to the police because it can save precious time, money and manpower. In fact some senior police officers believe that it'll become as important as finger printing or DNA in the near future.

Despite the importance of these super recognisers in crime fighting, computers are also playing their part. Facial-recognition software is constantly evolving and becoming better and better. However, right now humans still outperform the machines in this area. In principle, it should be relatively easy for computers to identify humans in video footage. We know that computers are fundamentally better at processing vast numbers of images. But the issue here is that much of the footage from security cameras and photographs is of low quality, meaning the machines are unable to fix on matches in the same way as humans can. So, why is this? Well, mostly it's to do with what is needed for facial-recognition software to work. Computers need reference points based on light, position and the facial expression of the person in the image. This is just for photographs. In video it is much more challenging for the computer because of the movement of the image and therefore the reference points are constantly changing. It is phenomenally difficult to develop algorithms which can cope with these requirements. And of course there's the fact that it's almost impossible to programme computers to do something we don't comprehend ourselves. What I mean is that we don't really understand how humans recognise faces so we have a long way to go before we can programme machines to do this. One reason behind this is that computers approach the task systematically. They use a series of steps to analyse the pixels which make up the facial image. Conversely, people recognise faces holistically, by this I mean, by looking at the whole face, rather than by analysing its parts. In the future though it's highly likely that computers will become more adept at doing this. More sophisticated cameras, for example, will produce better quality images and we'll also get better at training our computers to perform more like super recognisers.

6.10

E = Examiner   R = Ricky

E: Do you think using drones is a positive step in policing?
R: Hmm … that's an interesting question … I'm not … sure. A drone can be a good beneficial thing because it can catch criminals easier, the police too … If there are not enough policemen and women, then they can be substituted by drones. This means they don't have to worry about having an officer ready. But we must think of keeping police jobs. If the police use drones, will they still need officers? If there are no jobs for officers, then this will be a problem … hmm … Maybe … Drones can … As … assist officers but there is a law that they cannot … take … re … place … real humans.

6.11

E = Examiner   R = Ricky

E: Do you think the use of drones is a positive step in policing?
R: Hmm … I'm not completely sure. … My initial thought is that a drone can be a useful tool for police … for example, it could lead to catching criminals more easily. As well as that it could assist with police numbers too, by that I mean if there are not enough policemen and women, then they could substitute officers with drones. This means they wouldn't have to worry about having an officer ready … But, on the other hand, we must think of keeping police jobs. If the police use drones, will they still need law-enforcement personnel out in the streets? If there are no jobs for policemen and women then this will be a problem. Hmm … Maybe the answer is to have some rules about drone use … For example, that drones can assist officers but they cannot take the place … and the … jobs of real humans.

Module 7

7.1

1: I live in relatively small city in centre of China. Actually, it's same city where I was born and grew up.
2: I'm from Guadalajara. Is a fascinating place I think and has a great range of architecture.
3: I think that if I would move city, I would choose to live in Stuttgart because it's conveniently located.
4: I've always dreamt of living in a big city. I'd put my time going to the galleries and shops!
5: Abu Dhabi's a fantastic place to live, but sometimes in the summer the heat's overpowered.

7.2

1

E = Examiner   P = Peter

E: Where are you from?
P: I'm from Moscow city in Russia.
E: What's it like?
P: Well, it's a big city. There's a lot to see. I can give you lots of advices about what you can see. If you go ever, you must visit the Red Square. I think it's the most famous sight in Russia. You can also make a lot of shopping there. The products are really good.
E: What's your favourite thing about Moscow?
P: Hmm … It's difficult question because I like lots of things about the city. I think maybe my favourite thing is people. They're all so friendly and kindly.

2

E = Examiner   P = Peter

E: Where are you from?
P: I'm from Moscow in Russia.
E: What's it like?
P: Well, it's a big city. There's a lot to see. I can give you lots of advice about what you can see. If you ever go, you must visit Red Square. I think it's the most famous sight in Russia. You can also do a lot of shopping there. The products are really good.
E: What's your favourite thing about Moscow?
P: Hmm … It's a difficult question because I like lots of things about the city. I think maybe my favourite thing is the people. They're all so friendly and kind.

7.3

J = James   K = Karen

J: Good morning, how can I help you?
K: Hello. Um, I hope so. I'm not sure if this is the right number to call about the climbing club.

J: Well, this is for enquiries about membership, general information about what we do and who we are, meetings and competitions.
K: Oh, right. Well, I already know when and where the club meets. I do have an enquiry about the best footwear for climbing for people new to the sport, but the main reason for contacting you is that I'd like to know if I can join your club even though I've never climbed before.
J: OK. Let me tell you a bit more about the club.

1

J: Right, so we try to meet up twice a week, once on Wednesday evenings at about 7.15 and then again on Saturday mornings. We used to meet at 8.15 but some people complained that that was a bit early so we changed it to a bit later. We like to start the climbing sessions at 9.00 on the dot so we ask people to get there at 8.50. That means that everyone's there by the time we start.
K: I see. It sounds like you're very organised.

2

K: Can I ask about training? Because I don't have any experience, does the club offer any kind of coaching to help me improve?
J: That's a good question. We don't allow our members to explicitly teach each other because it could be dangerous, although you can watch and learn from other more experienced people. The girl that founded the club is amazing, so it's well worth watching her at our practice sessions. What your membership does offer you though is a reduction on the climbing course at the community active centre. They've got tonnes of sports courses and we've got an agreement with them for our members.
K: Oh, that sounds perfect! I think I'd like to sign up and become a member.

3

J: Alright. Now, I need to get your details. Can you give me your full name?
K: It's Karen Whittaker.
J: Thanks. And what's your mobile number?
K: It's 07865 322 475.
J: Great. So, we have three meeting points. There's the wall in the city park, the bridge by the river and the large car park at the back of the station. Which are the most convenient for you?
K: Um, the first two are quite near where I live.
J: OK. And finally, the cost of membership for you will be £65 per year. Oh, wait a minute, we actually have a special offer this month. If you sign up now, it'll cost £55.
K: OK. Oh, by the way, I'm a student. Does that make any difference?
J: Oh yes. In that case the fees are even lower than £55. The student rate is £45.
K: That's a bargain.

7.4

N = Narrator   A = Anna   E = Edward

N: You are going to hear a conversation between a customer and a cycling company. Listen and answer the questions.
A: Hello, City Cycling Group, Anna speaking. How may I help you today?
E: Oh, yes, hello. I'm calling because I'd like to become a member of the cycling group.
A: Of course. First of all, I'll take down your personal details and then I'll answer any questions you may have.
E: OK, great.
A: So, can I have your name please?
E: Yes, it's Ed.
A: Actually, I need to have your full name, Sir.
E: Sorry, of course. It's Edward Simmons.
A: Thank you. And where do you live? Again, I need to have your full address including postcode.
E: Right. It's number 57, sorry, number 47, Lexington Road, London, SW23 4GJ.
A: Can you spell the street name for me?
E: It's L-E-X-I-N-G-T-O-N.
A: Thank you. I'm also required to take a contact telephone number for you, Sir.
E: I see, yes. Um … my mobile number is 07865 943262.
A: Let me just check that. It's 07865 943263.
E: Actually, the last digit is a 2 not a 3.
A: Oh, sorry about that. Lastly, what's your email address so we can add you to our mailing list?
E: It's ed dot simmons at my mail dot com.
A: Thank you. Just one more thing, Mr Simmons. Could you tell me your level of riding experience? Would you say you were a beginner, intermediate or experienced cyclist?
E: Let me think … I've been cycling for as long as I can remember so I think I'd categorise myself as experienced.

A: OK. Now, have you got any questions?

E: Um, yes. Could you tell me about the Sunday club? I read about it on your website and thought I might like to join.

A: Of course. Firstly, I should say there's an extra fee. It isn't expensive, just a couple of pounds for refreshments on the day. Um ... this group is about enjoying the ride not challenging yourself which means the routes are on flat roads. However, I'm not entirely sure that it would be appropriate for you because the members are all retired. I'd recommend the Saturday club more because it's mainly young professionals so you might have more in common with this group.

E: Yes, I see what you mean. In that case, can you sign me up for the Saturday group instead?

A: Of course, Sir. That's all done and we look forward to cycling with you soon.

E: Great, me too. Bye.

A: Goodbye and thanks for calling.

7.6

A = Assistant   C = Customer

A: Hello, customer service, how can I help you?

C: I'd like to complain about the quality of one of your international bus journeys. I travelled from London to Warsaw with your company last week.

A: OK, of course. What was the problem with the journey?

C: Well, the bus wasn't in very good condition. I thought that it was going to break down because the doors were constantly making a strange noise, but that isn't really what I'm calling about. The thing I want to discuss with you is the attitude of the driver. Throughout the journey he didn't speak to the passengers in an acceptable manner. He actually shouted at people a couple of times and I think that is quite rude.

A: I'm sorry to hear about this, Madam. Could you tell me what time your bus departed London so we can work out who the driver was and follow up on this?

C: We left at 9.30 in the morning. I think the service number was LN304.

A: Thank you.

C: In my opinion, you should be more careful in your recruitment process as this kind of problem can really affect the quality of passenger travel. When we finally arrived in Warsaw, people didn't feel quite so stressed as they had during the journey. Although they didn't complain at the time, it was clear people were unhappy with the experience.

A: It does sound like a bad experience. Is there anything else I can help you with? Can I offer you some compensation or would you like to have a word with my boss?

C: No, thank you. Actually, that'd probably be a waste of time. I think it's best if I make a formal complaint about this.

A: Let me just see if I can put you through to my boss ... Um, I'm afraid the line's engaged at the moment, but we do have an incident report record so I'll write it up and pass it on.

C: That would be great, thank you.

7.7

N = Narrator   A = Assistant   S = Silvia

N: You are going to listen to someone calling a train customer care line. Listen and answer the questions.

A: Good morning, UK Trains, how can I help you?

S: Um, I'm not sure if this is the right number to call.

A: Well, this number is for general enquiries about ticket prices and timetables, specific complaints about the service, updates to our service, scheduled maintenance works and lost property.

S: Well, I haven't lost anything, I know that! I do have an enquiry about the recent changes to the London to Edinburgh timetable, but my main reason for calling is to complain about the late running of my train last Monday. I really feel that I should get a refund for my ticket or at least some form of discount, especially given the high cost of ticket prices these days.

A: Right. Well, can you tell me what the problem was with the journey?

S: Well, the delay was far longer than I consider acceptable. I got to the station just before 8.15 – that should have been when my train got into the station, but it was over half an hour late. It didn't leave until 8.50. At one point I thought I'd have to wait for the 9.15 train.

A: Mmm, I see what you mean. That isn't very good. I'd like to apologise on behalf of UK Trains.

S: And on top of that, more and more passengers arrived on the platform and all tried to board that same train. As a result, it was so overcrowded and not everyone had a seat. On a commuter service this really isn't good. Arriving over an hour late was one thing, but

being so uncomfortable on the journey was really unacceptable, especially with the high price of the tickets nowadays.

A: Yes, I can understand your point.

S: In my opinion, there needs to be more organisation from the station staff to prevent this kind of problem. There weren't enough staff at the station to stop the people pushing to get on the train. It isn't very safe having that many people in the carriages and this could be avoided if there were more staff.

A: I agree. So, because the train was over 30 minutes late, I think you're eligible for a refund for this ... Just let me get the correct form ... OK, so can you give me your full name?

S: It's Silvia Cannings.

A: Can you spell your surname for me, please?

S: C-A double N-I-N-G-S

A: Thank you. And your mobile number so we can contact you about the refund process if there are any problems.

S: It's 07865 322 475.

A: So, just to be clear that's 07865 322 474.

S: No, the last number is five not four.

A: Thank you. And have you got an email address?

S: Yes, it's silvia2000@fastmail.com.

A: Can you tell me what service you travelled on?

S: It was the 8.15 from London to Manchester. I travelled standard class in the quiet coach.

A: And when was your journey?

S: It was last Monday which was ... the ... er, 12th of March. Oh, sorry the ... 13th, yes the 13th.

A: Great. Now, I need to record the exact problem so can you confirm that the train was over 30 minutes late?

S: Yes, that's correct.

A: Now we can refund the full amount to you via the credit card you used to purchase the ticket or by bank transfer. Which would you prefer?

S: Bank transfer, please. And can you call me rather than emailing if you need to contact me for any reason?

A: Of course, I'll make a note of that. Now, how much did you pay for your ticket?

S: I paid £87.95.

A: OK. I'll get that refund processed for you immediately.

S: Thank you for your help.

7.8

E = Examiner   C = Candidate

E: Hello, what's your name?

C: Dieter Schmidt.

E: Where are you from?

C: I'm actually from Munich. It's a large city in the south of Germany.

E: And now you're living here in Sydney?

C: Yes, that's right. I go to a language school near George Street, just a stone's throw away from here.

E: How did you get here today?

C: Well, although I study in the city centre, I live quite far out in the suburbs. I live in Cronulla. I don't know if you know it, but it's in the far south of Sydney. So, I have to get the train here. It would be impossible to walk it, and there's no buses to take you into the centre. Today, I took the 8.45 train and then walked from Central station. It's only about a 10-minute walk from here.

E: How do you prefer to travel?

C: Well, actually I prefer to walk. I'm a people watcher and I love being out amongst other people. Sometimes from the train or bus you don't get to see much. I also really enjoy driving. If I had a car here, I think I'd see so much of the country, but I'm reliant on public transport unfortunately. Oh, and I really love flying. Just the whole experience of it.

E: Is that your favourite form of transport?

C: Yes, I think so. I think with flying the excitement of going to a far-flung destination and the experience of knowing you're thousands of metres in the air. It's amazing. Although I don't particularly enjoy going through airports. It's just all queuing!

E: Would you say that you're a well-travelled person?

C: Yes, I think so. I mean, I'm only 20 and I've visited quite a few countries. I think I've been to about a dozen countries. Of course, I've seen a lot of Germany and Europe in general but I've also been to the USA, Australia and Thailand. I would say that's quite a few places. I like backpacking and my parents were always fine with me going away and exploring with my friends in the summer holidays, so I had plenty of opportunity.

E: Thank you, now we're going to move on ...

Module 8

8.1

1

My neighbour's such a generous woman; she's always volunteering to help the families on our street. For example, she offers to babysit so that the parents can spend an evening in peace. She's extremely tolerant of young children, even when they're naughty. I'd imagine that it's because she used to be a teacher, so she's sensitive to the needs of children. Anyway, people are very grateful for her efforts, but she's so modest. She thinks her help is nothing special.

2

I think my grandfather is a very attentive person because he's always available to listen to people and he doesn't interrupt. He's also a tolerant man. I think this could be because he lived in different countries so he would have got used to integrating with people from a variety of backgrounds. I've learnt to be more conscientious in my studies from him because he believes in doing things properly.

8.2

1: We might establish a book club in my local library to encourage community spirit.
2: The cinema's developed a new anime online chat group for teenagers on their website.
3: It could be worth considering the overall policy on charity funding in this area.
4: Creating more clubs for the elderly would be a real advantage in this area.
5: These days, there are a multitude of new initiatives for young mothers to share parenting tips.
6: Going to the open-air gallery in the park was a great way to establish new contacts.

8.4

N = Narrator   I = Interviewer   S = Simon

N: You are going to listen to an interview about social networking. Listen and answer the questions.
I: And that's the latest news today. Next we're going to be speaking to our technology editor, Simon Smith. He'll be telling us all about the latest report in social networking that has been collated from over a million participants around the world. Good afternoon, Simon.
S: Good afternoon, Carol.
I: So, this report …
S: Yes, it's the biggest report like this I think we've ever seen, and it certainly raises some questions for social media sites. And indeed for us, the people that use them.
I: I hear that it's tapped into the motivations we have for using social media. What can you tell us about this?
S: It has. There were over 50 different groups surveyed and there were some interesting discoveries. **For example,** senior citizens, who you would think use social networks like Facebook to make friends and avoid being lonely, actually used them to do things like look at articles and watch videos. This group of people actually spends the most time on the internet too, which is in stark contrast to the situation ten years ago when a lot of older people weren't even online. **The research also found** that young people tend to use social networks for reasons relating to social acceptance – simply, they want to stay 'in' with their friends. This group tends to switch sites a lot, so Facebook might be popular for a short amount of time, but they'll move on to other sites like Instagram or Twitter pretty swiftly. Loyalty isn't a big feature of this group. **If we look at** mothers however, we can see a completely different story. Their loyalty is actually pretty high, and they tend to form close bonds with people in their online community. People that they haven't actually met. This is not simply to allay the isolation of staying at home with a small child, which is what we might suppose. Actually, it's to find out whether they are doing the right thing when it comes to caring for their young children or indeed their teens. These sites can be extremely supportive tools. **Lastly, let's look at another group** which showed surprising motivations for using social networks; people who are not in relationships. This group of people, again, you may think are quite lonely, but statistics show they post more and go out more than any other group. In fact, often their motivation is to get back in touch with people they've met. Perhaps from school or just from their busy social lives.

I: That's very interesting and not at all what I would have thought. How do you think this information will affect social networking sites at the moment? Do you think we'll see some changes?
S: Yes, I think so. I've been looking at some of the most popular sites at the moment, SoPals, EverywhereUs and Sweet. They all have their advantages and disadvantages but I can see all three of them going in different directions in the future. **Let's talk about SoPals firstly,** as it's probably one of the most well-known social networks around at the moment. **And why is it so popular?** Well, I think it's pretty easy to use and also it's seen a good uptake in lots of different countries. I think nearly every country in the world has access to it and there are millions of international users. **However,** the one thing many people are not at all happy about is the way in which SoPals quite brutally collects user data. There has been some talk in the press about who can access this data, and although the wider community might not be too bothered, there are some rights groups who are outraged. **On the other hand, they also have quite a good strategy for going forwards.** They are going to develop posts which are more temporary. So, say, they'll stay on for an hour and are then archived. This is something which is increasingly popular for younger users, so it sounds like a good move to me. **Now, moving onto EverywhereUs …** This is more of a context-specific social networking website. **One of its best points** is that it's geared towards close friends. This means that people are more likely to share more things. The app has been a great success. **However,** we can't say the same for the web version, which has had some dreadful feedback. They need to work on this in my opinion, **but I don't think it** will stop this site from getting bigger and bigger in the future. **One final site that I do want to mention is Sweet.** Now, this isn't really a site for the likes of me and you, Carol. It's actually a social network for teens. **Now, the reason why this site is becoming so popular** for this age group is that it supports so many different forms of media. So, you can post audios, pictures, videos, little voice messages, games. It's really booming with this age range. **It's not all perfect though.** I've got to say that the design is quite simplistic and child-like. Even for the age range. And also, there's no app yet. They'll want to get that developed if they want to be a big player in this market. **And … they obviously do want to be a big player as they're planning next year** to branch out to other demographics, such as young parents and older people. I can see this being a really successful move if they get the design spot-on. One thing I will say though is that social networking doesn't appear to be going anywhere. It looks to just grow and grow.

8.5

S1: I think there are always books that people take to their hearts. One example I can think of is *Gone with the Wind*. Now, I know that it might not be that well known now, but when the book came out in the 1930s in the USA, it took the country by storm. Everyone loved it and loved the characters. This in turn led to the creation of one of the most famous films in cinema history. They couldn't lose with something that had captured the public's imagination so vividly. Everyone wanted to be a part of the movie. It was so popular it's now considered one of the classics of cinema.

S2: The early days of cinema were all about silent films. It didn't matter what the actors and actresses sounded like, they were simply never heard! However, the development of sound in movies had a dramatic effect on the world of cinema and these actors and actresses within it. It not only saw the beginning of the end for silent films, but also a lot of famous actors and actresses were out of a job since they simply didn't sound good enough.

S3: Films, they want to communicate a message to you. This can be in a variety of ways. A good plot, good acting, all of these things go to making up an emotional experience for the viewer. Films now can even transport us into different worlds. Think of the effects in films like *Avatar* or *The Matrix*. These would never have been possible without the development of CGI, or computer generated imagery, which makes the impossible a reality on our screens.

8.6

N = Narrator   P = Presenter   H = Helen

N: You are going to listen to an interview about film adaptations of novels. Listen and answer the questions.
P: So today we have reviewer Helen Warner joining us to talk about adaptations of great novels. Great to have you here.
H: Great to be here.
P: So, are you a fan of big-screen movie adaptations?

H: Well, it's not a simple yes/no answer I'm afraid. When people write great books they do it to communicate a message and encourage the reader to think and create an imaginary world. When we see the film, the world has been created for us. We're straight-jacketed into someone else's vision. This really means that the film is only ever as good as the vision provided and can be quite destructive to the reader's interpretation, no matter how good. For me, that happened when I saw the adaptation of *Wuthering Heights*. Now, this was in the 1990s I think, but I absolutely loved the book. The film, however, gave me completely the opposite reaction. I think that's true of many of the film versions of that particular novel, such as the 1930s black and white version which was overly dramatic. However, sometimes the imagination shown in film adaptations can surpass anything my mere brain has ever thought of. This is usually because they have used CGI to really make something out of this world. For me, the visual imagination in *The Life of Pi* was simply amazing. It's a must-see film in my opinion. Another film I'd like to talk about, in terms of adaptations, is *The Girl with the Dragon Tattoo*. Now, the film is dark, and anything but dull, but for me it just didn't hang together. I came out of the cinema wondering what I had just seen! This never happened to me when I read the book. Now, I don't think it's a reflection on me ... I've heard the same from many people. I think, however, that one of the worst crimes of cinema is simply making an overly stylised film version with no substance. This describes *The Maze Runner* perfectly. There was really nothing exciting about it. Although that could be my age! So, in a nutshell, film-makers must do the message and our imaginations justice.

P: Let's move on to talk about the *Shadow Thief*. As we know this is a book remade for the big screen and it's coming out next week. What do you think of it?

H: Well, when the book came out in 1951 it was almost instantly a bestseller. I think it sold over 5 million copies in the first year. It's a really amazing achievement and a big challenge for any director. If you've read the book, you'll know that the whole story revolves around three main characters ... the revolutionary Maxim, the royal guard Dmitri, and city dweller Irene ... and their experiences during the final three days of the Russian Revolution. The book was absolutely breath-taking for anyone that read it and I hope the film will be too. Interestingly, the director hasn't followed the book to the letter. Dmitri in the book tends to come off as quite a callous person, but in the adaptation he's rather different. The director explores the reasons for his actions in a very sympathetic way. I don't think this is problematic though. Motivations are explored everywhere in this film and it gives much more depth to what is an exhilarating story. The film was actually meant to be out last year, however, a disagreement with the writer affected the development of the screenplay. This meant production had to be postponed. However, the premier is nearly upon us and the film will be showing in cinemas from next week. It's certainly been talked about by everyone ... more than any other film this year so let's hope it can live up to the hype.

P: And you've been to a pre-screening?

H: I certainly have. I'm sure many people thought a film version of such a well-loved and well-known book would be doomed to failure. I think this is why it's had so much build-up. People want to see if it lives up to all the talk surrounding it. And I have to say it absolutely does, and more. If you like your films complex and evocative, this is most definitely for you.

P: Well, lovely talking to you and thank you so much for coming in ... now ...

8.7

I'm a great fan of Hollywood films and American TV so just choosing one person is incredibly challenging – there are just so many people I'd love to meet ... let me think ... one famous person I'd definitely like to meet is Jennifer Lawrence because she's one of my all-time favourite actors. To be honest, I've been following her on TV for years now and having seen her in countless interviews it seems to me that she's really down-to-earth ... and she's also naturally hilarious. Every time she's attended an award ceremony she's fallen over and she always makes a real joke of it. I think the thing I like most about her is the fact that she's quite feminist in her outlook on life ... so as far as I'm concerned she's a very good role model. I'd really like to meet her to see if she actually lives up to what I imagine she's like ... and I'd also love to find out about the gossip from behind the scenes. I've always thought that she'd be really friendly and generous with her time for her fans ... She seems unlike many Hollywood stars in her disposition and I think this is because of her upbringing. She was extremely shy as a child but had a

close family. I imagine they kept her feet on the ground. If I actually met her, I'd probably be tongue-tied and really embarrass myself. If I could manage to keep calm, I'd like to ask her about her experiences in films like *The Hunger Games* and *American Hustle*. I'd love to know what her co-stars were like ... *American Hustle*, which I think was filmed about five years ago, stars some of my other heroes like Christian Bale and Amy Adams.

Module 9

9.1

E = Examiner   C = Candidate

E: What does it take to be a successful person?

C: That depends ... Mmm, that's quite a difficult question ... I think this is different for everyone, but it is also often culturally determined, or perhaps even as a result of our upbringing and surroundings. As far as I'm concerned, success can be achieved in all aspects of our lives as long as we know what we are trying to do. I'm not sure if this is the correct way to say it, but success happens when you know about or you are ... maybe ... aware of what your goals are.

9.2

J = John   P = Penny   I = Ian

J: OK Penny, let's have a think about what we can do for our presentation.

P: OK John, well I've had some thoughts about what we could do. So, our presentation is all about what it takes to be successful, so why don't we tackle world record breakers?

J: Hmmm, it's a possibility, but do you think that'd be sufficient? Those people are quite out of the ordinary. What do you think, Ian?

I: Actually, I side with Penny. Quite a wide range of world records exist from quite serious feats, to really unusual ones, and they all illustrate different traits that are needed to be successful.

P: Exactly Ian. We could start with examples of world record breakers and then identify their shared traits. Once we've gathered this information, we can develop a kind of blueprint for success and present it to the group.

J: So, kind of like an inductive approach.

I: What do you mean by that, John?

J: Well, here, extracting theory from observation of examples, rather than the other way round.

P: Yes, I suppose it is.

J: OK. Well, what examples shall we use?

I: We could use Usain Bolt. He's got quite a few records. And I think he's a great example of the motivation and single-mindedness needed to become the best.

P: I agree. And then we could look at someone whose record is more unusual. For example, the woman with the longest fingernails. They're over 7 metres long! I mean maybe this doesn't take the talent and natural ability that Usain Bolt has, but it must take a concerted effort. Imagine the time it takes to grow them! And also, there must be so many things she can't do.

J: I really like the Usain Bolt example, but do you think the other one is serious enough for our presentation?

P: I think so. It shows a different kind of dedication, but it is still dedication nevertheless. I think the seriousness will come across in our presentation style. As long as we have proper facts, figures and quotations, I think we'll be alright. We will need to think of more examples though.

9.3

S1: Hmmm ... well, I think that it's pretty challenging to work in a really frenetic environment. I think maybe it might energise you for a while ... you know, perhaps spur you on to work faster and better ... but there must be a high chance of burnout. How can you sustain working in fifth gear all the time? I just don't think we're hard wired for that kind of intense activity.

S2: There's plenty of evidence that working from home actually boosts productivity, but I'd be surprised if it did that for me. The problem with working from home is that there are a multitude of distractions ... you know ... watching TV ... wasting time online ... I think it might be hard to focus for extended periods of time. I know some people manage it, but ... well, I frankly have my doubts. Besides, productivity isn't everything. If you work from home, you might miss the environment of having others around you to bounce ideas off or just chat with.

S3: So now more forward-thinking companies like Google or Facebook have these kind of space-aged environments for their employees to work in. It's a real change from before because ... well, I think it gives employees a chance to think and change their environments to their frame of mind. Sometimes when you're doing something creative you just can't be stuck in front of a computer because you need to go out and give your mind some room to breathe. I think these kinds of companies know this.

S4: There are some jobs that I just couldn't do. I like to be around others ... I kind of enjoy being the centre of attention ... but there are so many jobs where you're completely isolated. I don't think I could spend that much time with my own thoughts, it'd probably drive me crazy. There is some research suggesting that people who work by themselves need to be quite self-reliant and practical people. I think this is probably true. I imagine the benefit is that you don't have to deal with uncooperative people, but for me that's not a good enough reason.

9.4

P = Professor Hickey   C = Charlotte   J = Jim

C: Hello, Professor Hickey. Can we come in?

P: Yes, certainly. Hello, Charlotte. Hello, Jim. Do come on in and take a seat. So, how's your research coming along?

C: Mine's progressing well, I think. All my questionnaires are completed and I'm analysing the results.

P: Excellent, Charlotte. Now let me check, your focus was related to the effects of sounds on productivity, wasn't it?

C: No, that's Jim. Mine is centred around multinational companies like Amazon.

P: Oh yes, that's right. So how many questionnaires have you managed to get completed?

C: Around 50, from about three different companies.

P: Excellent. And what about you, Jim?

J: Mine's not going so well, I'm afraid. I'm having some serious difficulties finding people who are willing to be interviewed and so far, I've only found one person. People simply aren't getting back to me.

P: Hmm ... well that is one of the main difficulties when it comes to undertaking qualitative research, especially face-to-face interviews. It might be an idea to review the methodology you're using. Think of other ways you can obtain the data you want. I'd personally suggest organising focus groups as people tend to feel less intimidated when they're not the sole focus of attention. You'll also gain a wider spectrum of results and save time.

J: Hmm ... OK. To be honest, I haven't got far. I've still got two sections to complete, so I just think it will hurt to move away from interviews. It's a shame though as my one interview gave me some really valuable insights. The employee talked about how much more productive they were when listening to music, and also they mentioned how being more flexible in many aspects of their work really made them work better.

C: I found that too. Flexible working was one of the most commonly cited reasons for productive working.

J: Yeah, but interestingly, I read an article about working environments recently and it talked about big companies having lots of different areas for employees. You know, like sleep pods and café areas and terraces, that kind of thing. Well, the article said that although employees seem to like it, it's not at all cost-effective.

P: Yes, that's the Bonner article. It's worth reading if you haven't already, Charlotte.

C: I will, thank you.

P: Look, Charlotte we'll come to you in a minute, but Jim I think we need to think about your situation. You absolutely must get your research carried out in the next few weeks or it's possible that you'll struggle to meet the deadline. You know if that happens, you automatically fail and we don't want that.

J: I know. I think you're right. Maybe I'll start working on organising some focus groups in order to gather some data as soon as possible.

P: And Charlotte, you say you're analysing the results from your questionnaires now. Are you finding any patterns?

C: Actually, I wasn't sure I'd find anything but I identified some really clear patterns, I wasn't really expecting that, but I'm pretty pleased.

P: And what have you found?

C: Well, that more up-to-date working environments – in all forms, so flexible working, forward-thinking workspaces, things like gyms and gardens – all of them contribute to making a more effective working environment and ultimately making a more successful company.

J: Hmm ... really? Can you say that? It's not what my research found. Remember that Bonner article. From my reading, I've found that only some of these practices are actually effective. I know I haven't conducted any primary research yet, but I don't think it's such a simple picture. I think there's a lot of discussion about these work places being great, but generally it's for recruitment purposes. It's not actually beneficial when working.

C: You mean that these new-style work practices and environments are a negative thing?

J: No, not so much negative as irrelevant to existing employees. They're just there to attract new people ... the best people ... because the idea of working in a place with gardens and pool tables seems attractive.

P: Jim, if you're going to make such strong assertions you had better support them with readings and research because remember, your work is only going to have academic value if it's based on evidence. Charlotte, from what I can see here your research so far is solid. I think you've got good questions on your questionnaire and you've collected some rich data. Remember to analyse the data very carefully when formulating your main points though. Jim, I want to see you next week as you're going to need to begin this research with some urgency so come back with what you've done next Wednesday afternoon.

9.5

1

E = Examiner   K = Kenji

E: Do you think that society is too focused on work and career success nowadays?

K: Mmm, that's a tough question. At one level I think it's good to be focused on work. I mean we spend long periods of time working so, as far as I'm concerned, it's really worthwhile at least attempting to be successful, because then hopefully, we're going to actually receive some ... I'm not sure if this is the right way to put it ... sense of satisfaction from the work we're engaged in. Having said this, it's, it's clear that certain individuals seem to have taken this too far and the results are increasing stress levels and more widespread unhappiness across the world.

2

E = Examiner   S = Steffi

E: Do you think that society is too focused on work and career success nowadays?

S: Mmm, that's a tough question. At one level for me ..., I think it's good to be focused on work. I mean ... we spend long periods of time working so ... as far as I'm concerned it's really, it's really worthwhile at least attempting to be successful, because then hopefully, we're ... we're going to actually receive some ... I'm not sure if this is the right way to put it ... sense of satisfaction from the work we're engaged in. Having said this, it's clear that certain individuals seem to have taken this too far and the results are increasing stress levels and more widespread unhappiness across the world.

Module 10

10.1

1: I used to be really scared about sleeping in the dark when I was younger. I think it stemmed from the fact that if I read or saw something even remotely scary, I'd think it could come true. I've always been told that I have a very ...

2: When I was at school our art lessons were focused on theory and the history of art, so we never really got our hands dirty actually doing art. The effect of this, I think on all of us, was to completely ...

3: Problem-solving is second nature to some people. Not for me though. My brain just isn't wired that way. I've no ability whatsoever to ...

4: I used to be really good at playing the piano when I was younger, but when I became a teenager I just gave up because all I wanted to do was to spend more time with my friends. Now, of course, I really regret ...

5: My aunt is quite an amazing individual. When I visit her house, I'm always in awe of how it looks. I don't know how she does it, but she has this capacity to buy completely random second-hand objects that seem to go perfectly together. I tell you, her house could easily be on the cover of an interior design magazine as she has such ...

10.2

Last year I went to a friend's New Year's Eve party which was fancy dress. Everyone was told on the invitation that they had to make their own costume and not buy one on the internet! So, I decided to make a princess costume. I chose to use a combination of silk and lace and I imagined it would look spectacular, like something from *Frozen*! I was pretty confident that I could do it because my grandmother taught me how to sew when I was a teenager and I had quite a lot of artistic flair back then. I made a couple of party dresses with my grandmother's help and I was quite proud of them at the time. Anyway, because of my previous experience, in my mind, I thought my costume would be fairly professional-looking.

The day before the party I got out my old sewing machine, set it up on the kitchen table and started work. After a couple of hours, I'd not managed to get very far and I wish I'd read the machine instructions beforehand. I'd forgotten what some of the controls did and had ruined most of the material. At that point I realised I only had a couple of options – buy a costume and pretend I had made it or call my friend to help me fix the mess I'd made. I decided to call my friend who arrived an hour later and managed to undo all my sewing and make the costume as it was supposed to look. I don't know what I'd have done without his help and patience.

I suppose if I had to do something like this again, I'd do a few things differently. First and foremost, I would be making sure I knew how to operate any machinery properly as this was what caused the most setbacks. Besides that, I think I should have drawn out the design more thoroughly. In my view, I believe that the costume would have been easier to make with a clearer design.

10.3

S1: There is undeniable talent and creativity involved in the most enduring music. One such example is Mozart. Mozart was undeniably talented in music from a very early age. He understood music and the workings of composition at an incredibly young age. His understanding of music was as a bird learns to fly; natural, effortless and awesome to watch. Great talents like his don't come along every day.

S2: Of course, music has changed a great deal in the last hundred years. In one way the diversity of music has changed, and as this has happened our taste in music has become more diverse. We the listeners are sponges, soaking up everything around us, no matter what it may be. So, nowadays we can't simply say 'I'm a jazz buff' or 'I'm into rock', generally we're into many different musical genres, and this can depend entirely on mood.

10.4

N = Narrator   A = Amy

N: You are going to listen to a lecture about pop songs. Listen and answer questions one to ten.

A: So in today's lecture we're going to be looking at the pop song … and whether nowadays they follow such formulaic rules that they could actually be written by a computer. Basically, have we come to a time when a songwriter could feed a generic topic into a machine that can produce something akin to the songs we see in the charts these days?

There are many schools of thought on this area. John Covach at the University of Rochester claims that music is more about cultural influence, and that songs need to be personally significant if they are to find the right audience. He talks about being at the cutting edge of culture, citing that hits of yesterday wouldn't be the hits of today … for example if Michael Jackson had released his initial hits nowadays, they wouldn't have been a success simply because they wouldn't capture today's mood. In this way, making a good pop song is like catching a wave. You need the right conditions, you have to time it perfectly, and you need to embrace and work with nature's forces. In this way, music is seen as a social construct. While it might be easy to write a pop song, the real success comes in ensuring that song resonates with a huge swathe of listeners.

However, there is another school of thought which believes that computers and understanding patterns have a larger role in the music industry. Susan Schmidt-Horning of St John's University is one of these people. She makes the case that people have actually reverse-engineered successful songs. In the same way that we can take a car apart and put it together again, so we can with a song. She looked at the case of rock and roll. Musicians would study certain instruments and recycle elements in newer songs. This can be done to many different extents, perhaps the most common and obvious example is sampling. This is when musicians take a part of one song and put it in a newer song. James Brown for example has

been sampled in over 900 songs. A famous example is Beyoncé's *Crazy in Love* which samples a 70s song by the Chi-Lites, *Are you my woman*? This can cause issues. Some people think this is akin to robbery, however most musicians credit and pay for the samples. The only issues come when the original credit is not given and permission isn't sought.

Now another point here is the fact that maybe we need to be looking further than simple reverse-engineering where we offer up the next Miley Cyrus or whoever to sing whatever is produced by this process. Another option is that the future of pop music will actually be a robot. Hatsune Miku is a humanoid persona voiced by a synthesiser. She can sing and perform, but she isn't human. Miku is a household name in Japan where she supported Lady Gaga on tour … and she's probably good for investors too … She's not going to cause problems. She won't age, or do something embarrassing or shocking for all her fans to see. And she can perform in two places at once!

But, let's not think that this means the music of the future is robotic. At present, we cannot definitively say whether robotic stars like Miku will become the norm, or whether they are simply a trend, which will be over as soon as it's begun. Even if this trend continues, humans still need involvement. In fact, Miku sources a lot of her music from fans. Perhaps she is in fact some kind of mirror, enabling fans to express themselves more freely. A simple reflection of her fan base. This would indicate that music is in fact becoming more fragmented, crowd-sourced and for the people rather than the elite. In sum, although we may be able to create a digital recipe for a song, that doesn't mean they are going to taste good to the diverse audiences that exist nowadays. If we really want to create something, the recipe needs to focus on popularity. A magic ingredient that just can't be quantified.

10.5

1: I can't imagine what the world would be like without painkillers. They're used so much these days, for things like headaches all the way through to post-operative treatments … I suppose people would put up with things a lot more because they'd not want to have operations or medical procedures that might hurt. I imagine we'd be using more natural pain relievers too like acupuncture.

2: In the next 50 years? Well, I think we might have cures for many of the diseases that exist today. And hopefully ones like polio and malaria might be a thing of the past. With the progress made in vaccinations I see that as a very real possibility.

3: It would be a very bleak place in my opinion. If we didn't have these essential medical services, we'd probably see people suffering just out on the streets. This would be a very difficult sight. Also there would probably be a much shorter life expectancy for everyone.

4: Yes, I think that might well happen. Life expectancy has risen and risen up to now, and I see no reason why that wouldn't continue. In the early 20th century, it was probably common for people to live to about 60, but now in many countries it's the norm for people to live into their eighties.

10.6

N = Narrator   J = Josh

N: You are going to listen to a lecture about medical innovation. Listen and answer questions one to ten.

J: So, in today's lecture I'm going to look at some of the most important medical innovations in the last 20 years. It may seem like quite a short time, but the 21st century has seen some incredible changes in medicine. Changes that many wouldn't have thought possible at the start of the century. We're going to look at some of these changes and consider how they have and might yet change our lives.

Let's start with the functional MRI. This is basically a kind of scan which can detect brain activity. This has actually made mind reading, to an extent, possible. This kind of imaging can tell us the way the brain functions. Not only can this imaging give us useful information on language and memory, it can also be used to detect certain illnesses like Alzheimer's or depression. Additionally, it works as a map for surgeons, helping them avoid critical regions when undertaking brain surgery. However, reading the scans is still quite problematic. Data is still being collected on the subjects who have had scans which will hopefully lead to a kind of database of what each scan means. It might even be possible to see how certain drugs for mental illness function, just by reviewing brain activity on the scan.

Another great innovation of the 21st century is the success of creating a functioning artificial liver, and functioning kidneys. Japanese researchers achieved the feat of growing a liver from stem cells in 2013 and a laboratory in the USA also grew an artificial functioning kidney in the very same year. Now many are predicting that manufacture of artificial organs may be a distinct possibility in the future. This would have an astounding effect on the many people who are on donor waiting lists for such organs. There may be no need to wait in the future, there will be a readily available store of artificial organs.

Connected to these innovations in organ transplant is the rather futuristic and fantastical idea of face transplants. As the face is probably the most noticeable part of our bodies, people who suffer from facial disfigurement due to accidents or disease are likely to suffer from extreme and ongoing emotional trauma. This may well change soon as the first full transplant of a face was carried out in 2010 in Spain. This procedure however has led to ethical concerns. One which I think is most relevant is the idea of identity transfer. This really is the idea that the recipient doesn't see themselves in the mirror anymore and rather feels like another person. Now this may be a real concern, but the likelihood is that they'll see a third face, not the donor's, and not the old face of the recipient. Getting used to this could be similar to what they have already been through due to disfigurement, but without the same emotional, and physical, depth of scar.

Lastly, let's look to possibly the most amazing medical breakthrough not just of our time, but possibly of ALL time ... And this is the mapping of our genes. This is actually the world's largest collaborative biological project with contributions from over 20 universities and research institutes throughout the world. Why is this so important? Well, it can tell us so much about things that are genetically determined in our lives. It can offer us the opportunity of personalised medicines based on our own individual makeup. It can give us knowledge of how people evolved and it can also indicate our chances of developing an inherited disease. These are just a few of its benefits. It also offers the chance for far more advanced treatments. However, again we have ethical concerns about this development. One of the main issues is how, in some hands, it could discriminate against people or certain types of people. A key example cited is one of 'ordering' the perfect child. Now, this may seem quite a trivial idea, but let's put it more practically. If we identify what triggers, say, colour blindness, which is a genetic disorder, by mapping those who are colour blind, it may be possible to eradicate it. But ... can we be selective in this way? These ethical questions really have no answer. It's just a case of your standpoint. There are also more pressing issues of who gets to see your genetic information. For example, would you make a choice of a future partner based on whether their genes could produce healthy offspring? Again, quite possibly. Yet we must not underestimate the enormous benefits that developments in genetic mapping will give us. Perhaps the issue is about protection of information rather than the act of gathering this data.

OK, so these are just a few medical innovations which are at present changing the way healthcare works. I'd like you for next week's seminar to give a short presentation on one illness or condition which has benefitted from gene mapping. Along with an outline of benefits, I'd like you also to look into issues of ethics and legality. If you've got any questions we don't have time now, but you can ask them in the seminar. Please make sure you've noted them down.

10.7

E = Examiner   J = Jina

E: Would you say that inventions always have positive effects on our lives?

J: Mmm, that's an interesting question. For me, the drawbacks of inventions can be overlooked in favour of the beneficial aspects. On the vast majority of occasions, it is reasonable to assert that inventions instigate positive changes in society. I mean, where would we be if the internet hadn't been created, for example? When it was launched in the late 1980s, we couldn't have imagined how it was going to revolutionise our lives. Yet, sometimes negative repercussions of inventions come to our attention a little later. I'm thinking about research which has revealed some of the adverse effects of social media on young people and youth culture. Things such as cyber bullying which is when children adopt threatening behaviour to others on sites like Facebook. So, I guess my view is that there's usually both good and bad outcomes.

Pearson Education Limited

Edinburgh Gate, Harlow, Essex. CM20 2JE and Associated Companies throughout the world

www.pearsonelt.com/expertielts

© Pearson Education Limited 2017

First published 2017
Third impression 2018
ISBN 978-1-292-12511-4
Set in Amasis and Mundo Sans
Printed and bound in Slovakia by Neografia

Acknowledgements

The publishers and authors would like to thank the following people and institutions for their contribution to the development of the material:

Carole Allsop, Sarah Emsden-Bonfanti, Joanna Preshous, Lizzie Wright, the teachers at the English Centre at The American University of Sharjah Souha Adlouni, Nouf Al-Salem (video), Rasheed Al-Siddiq, Fiona Aish, Marine Andre (video), Asmaa Awad, Jan Bell, Jason Bednarz, Freya Beesely, Ludmilla Boysan , Edward Burnham , Yuka Chibioni (video), Andrew Condor, Jude Conroy, Brendan Cox , Natalia Donmez, Tim Edwards, Nick Falkinder, Filippo Geraci (video), Mark Gillespie, Rebecca Gilligan, Nazli Gonca (video), Douglas Greig, Niva Gunasegaran, Rita Hanlon, Mark Hanson, Ramin Hashemian, Deborah Hobbs, Dr. Paul Hudson, Alexander Ingle, Daphne-Ann Kelly, Brian John Knight, David Knowles, Carl Lam, Jill Landry, Christien Lee, Sydney Liu, Sally Lloyds, Andrew Loader, Mark Long, Daniel Meager, Claire Murphy, Tom O'Brien, Sheila Parrott, Gonzalo Pastrana (video), Olivia Qin, Abdelghani A. Remache, Louis Rogers, Amber Roshay, Abdelhameed Safa, Kareen Sharawy, Li Shengyue, Kelly Smith, Helen Stobie, Jo Tomlinson, Amira Traish, Richard Vile, Joseph Vitta, Claire Wallis, Clare Walsh (video), Ian Watson, Liu Weili, Elaine Wilson, Mehtap Yavuzdogan, Yulia Yarmolinsky, Eden Zhange, Cee Zhao

We are grateful to the following for permission to reproduce copyright material:

Figures

Figure on page 78 from How energy is used in the home Pie Chart, http://www.sa.gov.au/topics/water-energy-and-environment/saving-energy-at-home/home-energy-use, The Government of South Australia website is licensed under a Creative Commons Attribution 3.0 Australia Licence. © Copyright 2016; Book Covers on page 127 from *The Hunger games*, Scholastic (Collins,S 2009),*The Hobbit*, New Ed., HarperCollins (J. R. R. Tolkien) © The Tolkien Estate Limited 1937, 1965, *Sherlock Holmes*, Penguin (Conan Doyle, A.); Figure on page 156 from Infographic 'Anatomy of Songs created by, https://wronghands1.com/, Cartoons by John Atkinson. ©John Atkinson, Wrong Hands.Used with permission; Figure on page 191 "Skills, education, and the rise of earnings inequality among the "other 99 percent" from Choosing our future: A story of opportunity in America, SCIENCE 344: 843(23 May 2014), Fig 1a (Autor,D.H. 2014) with permission from David Autor and from the publisher; Figure on page 195 from The experiences of international students in New Zealand, Ministry of Education New Zealand licensed for re-use under the Creative Commons Attribution 4.0 International licence, licensed for re-use under the Creative Commons Attribution 4.0 International licence

Logos

Logo on page 124 from http://www.couchsurfing.com/about/trademark/

Screenshots

Screenshot on page 15 from Star Walk, Vito Technology Inc. © 2009-2013 Vito, Star Walk app available for mobile devices, created by Vito Technology, Inc.; Screenshot on page 15 from Wordflex Touch Dictionary. Copyright © 2016 Robert Scheiner. All rights reserved.

Text

Extract on page 35 adapted from *A Buzz in the meadow*, Vintage Books (Goulson,D. 2014) pp.28-33, The Random House Group; Article on page 40 adapted from A healthy dose of nature, *BBC Wildlife* (Bird, W.), August 2015, © Radio Times / Immediate Media London Ltd; Article on page 51 adapted from Why we worry too much about health, *The Independent*, 26/01/2010 (Sharp, R.); Article on page 57 adapted from Our prosperity is in peril unless we shift from a wasteful world to a 'circular economy',11/09/2015 Mark Esposito and Terence

Tse Copyright © 2010–2016, The Conversation Trust (UK) Limited; Extract on page 67 adapted from My precious - Being Human, *New Scientist The Collection* 2 Issue 3, pp.71-74 (Bond,M. 2015); Article on page 73 adapted from How robots are taking over our homes — but not as you'd expect *Financial Times*, 30/07/2015 (Bradshaw,T.), © The Financial Times Limited. All Rights Reserved; Article on page 83 adapted from How underwater living could soon be a reality *Financial Times*, 06/09/2013, © The Financial Times Limited. All Rights Reserved; Extract on page 84 from *Neither here nor there: Travels in Europe*, Random House (Bryson,B. 2010), The Random House Group (UK) and with permission from Bill Bryson; Extract on page 84 adapted from Statistical bulletin: Migration Statistics Quarterly Report: November 2015, Office for National Statistics, licensed under the Open Government Licence v.3.0.; Article on page 89 adapted from The field of neurocriminology is reviving some controversial ideas. Can criminal urges really be blamed on the brain? *The Times*, 04/02/2010 (Leslie, I.); Article on page 99 adapted from Forensics: Assessing the Scene of the Crime, Dummies (Wiley), Copyright © 2016 & Trademark by John Wiley & Sons, Inc. All rights reserved; Article on page 115 adapted from If autonomous vehicles rule the world, *The Economist*; Article on page 121 adapted from How to be good, *Financial Times*, 08/05/2015 (Cave,S.) © The Financial Times Limited. All Rights Reserved; Article on page 131 adapted from Love of animals led to language and man's domination of Earth, *The Guardian*, 02/10/2011 (McKie, R.). Copyright Guardian News & Media Ltd 2016; Article on page 137 adapted from Multi-tasking: how to survive in the 21st century, *Financial Times*, 03/09/2015 (Harford,T.) © The Financial Times Limited. All Rights Reserved; Article on page 147 adapted from My father had one job in his life, I've had six in mine., my kids will have six at the same time, *Guardian*, 29/11/2015 (Adams,T.).Copyright Guardian News & Media Ltd 2016; Article on page 153 adapted from The science of imagination "double your brainpower" *The Independent* (Professor John Stein); Article on page 163 from Throwing the book at bad ideas, *Physics World* (Ball.P.). Copyright Institute of Physics (the "Institute") and IOP Publishing, Copyright Institute of Physics (the "Institute") and IOP Publishing.This article first appeared in the December 2015 issue of Physics World magazine and with permission from Philip Ball.

Illustration Acknowledgements

Illustrated by ROARR Design

Photo Acknowledgements

The publisher would like to thank the following for their kind permission to reproduce their photographs:

(Key: b-bottom; c-centre; l-left; r-right; t-top)

123RF.com: signout 34 (B); **Alamy Images:** AF archive 151r, Anatolii Babii 9, Caspar Benson 98, Blend Images 17, 108cl, Blue Jean Images 109, Andor Bujdoso 7br, colaimages 148tr, David Cole 75, Cultura Creative (RF) 45, 52, Cultura RM 7tl, Andrea De Martin 145, De Visu 119, Design Pics Inc 33tl, Dinodia Photos 65 (A), dpa picture alliance 65 (B), epa european pressphoto agency b.v. 161tr, fStop Images GmbH 66, Terry Harris 12r, Alistair Heap 108tl, imageBROKER 131, 164tc, Frederick Mark Sheridan-Johnson 34 (C), Tim Jones 115, Juice Images 116, Justin Kase z12z 107tl, John Kellerman 23tr, Ton Koene 23c, 49, Alexey Kotelnikov 18, Cro Magnon 107tc, Iain Masterton 103bl, Rachel Megawhat 151l, Wietse Michiels 57, Mint Images Limited 7bl, MITO images 89, Paul Paddison 92tr, PhotoAlto 67, Pictorial Press Ltd 153, Radius Images 130, Simon Reddy 103tr, Reuters 60, 65 (C), robertharding 12l, Chris Rout 47, Miguel Aguirre Sánchez 71b, Dmitriy Shironosov 23tl, 129, Eitan Simanor 103br, Robert Stainforth 68, Tony Tallec 29, Tetra Images 51, The Print Collector 25, The Protected Art Archive 161tl, Dmytro Zinkevych 160; **CartoonStock.com:** Clive Goddard 62; **Chris Madden:** 121; **Gianfranco Cignetti:** 76t, 141r; **Courtesy of Hi-Interiors:** 71tr; **Fotolia:** adimas 139, alex83ch 164tr, BestForYou 147, georgejmclittle 92cr, Jag_cz 41t, jutaphoto 91b, mountaintreks 96, nuruddean 91t, Romolo Tavani 55, The physicist 35, Oleg Zhukov 27; **Getty Images:** Thomas Barwick 113, Yvonne Hemsey 7tr, Hulton Archive 163, Carsten Peter 36t, Javier Pierini 73, Monty Rakusen 95, Sankei 151c; **Lou Fischer Bonneville Stories.com:** 140tl; **Mark Lynch / toonpool.com:** 100; **Reuters:** China Daily 140tr; **Science Photo Library Ltd:** Alfred Pasieka 19 (Brain); **Shutterstock.com:** Arkela 43, Castleski 143, Frenzel 88, gorillaimages 159, Chris Howey 103tl, kurhan 42, littleny 132tc, micro10x 132tr, Monkey Business Images 148tl, neelsky 34 (A), Vitalii Nesterchuk 28t, nitrogenic.com 83, Regien Paassen 33tr, reddees 105, Johan Swanepoel 99, Syda Productions 71tl, Kochneva Tetyana 82t, travellight 164tl, Julien Tromeur 8; **The Kobal Collection:** Killing Road Productions 87cr, Studio Babelsberg / Rose Line Productions 87tl, Umbrella / Rosenblum / Virgin Films 81tr, Walt Disney Pictures / A113 81tl, Zentropa / Film I Vast / Christian Geisnaes 87bl; **Mike Warren (mikeasaurus):** 76b, 141l

All other images © Pearson Education

Video produced by Silversun Media Group for Pearson Education